Dissertations and Theses From Start to Finish

THIRD EDITION

Dissertations and Theses From Start to Finish

Psychology and Related Fields

Debora J. Bell, Sharon L. Foster, and John D. Cone

AMERICAN PSYCHOLOGICAL ASSOCIATION
Washington, DC

Published by
American Psychological Association
750 First Street, NE
Washington, DC 20002
https://www.apa.org

Order Department
https://www.apa.org/pubs/books
order@apa.org

In the U.K., Europe, Africa, and the Middle East, copies may be ordered from Eurospan
https://www.eurospanbookstore.com/apa
info@eurospangroup.com

Typeset in Meridien and Ortodoxa by Circle Graphics, Inc., Reisterstown, MD

Printer: Sheridan Books, Chelsea, MI
Cover Designer: Naylor Design, Washington, DC

Library of Congress Cataloging-in-Publication Data
Names: Bell, Debora, author. | Foster, Sharon L., author. | Cone, John D., 1942- author.
Title: Dissertations and theses from start to finish : psychology and related fields /
  Debora J. Bell, Sharon L. Foster, and John D. Cone.
Description: Third edition. | Washington, DC : American Psychological
  Association, [2020] | Previous editions entered under: John D. Cone. | Includes
  bibliographical references and index.
Identifiers: LCCN 2019022625 (print) | LCCN 2019022626 (ebook) |
  ISBN 9781433831607 (ebook) | ISBN 9781433830648 (paperback)
Subjects: LCSH: Psychology—Research—Methodology.
Classification: LCC BF76.5 (ebook) | LCC BF76.5 .C645 2020 (print) |
  DDC 150.72—dc23
LC record available at https://lccn.loc.gov/2019022625

https://doi.org/10.1037/0000161-000

Printed in the United States of America

10 9 8 7 6 5 4 3 2 1

CONTENTS

FOREWORD

As one embarks on their journey toward the completion of a dissertation or thesis, they might reflect on their participation in one of academia's most time-honored traditions. They might marvel at the opportunity to add their own intellectual contribution to a centuries-old discourse among scholars or rejoice in their impending membership to our society's elite class of graduate-trained citizens.

Yet, few students do so. Instead, many students quite understandably think of their dissertation or thesis as an enormous chore (or perhaps more accurately as a pain in the neck) that they must conquer as the final hurdle in a lifetime of academic pursuits.

Fair enough. Dissertations and theses indeed are large undertakings that are meant to reflect the culmination of years of training, and they can be maddening in the level of detail, precision, exhaustive review, and thoroughness that successful completion requires. Many are scared away from graduate training simply by the thought of the dissertation or thesis. But the readers of this book—you—were not. You have made it this far through years of primary and secondary training, exemplary academic achievement as an undergraduate student, through the gauntlet of competitive graduate school admissions, and now have reached this final stage of your training because you have a passion for psychology and a tenacity, discipline, and successful record of accomplishments that few possess. You can do this! And with the help of this fantastic volume, you may even get through quite painlessly.

The authors of this book are esteemed scholars and fantastic mentors who have distilled years of wisdom and exceptional advice into a step-by-step road map to help get you through this final graduate task without breaking a sweat. Step by step, point by point, this book offers a remarkable blend of nurturing support and practical tips to help you with each step of the process, from the formulation of your hypotheses all the way through your final defense.

How do you select a topic? How do you manage your time? What is the best way to approach each small step in this important undertaking? How can you successfully finish while still having time for a personal life? It's all covered here in the outstanding pages that follow within this volume—a constant source of support, advice, and instruction that will become your best friend throughout the writing process.

Just imagine: One day, your thesis or dissertation will be complete. You will defend your work in front of a group of scholars who will tell you that you have passed, and your contributions will be bound and archived to contribute to scientific discourse for decades to come. You might even continue to contribute to the scientific literature with dozens or hundreds of subsequent studies to report in the future. But most only have the chance to write one thesis and/or one dissertation. Good luck making it the one that will make you feel proud for years to come, and launch you into the world of science.

We are excited for you to join us!

—*Mitchell J. Prinstein, PhD, ABPP*
John Van Seters Distinguished Professor
of Psychology and Neuroscience
University of North Carolina at Chapel Hill

PREFACE

It was almost 30 years ago that the first edition of *Dissertations and Theses From Start to Finish* hit the shelves. With that edition, we envisioned helping students negotiate the often mysterious and daunting process of completing a thesis or dissertation. Dissertation and thesis research has changed since that time. We have gone from a world in which literature was archived on paper and housed in brick and mortar libraries, data were collected in person, and data analysis, even with the support of mainframe computers, was often a slow process, to a world in which ready access to electronic data storage, analysis, and transmission allows research to proceed with what seems like lightning speed. Today, students have the opportunity, and the responsibility, to master larger bodies of literature, conduct more extensive and sophisticated research, and in essence, "do more" than in past generations. Likewise, the resources supporting a student's journey through the thesis and dissertation have exploded. In contrast to past students' reliance on their advisors, student colleagues, and university handbooks for advice on negotiating the dissertation or thesis process, current students need only do a quick internet search to access dozens of articles, web pages, and videos, some good and some not, designed to assist them.

Given the many changes, is a book such as this one still useful? On the basis of feedback from countless students and faculty over the years, we believe the answer is a resounding "Absolutely!" In the third edition of our book, we cover issues that generations of graduate students have faced as they tackled their theses and dissertations, as well as newer issues relevant to students today. Many aspects of doing a thesis or dissertation remain unchanged—students must still focus their research questions; manage their personal resources; design and conduct sound studies; and communicate effectively with research participants, thesis and dissertation committees, and broader scientific and lay audiences. They still have only 24 hours in a day, competing tasks, and varying levels of preparation for their roles as principal investigators for their project. In this book, we address these classic issues with contemporary examples, advice, and resources. We also examine ways in which dissertation and thesis research has evolved in recent years. For example, students are more likely than ever before to begin graduate study with prior research experience and assignment to a specific research mentor. Technological innovations (e.g., smartphone and activity tracker collection of real-time participant behavior and experiences, online studies that can reach around the globe) allow students to collect a large variety and volume of data, and powerful data analytic software facilitates nuanced examination of these data. The open science movement creates an increasing expectation that students' thesis and dissertation projects will involve collaborative, transparent, and reproducible research that is accessible to both the scientific community and broader public. We discuss the opportunities and challenges created by these changes, offer suggestions for handling them as part of the dissertation or thesis process, and provide additional resources for students to consider.

This revision continues our commitment to providing students with a written guide that is affordable, accessible, and easy to read and digest, while addressing both scholarly and pragmatic issues. We also continue to recognize that students have diverse research backgrounds and career goals, as well as identities, activities, and social networks that exist outside of their thesis/dissertation project. We write this volume to help students navigate the research process smoothly and develop research and professional skills that will serve them well throughout their careers and in their lives more generally.

Much like dissertation and thesis research, this book was a team effort. We have been fortunate to work with many graduate students over the years who have entrusted us with their professional development, helped us develop our repertoires as mentors, and provided many of the examples we include. We are also indebted to students and colleagues who offered candid and helpful feedback on what worked well and what was off-target or missing from earlier versions of the book, including Madison Beedon, Jasmine Berry, and Kelsey Irvin from the University of Missouri, and Kanjana Boes and the library staff from Alliant International University. Linda McCarter and Ted Baroody from APA Books, and copyeditor Hyde Loomis, have supported us throughout this revision, providing input on the clarity of text, tables, and figures, and attending to the technical details that ensure a high-quality product. Finally, we are immensely grateful to our families, whose emotional and instrumental support was critical to this project's success. Spouses Bob Ekle, Tom Barton, and Jan Cone were great as sounding boards for our book-related inspirations and frustrations as we prepared this revision.

Debora Bell's daughter Sarah chipped in as well, taking on additional chores so mom could write.

Seeing our efforts reflected in the lessons learned by the next generation provided the catalyst for this book. We hope in turn that our accumulated wisdom will help students find the joy and satisfaction (even amidst inevitable frustrations!) of contributing to the knowledge base and completing a major milestone in their professional development.

Dissertations and Theses From Start to Finish

1

What Are Theses and Dissertations, and Why Write a Book About Them?

This chapter introduces you to this book and the thesis and dissertation process, including
- what to expect in the book
- an overview of what theses and dissertations are and why you should do one
- helpful social, environmental, and resource supports

Read thoroughly if
- you are new to the thesis or dissertation process
- you want a quick overview of what you can expect to get from this book

Skim or skip if
- you are ready to dive right in!

Let's answer the second question in the chapter title first. It's been almost 30 years since we first conceived this book. When we started the first edition, students often began graduate school with minimal formal research experience. The thesis or dissertation may have been based on their first independent research projects, and these projects were often their primary, if not only, major research endeavors during graduate school. In addition, most students relied largely on the professor who chaired their thesis or dissertation for guidance on these projects.

https://doi.org/10.1037/0000161-001

Dissertations and Theses From Start to Finish: Psychology and Related Fields, Third Edition, by D. J. Bell, S. L. Foster, and J. D. Cone

Times have changed. Today, it is much more common for students to have considerable research experience by the time they get to the thesis or dissertation; for many it is no longer the first project or the pinnacle of their graduate years. For these students, the thesis or dissertation may feel like just another project in their evolving program of research, requiring skills they've already developed or at least observed in their lab mates. In addition, the number of resources available to support thesis and dissertation writing has exploded since the first edition of our book, including everything from online resources such as websites, blogs, and YouTube videos, to articles and books on the topic, to thesis or dissertation coaches and writing services! There are now journal articles and books, often discipline specific, that address certain aspects of graduate-level research projects (e.g., selection of a topic, organization for writing, time management, self-care). So why another edition of this book?

First, the vast array of resources can be overwhelming, as the focus, depth, and content of their support are different and sometimes even contradictory. Online informational resources are often too brief to offer much specific detail about any one aspect of the thesis or dissertation project, or they focus on only one aspect (e.g., organizing a proposal document). The stream-of-consciousness style of many blogs can take you down many informational rabbit holes before you find a nugget that is helpful to you. Writing support websites may offer some helpful hints, but many are really geared toward selling you a thesis or dissertation, which, for obvious reasons, we strongly discourage! Face it—the resources you find on the internet may not have been subjected to any quality assurance review; you may find useful information, but it is clearly a "buyer beware" marketplace. We believe that a single curated source of information that takes students through the thesis and dissertation process step by step still has a place on bookshelves and in libraries.

Second, there are key aspects of the thesis and dissertation process that warrant close attention from students new to the research process, as well as from students who are more seasoned researchers. If you are newer to independent research, as a beginning graduate student or even an advanced undergraduate, information on developing, implementing, and describing research will be quite useful. If you are already an active researcher, things such as the etiquette and formalities of university theses and dissertations, working with committees, or managing greater independence than you're accustomed to may still be new to you. Regardless of your experience level, considering topics such as how to assess your readiness, manage your environment, and balance your priorities can be critical in facilitating your research and graduate school success well beyond these two specific research projects.

We wrote the first two versions of this book to help graduate students in psychology and related fields more successfully negotiate the thesis and dissertation process from beginning to end. We included everything from deciding whether and how to embark on the journey to developing, implementing, and writing up the project; managing the myriad logistical issues involved in making it to and through a successful defense meeting; and then disseminating your results through professional presentation and publication.

We also wrote the book to serve as an archival source of the wisdom we have amassed from a combined total of close to 100 years of supervising theses and dissertations. All of us have told graduate students many useful (and sometimes not-so-useful!) things over the years to help them through the process. Until we systematized these suggestions, we, like other faculty members, had to tell each fledgling thesis or dissertation student everything all over again. The first edition of this book compiled the best of our ideas on how to make the process a less mysterious and more exciting educational experience, and the second edition added a few things we left out and updated our suggestions in light of new trends in the field.

In the 13 years since the second edition was published, research areas and methods, expectations and requirements for theses and dissertations, and technology have all changed in notable ways. The pages that follow address these changes. Although we aim our suggestions primarily at graduate students in psychology and related fields and focus more on quantitative than qualitative research methods, much of the content of the book will be useful across disciplines, research methods, and levels of research experience. Importantly, we hope that many of our suggestions will be generalizable beyond thesis and dissertation projects to an ongoing program of research, other types of formal proposals (e.g., grant applications), collaborative projects that require committee approval, dissemination to multiple audiences, and even your general approach to multifaceted and long-range tasks.

HOW THIS BOOK IS ORGANIZED

The 14 chapters of this book provide the tools needed to assemble good theses and dissertations. Of course, simply reading this book is not sufficient to fully prepare you for the thesis or dissertation process. The book will be most valuable as a supplement to an already adequate graduate education. We do not explain research ethics, designs, methods, or statistics. Instead, we help you apply what you have already learned in graduate school to the practical conduct of research and point you toward resources to supplement that knowledge as needed.

In this chapter, we talk briefly about what theses and dissertations are, what they look like, and some of the reasons for doing one. Then, in Chapter 2, we ask you to assess your own preparation and commitment. Chapter 3 helps you estimate the time you will need to complete your project and anticipate and manage the various events that can come along to derail your efforts. Chapter 4 discusses finding a topic and developing a research question and hypotheses. Because this is most often done in collaboration with one or more faculty members, Chapter 4 also contains advice about selecting a chair and committee members and about thesis and dissertation etiquette in general.

Chapter 5 provides an overview of the all-important thesis or dissertation proposal, and Chapter 6 follows with suggestions for developing your literature review. Chapter 7 discusses what to include in a good Method section, along with issues of research ethics and informed consent. Operationalizing and measuring your variables, collecting and analyzing your data, and presenting and discussing your results are covered in Chapters 8 through 12. Chapter 13 reviews strategies for handling your proposal meeting and oral defense. Finally, Chapter 14 discusses readying your research for presentation at professional meetings and submission for publication.

Each chapter begins with an advance organizer that gives you, in a few bullet points, an idea of what to expect in the chapter as well as advice to help you decide whether you should read the chapter thoroughly or can skim or skip certain pieces of the chapter. Most chapters end with a checklist that turns our suggestions from that chapter into concrete steps you can take to move your project forward. You can adapt these checklists to suit your project and use them to keep track of your progress.

At the end of most chapters, we also provide references to supplemental sources you might find useful if you want to explore the topics in more depth. These resources are ones we have found particularly useful for ourselves or our students. Although websites come and go, we provide references to a few websites that we believe offer particularly useful advice and may have some staying power. When our reason for recommending a specific resource may not be obvious, we provide a brief explanation of its topic and relevance.

The topics we cover follow the sequence you would normally encounter in the thesis or dissertation process. We think most readers will benefit from reading the chapters in order as they approach each new phase of their research. Some readers, especially if they've had a great deal of experience in a specific area, may want to focus more selectively on areas that are new to them. It will be useful to skim the entire book quickly before digging in so you have some idea of its contents and where to look for something should you want to focus on it or need it in a sequence different from the one we have chosen.

Now let's go back to the first question posed in the title of this chapter: What are theses and dissertations, anyway? First, we define them and talk a little bit about their history. Then we say something about what theses and dissertations in psychology actually look like.

DEFINITIONS, DISTINCTIONS, AND FUNCTIONS

Dictionary definitions of "thesis" and "dissertation" often do not distinguish between these terms. *Merriam-Webster* (n.d.-a) defines a *dissertation* as "an extended usually written treatment of a subject; *specifically*: one submitted for a doctorate." The same source defines *thesis* as "a dissertation embodying results of original research and especially substantiating a specific view; *especially*:

one written by a candidate for an academic degree" (Merriam-Webster, n.d.-c). Similarly, the *Oxford English Dictionary* defines *dissertation* as "a long essay on a particular subject, especially one written for a university degree or diploma" (AskOxford.com, n.d.-a) and *thesis* as "a long essay or dissertation involving personal research, written as part of a university degree" and gives the example of "a doctoral thesis" (AskOxford.com, n.d.-b). Not only is there no clear distinction between the terms "thesis" and "dissertation," but both definitions of the former include the latter!

In U.S. universities, it has become common to distinguish between theses and dissertations by referring to the work done for a master's degree as a "thesis" and that done for a doctoral degree as a "dissertation." This is not a universally accepted distinction, by any means, and some faculty members refer to dissertations as "doctoral theses." Throughout this volume, we use the term "dissertation" to refer to an original piece of empirical research done as partial fulfillment of the requirements of doctoral (EdD, PhD, or PsyD) programs in psychology and related fields. We use "thesis" to refer to empirical research conducted en route to a master's degree.

Despite terminological ambiguities, most faculty members agree on the general functions of theses and dissertations. One major purpose of both projects is to demonstrate the student's skill at conducting independent research that makes a contribution to knowledge on an important topic. Another is to assess the student's mastery of a specialized area of scholarship. Some see the dissertation process as examining mastery of technical aspects of research, including knowledge and ability to apply principles of research design, statistics, and so on. Thus, the dissertation process is an examination of your competence to function autonomously as a researcher. The finished dissertation also results in a new and significant contribution to the body of knowledge.

Theses, too, are expected to contribute to the body of knowledge. Thesis requirements place less emphasis on originality, however, and candidates are often given more guidance and supervision. Some thesis candidates conduct a systematic replication of already completed research, for example. In addition, thesis candidates rarely operate as independently as doctoral candidates must.

Not to be overlooked is the training function theses and dissertations serve. In undertaking such a project, you learn and grow in your research skills and knowledge of the field. You expand your skills in thinking critically, synthesizing and extending the work of others, and communicating clearly and professionally. Ideally, the process should also increase your respect for the empirical aspects of the discipline and your pride in participating in the development of new knowledge about important phenomena.

WHAT THESES AND DISSERTATIONS LOOK LIKE

You have probably asked yourself numerous questions about the form your thesis or dissertation is supposed to take. Must you use particular methods? How long is it supposed to be? What format are you supposed to follow?

Are there writing style requirements to follow? Let's look at some of these questions.

First, about methods. Although this book focuses primarily on empirical projects that involve quantitative research, not all theses and dissertations require this type of project. The traditional terminal degree in psychology, the PhD, virtually always requires an empirical project; frequently, these use quantitative methods, but increasingly, mainstream psychology research uses qualitative or mixed (i.e., quantitative and qualitative) methods. Some applied psychology programs offer an alternative terminal degree, the PsyD, or doctor in psychology. PsyD programs explicitly prepare students for careers as practitioners and thus may have somewhat different degree requirements than PhD programs. For example, many practitioner-oriented schools allow alternatives to the traditional empirical dissertation, such as a theoretical dissertation (or, more rarely, a case study) that addresses a clearly defined question and makes an original contribution to knowledge. However, many students in PsyD programs still complete an empirical dissertation. In a 1992 survey of directors of 40 "Vail-model" programs (i.e., professional clinical psychology programs, which presumably included a significant number of PsyD programs) in the United States, Sanchez-Hucles and Cash learned that despite the variety of acceptable dissertation formats, approximately half of the students in these programs elected to conduct empirical dissertations. Our recent informal consultations with colleagues in PsyD programs indicate that this is still true.

As for length, there is a great deal of variability within and between disciplines and within and between universities. Although we do not have objective data on theses, we do know something about the length of dissertations. We recently randomly sampled 100 dissertations completed in 2016–2017 selected from the ProQuest Dissertations & Theses database. Psychology dissertations had a mean length of 132 pages, including text, tables, appendices, and related items, with a range of 42 to 285 pages.[1] Interestingly, these numbers suggest that dissertations have become shorter in the past 15 years; when we sampled 2001–2002 dissertations, they averaged 44% longer, with minimum and maximum lengths close to double our current range (Cone & Foster, 2006). Likely this is due to the increased acceptability of publication-style dissertations. Our educated guess is that master's theses would average about two thirds this length, or about 88 pages.

As for format: Yes, there is a format you are supposed to follow. This format is dictated by your particular academic department and institution. We suggest that you get in touch with the people knowledgeable about such matters and learn about your local requirements. These people can usually be found in your department's graduate services office, your institution's graduate school or office of graduate studies, or your library. They typically have a website or written materials that spell out the acceptable format or formats. In addition, they can most likely provide you with other useful information,

---

[1]We are indebted to Madison Beedon for collecting these data.

such as timelines, committee requirements, document deposit requirements, fees, and so on. Theses and dissertations in psychology commonly follow the style and format guidelines set forth in the *Publication Manual of the American Psychological Association* (also referred to as the *Publication Manual*; American Psychological Association, 2020). This book has been written in that format, and many journals in the behavioral sciences adhere to it. You will see frequent references to the *Publication Manual* throughout this book.

Although the *Publication Manual* provides an often-followed format, it is not universally accepted, even in schools and departments of psychology. Furthermore, even where it is accepted, local deviations often exist (e.g., sections or chapters to include, their order, reference format, placement of tables) that you will do well to discover. We advise you to make learning the local norms one of your first priorities. You will save time and aggravation by writing and referencing in the locally accepted format right from the start.

A good place to begin to find out what your thesis or dissertation will eventually look like is to examine some of those completed by previous students working with the same committee chairs you are considering. These provide good, concrete examples of what you can expect. Ask faculty members for some suggestions. Be aware that completed projects vary in quality, and faculty members should be able to direct you to the better quality examples. Because norms for the format and content of a thesis or dissertation may also differ depending on your specific area of research, you should ask for examples that are most relevant to the type of research you are contemplating. Chapter 4 deals specifically with the selection of committee chairs, so don't worry if you haven't yet selected one.

What, in general, will your final document contain? It will most likely resemble a journal article, or sometimes a series of articles but with more detail. The traditional thesis or dissertation begins with a table of contents and then launches into a review of the literature. Following this are the Method, Results, and finally Discussion sections. A reference section contains details on the works cited in the text, and appendices provide supplemental material, such as equipment blueprints, consent forms, data recording forms, and sometimes even raw data. Recently, many departments have begun to encourage alternative formats that are closer to submission-ready journal articles but that still allow students to demonstrate in-depth mastery of relevant knowledge. These alternatives may include a journal-length document with an appendix containing an extended literature review or a portfolio-style project consisting of a series of two to three studies completed during doctoral study, often with an integrated introduction and discussion. The portfolio-style alternative is more common at the dissertation stage, once students have amassed a body of work, than at the thesis stage. We say more about these alternative formats throughout the book.

So, there you have it. You know what theses and dissertations are and what they look like. The remainder of this book discusses the nuts and bolts of the process you will follow to complete this major undertaking. Now, let's turn our attention to what is probably the most important question of this chapter.

WHY DO A THESIS OR DISSERTATION IN THE FIRST PLACE?

There are many reasons for doing a thesis or dissertation. In the final analysis, you are writing one because your graduate program requires you to do so to obtain a specific degree. There are other good reasons as well, of course. Some are pragmatic and directly related to your career plans: The project, as a way to showcase your conceptual, methodological, analytic, and communication skills, might be your stepping-stone to an academic research or teaching position or an applied job. Any publications that emerge from the project, as well as a rich data set that you may be able to work from for several years, can also jump-start your career and help you maintain momentum as you transition from trainee to professional.

Other reasons are more purely intellectual. Research offers many challenges and opportunities to think about and solve conceptual, methodological, and practical problems. Conducting research is a way to find out more about some psychological or other behavioral science phenomenon that piques your curiosity. Completing a thesis or dissertation can also provide the personal satisfaction of taking on and mastering a complex and challenging task and seeing how your intellectual skills have grown during the process.

Now that you are at this point in your program, take a moment to consider how you view this specific requirement. Is it merely a troublesome hoop to jump through on your way to a degree? Are you looking for the easiest, quickest way to get beyond it? Do you eagerly anticipate gaining useful skills during the project? Is it an opportunity for you to continue research you are already doing? Do you see it as having any relevance to the work you plan after graduation—for example, as a key part of your developing program of research or a chance to master and advance knowledge of an area in which you plan to practice?

As cognitive behavior therapists know, the way you think about the major research you are about to undertake will contribute to the enjoyment, ease, and speed with which you conduct the project and the amount you learn from it. If you are filled with curiosity about some aspect of psychology or about the process of doing research in psychology, good for you! You will probably have the stamina to stick with your project from start to finish. You will probably even have some fun along the way. You probably haven't gotten this far if you don't enjoy learning. For many of us, doing research is the ultimate learning experience. Even if the prospect of embarking on your thesis or dissertation is daunting and you're not sure it will qualify as "fun," it will be useful to concentrate on the positive aspects of the project and to view the hurdles you will encounter as challenges and growth opportunities rather than obstacles. With that attitude, although the project may never rise to the level of fun, it can be a very satisfying, rewarding, and esteem-building experience.

FIND WHAT WORKS FOR YOU

Before ending this chapter, a word of warning is in order. Some of the advice we offer will not be useful to you. Not every strategy works well for every student, and not every faculty member or department orchestrates the thesis and dissertation process with the same instruments and score. There are almost as many ways of getting from the beginning to the end of the thesis and dissertation process as there are graduate students. The key is finding ways of negotiating the process that work for you. In addition, rules and traditions differ from place to place. Take what we say with some healthy skepticism, and gather information along the way to see whether your local situation is different from what we present in this book.

Remember, completing a thesis or dissertation is, in some respects, a rite of passage. As with most such rites, some of the process may seem arbitrary and nonfunctional. If you acknowledge this up front and decide to do what needs to be done, whether it makes complete sense or not, you will succeed much more easily and have a lot more fun along the way. Remember to keep your eyes on the prize, and engage in lots of positive self-talk as you do.

In other words, don't get too intimidated or annoyed by the thesis or dissertation process. Yes, it's lengthy. Yes, it involves seemingly arbitrary requirements. Yes, you may never have done anything quite like this before. Yes, it may be scary. And yes, you, like many others, will probably complete the process and earn your degree. Remember, most of the project will involve skills you already have. In addition, your chair and committee will be there to help. One of our students put it very well:

> As I come to the close of my graduate process and the completion of my dissertation, one thought keeps coming back to me—that any goal is possible given two factors: 1) the ability to break things down into tiny steps, and 2) the support of family, friends, and the community. (Dionne, 1992, p. iii)

We know you are motivated, or you wouldn't be reading this book. Are you ready to act on this motivation? Let's turn to Chapter 2 to examine your preparation in some detail and find out what you might do to be even better prepared for the task ahead.

2

Starting Out

Assessing Your Preparation for the Task Ahead

This chapter guides you through a checklist to assess the skills and resources you'll need for your thesis or dissertation, including
- research, writing, and technical skills
- personal skills such as time management, interpersonal abilities, and adaptive self-talk
- social, environmental, and resource supports
- financial costs and resources

Read thoroughly to
- take a careful look at your professional and personal readiness for the project
- make sure you consider as many personal and environmental resources as possible

Skim or skip if
- you already know what skills and resources you'll need for the thesis or dissertation

In the previous chapter, we suggested that you examine your attitude toward completing a thesis or dissertation. Being in the right frame of mind is important both at the start and throughout a big writing project like this. There are other types of preparation, too. In this chapter, we describe how to

https://doi.org/10.1037/0000161-002
Dissertations and Theses From Start to Finish: Psychology and Related Fields, Third Edition,
by D. J. Bell, S. L. Foster, and J. D. Cone

assess your preparation. Our goal is to help you appraise your skills to do the job well.

ARE YOU READY?

To get you started, we provide a reality test. By now you have identified good reasons for undertaking a major research project and are convinced you want to do it. Are you really prepared, however? Complete the Research Readiness Checklist in Figure 2.1 to answer that question. When you complete the checklist, be sure to respond to each of the questions as truthfully as you can. Remember, this is a test of how realistically you are approaching this process. Be honest with yourself. A "no" answer will provide useful material for reflection when we talk about the implications of your responses. Write down your answers, and we will discuss how to interpret them in the next section.

Because this checklist is not an empirically validated measure, don't think of it as providing definitive answers concerning your preparation to navigate a complex research project successfully. Instead, use it as an inventory of the

FIGURE 2.1. Research Readiness Checklist

Yes	No	**How well do you write?**
☐	☐	1. Do you organize your papers effectively?
☐	☐	2. Do you get feedback from professors that your writing is easy to follow and that your logic is clear?
☐	☐	3. Do you prepare an outline before beginning to write?
☐	☐	4. Do you use correct grammar consistently?
☐	☐	5. Do you know APA Style well enough to write with only occasional checking?
Yes	**No**	**Do you have the necessary methodological preparation?**
☐	☐	6. Have you taken two or more graduate-level statistics courses within the past 3 years?
☐	☐	7. Have you taken a graduate-level course in test construction or measurement theory?
☐	☐	8. Have you taken a course in research design as a graduate student?
☐	☐	9. Have you critiqued empirical research papers in graduate school?
☐	☐	10. Have you been involved in empirical research as a graduate student?
☐	☐	11. Do you know how to use at least one major statistical software package?

FIGURE 2.1. Research Readiness Checklist (*Continued*)

Yes	No	Have you made the following general preparations?
☐	☐	12. Do you have at least 10 to 20 hours per week to spend on the project?
☐	☐	13. Will this time be available for at least 12 months?
☐	☐	14. Have you talked to at least three other people about their thesis or dissertation experience?
☐	☐	15. Have you examined theses or dissertations completed by other students in your program?
☐	☐	16. Do you have the physical space for uninterrupted writing, data analysis, and related activities?
☐	☐	17. Do you have the agreement of family and loved ones to support you in this effort?
☐	☐	18. Do you have access to faculty or adviser input on a regular basis?
☐	☐	19. Do you have access to adequate bibliographic resources (libraries, databases)?
☐	☐	20. Do you know how to use the databases, literature retrieval mechanisms, and other resources available at your school's library?
☐	☐	21. Do you own or have access to a computer?
☐	☐	22. Do you have reasonable time management skills?
☐	☐	23. Do you have reasonable interpersonal and political skills?
☐	☐	24. Do you know the formal rules governing the thesis or dissertation process at your school?
☐	☐	25. Do you know the informal rules governing the thesis or dissertation process at your school?
☐	☐	26. Have you asked other students about the costs of doing their research?
☐	☐	27. Have you investigated financial resources to defray thesis or dissertation costs?

important types of preparation you will need to make the journey a smooth one. Basically, this list is a task analysis of the skills and resources we believe you will need to complete the project effectively and in a timely manner. This leads to a word of warning: On one hand, do not let a "no" answer be a stimulus for an anxiety attack. A "no" does not mean you will fail to complete your thesis or dissertation. One of us, for example, would have said "no" to at least four items before beginning the successfully completed dissertation. At least a few "no" answers will be even more likely if you're embarking on your thesis, as theses often begin fairly early in graduate training at a time when you may be just beginning to master scientific writing, research design, or statistics. On the other hand, a full complement of "yes"es does not mean you will sail through the project trouble free. Use "no" answers to alert you to potential trouble spots that advance planning and preparation could help you avoid. Next, we provide some tips on what this preparation might involve.

INTERPRET YOUR CHECKLIST RESPONSES

To analyze your preparation, let's look more closely at the items on the checklist.

Writing Skills

Writing and methodology skills are probably the most important skills you will need to complete a thesis or dissertation successfully. We'll discuss methodology in a moment. First, let's talk about writing. If you said "no" to Items 1 and 2, you should seriously consider additional preparation before undertaking your project. Organization skills in writing (Items 1 and 2) are an indication of how clearly you think and convey your thoughts in written form. As Zinsser (2006) observed, "Clear thinking becomes clear writing" (p. 8). Failure to organize well can reflect trouble thinking in a logical fashion. And unfortunately, there are no quick and easy programs to teach this skill. So, if you have reason to believe you do not organize verbal material well, stop and reconsider. You might benefit from specific coursework or tutoring in organizing and sequencing written material. Examine offerings in the English department of your school. Have you ever taken a course in logic? If not, look for one in the philosophy department.

Alternatively, you may have written clearly and logically when most of your writing was for class papers or exams. A thesis or dissertation is a much different animal, however. It is typically longer and much more complex, covering more information in greater depth than papers you have written for other purposes. This project will require crystal-clear organization to guide readers (and you!) through the complexity of a comprehensive review that can include multiple literatures and descriptions of one or more specific studies and their results. You will also need to provide a clear description of your methods, as well as thoughtful discussion of your findings and their limitations and implications.

If you checked "no" for Item 3 (using outlines in your writing), now is the time to begin using outlines. Writing outlines helps organize your thinking and is a concrete step you can take to get any writing project underway. Again, your campus may offer writing courses, workshops, or tutoring that can help you develop this skill. But be warned that writing in the behavioral sciences is different from writing in other disciplines. Attending a writers' workshop for aspiring journalists or novelists may advance your general organization and logic, but the conventions of narrative flow in those disciplines will probably not transfer well to your thesis or dissertation. Look for learning opportunities that target scientific writing, or ask your adviser or committee chair for guidance.

Grammatical prowess (Item 4) is more specific than organization. If you have consistently received input during your university schooling that you have problems with sentence structure, paragraph organization, writing mechanics, proper choice of words, or spelling errors, give some serious thought to remediating before beginning your thesis or dissertation. Although some schools allow editorial consultation on theses and dissertations, most stop short of allowing the kind of input serious grammatical deficiencies would require. Unless English is not your native language, faculty will expect you to write the document yourself, not have an editor do it.

You can take several steps to improve your grammatical skills. First, consider taking advantage of a good course or textbook on syntax, grammar, and punctuation. When you have a basic foundation in syntax and punctuation, one next step toward grammatical proficiency would be to subject a sample of your writing to one of the several good grammar-checking programs that run in conjunction with your word-processing programs. Most major programs (e.g., Microsoft Word) have spelling- and grammar-checkers that include a number of options you can elect to occur automatically or on demand. There are also many stand-alone software programs (e.g., StyleWriter, Grammarly, WhiteSmoke) that operate in similar ways. Most are available online (although they often require purchase) and can be used with a variety of computer operating systems.

Stand-alone programs typically provide a more detailed assessment of your writing than a word-processing program. They can indicate whether you have violated one or more of hundreds of rules of grammar, made punctuation errors, produced too many long sentences, been too negative, or written in the passive voice. You will be amazed at the thoroughness with which these programs analyze your writing. Even if you are a good writer, you will benefit. We all have bad habits that are so automatic we're not even aware of them.

As an example of the type of analysis you can receive from a grammar- and style-checking program, look at the writing sample in Figure 2.2, which is from an earlier draft of this chapter. As you can see, StyleWriter provides a rather detailed analysis of this writing sample. It provides indexes of readability ("bog"), interest ("pep"), wordiness ("style" and "glue"), and reading level; identifies misspellings and use of passive voice; and counts words and average sentence length. Subjecting repeated samples of your writing to analyses of this type can lead to considerable improvement, as revealed by the revision of this sample in Figure 2.3, as well as the final, revised text that appears four paragraphs below.

Although your faculty adviser or chair will likely edit your writing as you prepare drafts of your thesis or dissertation, you will not get feedback this extensive. It is just not humanly possible for faculty to keep the thousands of rules available in their head and recall them at just the right moment. And

FIGURE 2.2. Original Sample With StyleWriter Corrections Suggested

A[1] final suggestion for improving your writing style (i.e.[2], organization, flow, stentence[3] structure,[4] grammar) is to model your writing on recent publications in the most prestigious journals in your field. Select a journal that publishes empirical reseach[3] much like what you will be doing in your thesis or dissertation, and start with one article from a recent issue of the journal. First, carefully review the article for writing style (don't worry about the content right now). Notice how the author(s)[5] organize the paper by concentrating on the headings and subheadings used. Within sections of the paper, notice how the different paragraphs are sequenced and how they present the flow of information in a logical way. Notice the sentence structure the author(s)[5] use.

Second,[6] attempt to reproduce the paper's organization, sequencing, flow, and sentence structure.[4] The best way to make sure you attend to these things[4] in enough detail to improve your own writing is to imitate[7] them. prepare[8] an outline of the paper and examine it for organization and structure.[4] Leave space on your outline to copy in text under each heading. Then copy, word for word, the sentences that support or expand each point in the outline. Note that electronic cutting and pasting misses the point of this exercise (you are building your writing skills, not your cut and paste skills!). Based on recent Research (e.g., Mueller & Oppenheimer, 2014), even typing may reduce this exercise's effectiveness in improving your writing. So, dust off your pen and paper and hand-write this outline. After[9] doing this for several papers you will be impressed[10] with how much better your own writing becomes. You can do the same thing[4] using dissertations or theses your chairperson nominates as particularly[11] well-written.

- Words: 286 • Bog: 34 Good • Pep: 16 Good • Passive: 13 Good
- Style: 41 Fair • Sentence: 17.9 Excellent • Jargon: 0.7% Excellent
- Glue: 41% Fair • Grade: 10.5 Fairly Easy

Sentences and words that require attention are highlighted in different colors. By clicking on highlighted words and sentences, you see an explanation from StyleWriter as to why the passage is flagged. In addition, StyleWriter advises you about changes to consider. Suggested changes and our responses are as follows:

- [1]Poor sentence readability ("bog" index, indicating readability = poor)
  - Advice: Edit highlighted words to improve readability (highlighted words: "suggestion," "organization," "publications"). Attend to other suggested edits/corrections.
  - Response: We edited some words.
- [2]Abbreviation/acronym use (increased bog)
  - Advice: Don't overuse abbreviations and acronyms.
  - Response: We made no change; this use of abbreviation is appropriate.
- [3]Spelling
  - Advice: Correct typo.
  - Response: We corrected the typo.

FIGURE 2.2. Original Sample With StyleWriter Corrections Suggested (*Continued*)

- [4]Nonspecific word choice
  - Advice: Be specific or edit out.
  - Response: We made no change to "structure," which we determined to be the appropriate word. We changed "thing."

- [5]Punctuation check
  - Advice: Should be a space before opening bracket.
  - Response: We removed the parentheses, which we determined to be unnecessary.

- [6]Poor sentence readability (bog index = dreadful)
  - Advice: Edit highlighted words to improve readability (highlighted words: "attempt," "organization," "sequencing"). Attend to other suggested edits/corrections.
  - Response: We edited the sentence by changing one word but left the remainder intact.

- [7]Complex word choice
  - Advice: Consider a more readable synonym.
  - Response: We substituted the suggested synonym.

- [8]Poor sentence readability (bog index = fair, style = poor)
  - Advice: Consider cutting "glue" (often unnecessary) words: "an," "of," "the," "and," "it," "for."
  - Response: We made no change; we deemed these words appropriate.

- [9]Poor sentence readability (style = fair)
  - Advice: Consider cutting glue words: "after," "this," "for," "will," "with," "how," "much," "better," "own," "becomes."
  - Response: We made no change; we deemed these words appropriate.

- [10]Passive word choice
  - Advice: Use active tense.
  - Response: Our original word choice is appropriate.

- [11]Unnecessary word
  - Advice: Can usually omit "particularly"
  - Response: We omitted "particularly."

even if they could provide this level of feedback, your adviser or chair's job is to teach independent research skills, not writing. About all these busy people will have time to do is comment that your writing needs improvement and, perhaps, point out a few examples of your run-on sentences, subject–verb disagreements, and preposition errors. The less time you and they have to spend correcting these issues, the more time and energy you and they can spend on the actual content of the project.

Two warnings are in order here. First, it is critical to use software (and especially your word processing program) to check your grammar as only part of your writing enhancement routine. In a detailed examination of how several word-processing programs handled common errors, one English professor noted that the grammar-check functions in most programs not only failed to consistently identify several of the most common writing errors

FIGURE 2.3. Revised Sample With StyleWriter Corrections Incorporated (or Not)

A final suggestion to improve your writing style (i.e., organization, flow, sentence structure, grammar) is to model your writing on recent articles in the most prestigious journals in your field. Select a journal that publishes empirical research much like what you will be doing in your thesis or dissertation, and start with one article from a recent issue of the journal. First, carefully review the article for writing style (don't worry about the content right now). Notice how the authors organize the paper by concentrating on the headings and subheadings used. Within sections of the paper, notice how the different paragraphs are sequenced and how they present the flow of information in a logical way. Notice the sentence structure the authors use.

Second, try to reproduce the paper's organization, sequence, flow, and sentence structure. The best way to make sure you attend to these details in your own writing is to mimic them. Prepare an outline of the paper and examine it for organization and structure. Leave space on your outline to copy in text under each heading. Then copy, word for word, the sentences that support or expand each point in the outline. Based on recent Research (e.g., Mueller & Oppenheimer, 2014), even typing may reduce this exercise's effectiveness in improving your writing. So, dust off your pen and paper and hand-write this outline. After you do this for several papers, you will be impressed with how much better your own writing becomes. You can do the same exercise using dissertations or theses your chairperson identifies as well-written.

• Words = 272 • Bog = 18 Excellent • Pep = 16 Good • Passive = 0 Excellent
• Style: 14 Excellent • Sentence = 17 Excellent • Jargon: 0.7% Excellent
• Glue = 38% Concise • Grade 9.7 = Fairly Easy

but also offered bad advice about fixing errors (Kies, 2018). The take-home message is that grammar-checking software is best used in addition to, rather than instead of, your own knowledge of good writing and the specific nature of the information you are trying to convey. We encountered this in Style-Writer's evaluation of our paragraph, and as we note in Figure 2.2, we chose to ignore some of the suggested edits.

Second, the informal style we use in this book is not appropriate for your thesis or dissertation. This book is full of "you" language and contractions, and it sometimes begins sentences with conjunctions ("And") and occasionally ends a series with "and so on." We attempt to be engaging as we speak directly to you in sharing our experiences and advice, but these informalities are not acceptable for the more formal, scholarly writing expected in theses and dissertations. Please do not use the writing in this book as an example of a style that would be appropriate in your document! At the same time, however, writing that is overly formal and full of jargon can come across as stilted and be difficult to read. Remember, you are writing professionally, but that doesn't mean you need to use the longest words and most complex sentences possible. Instead, aim for a writing style that is clear, straightforward, and succinct.

A final suggestion to improve your writing style (i.e., organization, flow, sentence structure, grammar) is to model your writing on recent articles in the most prestigious journals in your field. Select an article from a recent issue of a journal that publishes empirical research much like what you will be doing for your thesis or dissertation. First, carefully review the article for writing style (don't worry about the content right now). By concentrating on the headings and subheadings used, you'll notice how the authors organized the article. Within sections of the article, notice how the sequence and flow of paragraphs present information in a logical way. Notice the sentence structure the authors used.

Second, try to reproduce the article's organization, sequencing, flow, and sentence structure. The best way to make sure you attend to these details in your own writing is to mimic those of other authors. Use the article's structure to prepare an outline of a paper of your own (e.g., one you need to write for class, an early version of your thesis or dissertation). Leave space on your outline to write in text under each heading. Then, using similar sequencing, structure, and flow, try to write sentences that support or expand each point in the outline. Research indicates that typing may reduce this exercise's effectiveness in improving your writing (e.g., Mueller & Oppenheimer, 2014). So, dust off your pen and paper and handwrite this outline. After you do this for several papers, you will be impressed with how much better your own writing becomes. You can do the same exercise using theses or dissertations that your chair identifies as well written.

APA Style or other specific style requirements (Item 5) deal with even more specific verbal skills (American Psychological Association [APA], 2020). Happily, although these skills are important, their absence is not fatal in the budding behavioral scientist. Your institution may have a subscription to Academic Writer, a comprehensive online platform that provides instruction and support for APA Style writing (for more information, visit https:// digitallearning.apa.org/academic-writer). Academic Writer helps students learn to conduct research, create APA Style citations and references, and structure and format their papers in APA Style to help make the process straightforward and painless. Better yet, buy the *Publication Manual of the American Psychological Association* (seventh ed.; APA, 2020) and learn the proper formatting yourself. Anyone competent enough to complete graduate work can master APA Style with a little help from this clear and detailed manual.

In addition to Academic Writer, APA also provides a series of online resources with answers to frequently asked questions, online courses and tutorials, and an APA Style blog (https://blog.apastyle.org/apastyle/). If you are at a school that uses some other style, ask at your library, department, or dean's office for a style sheet, website, or manual that indicates what is acceptable. Again, a quick online search should reveal several software programs to help you conform to your particular style requirements.

Methodology Skills

Items 6 through 11 deal with the adequacy and recency of your methodological and data analytic preparation. It is probably safe to say that taking two or more data analysis classes (Item 8) is an essential requirement for satisfactory thesis or dissertation completion in most departments. Of course, the specific types of courses you need may differ depending on the type of research methods you will be using—that is, quantitative, qualitative, behavior analytic, brain imaging, and so forth. If you are not currently fluent in the statistical concepts and tools covered in the usual two-course graduate statistical sequence, you may have to take some remedial steps. Part of the material covered in such courses can be found in Chapter 9. Look it over. Does it seem comfortably familiar? Could it be, with just a brief review?

If it has been some time since you completed your statistics coursework, or your particular research will require skills outside of those typically covered in your program's statistics courses, you might want to appraise your current skills more systematically. If your graduate program includes tests in statistics as part of its comprehensive exams, ask your adviser if you can take the current version of the test. Explain that you want to know whether you need to take a refresher course. You might accomplish this by auditing the major methodological courses, all or in part. YouTube videos with statistics tutorials provide another way of beefing up or reviving your understanding. Now is also a good time to identify whether you need any advanced or specialized data analysis courses or workshops. If so, begin planning how and when you will take them.

Before you let statistics phobia scare you away from doing a thesis or dissertation, remember that we said "fluent"; we did not say that you must be an *A+* whiz in statistics or that you must find the material easy. Many students, in our experience, find statistics to be the most challenging and intimidating part of research. Even students who earn *A*s in stats classes may find that they need to review the material or that they sometimes get stumped when it comes to applying what they learned to their own projects. Nonetheless, with adequate guidance, they master this aspect of their thesis or dissertation. A committee member with specific analytic expertise can provide invaluable guidance. Many departments and institutions also offer statistical consulting services that students find helpful. The key is obtaining adequate guidance if you have mastered basic statistical concepts, and additional training or tutoring if you have not. Thousands of psychologists in training have mastered their fear of numbers, and so can you.

An affirmative answer to Item 7 (measurement theory) is most important if you are planning a project that will require constructing your own measure(s). Are you working in an area with nonexistent or inadequate measures of the variables you will be studying? For example, are you planning to survey the attitudes of a group of migrant workers, or interested in emerging adult dating relationships among transgender individuals, but you have found there are no good measures? If your answer is "yes" to similar questions, you should be fluent in measure development or test construction concepts. The intricacies of scale construction and validation are myriad and should not be approached lightly. Even if your research does not involve the actual construction of new measures, it is well to be an educated consumer. Making the most informed choice of instruments for the variables you will be studying requires more than passing familiarity with psychometric concepts. If you are unsure of your preparation in this area, take a look at the material in Chapter 8.

Have you taken a class in research design (Item 8)? This is important for understanding how to design studies that maximize both internal and external validity. If these terms are unfamiliar to you, we strongly recommend that you review research design principles. Another outcome of design classes is that you learn to speak the language of research, and to speak it correctly. Ill-prepared students often use the term "confound" when they mean "methodological problem." Others refer to the "reliability" of a research design or confuse dependent and independent variables. Or they state that they will test "mediation" when they really mean "moderation." Correct use of terminology is important for discussing the methodology of your own study as well as others' work. In addition, an incorrectly used term in a proposal or defense is a signal to committee members that you may not know what you are talking about, and indeed, you may not! This kind of problem can lead to serious flaws in your research conclusions, if not your design, and invites probing and sometimes antagonistic questioning by committee members. Fortunately, both the flaws and their discussion can be prevented if you make sure you understand research terms and use them precisely.

Which brings us to Item 9—having some experience reading and evaluating the research literature. All published articles are not equal in terms of their methodological rigor. Part of your job in creating a good study is to sort the good from the mediocre (we can hope the bad never made it into print!) and to make sure your study is in the "good" group. You will need to be appropriately critical of what others have done (in your literature review) and what you yourself have done (in the Discussion section). As with most things, practice makes perfect. Experience in critically reading and evaluating empirical literature in graduate courses can help you build these skills and has the added advantage of sharpening your thinking skills generally. If your adviser reviews manuscripts submitted to journals, you can also ask to assist with those.

To some extent, answering positively to Item 10 (research experience) may cover you with respect to Items 6 to 9. If you have been especially active in a program of research that serves as the basis for your own study, you will likely be familiar with the methodology required for conducting that research. If you have been involved less extensively or if your plans have led you to another area, you might not be as well prepared. In this case, a thorough appraisal of your competence in research design, measurement, and data analysis might be in order.

Most graduate programs expose students to computer software designed to make the number crunching part of research very efficient (Item 11). Among the more popular are SPSS, SAS, Mplus, and R (R is free!). Find out which of these are available to you and can be used to analyze the data you will eventually produce. If you do not know yet exactly which tests or procedures you will need, just familiarize yourself with what is available for now. You can get more specific after you design your project and know the type of data you will be analyzing.

In summary, your writing and methodology skills are the most important determinants of your success in the research process. Before moving on, however, let's look at the implications of some of the other items on the Research Readiness Checklist. Consider Items 12 and 13, for example. Some otherwise realistic candidates are amazed at suggestions that they will need at least 10 to 20 hours a week to devote to the effort. And the thought that this might have to extend over a year or more completely dumbfounds them! In truth, these are probably conservative estimates—at least for dissertations. Of course, these estimates are subject to local variation, and that is where Items 14 and 15 can be useful. What have others at your school said about the time required to complete their thesis or dissertation?

Environmental and Social Support

What about the physical space to pursue this mammoth undertaking (Item 16)? This is clearly not the time to be eyeing the kitchen table, figuring you can work around the salt and pepper, morning paper, and your family's or roommate's meals! You are going to be at this a while, so choose your work space carefully. Find some quiet place that will afford uninterrupted privacy for sustained periods of time. If you are fortunate to have a private or semi-private office on campus, consider arranging private writing shifts with office mates and then closing the door (and perhaps using a "Do Not Disturb" sign) during your scheduled writing time. Many university libraries also provide locked carrels or private workspaces that scholars can reserve for long-term projects. We have even had the occasional student who rented an office specifically for doing their dissertation. They planned to do no other work in this office.

Designating physical space exemplifies an important behavior management principle. Behavior that is under the control of narrowly defined stimulus conditions will, other things being equal, become increasingly focused. Researchers in self-control have talked about stimulus control for decades (Stuart, 1977). People with weight problems are told to eat only at the dining room table and (sometimes) only with a white placemat in front of them. Insomniacs are told to sleep only in bed, and only to sleep in bed, thus bringing sleeping more clearly under the stimulus control of the bed. Behavioral psychologist B. F. Skinner had a special desk in his house for writing. He spent several hours at this desk each day and permitted himself no other activity (e.g., bill paying, personal correspondence) at this desk. One of us has a student who still claims that she cannot enter a particular coffee shop without having an almost overwhelming urge to pull out her computer and get to work. Although this setting certainly was not private, the student and her colleague had spent every Saturday morning for more than a year frequenting that coffee shop for their thesis writing, and no other activity (including simply relaxing with a cup of coffee) felt appropriate in that location.

Related to bringing your writing under the stimulus control of a particular location is bringing it under the control of a particular time of day as well. In his later years, Skinner wrote each day between 5 a.m. and 7 a.m. By being consistent in the time you work each day, you increase the chances that a whole host of additional temporally related stimuli will control your writing. The outside light and sounds are likely to be constant (and thus less distracting), as is your biological state. In selecting your writing time, it is helpful to ask yourself when you are most apt to write well. When is your thinking (including your organization, logic, creativity, and concentration) at its sharpest? Do you work best with longer stretches of time or with more frequent but shorter time blocks? Do you prefer to immerse yourself in just one task or work better when you're able to move between a few different tasks?

It is also useful to anticipate interruptions. You should be rigid in writing during the same time each day. Others will test your consistency and want you to do things with them (e.g., meetings, shopping, trips with the kids to the park) during your sacrosanct research and writing time. Although consistency might be, for some, the hobgoblin of little minds, it is more often the godparent of successfully completed theses and dissertations.

You will be much more likely to produce this consistency if you carefully cultivate the support of family and loved ones (Item 17). Do not neglect these important people. Be up front and realistic with them about your need for sustained periods of molelike behavior. At the same time, arrange occasions when you can be exclusively with them. Children and other family members will be much less likely to interrupt your work if they know you have committed to spend specific times with them and you keep your commitments.

Finally, your faculty adviser or chair, and often other faculty, will provide indispensable instrumental and social support (Item 18). To assess your preparation for the upcoming project, take realistic stock of your ability to access these faculty. Do you and your adviser already meet on a regular basis? If so, this is a great start, but will the current arrangements be sufficient to support all stages of your project? Consider whether you'll need to develop other routines with your adviser. For example, if your weekly meetings cover everything—your assistantship, clinical work, collaborative work on your adviser's research—you might want to schedule specific dissertation-only meetings to make sure the dissertation doesn't get set aside in favor of more immediate deadlines. Can you reach your adviser between meetings for help with data collection problems or an analysis that just won't run? The students of one of our colleagues knew that for impromptu meetings, it was always best to catch up with this colleague during a midmorning walk. Understanding which faculty relationships you have now, which additional relationships you'll need to develop, and how to get what you need from faculty will have a major impact on the success of your thesis or dissertation. We discuss these issues more in Chapter 4.

Library and Computer Access and Skills

Of course, it is crucial that you have access to the literature and the technology that will support your writing (Items 19–21). Does your library have the bibliographic databases you may need for your literature review, such as PsycINFO or MEDLINE, and do you know how to use them effectively? Your library probably has a resource librarian who can help you learn to use databases in ways you never thought possible. Learning how to search effectively and efficiently will save you time while helping ensure that you haven't missed key papers in your research area.

Once you identify sources that are relevant to your work, does your institution have the books and journals you need, or can you borrow them through interlibrary loan? Institutional subscriptions to electronic journals can be a huge time saver as they allow you to access articles immediately, skim them for relevance, and download the ones you want to keep. No more traipsing up and down the stacks in your library just to discover that the volume you need is missing or that the article isn't really relevant after all.

Time Management Skills

Chapter 3 has lots to say about time management skills (Item 22), an area in which most of us can improve. We also discussed some of the elements in successful time management in the Environment and Social Support section of this chapter. Suffice it to say here that most deadline workers and procrastinators face major challenges in completing their thesis or dissertation. It's time to start learning new work habits now.

Interpersonal Skills

Items 23 through 25 are related to how well you are likely to get along with others in your research endeavor. Interpersonal and political skills contribute to effective interaction with the key players in this work. The most important, of course, after loved ones, is your chair. Do you have the interpersonal skills needed to work effectively with this person? Are you willing to submit innumerable rewrites in response to what seem to you to be petty criticisms? Often students do not appreciate that multiple revisions are required to make a scientific document clear, coherent, and sufficiently detailed. It is said that Sir Isaac Newton knew well the importance of multiple rewrites. He took great care in revising his papers and would write, cross out, correct, copy all over again, cross out, recorrect, and recopy. When he finished this process, he would start all over again—"Thus, he made at least eight drafts of the *Scholium Generale* for the second edition [of his *Principia*]" (Koyré, 1965, p. 262). Are you ready for a similar level of care?

Do you know how to accept suggestions and assert your disagreements in positive, constructive ways? Or do you typically react defensively to suggestions for change? Do you know how to read the relationships between and among committee members? Are you likely to select members whose failure to get along interferes with your thesis or dissertation? Can you recognize grandstanding in committee meetings so that when it happens in yours, you handle it effectively? If your project requires the support of people in off-campus agencies, do you have the interpersonal resources to obtain and maintain this support? Can you move in and out of these agencies in effective, nondisruptive ways? Of course, your committee chair is often a key player in managing these relationships, but learning to handle them effectively yourself will help you manage situations when your chair is not present (or is part of the challenge!).

If your interpersonal skills are a bit rough, make a list of the situations in which you have difficulty. You may be able to recruit an assistant to help you with agency interactions, for example. The assistant can do most of the interacting if you are not good at it. For situations you must handle yourself, seek advice from other students or faculty who are good at handling them. Rehearse effective approaches with a friend and get feedback on your performance.

Formal and Informal Rules

At all schools, there are both formal and informal rules governing the entire thesis and dissertation process. There are forms to complete, fees to pay, deadlines to meet, and formats to follow, among other matters. For example, how much time are committee members given to review the proposal before the proposal meeting is convened? Two calendar weeks is not an unusual amount of time for this. Is there a time period such as this at your school? In addition, many schools publicize the occurrence of doctoral defenses. These are open meetings to which all members of the academic community are invited. To give notice in a timely way, it is often necessary to impose deadlines for specifying a time and place for the meeting. Is this true at your school? Some schools circulate a form among committee members indicating the time and place of the defense. At that time, the committee member is asked to sign the form agreeing to be available and acknowledging receipt of a copy of the thesis or dissertation. Does your school do this? Find out early what the formal rules are. Ask for a copy of them from your department or campus graduate office, or find them online, and ask for clarification of any rules you don't understand.

Then there are myriad informal rules. Becoming aware of these will make your life go more smoothly. For example, when should you approach a faculty member about serving on your committee or even being its chair? Do faculty expect you to have a well-developed idea and literature supporting it before you contact them? If you are in a program that uses a mentorship model, what happens if you'd like to do your thesis or dissertation project with someone other than your mentor? What if you have discussed ideas with several faculty and like the ideas of one best but really want to work with another? Is it OK to use the ideas provided by one faculty member and choose another as chair? How complete and carefully proofread do drafts need to be before you present them to your chair? to your committee? Are there certain blackout periods during which proposal meetings generally cannot be scheduled (e.g., during the last or first weeks of the term or during the summer)? Is your preferred chair planning a sabbatical anytime during your project's tenure?

Start finding out about these informal rules and occurrences before getting too far down the path. Talk to other graduate students who have nearly completed the journey. Ask your adviser, mentor, or potential committee members what they know about such rules. There will be no published list of these rules, and although the informal rules are often as important as the formal ones, faculty and more advanced students may not think to mention them unless you ask.

Costs and Resources

It costs money as well as time to do research. Schools and faculty vary widely in the financial support they provide for student research; financial support can range from none at all to complete support of all of the student's costs in conducting the research. The latter is most common when a faculty member has large grants and the student's project is subsumed under the objectives of the funded research.

You should anticipate several potential expenses by the time your thesis or dissertation is complete. You may need to pay to photocopy consent forms or questionnaire measures, especially if you're completing data collection in the field. You will need a computer and printer to prepare your documents and analyze data; do you have access to campus computers, or will you want or need your own? Will you need to upgrade what you have in order to run specialized software? Additional costs to consider, depending on your project, may be payments to participants and research assistants and costs for procuring copyrighted measures, software and equipment, postage, and advertising. You may also have travel expenses and possibly costs related to research or writing space. You will probably also have to pay fees to process the document, apply for graduation, and the like.

How will you finance these costs? Although you may not know your exact topic at this point, it's not too soon to do a little investigation (Items 26 and 27). Some faculty and departments have funds they can draw on to assist students. If your project is one with direct practical application at an agency with which you or your faculty members have contact, it might provide support in various ways, including space, participant recruitment, clerical assistance, and access to funding via sources unique to it. Some schools have competitive grants for thesis and dissertation assistance. Many national organizations, such as APA and the National Institutes of Health, offer dissertation grants and fellowships. Likewise, private foundations often fund specific types of projects. Your university's grants and contracts office is a good source of information about funding resources, especially once you have narrowed down your topic. Websites are another (e.g., see https://www.apa.org/apags/issues/funding.aspx for extensive information from APA's graduate student organization about student funding in psychology).

Finally, other students who have obtained funding are great sources of information, as are their mentors. For now, just get an idea of how other students have handled the costs of their research. If it looks like funding opportunities are likely to be few and far between, think about cutting back on your discretionary expenses and putting away some money to help with thesis and dissertation expenses when the time arises. Several students we know have raised funds from family and friends by asking family for thesis or dissertation fund money for every gift-giving holiday or by establishing a GoFundMe account (https://www.gofundme.com).

EXAMINE YOUR COGNITIVE ECOLOGY

In assessing your overall preparedness, it is useful to identify and dispel some common assumptions that will impede your progress. Mahoney and Mahoney (1976) referred to the process of cleaning up irrational thinking as *cognitive ecology*. Some irrational thoughts have to do with estimating what it will take to get the job done. Even after everything you have read so far, you may be saying to yourself that if you start now, you can expect to be finished with the entire process in 6 months. Or you might be saying you can get all the subjects you will need from two elementary schools, or that it will take 2 weeks to get permission from the principals to contact their teachers. If there is anything close to a Newtonian principle governing research, it is that estimates such as these are almost always wrong. In fact, this is true of research in the behavioral sciences generally. Estimates are so often in error that we have found it helpful to invoke the "rule of threes" whenever we make them. Multiply everything you think you'll need by three, and your estimates will be much more on target.

A related irrationality is thinking that everything will run smoothly. It won't. Plan for the unexpected. It is going to happen anyway, and you might as well be ready for it. In addition to needing 3 times more of just about everything to complete the job, you can expect participants to break their appointments, equipment to fail, data to be lost, and your chair to take another job and leave the university, among other difficulties. Are you ready for these events? Assess the likelihood of each, and prepare contingency plans. If the event is significant and its likelihood great (e.g., your chair leaving) and you cannot develop a plan for working around it with your particular project, you might want to consider an alternative project.

Another irrational thought is that your study must be *the* definitive work in the area. We are not saying there is anything wrong with ambition. The problem is the paralyzing implications of what we call the Nobel laureate syndrome: If you think yours has to be the definitive study, you are never going to be satisfied that you have researched enough literature, framed the question and hypotheses properly, selected the absolutely best design, or controlled all the important variables. Keep in mind that there is rarely one "right" or "best" research idea or project. Knowledge grows by increments. Scientific breakthroughs and paradigmatic revolutions (Kuhn, 1970) are rare, and it is even more rare that they are the result of single studies. There are probably many good ideas you could pursue, and ultimately you need to consider your options, their pros and cons, and commit to just one.

The "myth of methodological perfection" is a related collection of thoughts that impedes research progress. Every study has its faults. These may not be recognized until the scientific community has scrutinized the work closely, but the faults are there. At a minimum there are trade-offs, the most common being that between internal and external validity (i.e., between scientific control on one hand and generalization to the messy real world on the other). To expect your study to be different is simply unrealistic. We are not saying you should strive for anything less than excellence in pursuing your research. But to insist on methodological perfection when this is unattainable is likely to lead to an unfinished project.

If you still think your research has to be a methodologically perfect, definitive study, you would do well to analyze the function of such thoughts. What are you gaining by thinking them? Do they insulate you from your own and others' criticisms of your lack of progress? After all, who could be faulted for wanting to do the perfect study and for refusing to be part of anything less? Are these thoughts keeping the research process deliberately drawn out so you can stay in school and not have to face the cold, cruel world of job seeking and economic self-sufficiency? The trick is to balance high standards with realism and pragmatism that stop short of immobilizing perfectionism and to see your thesis or dissertation to completion instead.

GET READY FOR THE TASK AHEAD

We hope you take this appraisal seriously. Answer the questions on the Research Readiness Checklist as forthrightly as possible, and take the steps needed to prepare for a successful thesis or dissertation. There is no shame in acknowledging areas of needed improvement. Theses and dissertations are complex projects that require many skills. Remember, you do not have to be perfect to complete yours. It is normal to have to work on areas in which you have less experience or expertise. In fact, assuming that your career will be one in which knowledge, technology, and best practices continue to evolve, "getting up to speed" will be a lifelong professional activity. Most of us make it through the process, and the most successful among us are often not the ones who know the most going into a project, but rather those who view it as another opportunity to learn and grow. If you have a history of academic success (and most likely you do), apply the skills you have, and work on those you lack, you, too, will make it through.

Now that you have completed this self-assessment, there is one more skill to consider before you plunge into your project—time management. We turn to that subject in Chapter 3.

✓   **TO DO . . .**
ASSESSING YOUR PREPARATION

☐ Complete the Research Readiness Checklist.

☐ Interpret your responses.

  – Writing skills

  – Methodology skills

  – Environmental and social support

  – Library and computer access and skills

  – Time management skills

  – Interpersonal skills

  – Formal and informal rules

  – Costs and resources

☐ Examine your cognitive ecology.

☐ Plan for needed skill building.

SUPPLEMENTAL RESOURCES

Guides for Thinking About, Writing, and Doing Theses and Dissertations

Miller, A. B. (2009). *Finish your dissertation once and for all! How to overcome psychological barriers, get results, and move on with your life.* American Psychological Association.

Munsey, C. (2009). Summer session: 8 tips for funding your dissertation. *APA Monitor on Psychology, 40*(7), 64. https://www.apa.org/monitor/2009/07-08/dissertation.aspx

Writing Software

Academic Writer (http://digitallearning.apa.org/academic-writer)
StyleWriter (http://Stylewriter-USA.com)

Grammarly (https://www.Grammarly.com)
WhiteSmoke (http://www.whitesmoke.com)
Paper Wizard for APA (https://www.wizardsforstudents.com)
PERRLA for APA (https://www.perrla.com)

Books About Writing More Generally

American Psychological Association. (2020). *Publication manual of the American Psychological Association* (7th ed.).
Darley, J. M., Roediger, H. L., & Zanna, M. P. (Eds.). (2003). *The compleat academic: A practical guide for the beginning social scientist* (2nd ed.). American Psychological Association.
Harris, S. R. (2014). *How to critique articles in the social sciences.* Sage.
Silvia, P. J. (2014). *Write it up: Practical strategies for writing and publishing journal articles.* American Psychological Association.
Silvia, P. J. (2018). *How to write a lot: A practical guide to productive academic writing* (2nd ed.). American Psychological Association.

Websites: Writing and Graduate Student Resources

https://www.apastyle.org/—APA Style information, including frequently asked questions, blog, and information about Academic Writer
https://www.apa.org/apags/—American Psychological Association of Graduate Students website with links to multiple resources supporting thesis and dissertation research
http://asgs.org/—Association for Support of Graduate Students website

3

Time and Trouble Management

This chapter guides you to
- start with carefully worded goals that have specified completion dates
- state clear steps to a completed thesis or dissertation with specific measurable behaviors and completion dates
- schedule the steps and monitor your progress
- minimize procrastination and avoidance

Read thoroughly if
- you could use help with setting realistic goals
- you want a review of basic time management principles and progress monitoring procedures as they relate to completing a major writing project

Skim or skip if
- you are someone whom others would describe as a person who is well organized, keeps commitments, and manages time well on large projects
- you regularly set and meet specific goals in your everyday school, work, and social life

In Chapter 2, we warned you to expect the unexpected to occur sometime in the course of doing your thesis or dissertation. The present chapter deals with some of the most common general problems you might encounter in conducting a thesis or dissertation and suggests ways to avoid or overcome

https://doi.org/10.1037/0000161-003
Dissertations and Theses From Start to Finish: Psychology and Related Fields, Third Edition,
by D. J. Bell, S. L. Foster, and J. D. Cone

them. Later, Chapter 10 helps you plan the specifics involved in implementing your research. Our goal is to help you anticipate and plan the many steps involved in successful research so that you encounter fewer surprises.

The first issue is how effectively you manage your time. Our focus is the logical outgrowth of Einstein's definition of *time* as the occurrence of events in sequence (Barnett, 2005). It follows from this definition that effective use of your time means that you are managing sequenced events in an effective way. But what do we mean by "in an effective way"? A synonymous phrase might be "in a way that gets desired results." Managing events effectively can be viewed as arranging things to get the results you want—in this case, a completed thesis or dissertation.

START WITH GOALS

Successful completion of a research project starts with clear overarching and intermediate goals. Carefully worded goals contain certain common elements. Most important, they state what you want to accomplish and by when. For maximum effectiveness, the "what" should be stated in terms of measurable behavior. "Complete my dissertation by June 30, 20XX" would be an example. Another is "Obtain permission for study from elementary schools by March 1, 20xx."

The most difficult part of such goal setting is deciding the "when" element. Sometimes this is decided for you. For example, many universities require that the doctorate be completed within 5 years after the comprehensive exam. Or you may have a form of financial support that ends at a specific time, whether you are finished or not. Government scholarships to students from foreign countries often include a completion date as one of the terms of the award, after which the student must return to the country to perform some type of work; obviously, this type of contingency is more exacting than the one that involves simply stopping further monetary support at the end of a specified period. The end of monetary support, in turn, is more exacting than an open-ended completion date with no contingencies. Careful planning and the effective use of your time are extremely important if you must finish your thesis or dissertation by a specific date.

LIST YOUR STEPS AND ESTIMATE YOUR TIME REQUIREMENTS

Your thesis or dissertation, like any sizable project, will include numerous intermediate goals or smaller steps to identify, sequence, and accomplish in order to complete the larger effort. You can increase the ease and manageability of your research by carefully identifying and sequencing the steps involved. So, how can you identify the steps?

First, sit down and reflect on everything you know about the requirements. Remember to consider both formal and informal rules. If you don't know them, find out now. List them in terms of things you have to do, beginning with a verb that specifies the action you need to take. For example, participants have to be recruited. Write this as "Recruit participants." Work space has to be obtained. Write this as "Find [or obtain, or acquire] a place to work." Bound copies of the final version of the document might need to be presented to the librarian at your school. Write this as "Turn in ___ bound copies to the library."

Why start each item with a verb? A verb implies action and makes it pretty clear who is responsible for the action—namely, you. Compare "Recruit participants" with "Participants need to be recruited." The first is clearly an instruction to you. The second is merely a declarative sentence. So, participants need to be recruited. Isn't that interesting! When you watch the way you talk, you also watch how you behave in other ways. And decisive language is associated with decisiveness in other behavior. Compare the forcefulness of "*Try* to recruit participants" with "Recruit participants." Have you ever invited someone to a party and heard "That sounds great! I'll try to be there"? How much money would you bet on their appearance? Get clear on your intentions, and then move decisively to accomplish them.

We routinely require our students to develop lists of intermediate goals with respect to their project. These are lists of the sequenced steps necessary to take students from where they are at the beginning to a completed thesis or dissertation. Many students find this worthwhile because it concretizes the whole undertaking and helps make it real. We do not restrict the number or sequencing of the steps. Although we generally encourage small, easily accomplished events using the "little steps for little feet" principle, students vary considerably in selecting the number and size of the steps in their lists. Some prefer fairly large chunks—for example, "Write proposal." Others prefer smaller chunks—for example, "Outline proposal," "Write first five pages of proposal," and "Turn in first draft to chair."

There are two approaches to sequencing the steps in your list: backward chaining and forward chaining. With backward chaining, you begin with the last step (e.g., "Turn in copies at the library") and work backward to the first step. This is most helpful in the planning stages, especially if you must be finished by a particular date. If an exact completion date does not concern you, you might take the more leisurely forward chaining approach, starting where you are and listing all the steps between that point and the final one, adding dates for each as you go. If you find it too overwhelming to set goals covering the entire thesis or dissertation, pick an intermediate goal (e.g., "Obtain approval of the proposal") and develop steps for that part of the process.

We have seen as few as six steps and as many as 46 in students' goal lists. Some inventive sorts have even put their lists in the form of a flowchart with alternative courses to pursue depending on outcomes at various decision points. For example, one student listed these alternatives after "Defend dissertation successfully": "If 'yes,' leave on much-deserved trip to Europe with spouse and family. If 'no,' start looking through the help-wanted ads." A little levity can be a great help at all stages in the process!

As you produce the list of things you must do to complete your project, think of each item as a goal in itself. As mentioned previously, write each step in the form of a goal, including both the behavior to perform and the date by which you will perform it. If you have started with the date by which you want to be finished, it is relatively easy to back up from that date and estimate how long each step should take.

Be realistic in estimating your time. As we noted earlier, most students grossly underestimate the amount of time it will take to turn a research question into a complete proposal. "Two months should be plenty," they might say. Even if the student is the world's fastest writer and has all of the relevant literature in hand, what about the time required for the chair to read between two and six drafts of the literature review and the Method section? How about the time required for committee members to read the proposal? In planning time requirements, first be honest with yourself about how fast you can accomplish things. Second, be sure to consider steps in your time line that rely on others (e.g., your committee chair, the institutional review board, research assistants). If you are in doubt about time estimates and the sequencing of steps, ask other students about their experience. Ask your chair for estimates, as well.

SCHEDULE THE WORK

Once you have identified and assigned realistic completion times to each of the steps in the process, you may find it useful to represent these visually. There are numerous approaches you could take, from simple Gantt charts to more complex PERT (program evaluation and review technique) analyses. These tools provide a structure for planning. For example, a Gantt chart lays out a list of tasks with a visual time window for accomplishing them. Many spreadsheet and project scheduling software packages (e.g., Microsoft Project, Google Docs, Excel) include Gantt charting and often combine it with project scheduling functions. These vary considerably in complexity and thoroughness, ranging from simple time line charts to analyses that include cost estimates, conditional completion probabilities, and so on. Watch out here. Getting into sexy new software can be tempting—and time consuming. Keep your eyes on the prize: completing your thesis or dissertation. Unless you are already a project-scheduling whiz kid, it is probably enough to produce a modest Gantt or time line chart. See the supplemental resources at the end of this chapter, or search online using "Gantt chart." Numerous YouTube videos show how to create them, as well.

Figure 3.1 shows a partial Gantt chart for a research project. It lists the identified activities or steps in the project down the left side of the chart in the order they are to be accomplished. Across the top of the chart is a progression of time units (in this case, weeks) used in scheduling the steps. The example also includes crosshatched shading to indicate when the activity is scheduled

FIGURE 3.1. Gantt Chart for Children's Social Skills Research Project

ACTIVITY	Week								
	1	2	3	4	5	6	7	8	9
1. Assess children in classes	P	A							
2. Identify target children and desired playmates (DPs)	P	A							
3. Randomly assign to groups	P	A							
4. Interview DPs of target children in template-matching group (TMG)	P	A							
5. Develop templates		P							
6. Interview choosers of target children			P						
7. Design target behaviors for TMG		P							
8. Design treatment plan			P						
9. Conduct direct observations					P			P	
10. Implement treatment					P	P	P	P	
11. Repeat in-class assessments									P
Legend: Planned	P								
Actual	A								

to occur and darker shading added when it actually occurs. We provide entries in the chart for the first four activities. As you can see, the darkened cells under Week 2 show the activities occurred a week later than planned. As the project progresses, information is added to the chart for each activity.

A visual representation of the steps and their temporal relationships to one another makes you aware of the completeness of your planning. It also shows the interdependence of the tasks you need to accomplish. The whole job becomes clearer. The chart also becomes a tool you can use in communicating with others when describing your project, especially useful when meeting with representatives of off-campus agencies from whom you hope to recruit participants. It also impresses your committee in proposal meetings. Not only does it aid you in explaining exactly what you plan to do, it also shows your committee that you have thought of everything. Well, almost everything!

The added advantage of even simple computer scheduling software is that you can get immediate feedback on the consequences of changes in your plans. If you are familiar with spreadsheet software, you know the tremendous power afforded by the automatic recalculation of related values when a single value in the data set is changed. Suppose you decide that you want to take a week off in the middle of your project for some unplanned R and R. You know, like when a great aunt has decided she just has to go to Hawaii and thinks you're the only one who can accompany her (at her expense, of course). What impact will this have on the entire project? Is it a simple matter of moving every time line a week back? Or is it more complex because of the parallel nature of some of the activities and their conditional dependence on one another?

When you produce a schedule, remember that it is not set in stone. Logistics problems may force you to alter your plans once you begin the project. This is to be expected. You may not yet know enough about an activity to estimate time frames, and you may need to alter your deadlines as you master this skill. Scheduling software helps by showing the impact of such alterations on the rest of the project.

PLAN YOUR SCHEDULE TO FREE YOURSELF

At this point, you may be asking, Why all this fuss about scheduling, time lines, charts, and so on? You want to get on with your research. Is all this fancy planning just a socially acceptable form of avoidance? It certainly can be, of course. However, an ounce of planning can avoid a pound of problems later on. In the Army, one of us had a sergeant who admonished new recruits daily with the five Ps: *Prior Planning Prevents Poor Performance*. A little time spent up front identifying, sequencing, and time lining the steps in your research project will save inordinate time and frustration later.

To this point we have focused on scheduling the steps involved in completing your thesis or dissertation project. Having a well-designed plan is critical to finishing it, to be sure. However, although it may not seem like it, the thesis or dissertation is only a part of your larger life. To complete it successfully requires making it a regular part of your life. How and when will you fit it into what is likely a pretty full schedule already? We suggest taking an inventory of how you are currently spending your time. We recommend looking online for an inexpensive and easy-to-use app for your cell phone that will beep at random times, allowing you to note what you are doing at the moment. The app organizes the data from these observations into categories (e.g., eating, sleeping, studying, using social media, exercising) and produces graphs showing how much time you spent on what, along with a distribution of your time throughout the day. Wow, you didn't realize you are spending an average of 74 minutes a day on social media!

What are the other consumers of your time? This kind of information alerts you to current priorities and their relative importance in your life. It also clarifies whether your present schedule permits you to work on the thesis or dissertation on a regular basis or whether you are going to have to adjust other activities to make time for it. In our experience, students who make time in their daily schedule for their thesis or dissertation finish earliest and with the least pain. Remember the old story about the tortoise and the hare? Remember who won the race? Slow and steady works for theses and dissertations, too.

Equally important is the liberating effect of having a schedule and sticking to it. Within the time set aside for your research, you have already identified and scheduled all the steps necessary to completing it. This was the hard part. Now, all you have to do is accomplish each step as it comes up in the schedule.

This is why we encourage students to make the steps many and small. A good rule of thumb is to make them small enough to accomplish in a day or, at most, a week. If you do this, you can enter the steps in your appointment calendar or cell phone, entering each on the day you have scheduled to accomplish it.

Be sure to specify the outcome you want to produce in behavioral terms or in terms of products having a close relationship to behavior. For most people, "Read five articles" is preferable to "Spend 2 hours reading," and "Read and outline five articles" is even better. A few students, however, have told us they find time goals more useful than specific product goals, probably because they already use their time productively. The key here is keeping on schedule by working steadily and taking the steps toward completion one by one.

Once you enter all the steps into your calendar, you can stop worrying. All you have to do now is complete each small task as it comes up on your calendar or daily to-do list. It's like the old joke: How do you eat an elephant? One bite at a time! That is exactly how you complete a major research project. In fact, one of us wrote sections of the first edition of this book by planning to complete five pages every week. By sticking to that plan, she produced about one chapter a month and finished her writing on schedule. Note that she had a specific behavioral product as a goal—five pages written. She did not say, "Work on the book for 5 hours a week."

We once had a student who sat down at the beginning of each semester and scheduled all of his classes and all of his study, paper-writing, and project times for the classes. Each day of the semester was scheduled. When other students asked how he could stand to live under such a confining schedule, he replied that, on the contrary, he found the entire process quite liberating. Now he didn't need to spend any more time figuring out how he was ever going to get all that work done or worrying about whether he would. He could use that time more productively in (planned!) recreational pursuits, safe in the knowledge that by having a plan and sticking to it, all his work would get done.

The lesson here is clear: When you know what you have to do and do it according to schedule, you free yourself for guilt-free enjoyment of other parts of your life. This method does not work for everyone. For example, you might find that such detailed scheduling raises your stress level and that missing one scheduled task (an almost inevitable occurrence at some point during your project) throws you into a tailspin of guilt and self-doubt. Remember, the end goal is to make progress on your thesis or dissertation; knowing how to balance rigor and flexibility in your schedule—how to meet your own needs and style as well as the unexpected curveballs that life often throws— will help you achieve this goal.

A final point to remember when constructing your initial schedule is to allow time for social support. This can include time with significant others as well as time spent on social media. Schedule the latter for a less productive period of the day, and do your email then, as well. Also, if your time with significant others is going to be severely limited during particular periods, discuss this with them in advance, when first making your schedule. They need advance warning and the opportunity to plan activities for themselves during those times. Whenever possible, give them some say in the schedule itself. By being empowered at this stage, they are less likely to feel excluded and resentful later.

Balancing professional and personal commitments and priorities is never easy. It is a challenge during the thesis or dissertation process to make time for health-, friend-, and family-related activities while reserving enough time to complete your research and education in a timely fashion. The importance of balance is highlighted by some researchers in time management who argue that time is a limited commodity. Getting more done within the time available results less from managing time than from managing one's energy, including its physical, emotional, mental, and spiritual aspects (Loehr & Schwartz, 2003).

MINIMIZE PROCRASTINATION AND AVOIDANCE

We alluded earlier to the overuse of scheduling and planning as a way of avoiding getting on with the project. Many other behaviors are even more easily seen in this light. There is no cleaner, better organized apartment than that of a dissertation candidate, for example. Because it is so common among those doing theses and dissertations, procrastination and avoidance (or P and A) should probably be a category in the *Diagnostic and Statistical Manual of Mental Disorders* (American Psychiatric Association, 2013)!

We all avoid things to some degree or other. In the extreme, however, P and A prevent the project from ever being completed. Thus, where dissertations are concerned, the master of P and A becomes the ABD (All But Dissertation, or ABT for master's students). To minimize these behaviors, put this statement on your wall in very large print:

THE MASTER OF P AND A BECOMES THE ABD!

Or, as an alternative,

PUT OFF PROCRASTINATION!

These can then serve as daily reminders to keep with the program. Some of our students have taken this suggestion to heart and routinely post their goals on their refrigerator or computer to remind themselves to keep their eyes on the prize.

If you follow the suggestions earlier in this chapter, you are already dealing with P and A. If you have identified small enough steps, sequenced them properly, and written them in your calendar or phone, you have arranged the components of a momentum-gathering machine that will propel you through the thesis or dissertation process. This is because of the energy that is liberated by completions. Ever notice how simply getting something done gives you the motivation to do other things? This is how it works with research projects, as well. By getting each day's small step completed, energy will be liberated enabling you to do more steps. The momentum builds and carries the project forward.

With major research projects, the most common time for procrastinating is in the writing stages—namely, producing a proposal and a final version of the thesis or dissertation. Several factors can operate here. If, despite following our sage advice so far, you are still procrastinating, perhaps you are victimizing yourself with some of your verbal behavior.

You might say to yourself, "I can't seem to get started. It's so overwhelming." Feeling overwhelmed is a clue that the size of your task doesn't match your energy level. Perhaps you have not broken your task into small enough steps, or perhaps you're trying to tackle a task that takes more attention and brainpower than you have at the moment. Think about what you can accomplish today toward your goal: read five articles? type your references? outline your Method section? Overwhelming tasks can be turned into manageable ones by the simple device of breaking them into small, readily accomplishable steps. If you still can't face the one you planned, do something on the project that seems more appealing. For example, you may not be able to write a coherent Discussion section when you're worn out from the day's activities or fighting a cold, but maybe you can update your reference list. Accomplishing that task may give you the energy to tackle the one you originally planned. Do *something* to get into the task.

Alternatively, you may say to yourself something like, "I can't work on my research unless I have huge chunks of time, and I won't have those until next summer." This is a creative excuse for doing nothing until next summer. The truth is, although you might be more efficient if you had large chunks of time, you can still get something done without them. In addition, can't you find at least one 3-hour block of time each week to work on your research? One of us, for example, has set aside a morning a week for the past 2 decades to work on scholarly writing. This time is as sacred as classroom teaching. (After all, would you cancel a class you were teaching to do schoolwork for another class? to clean your apartment? to go grocery shopping?) Over the years, many articles and book chapters were written during these periods. As we have pointed out repeatedly, people complete theses and dissertations by steady work—one page at a time.

It is also important to schedule your thesis or dissertation and competing activities to take advantage of times you work best on academic tasks. Remember the example from Chapter 2 about B. F. Skinner's writing regimen? By doing the same thing at the same time and in the same place over and over, Skinner enabled the temporal, spatial, atmospheric, and biological stimuli to take charge, supporting a lifetime of productivity; the same type of structure can support your thesis- or dissertation-completing behavior. Our students have varied tremendously in how they work best. You know the conditions in which you are most effective. Use them to your advantage to get your thesis or dissertation done.

Then there's "I don't know enough [or haven't read enough, or haven't worked out the problems well enough, or don't have good enough hypotheses] to write anything." This is a variation on perfectionist thinking: "I can't do it if it isn't perfect." You obsess about doing it, and nothing gets written. No written draft will ever be perfect the first time around . . . but it also won't be perfect the 10th time! Just write it, planning for it to be imperfect. Then, build in time for revision to improve the first draft, perhaps using the grammar-checking or editing software described in Chapter 2.

More problematic are self-doubts: "I'm not smart enough" or "will never do enough or well enough to satisfy my adviser" or "will be found out as the 'imposter' that I am" (Rudestam & Newton, 2015). This kind of self-talk robs you of your confidence and involves unnecessary emotional behavior and self-directed negative thoughts. It is important to distinguish between the nature of the thesis or dissertation task (the reality you face) and what you conclude about yourself (your own personal fiction or philosophy). Yes, the project is a challenge; it is scary, and it is the door to your future, which may be even scarier! Yes, it is a long and often demanding task that will require you to work hard and push yourself. Yes, drafts that you worked very hard on will come back to you covered with "constructive" comments. And you might choose to beat yourself up over these. Yes, there will be times when you feel lost, because you *will* (temporarily) be lost. But—and this is a big "but"—that does not mean you are stupid, an imposter, or not up to the task. Most people doing a thesis or dissertation experience these fears. Don't beat yourself up if you find them difficult. Instead, pat yourself on the back—at least such experiences show you are normal!

You might also say, "I can work only with deadlines." Some people learn to goof off unless a deadline is imminent. Then, they pull all-nighters to produce a paper, study for a final, complete a grant proposal, and so on. These people find themselves in deep trouble with the thesis or dissertation, because these projects involve working toward a long-term goal with many steps and (usually) few immediate deadlines. As you have probably realized, a proposal or final draft is not a project to be pulled off over a single weekend armed with carafes of coffee or bottles of amphetamines.

We suggest two solutions for the deadline worker. First, create a series of real and meaningful deadlines for completing portions of your thesis or dissertation. Perhaps your graduate program has these. Some programs, for example, have a rule that clinical students cannot apply for internships without an approved dissertation proposal. If your program does not, perhaps you and your chair can create a similar contingency for you anyway. For example, if you are applying for academic jobs, perhaps you and your chair can agree that letters of recommendation will be sent only after a certain step (e.g., data collection, data analyses) is completed. Other professional time lines, such as dates for submitting abstracts to conventions or presenting your results at a job colloquium, may also serve as deadlines for you.

A second strategy involves breaking the deadline habit altogether. If you intend to pursue a professional career that involves research and scholarly writing, you will need to reduce your procrastination. So, why not start now? If you create and stick with schedules, as outlined in this chapter, you will kick the habit. Remember, "Put off procrastination!"

One useful approach is to arrange your schedule according to the Premack principle, so named after the psychologist who popularized it. The simple fact is that we can strengthen low-probability behavior by following it with behavior of a higher probability. This is the behavioral principle behind the old "first work, then play" maxim. Do something on your research, then do something you really want or need to do (e.g., shopping, sleeping). Build this work first, play second rule into your lifestyle, and your project will be finished much more painlessly. Another good technique is to post a graph showing pages written per day or week on your refrigerator door. People can notice it and make comments appropriate to the data.

It's a good idea to build rewards into the research completion schedule initially. After turning in the final draft of your proposal to your committee members, for example, plan a getaway trip with a loved one. But do not leave unless the draft has been completed. If you make your accomplishments rewarding for significant others, too, they will keep supporting you in the overall effort. If you build the rewards into the schedule in advance, you will have them to look forward to. In this way, you will control a lot more on-task behavior than by waiting to finish the task and then deciding what nice thing to arrange for yourself and others.

Finally, ask members of your social support system to encourage you to make progress. Tell your peers about your accomplishments so they can congratulate you. Share your progress on Facebook. If you are reluctant to shamelessly solicit positive comments so directly, use a modeling approach. Compliment your peers on their accomplishments. In other words, model what you want them to do for you. This is a practically guaranteed way to increase social reinforcement for your own efforts.

Some students band together into thesis or dissertation support groups to help keep each other on track. We know students who meet for a day each week to work on their thesis or dissertation. They might, for example, meet at the library or work independently at one student's apartment. Another student joined an online dissertation support group that provided her with many good ideas for breaking her habits of procrastination. There is some evidence that students engaging one another via Twitter can lead to increased involvement in educational activities and higher grades (Junco et al., 2011).

Members of a dissertation support group might similarly benefit from using Twitter between (or instead of?) group meetings. Be sure to emphasize communications that reinforce accomplishments, not ways to commiserate with one another or provide support for "good reasons" for not making progress! As Silvia (2007) noted, "Support groups shouldn't be unconditionally supportive" (p. 54). If you decide a group would be helpful, see his excellent suggestions for "agraphia groups."

Other challenges can arise during thesis or dissertation writing that have the potential to disrupt the process. Many people soldier through them with the help of friends, advisers, peers, and books such as this one (see the list at the end of this chapter for other resources that may be helpful). Professional guidance is also available in the form of thesis or dissertation coaches or mentors and therapists who specialize in working with students. Search the internet using terms such as thesis or dissertation "mentor," "doctor," or "coach." Be careful here: We are not suggesting you engage someone to write the thesis or dissertation for you. There are such services on the internet. It would be unethical to have someone else write a thesis or dissertation for you, and it is very unlikely you would be able to pass it off as your own work. That said, if time management or emotional issues seriously interfere with your thesis or dissertation progress, it is worth your time to consider whether professional help might assist you in getting unstuck and moving forward.

As we keep repeating, the key to completing a thesis or dissertation is forward movement. We have offered lots of ideas about scheduling and planning, but many different roads can lead to the completed thesis or dissertation. Find one that works for you, using your knowledge of yourself and your way of managing time.

✓   **TO DO . . .**
MANAGING TIME AND TROUBLE

☐ Set overarching and intermediate goals specific to your thesis or dissertation completion.

☐ List your steps and estimate your time requirements.

    – Identify subgoals and activities.

    – Break down big tasks into small steps.

    – Sequence the subgoals, activities, or steps.

☐ Schedule the work.

    – Post the schedule in a prominent spot where you and others will see it often.

    – Schedule thesis or dissertation times that capitalize on your energy levels.

☐ Plan your schedule to free yourself.

☐ Minimize procrastination and avoidance.

  – Avoid common unproductive thinking patterns.

  – Use the Premack principle: Strengthen a low-probability behavior by following it with a high-probability behavior.

SUPPLEMENTAL RESOURCES

Bolker, J. (1998). *Writing your dissertation in fifteen minutes a day.* Henry Holt.

This nifty volume focuses mostly on the writing process, including how to think about writing and how to manage the writing process.

Ferrari, J. R. (2010). *Still procrastinating? The no regrets guide to getting it done.* Wiley.

Based on 20+ years of the author's research on procrastination, this book discusses self-sabotaging tendencies, others' enabling behaviors, and other factors that affect procrastination and looks at specific issues around procrastination in school and at work.

finhamict. (2016). *Creating a Gantt chart in Google Sheets* [Video file]. https://www.youtube.com/watch?v=ibdDmhipDOQ

This video shows how to use Google Sheets to produce Gantt charts and also refers to Excel and other options.

Jaffe, E. (2013). Why wait? The science behind procrastination. *Observer*, *26*(4). https://www.psychologicalscience.org/observer/why-wait-the-science-behind-procrastination

This reader-friendly article summarizes research showing that procrastination occurs in all of us and includes practical suggestions to minimize procrastination and keep you motivated.

Lakin, A. (1974). *How to get control of your time and your life.* Signet Books.

Silvia, P. J. (2018). *How to write a lot: A practical guide to productive academic writing* (2nd ed.). American Psychological Association.

Tracy, B. (2004). *Time power: A proven system for getting more done in less time than you ever thought possible.* AMACOM Books.

Zimbardo, P., & Boyd, J. (2008). *The time paradox: The new psychology of time that will change your life.* Simon and Schuster.

4

Finding Topics and Faculty Collaborators

This chapter addresses how to
- select your research area and topic
- identify a committee chair, if you don't already have one, and clarify expectations for the student–chair working relationship
- develop a research question and hypotheses
- round out your committee

Read thoroughly if
- you haven't yet identified your topic, research questions, or hypotheses
- you have questions about how to select a research mentor and other faculty collaborators who complement your strengths, style, and needs
- you need ideas about how to match your research interests to faculty expertise

Skim or skip if
- you already have a strong and effective relationship with a faculty mentor and know how to form your committee
- your research aims, questions, and hypotheses are already well defined

https://doi.org/10.1037/0000161-004
Dissertations and Theses From Start to Finish: Psychology and Related Fields, Third Edition,
by D. J. Bell, S. L. Foster, and J. D. Cone

At last we arrive at the steps involved in getting your project underway. Remember that we have sequenced the chapters of this book in the order in which we think most students deal with the topics in writing their theses and dissertations. This order is not sacrosanct. For example, we deal with finding a topic and chair in the present chapter and with writing a literature review in Chapter 6. But suppose you do a literature review for a course and this leads to a researchable topic. In that case, reading Chapter 6 first might be more functional for you. Nor do these activities necessarily proceed in a linear sequence, one after the other. We tell you how to word your hypotheses precisely in this chapter, but in our experience, students generally refine and finalize their hypotheses as they study the literature (Chapter 6) and develop their methodology (Chapter 7). As we will say many times, find the sequence and method that work for you.

Now, let's start with the two most important decisions you will make in planning your thesis or dissertation: what to study and who will guide you in studying it. We consider these together because we believe the two decisions are closely linked. Many of you were admitted to work with a specific faculty mentor, and so your topic and specific research questions will emerge from work in this person's lab. For others, your research interests will guide whom you select to advise the project. In most instances, the process of identifying your topic and faculty collaborators is a reciprocal and iterative one—your research interests shape your choices about the faculty you seek out for research experiences and advising relationships, and interactions with these faculty help shape your research interests.

Regardless of how you settle on a research topic and thesis or dissertation chair and committee, perhaps the most important consideration is the match between what you want to do and what your team of faculty collaborators can help you do. As we discuss each component of finding your topic and your faculty team, we'll come back to these ideas of multiple pathways to your end goal and the importance of match.

SELECT A RESEARCH AREA

Let's talk strategy for a minute. Students often ask when the process of selecting a thesis or dissertation topic should start. We generally answer, "The earlier the better." Many students begin this process prior to graduate school. As undergraduates, they might have taken a particular course that piqued their interest in a research area. They might have worked as a research assistant on a faculty member's or graduate student's research project or conducted their own honors thesis. Or perhaps they had a postbaccalaureate research position that allowed them to dig in to a specific research interest. For these students, the thesis or dissertation is the logical extension of a program of study that began years earlier.

Many students don't have this experience, however. The direct research experience they had, if any, was probably in an area unrepresented by faculty in their current program. Or it may have been an area that was great for an undergraduate learning experience but doesn't hold enough interest or impact potential to become a graduate-level line of research. Even students who attended graduate school to work with a specific faculty member in a specific research area may find that their interests have shifted or their initial faculty mentor left the department.

Regardless of their starting point, coming up with a researchable idea is the most difficult step for many graduate students. This difficulty can come from two mistaken assumptions. One is the "Nobel laureate" error described in Chapter 2. The other is the "undergraduate research paper" error in which students think that any topic they come up with is, by definition, a good topic. Although professors often tolerate unusual or wacky topics for undergraduate research papers, you can expect more than a little skepticism about these topics as a fledgling professional.

Why are these assumptions problematic? The Nobel laureate error reflects unrealistically grand thinking, whereas the undergraduate paper error reflects unrealistically miniscule thinking. As faculty members chairing these projects, we often prefer the Nobel laureate error. It is easier to trim the fat off a bloated research idea than to build up an anorexic one. Both errors reflect poor reality testing, but the first at least shows the candidate is willing to work! These errors are more common among those who have not had much firsthand exposure to actual research.

If you have been active in research up to now, you probably already have some ideas about the question(s) you want to address with your thesis or dissertation. They probably came as the logical extension of some research you have already been conducting or collaborating on with faculty and other students. If not, the challenge of coming up with a workable research idea grounded in the literature may be a bit more formidable. If you are a master's student, your chair might give you a specific idea. Alternatively, you might replicate and extend work already published. If you are a doctoral student, your idea should be original, and your study must make a novel contribution to the literature.

In reality, coming up with a viable research project for your thesis or dissertation involves two steps. The first is to identify the general topic or area in which you want to do research (e.g., information processing, childhood aggression, social support, implicit bias, addictions). This is relatively easy and can give you something to say when people ask what your research is about. Once you have a topic, you are ready for the second step—coming up with a research question and hypotheses that you have (or will develop) the skills and resources to examine. Because research questions and hypotheses are much more specific than the general topic, they require more thought and a more in-depth understanding of the literature. For these reasons, most students find developing specific research questions more difficult than arriving at a general research area.

Select a General Topic Area First

Even at this stage, selecting a topic area is closely intertwined with considering faculty interests and expertise. The area you pick must meet two key criteria. First, it must interest you enough that you will be willing to spend months or even years reading about it, writing about it, and analyzing data having to do with it. Second, it must be an area in which you can find a faculty member interested in chairing the project. If you are in a mentor-model program, in which you were admitted to work with a particular faculty mentor, you probably already have a general idea of your topic area because it is constrained by your mentor's interests and expertise. Your task in this case is to decide which of the many possible avenues of inquiry in your mentor's lab will be most interesting and feasible for you. If you aren't in a lab where the general topics are already apparent, your task will be a bit more open-ended. We suggest that you identify at least a general topic area and then seek out faculty with an interest in the area, but many students reverse this process, finding a faculty member with whom they like to work and then identifying a topic jointly.

To identify a topic area that interests you, think about your classes and professional experience. What topics pique your interest? What do you find yourself stopping to read when you are supposed to be compiling research for a class? What catches your attention when you're scanning the literature? What academic topics come up frequently when you are talking shop with other students and faculty? What class paper did you enjoy writing the most? Did you write it recently enough that you are current in the literature in that area? If so, you might have a head start on the literature review for your thesis or dissertation. We say much more about literature reviews in Chapter 6.

Some students are very strategic about their choice of topic. They think ahead to the kind of work they plan to do in their career and use that to guide their selection. Others start with a master's thesis and move on to do their dissertation in the same area. Still others let their experience guide them to a topic. Identifying the things you think, read, and talk about or plan to do is a good way of clarifying areas that interest you. Most likely, you will find several of these.

In the best of cases, students start this process at the beginning of their graduate career, if not before. Then, their graduate program contributes in significant ways to their own research. Each course they take has some relevance. If students start the process early, they are able to see that relevance more clearly as they advance through the program. It is a good idea to keep an idea log in which you jot down potential research ideas as they occur to you in courses or throughout your graduate program. One of us still keeps a log in which he records ideas for articles, book chapters, research projects, or possible grant ideas as they come to him in the course of everyday life. Allow time and space for brainstorming and creativity; this list will provide several avenues for research that you can explore later.

If you are starting early and do not find a good match with a particular professor or research program, try another one. There is nothing wrong with having a deliberate plan to work directly with several faculty in the early stages to find out their styles, the type of work they do, and some of the problems and rewards associated with it. Even in mentor-model programs, it is possible and sometimes even desirable to work with multiple faculty or to change mentors over the course of your graduate training. Some of the most productive students we have known have systematically worked with numerous faculty during their graduate years. This helped them gain research experience from a variety of perspectives and led to several viable possibilities as they pursued their own research.

If you choose this route, make sure you and each faculty member discuss expectations so that you both know whether the relationship is intended to be a long-term exclusive one, a short-term one to work on a specific research project or skill set, or something else. There is little worse in graduate school than finding out that a faculty member (from whom you might like a recommendation letter someday!) is surprised and disappointed by a "premature" departure that disrupts his or her research program, or discovering that the faculty member you were hoping would advise your thesis or dissertation doesn't have the time because they thought you were just a short-timer in their lab.

Avoid Going It Alone

Some students, particularly those at the doctoral level, have the impression that their research is supposed to be a solo affair. They spend months developing a research idea and proposal and then approach a faculty member to try to sell it. Yates (1982) described his own experience doing just this and being devastated when his ideal committee chair rejected the idea as infeasible. In situations like this, you are faced with either rejecting the faculty member's advice and trying to find another who will agree that it is a terrific idea, or bagging the idea and starting over. Neither alternative is high on the hit parade of fun things to do in graduate school—the first idea disregards the initial mentor's opinion (which is likely based on considerable experience and expertise, and sometimes on their own hard-learned lessons), and the second just wastes time.

True, the dissertation is a test of your preparation to conduct independent research. This is not quite so true of master's theses, however, and with neither do you have to generate and develop ideas completely on your own. In fact, solo work at the training stage runs a real risk of producing unworkable proposals. Another all-too-frequent occurrence is that you cannot find a faculty member with the expertise and interest in your topic to shepherd you through the rest of the process. We have known students who have gone systematically to every single faculty member of a department with an idea, only to find no one who would agree to chair their committee. Thesis and dissertation research is challenging enough without making it into a course in the art of selling as well. We strongly recommend that you avoid going it alone.

Collaborative research isn't just for training; even seasoned researchers frequently engage in collaborative work that draws on colleagues' expertise in relevant content areas, methodologies, and analytic methods. If you're planning to pursue a more applied career, skills in collaboration will serve you well there, too. Use the approaches described in the previous section to develop ideas in conjunction with a faculty member. If they have joint ownership of the idea, you will likely form a cooperative relationship that will aid you enormously in successfully completing your research.

However, collaborative research comes with its own challenges. If you and your research mentor or research team develop your thesis or dissertation plan together, you will need to address issues such as ownership of the ideas and the data. This can be a sensitive topic, particularly because with many mentoring styles, the mentor guides a student toward a promising area but allows or requires the student to actually identify the idea. So what piece of the idea does each person "own," and can either person claim primary ownership? If your adviser's lab provided the necessary equipment or funding for data collection, who owns the data? Are you borrowing it simply for the purpose of your thesis or dissertation, or will you be able to use the data in the future for other analyses or publications? Ironing out the answers to these questions ahead of time will save headaches and heartache later.

Using archival data, either from your research mentor's lab or from large national or international data sets (e.g., Australian Twin Study, Adolescent Brain Cognitive Development Study, National Longitudinal Study of Adolescent Health), is another option for your thesis or dissertation. Using a preexisting data set can allow you to address research questions in a way that would be impossible if you had to collect your own data. For example, with archival data from your mentor's 10-year longitudinal study, you can examine the development and course of depression without having to remain in graduate school for decades. Using twin registry data could allow you to learn to use behavioral genetics approaches to address your interest in genetic and environmental risk for addiction. As with collaboratively developed ideas, using archival data requires that you address several issues up front. What data can you use, and for what purposes? Will you be able to publish the results of your thesis or dissertation, and who else must be an author? For shared data sets, there often are specific rules about who can use the data and how, and you may need to have your research proposal approved by the data's owners before you can even think of submitting a thesis or dissertation proposal to your committee.

Some students seek out archival data thinking they can save time and money by working with existing data sets. Although access to archival data has its pluses, it also adds an extra challenge to developing a proposal. This is because archival data sets do not come with a research question—you still have to develop an idea that is grounded in the research literature and interests you. In addition, you have to make sure that the idea can be addressed soundly with the data from the archival data set, which likely was not designed specifically to explore the idea you develop. We have known several students who came up with a good idea only to find that the archival data they wanted to use lacked good measures of the constructs they wanted to explore. This happens most often when neither the student nor the chair knows the data set well. This again underscores the importance of having a chair who can help you develop your topic and methodology—a topic we now consider in more depth.

IDENTIFY YOUR CHAIR

Identifying a chair for your project is a crucial step in the thesis or dissertation process and goes hand in hand with selecting a topic. A good chair will provide expertise in your topic area, specific feedback on your work, and support—as well as an occasional kick in the pants if you need it to keep going. A poor chair will provide few of these and may, in fact, make your life miserable as you negotiate the thesis or dissertation process. For many students, identifying a chair is merely a formality; their thesis or dissertation chair is the primary mentor they've been working with since admission to the graduate program. If you do not already have a chair for your thesis or dissertation, Table 4.1 provides information you can use to help select one. Take some time to investigate multiple potential chairs before making your selection. Here, we highlight some of the primary issues that can help guide your working relationship with your committee chair and, consequently, facilitate the success of your thesis or dissertation.

Understand the Chair's Role

Although the specifics of the committee chair role vary from school to school and from chair to chair, some general functions are reasonably consistent. Overall, the chair provides the first line of quality assurance for the project, from inception to final write-up. First, the chair helps the student develop the research idea, methodology, and analysis plan and oversees the student's implementation of the project. Second, the chair reads and critiques multiple drafts of each section of the thesis or dissertation proposal and the final write-up. Third, the chair approves the proposal for, and the final version of, the project before permitting the student to submit these documents to other committee members. Finally, the chair oversees the proposal and oral defense meetings, ensuring that the meetings stay on track and productive so the student can focus on the content of the meetings.

TABLE 4.1. Selecting a Committee Chair: For Students Admitted to Graduate School Without a Research Mentor

Action	Research area	Work style and mentorship style
Assess your preferences and needs.	What research areas interest you? What skills do you want to learn as part of your thesis or dissertation (e.g., methodological or analytic approaches)? How do your research interests correspond to your longer term goals? Are you looking for someone to chair a specific project or two or a mentor for a longer term program of research?	How do you prefer to work? Do you prefer flexibility or structure? Do you work well with minimal feedback or require detailed instruction? What aspects of your work style could be improved?
Take courses from potential chairs.	Is the area as interesting as you initially thought? Is the potential chair knowledgeable and enthusiastic about the area?	Does the potential chair provide helpful feedback on written work? Be aware that the potential chair's instructional style may not match their research mentorship style.
Read published research by potential chairs.	Is the area as interesting as you initially thought? Can you imagine yourself conducting similar research?	Does the potential chair publish work that is coauthored with students?
Get involved in potential chairs' labs before you begin graduate school or as a beginning graduate student.	Is the area as interesting as you initially thought? Can you imagine yourself conducting your own thesis, dissertation, or broader program of research in this area? Does your research involvement stimulate specific research questions you'd like to pursue?	What is the general work style and climate of the lab (e.g., work and resource sharing, relationships among lab mates and mentor)? How does the potential chair provide oversight and feedback on lab tasks? How well does the lab climate fit with your preferences and needs? Be aware that your experience as a lab volunteer may differ from that of thesis or dissertation advisees.

TABLE 4.1. Selecting a Committee Chair: For Students Admitted to Graduate School Without a Research Mentor (*Continued*)

Action	Research area	Work style and mentorship style
Ask other students about potential chairs.	What research areas or questions are currently being explored in the potential chair's lab?	What is the potential chair's advising style (e.g., expectations, feedback, availability, support)?
	What research ideas are of interest in the lab but have not yet been explored (and might be areas for you to pursue)?	Seek feedback from students who are successful and whose aspirations are most similar to yours (e.g., in productivity, career goals).
	How flexible is the potential chair in supervising research that extends beyond their core area?	
Talk with potential chairs once you've gathered information from other sources.	What research areas or questions are currently being explored in the potential chair's lab?	Is the potential chair willing and available to take on an advisee?
	What research ideas are of interest in the lab but have not yet been explored (and might be areas for you to pursue)?	What expectations does the potential chair have for thesis or dissertation advisees?
	How flexible is the potential chair in supervising research that extends beyond their core area?	What is the potential chair's advising style (e.g., type and specificity of feedback, routine availability)?
	What resources are available for student research in the lab (e.g., lab equipment and materials, participants, participant payments)?	What is the anticipated match between your and the potential chair's interests and needs?
	Be prepared to talk about your research interests, specific ideas, and preparation.	Be prepared to answer questions about your work style, strengths, areas of needed growth, and so forth.
Follow up with prospective chairs.	After identifying a good match on research interests and work style and establishing the chair's availability, finalize the agreement to chair the thesis or dissertation.	
	Clarify any remaining details regarding expectations for the student–chair working relationship.	

Departments usually have rules about who may and may not serve as a thesis or dissertation chair and committee member. Some institutions allow only individuals who have adequate recent publication records or who have been on the faculty for a certain period of time to assume the dissertation chair role. These rules are based on the assumption that inexperienced faculty members or those without active programs of scholarship lack the skills to ensure that a doctoral project has sufficient scope, grounding in the literature, and methodological rigor. Rules regarding who may chair master's theses are often (but not always) more liberal than those regarding dissertation chairs. Furthermore, some schools require special permission if the student wishes to work with a faculty member outside the student's specialty area or department. Working with a chair who is not a faculty member at all may also be prohibited or allowed only under special circumstances (e.g., when a faculty member is willing to act as a nominal chair or as a cochair). Finding out these rules in advance will help you avoid getting your heart set on working with someone who is not eligible to chair a thesis or dissertation.

That said, if you really do have your heart set on working with someone like this, find out what role the person may be able to fill, such as cochair, extra committee member, or consultant. Making use of available expertise will help make your project its best and is also a great opportunity to hone skills in collaboration and consultation that should hold you in good stead throughout whatever career path you take. Finally, find out what forms require signatures, and have those ready for your chair and committee members to sign when they agree to assume those roles. This formalizes the agreement and makes it easier to remember later!

Consider the Nature of Chair–Student Collaboration

A thesis or dissertation is a collaborative project between the chair and the student. When a dissertation is archived in *Dissertation Abstracts International*, the chair's and student's names are both listed. Faculty with national and international reputations will be careful about the type of work their name is associated with. Assuming the responsibility of chairing a thesis or dissertation committee is not something most faculty members take lightly.

For your collaboration to succeed, you and your chair need to work reasonably well together. This is especially true if you have little research experience and need a good deal of guidance (often the case with a master's thesis). A first step in assessing how well you might work with a faculty member is to examine the match between what you want from your chair and your chair's notion of the best way to implement their role.

Most chairs work closely with their students in guiding the master's thesis, as this is often the first major research project of the student's graduate school career. At the doctoral level, chairs vary from seeing the dissertation as a totally collaborative process in which they are fully involved to wanting students to report in only when drafts are complete or if they encounter major problems. What do you want from your chair? Do you want someone who will guide you from a research area to a specific topic (which will probably be something interesting to the chair), or do you want someone who will be happy for you to follow your own inclinations? Will you work best with a chair who is highly structured (e.g., sets deadlines, meets regularly with students) or with one who is more laissez-faire? Do you want to work with someone who is interpersonally warm and supportive, or are other characteristics (e.g., expertise, professional connections) more important? In short, think about what kind of structure, how much input in terms of topic development, and what sort of interpersonal style you prefer. You can then appraise how well the faculty member's style matches the way you prefer to work.

Of course, when considering your preferences, you must also consider what you need. You might prefer a warm chair who allows you to set goals and deadlines, but will you be self-directed enough to push through difficult analyses or writer's block without regular deadlines from your chair? Clearly, what you ultimately want is to finish your thesis or dissertation, so select a chair whose style complements your own strengths and compensates for your weaknesses.

Think About the Chair's Expertise

Some students and faculty assert that your chair must know a lot more about your topic than you do. Others disagree, maintaining that the role of the chair is to critique your methodology and the logic of your arguments, not to be an expert in your topic area. Good methodological and analytic skills should be applicable to any topic area, they say.

We believe there is merit to both arguments. Sometimes students produce excellent research working with chairs who know little about the students' area at the outset of the project. Nonetheless, we believe it is ordinarily in the best interest of both students and the profession for thesis and dissertation work to be supervised by chairs who have expertise in the topic area. Furthermore, we generally recommend that students develop their specific research questions jointly with a faculty member, working within the faculty member's area of interest. Although a strong foundation in methodology and analysis often transfers across areas, many specialized data collection and analysis methods (e.g., brain mapping, ambulatory assessment, actor–partner interdependence modeling) require more unique knowledge and skill sets. Working within a faculty member's research area is particularly important for students conducting research for master's theses, who enter the process with less experience and skill than doctoral students and who generally need more guidance at all stages of the project.

We strongly recommend that you work on a project within your chair's area of expertise on the basis of our opinion that this will lead to a better product with less time and agony. Faculty members who have worked in an area for at least several years know the literature well. They know what research has and has not been conducted and what is currently being done. This knowledge can prevent you from spending months designing what you think is the ideal study, only to find that someone published your magnum opus the year before in the *Journal of Personality and Social Psychology*. Furthermore, such faculty members are likely to guide you into a study that makes a contribution to the literature.

Just as important, knowledgeable faculty members know the ins and outs of doing research in the area. They know effective participant recruitment methods, pitfalls in common designs and procedures, and methodological norms in the area. Thus, you are unlikely to begin a master's thesis that has the scope of a small grant because you are unaware of how time consuming your procedures will be. Nor are you likely to design a study with a fatal flaw that is due to ignorance (both your own and your chair's) of the topic area. A chair who knows the literature may be able to point you to relevant articles, chapters, and books. A student of ours, for example, when getting ready to begin her literature search, was thrilled to learn that her chair and lab mates had a folder on their department's computer server that was full of recent research relevant to her study. Although this didn't substitute for her own literature review, it provided a great starting point with the articles that her research colleagues had found most useful.

Another reason for working in faculty members' areas is that these chairs will have more investment in your project. Faculty members who care deeply about what you are studying are likely to spend more time with you, to think about the project more fully, and generally to keep a sharper eye on your progress than those who do not. A sense of ownership often promotes accountability among collaborators, and if you share that ownership with your chair, you may reap the benefits of more timely and in-depth feedback and support.

Finally, working within your chair's area may have practical benefits. Faculty members often have laboratory space, equipment, and sometimes even monetary resources (e.g., grant funds to pay participants or buy MRI scanner time) that you can use. This can be especially helpful if your study requires participant payments or expensive equipment or supplies such as video equipment, an EEG machine, or IQ test kits. In addition, you may be more likely to get a job or internship if your chair is well known and respected in the field, especially if you do such a good job that he or she writes a stellar letter of recommendation about what a great catch you would be.

Of course, working in a faculty member's area is not without potential drawbacks. Some faculty members may be too controlling, requiring you to do what *they* want, the way *they* want it done, without regard for your ideas or intellectual development. You may find yourself following your chair's instructions rather than developing the skills you need to function autonomously as a researcher. Even at the master's level, which involves considerably less independence than the doctorate level, you should be learning new skills rather than functioning as cheap labor and learning how to be a researcher rather than just a research assistant. Failure to develop research skills at this stage is a particular drawback if you plan a career that involves research, in which you will be expected to function independently and pursue your own line of inquiry. These problems are not inevitable, however, and we believe that for most students, the advantages gained by working in an area the chair knows well far outweigh the possible problems.

If your chair is not an expert in some aspect of your project, consider recruiting one or more experts in your area to serve on your thesis or dissertation committee. Look for these experts among members of the department, your academic community, other nearby academic institutions, and community sites. Consulting with these individuals on substantive areas can fulfill some of the functions a knowledgeable chair would normally serve.

Clarify Expectations for the Working Relationship

Good working relationships between committee chairs and students are based on a shared understanding of expectations regarding the project and each person's role. If you already have a research mentor, the beginning of a thesis or dissertation project is a good opportunity to discuss these expectations with your mentor. Expectations change as you progress through the program, and so you can't assume that the ground rules established for your last project will continue to apply. If you don't have a committee chair yet, appraising potential chairs' expectations and work style can help you select a chair and prepare for an effective working relationship.

Standards and Feedback

In most departments, some faculty members expect very high levels of detail and rigor, whereas others are less critical and require fewer rewrites, less extensive methodology, and so on. We admit our bias here; we believe that high standards have several positive consequences for students. First, if you produce a product that satisfies a chair with high standards, you will be better prepared for your proposal meeting and oral defense, because you and the chair already will have considered and made good decisions about many of the major issues your committee members are likely to raise. Beyond the project itself, we believe that students who have met more rigorous standards in their thesis and dissertation projects are more likely to be well prepared for the rigors of a competitive job market.

Beyond considering faculty members' standards, consider whether your chair will provide specific feedback and suggestions. Few things are more frustrating than working with someone who tells you to do better but does not tell you specifically what you need to do to improve. You should not expect faculty members to find specific articles for you, make all your decisions, or rewrite your poor sentences. And especially later in your graduate training, your mentor will expect you to be able to write clearly, conduct data collection and analyses appropriately, and prepare all components of the thesis or dissertation document without micromanagement. However, you should find out what your chair will expect, what level of feedback they will provide, and what you need to do to improve as you progress through the project.

Find out your chair's preference for electronically submitted or paper drafts. Some faculty prefer paper copy; others prefer digital versions they can edit on the screen. If they prefer electronic drafts, find out

- what computer program they prefer (and whether it is compatible if you use a different operating system),

- whether and how they expect you to keep track of edits and additions (e.g., Do they like or dislike "track changes" functions? Do they want you to submit clean copies of revisions or fully marked manuscripts that allow them to see the progression of edits?), and

- how they want you to submit drafts (e.g., email; shared folder in Dropbox, Google Docs, or similar electronic repository).

These will be important things for you to know, especially if you are new to developing a major collaborative paper electronically. Alternatively, if you will be working with a faculty member who prefers paper drafts, it will be important for you to consider how to keep track of information contained in the multiple paper drafts that will pass back and forth between you and your mentor.

Timeliness and Availability

Most students receive feedback on several drafts of each section of the thesis or dissertation before their chair gives their final seal of approval. The timeliness of this feedback is important: A chair who sits on drafts of your introduction and Method section for months may seriously delay your progress. Similarly, your chair should be available to meet with you within a reasonable amount of time to discuss problems you encounter.

What is a good turnaround time? We strive for a 2-week turnaround on drafts, recognizing that it will take longer during very busy periods (e.g., final exam grading periods, weeks when we will be out of town, right before deadlines when all students want to finish their projects). Quick email queries can be answered in a day or two. However, a "quick" email query may open a much larger question that needs in-person discussion. If a student has a problem to discuss or needs an appointment, we ordinarily schedule it within a week to 10 days. Waiting 10 days for a meeting or 2 weeks for a draft turnaround may seem like an eternity! With 24-hour access to information that email, social media, and other technology can provide, many students have become accustomed to immediate feedback. However, research and writing don't work that way. Several things can get in the way of mentors being available and providing feedback as soon as you would like. Popular chairs may have many students vying for their time. Some faculty are busy with grant-sponsored research or extensive administrative or travel commitments.

Others have active consulting or clinical practices that compete with students' needs for time. No matter how scintillating your prose, it is just one of your mentor's many job duties and is unlikely to get any special treatment. Finally, faculty work very hard but are not (or should not be) available 24/7. Just like anyone, they will take time away from the job for family, personal time, and sometimes even sleep! Also, many faculty are on 9-month contracts with their school and may not be available during the summer months. Think about these things as you and your chair set expectations for your work together.

To balance busy schedules with a desire for quick turnaround, one of us has begun to routinely schedule both student due dates and chair reading and editing time blocks at the same time. For example, if the goal is to have feedback on a student's first draft of the thesis or dissertation introduction by May 1, one of us blocks out time in her schedule to read and edit the intro during a specific available time in late April. The student knows that in order to take full advantage of the scheduled time slot, they must submit the draft before that time. Another one of us informs students about upcoming trips because long plane rides provide uninterrupted times to read drafts. As with restaurant reservations and dentist appointments, scheduling in this way minimizes the time a draft spends sitting in queue, with the understanding that if a student misses the reserved time slot, they will need to reschedule for the next available time slot.

Independence and Support

We hope that every aspect of your project proceeds smoothly, but we recognize that this is almost always an unrealistic wish. It is important to understand how much independence your committee chair will allow or expect you to take in handling problems that arise, as well as when and how they will offer support. What if your chair and committee members don't work well together? Will your chair back you up if a committee member makes unreasonable demands? Will the chair help you out if something goes wrong in the external agency in which the study is being conducted? Chairs sometimes walk a fine line between encouraging developmentally appropriate independence and preventing students from feeling abandoned. Explicit discussion with your chair will help clarify how these things will be handled. Chair support may be particularly important if your study involves procedures that are difficult to implement and you need help gaining agency support or meeting with the human participants research review committee, or if your department is a hotbed of interpersonal feuds and thesis or dissertation meetings become shouting matches between faculty with students as hapless bystanders.

Finally, remember that your project is both an examination of your competence as a researcher and a learning experience. In general, the master's thesis is considered more of a learning experience than an examination, whereas the reverse is true for the doctoral project. Consider how your working relationship with your chair will be an opportunity for you to learn about research as you negotiate the project. Will it facilitate your growth as a researcher? Will your chair do most of the work for you, will you have to find your own way with little guidance, or will you be challenged to learn and grow in your research skills under the tutelage of a skillful mentor? We cannot emphasize enough the importance of establishing clear, direct communication with your chair regarding expectations and roles. Knowing what is expected makes the process less ambiguous for all concerned. Faculty members may or may not provide this explicit information, so think about how you can tactfully and directly communicate about issues involved in planning the project. Setting expectations at the outset can help you use the expertise, strengths, and resources of your committee chair most effectively and help prevent later problems that are due to mistaken assumptions by either you or your chair.

Anticipate Trouble Spots

Several issues can be troublesome when you are seeking a chair or considering a change. In the sections that follow, we list three common problems students face, along with our ideas for how to cope with each.

Switching to a New Mentor Without Alienating the Original Mentor

> I worked in Dr. McGee's lab and did my master's thesis with Dr. McGee, but I want to work with Dr. Jones on my dissertation. Is there any way to do this without alienating Dr. McGee?

Many students fear that leaving someone's lab means they will forgo goodwill and letters of recommendation from that faculty member. This is not necessarily so. In many schools, even those with mentor-based admissions, students are allowed (in some cases, encouraged) to shift mentors if their interests change or they wish to get exposure to another research area. Most faculty understand this, although they may be sorry to lose a student they have invested years in training.

In these situations, we recommend discussing the issue with the faculty member you wish to leave, saying something to the effect of,

> I'm thinking about my dissertation topic. Although I've learned a lot from working with you, my interests are really in the area of [*or* I'd really like to get close mentoring in the area of] ___. I'd like to talk to Dr. Jones about possibly working together on this, but I wanted to talk with you first to get your reaction.

The gracious faculty member will say, "I'd love to have you, but it's your choice," and there will be no negative repercussions. In fact, faculty members may appreciate your consulting them before approaching someone else. Many faculty members already know what you are telling them—that your interests have shifted, that you need to add a component to your training that another faculty member is better suited to provide, or that your work style aligns better with that of another faculty member. Less gracious but equally direct faculty members may tell you that they put a lot of time into your training and that your "payback" is to do your thesis or dissertation on a topic that interests them. In our experience, these less gracious faculty members are in the minority, partly because (a) switching to a different thesis or dissertation chair may not always mean ending the first relationship (e.g., collaborative research may continue if the relationship itself is good), and (b) the payback of a thesis or dissertation is still probably more work for a chair than the benefit they will reap from your project! With this faculty member's reaction in hand, you can decide whether maintaining their goodwill is worth altering your topic and professional development plans.

Selecting a Chair Who Is Not the Obvious Choice

I want to study the influence of sunlamps on worms' turning behavior. This is in Dr. Barton's area, but I don't want to work with Dr. Barton.

Working with a chair who is not the obvious choice is a problem for at least two reasons. First, unless someone else shares Dr. Barton's expertise, you may not find a faculty member qualified to chair your project. Second, Dr. Barton will likely find out about your topic and figure out that you chose another chair for a reason. Dr. Barton may or may not make an issue of this. Moreover, colleagues who are close to Dr. Barton may not be willing to serve as your chair or as a committee member. In addition, years later people may wonder why you chose someone other than the department's known expert to be your chair. Were you trying to take the easy way out?

We suggest that you consider two questions in thinking through this issue. First, determine your reasons for not selecting Dr. Barton. Is there any way you could arrange the process to minimize the problems you anticipate? Small problems can be discussed with the faculty member when you shop for a chair: "I'd love to work in your area, but you seem very busy, and I know I'll need a fair amount of guidance. If we decide to work together, would it be possible to schedule regular meetings?" Logistics problems can often be solved by open discussion in advance; problems involving irresponsible behavior and a negative interpersonal style are not so easily broached and prevented through advance problem solving, however.

A second question revolves around a realistic appraisal of the consequences of choosing someone other than Dr. Barton. Will Dr. Barton really care? Will Dr. Barton do anything? Will Dr. Barton's feelings or opinion have any impact on your life after you complete your degree? Many students catastrophize about the impact of not choosing Dr. Barton, when Dr. Barton may be happy not to have another student or may dislike the student as much as the student dislikes Dr. Barton! At the same time, if you intend to pursue an academic career in Dr. Barton's area and Dr. Barton is a national expert, it may be wise to put up with Dr. Barton's idiosyncrasies in exchange for their expertise.

Alternatively, you could do your research on another topic. Surely you can find another idea that interests you and that would allow you and Dr. Barton to save face when you select another chair. You can always change your research interests again after you complete the thesis or the doctorate.

Finally, it may be possible to negotiate a cochair arrangement. Faculty often have the same thoughts that students do about working together—they know who is best at managing what sorts of projects, student needs, and so on. All of us have (or have been) colleagues gracious enough to serve as cochair for students who needed help with specific writing issues, wanted close supervision of specific data collection or analysis methods, or wanted to pursue a topic that was at the intersection of two faculty mentors' areas. Comentorship arrangements come with their own challenges, but sometimes they provide a good solution to the dilemma of whom to pick as chair.

Encountering Difficulty Finding a Chair

I can't find anyone to chair my project.

If you don't seem to be able to find a chair, consider the cause. In our experience, the most common reason for this problem lies in the student's choice of topic. Faculty members may turn you down because they think your topic is trivial, poorly thought out, or outside their areas of expertise. Students who have their heart set on a particular research question, develop it without faculty guidance, and present it to faculty members as a fait accompli are particularly likely to be turned down on topical grounds. The solution, of course, is to approach faculty members earlier in the process, talk with them about topics that fit their interest areas as well as your own, and let them know you are flexible and open to feedback about what is important and what is not.

Another reason for failure to find a chair lies in the student's failure to investigate fully: You get your heart set on a particular faculty member and then discover that the faculty member cannot take on another student, is going on sabbatical, or for some other reason is unavailable. You then conclude that you "can't find a chair." As disappointing as it may be, you may need to explore other topic areas that would increase other faculty members' interest in working with you.

For students admitted to mentor-model programs, these first two reasons are less likely because topic–mentor match issues should have been addressed at admissions. If you are in such a program and still have difficulty finding someone to mentor your work, consider whether your interests have changed since admission. If so, you may need to increase your flexibility or consider changing mentors.

Finally, some students cannot find a chair because their academic or personal problems drive prospective chairs away. Students who have had repeated difficulty in their training program may find that few faculty members are willing to undergo the projected agony of working with them. If this is your difficulty, you should honestly appraise the situation. First, you will need to identify your contribution to these problems. Have you been unreliable, antagonistic, abrasive, or inflexible? Do you lack basic graduate-level academic skills and need extensive remediation? Second, you will need to decide whether a change in your skills, behavior, or attitude can be achieved in a relatively short amount of time. This may require a commitment to high-quality counseling, therapy, or other professional assistance.

If you are able to achieve these two goals, communicate this good-faith effort to a faculty member, show them at least one demonstrable change you have made, and ask for another chance. It is very difficult to shift a negative reputation, and you may need to work harder and make more compromises than other students in order to talk a faculty member into taking you on as a student and to overcome their negative expectations of you. But have hope—it is possible to earn a second chance and succeed. All of us can remember students who overcame negative histories and reputations, graduated, and went on to satisfying careers.

If you do not believe you can make the changes required to be successful in your graduate program in a reasonable amount of time, consider either taking a leave of absence to work on the problem or exiting graduate school gracefully and finding a career that suits you better. Although the latter is a drastic step, repeated problems in graduate school are likely to predict similar problems in job situations that have comparable requirements. Is it really worth staying in a profession for which you are not well suited? Or would you be better off to cut your losses and find something else that capitalizes on your strengths?

DEVELOP YOUR RESEARCH QUESTION

Let's assume you have successfully identified a topic area for your research (e.g., dental phobia, child sexual abuse, depression, HIV prevention), hopefully in collaboration with a respected faculty member who will chair the project. You next have to narrow your idea to something doable. To do this, you frame some sort of researchable question within that area. The *form* such questions should take is fairly specific. We address form in the next section. First, we take up the *source* of such questions.

In general, you should ask a question that interests the scientific community. It is not a good idea to propose a particular study merely because there is a lack of research on a topic. There might be good reasons why no one has published anything on the question. More important, such a rationale does not indicate why the question should be asked or answered in the first place. In other words, your question should have a place in the literature. You should know how it fits conceptually and methodologically with and extends the literature. After all, science is the cumulative process of knowledge generation. And a central part of all scientific disciplines is to generate knowledge that matters—that improves our understanding of some phenomenon and can be applied to improve quality of life (e.g., for the people who benefit from more effective educational approaches or medications, safer cars or neighborhoods, or healthier food choices). In fact, research funding agencies such as the National Institutes of Health and the National Science Foundation require a statement of broader impact or relevance for all research projects. You should be prepared to provide the same sort of statement.

What will answering your research question tell us? Why is this important? What can we do with the knowledge? True, it may be useful to know what percentages of students in a given school show particular cognitive deficits associated with learning disabilities. This will have little relevance beyond that particular school, however, and tells us nothing about how to address the issue. Of far more interest to others concerned with children would be the correlates of those problems. If you really want to strengthen the study, you will pick variables that have theoretical and even applied relevance for understanding and addressing learning disabilities. Remember, the purpose of research is to produce generalizable and meaningful knowledge. Your research will do this best if it builds on the research and theory that preceded it. We will have more to say about this when we talk about hypothesis formulation later in this chapter.

Poor Sources of Research Ideas

Before we turn to good sources of research ideas, a word of warning: Bad ideas for research questions do exist. Some people are happy to share them on the internet—generally a poor source of research questions. A recent search using in the term "psychology dissertation ideas" revealed a variety of websites ready and willing to provide topics, sometimes for free, sometimes for a price. These websites have multiple problems. First, it is not clear who is generating the questions and how well that person knows the research literature that should form the basis for the topic. Second, internet topics may not match the area in which you wish to work. Third, most of these topics lack the specificity that characterizes good research questions—indeed, some are so broad that they suffer from the Nobel laureate syndrome! We advise you to stick to more tried-and-true methods of developing researchable questions using the literature and knowledgeable mentors and colleagues to guide your thinking, not the internet and other mass media sources.

Another way to come up with a questionable research idea is from your personal experience. A student recovering from alcoholism decides to study families of alcoholics. A student with chronic test anxiety chooses to relate test anxiety and types of question to performance on math exams. Many of us are in the behavioral sciences, especially psychology, because of an interest in some aspect of our own experience. Don't get us wrong; this is not a bad reason for being in psychology. It may even evoke the passion that can fuel an energetic research endeavor. But it is probably not a good idea to plan thesis or dissertation research around something with a high degree of personal emotional relevance and reactivity. Save these issues for therapy. Research is difficult enough without having it serve as the stimulus for a lot of personal soul searching every time you pick up the pen or run a participant.

Besides interfering with your progress, you are unlikely to approach personally loaded issues from the detached, objective, analytic perspective necessary in science. You are likely to have a position on the subject that can interfere with the satisfactory completion of your research by introducing bias on a number of levels (Sonuga-Barke, 2017). One example of potential research bias is the "researcher allegiance effect" (Munder et al., 2012). If you are convinced from your personal experience that test-anxious students do worse on multiple-choice than essay questions, for example, you may design your study in subtle ways to ensure this outcome. For example, you may inadvertently share your expectation with the research assistants who score the essay questions or even with your research participants. Research has shown that communicating this information can produce data that are consistent with researchers' expectations, particularly when the data are subjective (e.g., desired outcomes communicated to them by the experimenter; Luborsky et al., 2002; Munder et al., 2012). Of course, we do not suggest you would do this deliberately. Nor is this is a problem only for research in personally relevant areas; it is simply that it is more likely in such research.

Choosing a research topic that evokes strong emotional reactions can also interfere with your objectivity in other ways. For example, otherwise helpful suggestions from committee members might be hard to accept if they don't fit your personal understanding of the problem. This can result in your appearing rigid, defensive, and inflexible, characteristics faculty do not view positively.

In fairness, issues of personal relevance can be a good source of research questions under some circumstances. Your motivation is likely to be higher for such topics, and you might know the area in unique ways that might challenge the conclusions of current investigators. The bottom line is that you should consider issues of personal relevance as a source of research ideas only if you can approach them objectively. If you have resolved the emotional aspects of the issue and can approach it in a detached, relatively disinterested and unbiased manner, go ahead. You might make a truly useful contribution.

Better Sources of Research Ideas

As you might have guessed from some of our earlier comments, possibly the best source for new research is research you are already doing because you will have both knowledge about and experience in the area. Moreover, if you have been collaborating with a particular faculty member on the research, that person will probably have provided suggestions you can develop into a satisfactory proposal. Finally, research often stimulates more questions than it answers, and one of these questions might provide the basis for a thesis or dissertation proposal.

In addition to your own research experiences (or those of your faculty mentor), you can gain valuable ideas from student and faculty colleagues on your campus or at professional meetings. Ask to attend lab meetings, journal clubs, and guest lectures across campus, and attend regional or national conferences and meetings. Even if not directly in your area, these presentations and discussions can help spark ideas. The discussions (e.g., in lab meetings and journal clubs) can also offer valuable insight into how researchers manage the challenges of settling on a research question, going from untenable ideas to realistic questions, and so forth. You can also find many useful webinars or video-recorded presentations on the internet, often on the websites of professional organizations (but remember our cautions about internet sources, and be sure that you are accessing the most current information from trusted experts in the field).

Literature published within the past 2 to 3 years is also an excellent source of research questions. Most journal articles end with suggestions for future research. Look for these. If one of them excites you, spend some time thinking about how you might develop the suggestion into a research proposal. Discuss the idea with faculty members and chair candidates and get their reaction. If it is generally positive, and after you have thoroughly researched the topic, get in touch with the author of the article and find out what they are doing currently in the area. Inquire nonchalantly about the specific question you hope to pursue, asking whether the author has already researched it or knows of anyone who has. If the answer to both questions is no, probe a bit and see whether the author knows why. After all, it seemed like a good idea to you!

This little bit of detective work could be very worthwhile and could save you much wasted time and possible embarrassment. The author might have discarded the suggestion because a colleague pointed out an inherent flaw in its logic. Or at a presentation at a professional meeting, several people in the audience strongly questioned the ethics of pursuing the research in the manner suggested. Or you might hear that several people have indeed followed the author's suggestion and will present their results in the very next issue of the *Ratatat Review*. Wouldn't such news be worth the email or phone call?

Another good source of researchable questions is to apply a paradigm used with one population to another population. For example, Lord (2005) was interested in indirect aggression (e.g., malicious gossip, statements designed to harm individuals' relationships with peers) in older adults. To measure aggression using methods other than self-report, she adapted peer nomination instruments used to identify perpetrators of aggression in elementary school settings and used them with participants in retirement communities, a novel adaptation that worked well for her study. Research on the leadership styles of executive women might suggest similar studies with executives who are members of an ethnic group underrepresented in the profession you are studying.

Of course, just because something was a good idea in one context does not mean you can apply it easily in another. Children are not simply little adults, and individuals from one underrepresented group are not necessarily like those from another underrepresented group. Your research will be most meaningful if you can integrate what you know about the paradigm (as used with, e.g., adults or women) with the theoretical and empirical literature on the new population.

Reviews of the literature in particular areas provide another worthy source of questions. *Psychological Bulletin* contains such reviews in psychology. *Annual Review of Psychology* is another source of such reviews, as are *Clinical Psychology Review* and *Developmental Review.* Many edited books contain literature reviews. The authors of reviews appearing in these sources often point out gaps in the research knowledge and correctable flaws in existing studies. Why not propose research that remedies some flaw that has already been acknowledged as important by the scientific community?

Replications of already-published research provide an avenue in some cases. There is much to recommend replications. If the original study was done in an exemplary way, you will learn much from modeling it. In fact, exemplary studies are the only ones you should attempt to replicate directly, as there is no virtue in repeating the errors of your predecessors. As we mentioned earlier, a proposal to replicate a study will be more acceptable for a master's thesis than for a dissertation. Check the local norms to see whether replications are acceptable master's thesis possibilities. Replications that extend the original study in novel ways that will add new knowledge are more likely to be accepted as dissertation topics. Be aware, however, that recent research has highlighted the high frequency with which findings from published research are *not* replicated (Nosek et al., 2015). If you attempt a replication, be prepared for this.

You may also identify relatively unexplored links between literatures and be able to connect them. Many professionals (e.g., sociologists, scientists in the communication field, physicians) study the same problems that psychologists do. Even within psychology there are numerous aspects of the discipline that are not integrated. Pulling together separate but related strands is a challenging but often rewarding way of devising something truly novel.

A final source of ideas comes from other theses and dissertations. We know some faculty who deliberately steer students away from consulting previous theses and dissertations. Partly this is because faculty members sometimes distrust the quality of research supervised by other faculty. Partly it results from the realization that theses and dissertations have not been subjected to the same peer review process as most published papers and cannot therefore be as confidently consulted as exemplars of competent research. These faculty argue that if the research is good enough, it will be published, and students will encounter it in the literature. Our own view is that existing theses and dissertations can be a good source of some kinds of information for prospective researchers. We routinely suggest that students consult one or two carefully selected theses or dissertations or thesis or dissertation proposals. This assignment stimulates reality testing as well as pointing to exemplary projects that could serve as models. We also recommend completed theses and dissertations as references if students are proposing a study that extends a program of research taking off from the previous thesis or dissertation.

Where can you locate potential model theses and dissertations? One option is to look at thesis or dissertation repositories, such as your campus library (for theses and dissertations from your institution), PsycINFO's dissertation archives, or ProQuest (https://www.proquest.com/products-services/dissertations). However, it may be hard for you to determine the quality of theses and dissertations you find through these sources (remember our "carefully selected" admonition). Asking your research chair is probably a better option. And as mentioned in Chapter 1, theses and dissertations completed under the direction of a potential chair can be an excellent source of concrete information about the finished product that chair is likely to expect. We do not suggest them as sources of ideas, however. Browsing through published literature reviews will probably yield more ideas per hour than theses and dissertations on the library shelf or in ProQuest.

Putting the Research Question in Researchable Form

Once you have decided the area of your topic and the general question to be asked, it is time to word the question so that it can be studied. Well-worded questions share five criteria (Leong et al., 2012). First, the easiest criterion to remember is that the question should be just that: Phrase what you are going to study in the form of a question. Second, the question should specify the key constructs or variables of interest. What, specifically, are you interested in? Constructs like "parenting" or "adjustment" are pretty generic, so it's preferable to be more precise. Are you interested in parent supervision, displays of warmth, depression (if so, symptoms or disorder?), delinquent behavior, or relationship quality? Note that in some research approaches, such as qualitative research, specification of constructs may be the focus of the research itself. In other words, because qualitative research is more inductive, you may not identify, for example, specific indexes of adjustment up front but rather look for emerging themes in your data.

Third, the question should clearly indicate what you want to know about these constructs. If your research is descriptive or qualitative, you may be interested in the nature of a phenomenon, such as the prevalence and characteristics of corumination among adolescent friend dyads or college students' reactions to campus violence. In qualitative research, questions are typically open ended and nondirectional and relate to understanding a phenomenon and its meaning and process (Cresswell, 2017). For example, you may be interested in how college students respond to campus violence and so may ask questions such as "How do undergraduate students at Allstates University react to campus violence incidents?" or "What is the meaning of recent legislation to allow individuals to carry concealed guns on college campuses to undergraduates at Allstates University?" In qualitative research, research questions often evolve as the data suggest themes and more specific questions.

In quantitative research, research questions typically suggest a relationship to be examined. For example, suppose that your general research area involves child sexual abuse, and you wish to study the adequacy of children's memory for specific events. Your question might be, "Are children who have not been sexually abused more likely to describe sexual behavior when interviewed with sexually anatomically correct (SAC) dolls than when interviewed with dolls not having secondary sex characteristics?" This is phrased in the form of a question, but does it imply a relationship to be tested? The children are to be interviewed with dolls that do or do not have complete anatomical features. Your independent variable is thus the secondary sexual characteristics of the dolls. The verbal behavior of children exposed to dolls with or without these features will be examined for references to sexual behavior; such references constitute your dependent variable. The research question suggests a relationship between the independent and dependent variables. Thus, it meets the third of our criteria.

A fourth criterion, specific to quantitative research, requires that the research question imply the possibility of quantitative empirical testing. If the question meets the third criterion, namely, suggests a relationship, it is halfway to meeting the requirements of the fourth criterion. It is not enough to suggest a relationship, however, unless that relationship is empirically testable. The principal ingredient of testability is the specificity of the variables being related in the research question. Can the variables be operationally defined? If the variables cannot be operationalized and measured, the research question cannot be answered. If they can be operationalized, an empirical test of the relationship suggested by the question can be performed (see more on operationalizing variables in Chapter 8).

A fifth and final criterion we like to add is that the question should specify the participants. Our sample questions clearly state this: "undergraduate students at Allstates University" and "children who have not been sexually abused." Specifying participants in your research question helps focus your study and set the stage for your methods.

Admittedly, these criteria are somewhat arbitrary. Good research can be done without following them exactly. For novice researchers, however, we have found these criteria to be quite helpful in evaluating and advancing their research ideas because the criteria require specificity and provide clear direction for thinking through the research topic and methodology.

You will probably need to spend some time refining and reworking your research question to make it clear and specific enough to guide your research. This process will force you to think through exactly what you want to know. You may start with a vague question, such as "How do parents and teenagers communicate about sex?" This implies no relationship, which is perfectly appropriate for qualitative research, but not ideal if you're planning a quantitative study. In discussion with your chair, you might revise the question to specify independent and dependent variables: "Does general parent–child relationship quality predict whether and how parents and teens communicate about sex?" or "How does parent–adolescent communication about sex relate to impulsive teenage sexual behavior?" You might revise the research question even further as you decide what specific aspects of parent–teen relationship quality, communication, and sexual behavior you want to study, and with what specific population.

Now that you have a question to study, let's talk about the availability of participants. Participant access is so important that we have had colleagues who advise students to get participants first and then decide what research they want to do. This falls into the pragmatic school of thesis and dissertation advising! If participants are not available, the greatest idea in the world is not going to make a suitable research topic. Are you working (or doing a practicum or internship) in a setting with a population suitable for your study? Is your parent, spouse, or good friend connected with such a setting? Does your potential chair have connections you could tap to gain access to participants? As a reviewer of this book pointed out, outsiders to a system usually lack the power to collect data within that system in ways orderly enough to make research possible. So be sure you are sufficiently well connected to ensure access to the participants you will need.

This issue is particularly important if your research question requires a select group of people (e.g., cancer survivors, displaced executives). The issue is less important if you could do your study with a more readily available population (e.g., college students). A more available population should not be used just for the sake of convenience (many journals routinely reject studies that include only college students unless they are the specific population of interest), but it can be useful for a proof of concept study. For example, your longer term goal may be to pursue your research question with youth or adults with schizophrenia, but you can start with a thesis or dissertation project that uses "emerging adult" college students (who are really just a year or two out of adolescence) or college students screened for high psychotic symptoms.

DEVELOP CAREFULLY WORDED HYPOTHESES

The wording of hypotheses is another area that will differ depending on whether you will conduct a quantitative or qualitative study. Qualitative studies, inductive in nature, do not begin with hypotheses but instead investigate themes that emerge from the data. For qualitative research, however, *hypotheses*—the declarative sentences that conjecture a relationship between two or more variables (Leong et al., 2012)—are a central feature. Well-stated hypotheses are derived directly from the research question that specified your participants, variables, and relationships to be tested. For example, our previous question asked "Are children who have not been sexually abused more likely to describe sexual behavior when interviewed with SAC dolls than when interviewed with dolls not having secondary sex characteristics?" For this question, we might hypothesize that "Nonabused children interviewed with SAC dolls describe sexual behavior more frequently than nonabused children interviewed with dolls without secondary sex characteristics." Hypotheses start with the basic research question and develop a specific prediction about the nature of the relationship between the variables identified in the question. Hypotheses are also stated in the present tense, predicting relationships that exist in the state of nature today. Preferences vary regarding the use of present or future tense (predicting a possible future relationship) in the wording of hypotheses, so be sure to check with your committee chair about their preference.

At this point you may be thinking that to come up with some hypotheses, you'll just say how you think your results will come out. That is easy enough, right? Well, not quite. You need a rationale for making predictions. That rationale can come from one or both of two sources: (a) previous empirical research (including applied and program evaluation research) and (b) theory. If your research question has been informed by previous research, the nature of hypothesized relationships will have been suggested by that research, and your specific hypotheses should then be fairly obvious. Similarly, theory may suggest certain relationships that can be tested.

Having said all this, it is important to acknowledge that some research areas are so new that hypotheses are difficult to develop. Similarly, some fields (e.g., ethology) have a stronger descriptive tradition than others. If you are having trouble coming up with hypotheses and know your literature and associated theoretical framework, talk with your chair. Avoid making something up. Science involves originality, but not creative fiction.

In addition, don't expect yourself to know what you predict until you've read the literature. You may think you can predict the outcome after reading a few articles, only to find as you delve more deeply into the topic that the literature suggests contradictory findings or leads you in slightly different directions. This is a normal part of the scientific process. Refine or modify your hypotheses as you think and read more about the topic. Might differences in the populations, methods, or analyses explain contradictory or nuanced findings in the literature? Use this information to help guide your hypotheses on the basis of the populations, methods, or analyses you will use.

A few words about types of hypotheses. Most commonly we read about the "research hypothesis" and the "null hypothesis" (Ray, 2011). A *research hypothesis* asserts a relationship that the researcher hopes to observe in the study. A *null hypothesis*, first identified as such by British statistician and geneticist Sir Ronald Fisher, basically states that there is no relationship. Although you are interested in your research hypotheses, statistics cannot confirm them: Statistics can only disconfirm the null hypothesis. The preferences of thesis and dissertation chairs differ, but most prefer students to include their research hypotheses in their proposal (the null versions are inferred quite easily from these).

It generally is not considered acceptable to proffer a null hypothesis as an expectation for the results of your project. Thus, the hypothesis "Boys and girls do not differ in their interest in science-related stories" would not be considered legitimate. This is because statistics can only disprove the null hypothesis, not prove it. Look for relationships you expect to exist, not the absence of relationships. Of course, it is perfectly legitimate to hypothesize that you will find different relationships in one group or condition than another.

Thus, the following is a legitimate hypothesis: "Gender difference in interest in science depends on the type of science stimulus, such that boys express more interest in science toys than girls but boys and girls express similar amounts of interest in science-related stories." This hypothesis is legitimate because it predicts a significant interaction between gender and type of science stimulus, something that can be tested with inferential statistics.

As with research questions, carefully phrased hypotheses indicate the specific relationships to be examined. They also suggest the nature of the relationship. Thus, the hypothesis "There is a relationship between education level and preference for liberal causes" is less desirable than "There is a positive relationship between education level and preference for liberal causes." Clearly worded hypotheses also include a third criterion important to some researcher—the nature of the research design. In this example, a correlational design is implied. Our earlier example, in which we hypothesized that "Nonabused children interviewed with SAC dolls describe sexual behavior more frequently than nonabused children interviewed with dolls without secondary sex characteristics," implies an experimental design. Another recommendation is to include in the hypothesis the population in which the relationship is to be studied. Thus, the hypothesis "There is a positive relationship between education level and preference for liberal causes in executive women" meets this criterion.

This is probably a good place to stop adding more information to your hypotheses. It is common for novice researchers to go further, however. A common mistake is to include the specific measures of one's variables in the hypothesis—for example, "There is a positive relationship between education level as assessed by the Horace Mann Scale of Educational Attainment and preference for liberal causes as measured by the ACLU Scale for Consistently Clear Thinking in executive women." It is certainly true that this hypothesis is more specific, if somewhat unwieldy. Although some might disagree, we believe that excessive operationalization at this point misses the point of the research. The purpose is to study relationships between variables or constructs in order to build a science, and keeping the hypotheses phrased at this level reminds your readers (and you!) about the big picture. So unless the purpose of your study is to examine a particular methodology or validate a measure, we recommend that you stick to variables or constructs and save the details of the specific measures that you will use to operationalize your constructs for the Method section. In general, phrase your hypotheses at the level at which you want to generalize your findings.

Another mistake to avoid is including the name of the particular statistical test in the hypothesis. Thus, the hypothesis "It is predicted that a one-way analysis of variance (ANOVA) will reveal differences among attorneys, psychologists, and accountants in degree of extrinsic religiosity" loses sight of the basic issue. In this case, we are apparently interested in differences among these professional groups in extrinsic religiosity. How we test for differences between them is a methodological detail that does not belong in the hypothesis and can detract from the primary focus. Again, unless the particular analytic strategy is the focus of your research (e.g., comparing variable-centered analysis approaches such as ANOVA with person-centered approaches such as latent class analysis in explaining a relationship between career choice and religiosity), save analytic details for elsewhere in your document.

Students often ask, "How many hypotheses should I have?" Our answer is "not many." We sometimes see proposals with 10 to 20 hypotheses. Often these involve administration of some personality inventory and predictions developed for each subscale of the inventory. So many hypotheses are a clear sign that the student (a) has bitten off more than they can chew, (b) has not given the study enough forethought to narrow the hypotheses to a number that is manageable and that can be analyzed with sufficient statistical power to detect findings, or (c) has lost sight of the forest. Remember Occam's razor when doing your thesis or dissertation: Keep it parsimonious. More than likely, if you have developed hypotheses for 10 to 20 measures, a factor analysis would find the measures to be correlated and reducible to a smaller number of three or four independent factors. Science advances when the same phenomena are explained with fewer concepts or variables. Ask yourself whether all the hypotheses you are formulating are really tapping different things. If not, combine and reword them to focus on the essence of the problem being studied. If they are tapping too many different things, you have bitten off too much. Go back to the literature or consult with your chair to whittle your project down to a manageable size.

Sometimes you and your chair will decide that these 10 to 20 specific and detailed predictions are important to examine. Maybe they refer to specific moderation or mediation effects you expect to qualify an overarching prediction. In this case, you should be able to "chunk" your predictions into a smaller number of overarching hypotheses. The specific ways in which you predict that moderation or mediation effects qualify the general relationship can then be spelled out as subhypotheses. This can help you keep the forest (i.e., overarching hypothesis) in sight while still pointing to some important species of trees (i.e., subhypotheses) and allows you to manage power and alpha correction more effectively. Exhibit 4.1 provides an example of how one of our students chunked several hypotheses into a few overarching hypotheses and their specific subhypotheses (Hausman, 2017).

Another useful way to manage a larger number of hypotheses is to think about them as falling into three categories: preliminary, primary, and supplemental. *Preliminary hypotheses* are the foundational basics that you need to establish in your study. *Primary hypotheses* are the real meat, or conceptually interesting focus, of the study. And *supplemental hypotheses* are other things that may be of sufficient interest that you want to call readers' attention to them but that aren't really your primary focus.

For example, in your study of relationships between career choice and extrinsic religiosity, you may want to use a relatively new (but, in your opinion, better) measure of religiosity. You will need to establish that the new measure

---

EXHIBIT 4.1

Sample List of Hypotheses for a Study of Positive Affect in Youth

Preliminary Hypotheses

Hypothesis 1: Dampening of positive affect will be related to affective experience, including

a. lower positive affect and

b. higher negative affect.

Hypothesis 2: Dampening will be related to higher maladjustment, including

a. higher internalizing symptoms (higher depression, anxiety, anhedonia) and

b. higher externalizing symptoms (aggression, disruptive behavior).

Hypothesis 3: Dampening will be related to lower positive adjustment, including

a. lower life satisfaction and

b. lower social competence (higher peer problems, lower prosocial behavior).

Primary Hypotheses

Hypothesis 4: Levels of internally experienced and externally expressed dampening will vary across context:

a. Youth will dampen expression of positive affect more in social than nonsocial contexts.

b. There will be no differences in dampening of internal experience of positive affect across context.

Hypothesis 5: Levels of internally experienced and externally expressed dampening will vary by gender:

a. Girls will dampen experience of positive affect more than boys across contexts.

b. Girls will dampen expression of positive affect more than boys across contexts.

Hypothesis 6: Dampening's relation to depressive symptoms will differ across contexts, genders, and whether it is internally experienced versus externally expressed:

a. Dampening experience will predict depressive symptoms across contexts.

b. Dampening expression will predict depressive symptoms in nonsocial but not social contexts.

c. Dampening expression and experience in social contexts will predict depressive symptoms more strongly for girls than for boys.

d. Dampening expression and experience in nonsocial contexts will predict depressive symptoms to the same degree for girls and boys.

Note. From *The Costs and Benefits of Dampening of Positive Affect in Youth* (unpublished doctoral dissertation, p. 70), by E. Hausman, 2017, University of Missouri. Adapted with permission.

is sufficiently reliable and valid for your purposes, but this isn't the most interesting piece of your study (unless you're the author of the newer measure!). Some thesis or dissertation chairs may want you to articulate hypotheses about the reliability and validity of the new measure; labeling them as "preliminary" hypotheses signals to readers (and reminds you and your adviser) that this is merely the foundation for getting to the main focus of your research.

Likewise, you may plan to collect and analyze data that are not the primary focus of your project but are important enough to include in the thesis or dissertation document. Maybe you are interested in how relationships differ across age or how they relate to life and career satisfaction, but your methods or sample size will allow you to take only an exploratory look at these issues. Laying out these predictions as "supplemental" lets you show your committee how you are thinking about expected findings but also lets them know that these issues aren't your primary interest.

A word of caution here: By including more than just your primary hypothesis in a thesis or dissertation, you run the risk of failing to distill the project down to its core, important elements, muddying your thinking and writing and diffusing the potential impact of the research. You also run the risk of letting your project get too big, which makes it harder to finish in a timely manner. You and your chair should think very carefully about whether including these extras will enhance or detract from your progress and the project. In general, we advise reserving supplemental analyses for later, using them if needed to help you understand your findings once you have conducted the study and analyzed the data. Don't overcommit at this point. Most projects grow as researchers develop their methodology.

Figure 4.1 summarizes our recommendations concerning hypotheses for quantitative studies. This information should help you determine when your hypotheses are adequate.

You now have some idea of the design you will need to use to explore the relationships implied by your hypotheses. Moreover, the nature of your hypotheses will direct the selection of statistical tests. A final issue warrants addressing at this point: Are you adequately prepared to carry out the research as you have now clarified it? For example, novice researchers sometimes launch into an area in which there are no adequate (or any) measures for its principal variables or constructs. The first thing they propose is to develop a measure to use in the research. Our favorite questions of such ambitious persons are as follows:

- What courses have you taken in scale construction and measurement theory? in factor analysis? in item response theory?
- How many years have you budgeted to complete this project?
- Are you prepared to do a thesis or dissertation just developing the measures you need?

The moral here is to avoid research questions that are too ambitious for your skills or that will require you to develop or master excessively complex new technical material. If you are thinking about your thesis or dissertation as a single, stand-alone project, pare down your scope to something manageable. Alternatively, think about your larger program of research, and identify specific steps that can serve as your thesis, dissertation, and other projects and that you can tackle as part of your other work with your research mentor, as a postdoc, or in your career.

FIGURE 4.1. Hypothesis Checklist

Yes	No	
☐	☐	1. Do your hypotheses suggest the relationship between two or more variables (and avoid predicting null results)?
☐	☐	2. Do your hypotheses specify the nature of the relationship?
☐	☐	3. Are your hypotheses stated in the present tense?
☐	☐	4. Do your hypotheses imply the research design to be used to study the relationship?
☐	☐	5 Do your hypotheses indicate the population to be studied?
☐	☐	6. Are your hypotheses phrased at the level at which you wish to generalize your findings (i.e., do they talk about constructs rather than specific measures)?
☐	☐	7. Do your hypotheses stipulate the relationships rather than names of specific statistical tests?
☐	☐	8. Are your hypotheses free of other unnecessary methodological detail?
☐	☐	9. Do you have a manageable number of hypotheses (e.g., 4–6 or fewer)?
☐	☐	10. Where appropriate, have you chunked your hypotheses to distinguish between major hypotheses and subhypotheses or between primary and preliminary or supplemental hypotheses?

RECRUIT COMMITTEE MEMBERS

Once you have a specific research topic, some idea of your likely hypotheses, and a chair, the time has come to assemble the rest of your team—your thesis or dissertation committee. Such committees vary in size, composition, and specific duties depending on the institution and the degree. Committee members' general roles are reasonably consistent, however: They provide suggestions for improving the proposed study and, later, the final written project; serve as additional checks on the quality of the proposal and final document; and participate in examining the student during the oral defense. In the thesis defense, the committee ordinarily wishes to ensure that the student understands and can talk intelligently about the research. In the dissertation defense, the committee also assesses the student's competence to function as an independent researcher. Thus, committee members serve partially as consultants and partially as examiners—two vastly different roles. The balance between assistance and inquisition varies from school to school and committee to committee and also depends on whether the project is a thesis or a dissertation.

Ideally, committee members provide expertise that supplements the chair's and contribute new insights and ideas that will enhance the research. One of us, for example, will agree to serve on a committee only if she has some expertise regarding the population, the independent variable, or the major dependent variables of the proposed investigation. Committee members' theoretical perspectives and points of view should be reasonably compatible with the student's, and members should have some interest in the topic. Students working closely with an outside agency might consider inviting a doctoral-level person in the agency to serve on the committee. Depending on the institution, this person may count as an official committee member or may be included as an extra member. Regardless, this person can serve an invaluable role by becoming the student's advocate and liaison within the agency and also providing valuable information to the student and other committee members about agency regulations and reasonable requests for agency resources. Adding a statistics expert to the committee may be useful if you will be using complex statistical procedures and will need more than occasional consultation with this individual.

Committee members should also get along reasonably well interpersonally with the chair. Further, committee members should be fair, direct, and trustworthy. Although committee members who praise the student privately and then torpedo the project in the oral defense are rare, the experience is traumatic enough that you should gather sufficient information about prospective committee members to ensure this won't happen to you. Similarly, committee members should contribute something to your project; as nice as it can be to hear positive feedback such as "this is great!" such generic comments do nothing to help you become a better researcher, critical thinker, writer, or professional. Look for committee members who will provide specific, constructive feedback.

Before considering specifics in selecting committee members, find out the written and unwritten rules about committee members' involvement in preparing the proposal and the final written document. Many departments follow a "strong chair" model in which committee members read the proposal and full write-up only after the chair approves these documents. This approval follows extensive work between student and chair to fashion the document into acceptable form. The chair, not the committee, consults with the student on the hypotheses, design, measure selection, and other details. Committee members voice their opinions after the chair is satisfied with the proposal, although they are expected to be available for consultation on specific aspects of the project that fall within their areas of expertise (e.g., specific measurement issues, statistical treatment of the data).

The strong chair model is not the only one, of course. In some schools, committee members assume roles much closer to that of the chair, sometimes reading drafts of the proposal and final project as the student prepares them (the "strong committee" model). Our experience in these situations is that members' roles often are ambiguously defined, leaving the student to figure out when and how committee members should be involved. When this is the norm, clarify the process by asking your chair to specify what role they want committee members to serve. Getting chairs to be specific is important: When and what should committee members agree to read? How many drafts? Will there be a formal proposal meeting? Then communicate these expectations to prospective committee members.

Another risk when roles are ambiguous is that the student gets caught between different members' ideas about how to handle particular research issues. This can result in students running from chair to committee member and back again, sometimes misquoting or forgetting what each person has told them about the issue, or being forced to defend each committee member's recommendation to the other. In these cases, we recommend a family therapy approach: Arrange a meeting among all involved parties and hash out the issues, including both project content and decision-making processes, face to face.

Investigate Prospective Committee Members

Many of our suggestions about committee chairs apply equally to committee members. Find out the formal rules about the composition of the committee and who can and cannot serve as a member, consider your past experiences with potential committee members, and talk with students about their experiences with different faculty as committee members. Take information from the rumor mill with a large grain of salt. We have been told on occasion that we do not get along with some of our favorite colleagues on the basis of misinterpretation and speculation. Check out better sources of data (e.g., good students' experiences with different committees). In addition, ask your chair about prospective committee members. If your mentor has worked with them, the mentor will know how each can contribute to your particular project. It is imperative to discuss prospective committee members with your chair *before* issuing invitations. This is because your chair may have specific recommendations and may work better with certain colleagues than with others.

Your chair will also guide you regarding when to approach committee members. In general, we advise students not to form a committee until they decide on a research question, develop their methodology, and have a reasonable timetable for completing the proposal and conducting the study. Knowing the specific topic is important for obvious reasons. Knowing the time frame of the project is important, too, because faculty members go on leaves of absence and sabbaticals, do not want to be on a dozen thesis or dissertation committees that will be meeting during the same week, and so on. Many who are not paid by the school during the summer do not meet with students or participate in proposal meetings or oral defenses during this period. Replacing a committee member can be difficult. Form a committee of individuals who plan to be available during the time frame you propose.

Approach Prospective Committee Members

We recommend some version of the interview-and-invite strategy that you may have used to select a chair. You should balance the need for information (yours and the potential committee member's) with the goal of providing and collecting the information efficiently. If you know the potential committee member already through courses, prior research, or other contacts, you may be able to cut to the chase and invite them via email. If you and the potential member are less familiar with one another, consider a stepped process with an initial conversation, additional information, and finally an invitation.

Contact prospective committee members by telling them first that you would like to talk to them about possibly serving on your committee. Provide a brief overview of your topic, proposed method, and timetable for completing the proposal and the final write-up. Ask potential committee members if they would like to see a brief summary of the project in writing. You may also want to tell prospective committee members what you believe they could contribute to the project. If you wish potential committee members to be available for specific tasks (e.g., to consult on statistics, to help you gain access to participants), tell them about these requirements (e.g., "I'm hoping you will be able to help me network with schools"). Ask about any special requirements they might have for your project. A committee member who is a statistician, for example, may wish to discuss your statistics with you only after you have discussed them with your chair. As with the invitation to your chair, issue or finalize your invitation after you have gathered the information you need to make sure the potential committee member is a good fit for your project.

Once your topic and committee chair are in place, it's time to start writing! We turn to your thesis or dissertation proposal in Chapter 5.

✓   **TO DO . . .**
DEVELOPING A TOPIC AND ASSEMBLING A TEAM

Develop Your Topic
☐ Select a general research area.

☐ Work with faculty to develop your topic ideas.

☐ Develop the research question.

   – Consider research in which you have been involved.

   – Avoid personally loaded topics.

   – Use the recent literature.

   – Use other theses and dissertations cautiously.

☐ Put the research question in researchable form.

   – Phrase the question as a question.

   – Identify constructs of interest.

   – Make sure your question specifies what you want to know about your constructs (e.g., their prevalence or process for qualitative research, a relationship to be examined for quantitative research).

> - Make sure the question can be answered by your study (e.g., for quantitative research, is empirically testable).
>
> ☐ Develop well-worded hypotheses for a quantitative research project.
>
> - Evaluate these hypotheses using the checklist in Figure 4.1.
>
> **Assemble Your Team**
>
> ☐ Identify formal rules about chairs and committee members.
>
> ☐ Identify informal rules about the chair's and committee members' roles.
>
> ☐ Identify what you want from the chair–student collaboration.
>
> ☐ Identify your committee chair.
>
> - Obtain a commitment from chair if you don't already have one.
>
> - Clarify expectations about the relationship.
>
> - Anticipate and prevent trouble spots.
>
> ☐ Investigate prospective committee members.
>
> - Talk with your chair.
>
> - Talk with classmates.
>
> ☐ Approach prospective committee members.
>
> - Provide an overview of your study and timetable.
>
> - Obtain a commitment from committee members.

SUPPLEMENTAL RESOURCES

Cooper, H. (Ed.). (2012). *APA handbook of research methods in psychology*. American Psychological Association.

This three-volume set covers virtually everything you will want to know about planning and conducting research in psychology.

Cresswell, J. W. (2017). *Qualitative inquiry and research design: Choosing among five approaches* (4th ed.). Sage.

Darley, J. M., Roediger, H. L., & Zanna, M. P. (Eds.). (2003). *The compleat academic: A practical guide for the beginning social scientist* (2nd ed.). American Psychological Association.

Provides insights into faculty–student research collaboration from the faculty perspective and useful for those planning an academic career.

National Institutes of Health. (n.d.). *Grant writing tips sheets*. https://grants.nih.gov/grants/grant_tips.htm

Provides links to documents, podcasts, and videos about various aspects of grant writing.

Pedhazur, E. J., & Schmelkin, L. P. (1991). *Measurement, design, and analysis: An integrated approach*. Erlbaum.

A classic but still highly useful resource.

5

Formulating and Communicating Your Plans

An Overview of the Proposal

This chapter provides an overview of the thesis or dissertation proposal, including

- the function of a proposal
- typical elements in a proposal
- outline of the process involved in proposing your project

Read thoroughly if
- you are going through the proposal process for the first time
- you want to make sure you know what pieces to include in the proposal

Skim or skip if
- you are already relatively knowledgeable about the proposal process

At this point, you know what you want to do and have chosen people to guide you in doing it. Next, you need to formalize your plans in the form of a written proposal. In this chapter, we provide an overview of the content and structure of the proposal. The specific components usually included are covered in Chapters 6 through 9. Chapter 13 discusses how you present and defend this proposal during a meeting of your committee. First, some thoughts about what thesis and dissertation proposals are supposed to accomplish.

https://doi.org/10.1037/0000161-005
Dissertations and Theses From Start to Finish: Psychology and Related Fields, Third Edition,
by D. J. Bell, S. L. Foster, and J. D. Cone

UNDERSTAND THE FUNCTIONS OF THE THESIS
OR DISSERTATION PROPOSAL

Your proposal specifies what you expect to do and how you expect to do it. It is important from several perspectives. First, the proposal is typically the first significant piece of writing you will do on your thesis or dissertation. In a sense, it serves as the training ground and testing period for the research. Producing the proposal will give you firsthand insights into the complexity of the investigatory process and the particular research area you have chosen. It provides a place to articulate your planned research, as well as any challenges or difficulties you may encounter and how you plan to address them. In this way, your proposal provides your chair and committee members with evidence of your preparation to carry out the research and of how you operate as a scholar. In some departments, the proposal may also serve as the basis for a grant application (e.g., for a fellowship from the National Institutes of Health or other national agency, for support by a private foundation); in this case, you are convincing not just your committee, but also funding agencies, of your preparation and potential.

Because the proposal sets the tone in this fashion, you should approach the process in ways that communicate how you wish to be perceived by your committee members. Do you want to be seen as a passive learner who waits for guidance and reassurance at every turn? as someone who knows it all and resists feedback? Or are you more interested in being seen as a proactive learner, self-motivated and self-reliant but with good judgment about when and when not to seek consultation, openness to feedback from your committee and other experts, and the ability to use that feedback constructively? You likely will need more guidance for your thesis and will be able to operate more independently for your dissertation, but for each project, it's a good idea to develop your skills as a proactive, motivated emerging scholar.

Another reason the proposal is so important is that once accepted by your committee, it serves as a blueprint for what you intend to do. Your proposal specifies exactly how you plan to complete your research. In some schools, the proposal is considered an informal contract; if you follow your procedures to the letter, your committee cannot, after the fact, ask you to run more participants, follow an adapted procedure, or run another control condition. Some schools actually have committee members sign an approval (following the addition of changes suggested in the proposal meeting) that is then filed with the amended proposal in the dean's or some other administrative office. Years later, when the weary doctoral candidate returns from Fiji with her completed dissertation and none of her original committee members are still on the faculty, there is some proof that the university really did consent to a longitudinal study on the underwater aerobic exercise of South Sea island octogenarians.

Not all faculty and departments view the proposal as a contract, however. Even those who do are quick to point out that approving the proposal does not mean the final project will also be approved. You must also conduct the study well, analyze the data appropriately, produce an acceptable final version of the thesis or dissertation, and so on. Furthermore, most researchers change something that they proposed once they actually implement the study; in fact, there are times a committee will expect you to alter your study rather than sticking strictly to the proposal (e.g., if you discover that your experimental manipulation is not working as intended). Thus, it will behoove you to assess local norms about how binding the proposal is, both for students and for faculty.

The proposal seems a formidable obstacle for many students. But believe it or not, you have probably done a great deal of the work for it already. What you need to do now is organize all those notes you have taken, all those references, and all those measures you've been collecting as you researched your topic and turn them into a single document. In the next section, we give you an overview of what to put into the proposal.

Your written product is your opportunity to show what you can do as a scholar. Be aware, however, that although creativity and originality are valued characteristics in conceptualizing and conducting research, they are not popular when writing about it. The proposal is no place for you to challenge the departmental rules and come up with your own "improved" way of doing things. Find out the proposal requirements of your department or school. If your institution allows multiple formats, find out which your committee chair prefers. Do it their way, and save your creativity for more important challenges.

KNOW THE ELEMENTS OF THE THESIS
OR DISSERTATION PROPOSAL

So, what goes into a proposal? Departments and faculty vary in how detailed they wish the proposal to be. At one end of the continuum, students present a very brief document, such as a grant application or an abbreviated literature review and a Method section with very little detail and few appendices. At the other end, the proposal is essentially a draft of the first half of the final thesis or dissertation, with all relevant supplemental material in the appendices. If you haven't already done so, ask your chair to recommend a couple of proposals for you to use as models. Compare them to the final thesis or dissertation version of the same studies to appraise the level of detail the candidates provided in the proposal.

In most cases, we tend to lean toward including more rather than less detail in the proposal, consistent with the contract view. A good rule of thumb is to include everything that will go into the complete thesis or dissertation eventually. Your ideas, references, and insights are relatively fresh and available now, not lost in the synaptic jungle of your brain or the disorganization of your writing space. Put them into the proposal, and you won't have to worry about losing them or re-creating them afresh after you have collected and analyzed your data.

Furthermore, putting the details of your study in writing allows you to benefit from faculty feedback on your specific ideas and plans. The more complete you are now, the more your committee will share their wisdom and experience about the best ways to measure your key constructs, minimize participant attrition, or set up specific analyses. Also, there will be less room for a committee member to say at your oral defense, "Oh—I assumed that of course you would do this my way. You didn't? You really need to run all those participants again to correct that egregious error."

The exception to this advice is in departments that encourage students to prepare their proposals as grant applications that they will actually submit to a funding agency. These documents are typically much shorter, with presentation of research aims, goals, methods, analyses, and timeline often limited to 5 to 10 pages. Clearly, in this instance, students learn to describe their research very succinctly, with an emphasis on the significance and potential impact of their work. However, one challenge of this approach for the committee is ensuring that students have considered all relevant aspects of the literature that underlies their research and details of the methods and analyses they plan to use. Departments that use this approach often require that students demonstrate their mastery of the relevant literature, methods, and analyses in other ways, such as prior research experience, publication, and oral presentation of their work. It is also important to remember that whereas a grant application may be acceptable at the proposal stage, it will not suffice for the final document. Students should expect to prepare a fuller document prior to their defense.

Although formal rules and chair and committee preferences can vary, a good way to organize a proposal is in terms of three major sections: introduction (literature review), Method, and Results (analysis plan). Portfolio-style projects typically include separate sections for the methods and proposed analyses for each study. However, the introduction for these projects may vary, with some documents including one integrated literature review, others including a separate introduction for each study, and still others including both an overarching literature review and briefer introductions for each study. For grant application–style proposals, the corresponding sections may be labeled "Significance and Aims" (including the literature review and study aims and hypotheses) and "Strategy" or "Approach" (including methods and analysis plan). Regardless of specific section or chapter names and scope, these are the meat of most scientific articles, and the format should be familiar to you.

Of course, theses and dissertations are often longer than published articles and may include some unique features. They may be organized into chapters (with required chapters often spelled out by your institution or department), and of course some material will go before (e.g., title page, table of contents, abstract) and after (e.g., references, tables, figures, appendices) these major sections. Nonetheless, the introduction, Method, and Results sections constitute the heart of the proposal. The material that follows provides an overview of each section. Chapters 6 through 9 go into more detail about these sections of the proposal.

Introduction (Literature Review)

In the introduction, you describe your research area and review the relevant literature. Two general variations of the thesis or dissertation literature review predominate: the two-chapter and the one-chapter model. In the two-chapter model, the first chapter (usually the first chapter of the document) is relatively short and introduces the topic, provides a brief overview, and then states the research problem and sometimes the specific aims of the research and the hypotheses you propose to test. A longer second chapter provides a critical, integrative review of the literature. The challenge of this model is to present sufficient information in the first chapter for readers to understand why the research question is important without being redundant with the longer chapter. The format of this first chapter is similar to that required for most grant applications (which allow much less space!) and is thus a useful format to perfect if you envision writing grants to support this or future research.

The more streamlined one-chapter model combines the material of the two-chapter version into one and may reverse the order of the major sections. This format often begins with a brief introduction to the topic, then launches into a focused literature review that concludes with a statement of the problem and hypotheses. Alternatively, it may begin with a brief (e.g., one- or two-page) overview and statement of the research aims and then move to the literature review. With either order, it is most common to conclude with your specific research question and hypotheses.

An increasingly common version of the one-chapter model is an introduction that approximates the length and format of the introductory section of a journal article (four–eight pages) or, more rarely, a grant application (one–two pages). This brief introduction is sometimes accompanied by a lengthier, more comprehensive review in an appendix. For example, at one of our institutions, publication-style proposals are encouraged for both the thesis and dissertation, with a comprehensive literature review appendix required for the thesis but not for the dissertation. The rationale is that at the thesis stage, students need to demonstrate their ability to review, consolidate, and use the literature to guide their research, whereas by the time they reach the dissertation, they have already demonstrated mastery of this skill and can focus more exclusively on publication-style writing.

Whichever version you and your committee chair choose, it is helpful if your proposal contains a complete review of the literature relevant to your specific topic. In other words, write the literature review that you will include in the final version of your thesis or dissertation (the final write-up will also include the few new studies that get published while you are conducting yours). Although some schools accept more abbreviated reviews for the proposal than for the final document, we strongly recommend writing a complete review at the proposal stage.

What is our logic? You will need to do all the work required for a complete review anyway in order to write your proposal. Otherwise, you won't know whether someone has beaten you to the punch and already explored your idea. A thorough review of the literature also acquaints you with all the nitty-gritty procedural and design details of research in your area, thereby helping you avoid the mistakes others have made. The precision required to write a review will force you to think through these details in much more depth than if you just read the literature and give a brief overview in the proposal. Similarly, writing helps sharpen your thinking. Integrating findings from diverse studies forces you to look for themes and to compare and contrast different studies. This process requires that you both think broadly about and attend to details of studies that you might otherwise gloss over. One of us calls this "going to the cognitive gym": You will get a brain workout, it will not always be fun, and it will take time and effort, but the results will be worth it.

Finally, if you write a thorough literature review and Method section, your final project is halfway written! If you leave the review for later, you'll have a demanding writing task left to do at the end of the project. You are not likely to be highly motivated to reread all those articles you've forgotten about while you were collecting your data.

In the literature review, we recommend using the funnel approach: Start with the general literature in your topic area, and gradually narrow your focus to the specific area of research and precise research question you are going to explore. After introducing the subject and reviewing relevant literature, you will lead readers skillfully to the point at which the rationale for your specific study should seem readily apparent to any who stayed awake through the previous material.

How long should the review be? In our experience, the "best" length varies widely, depending on departmental norms and on how many pages you devote to the wide end of the funnel (i.e., how much you summarize background material before reviewing it in depth). Our guess is that the modal length of a literature review for a thesis (in the introductory chapter or appendix) varies from about 10 to 30 pages. Dissertations are more variable, with publication-style literature reviews being much shorter (e.g., four to eight pages) and full book-style reviews of complex dissertations sometimes being as many as 50 pages.

Method

Using a cookbook analogy, if your introduction has been carefully composed, readers now know why you have decided on chocolate mousse cake for the dinner party you are planning. Your logic and organization in choosing the main course and wine and other accompaniments have been so compelling that no one would dream of selecting any other dessert. Now for the recipe!

The Method section can be thought of as the "how it is going be done" section of the proposal. The rules of thumb for this section are justification and replicability. Your Method section should provide sufficient details so that anyone reading it would be able, first, to evaluate the sufficiency of your methods to address your research questions and, second, to replicate your study in all essential aspects. In other words, the cake should have the correct ingredients and should come out exactly the same each time someone reads the recipe and attempts to bake it.

Several subsections are included in nearly any Method section. The first subsection is usually labeled "Participants." Subsequent sections cover design, independent variables, measures (dependent and other), apparatus, setting, and procedures. Exactly what content you cover, and in what order, will depend on your study. Chapter 7 provides more details about what to include in the Method section of your proposal.

What about length? As long as it takes! This smart-aleck response from committee chairs (one that we have all both gotten and given) does have some merit. The length of the Method section depends on how detailed you are, how complex your procedures and design are expected to be, and how much material you locate in the Method section and how much in the appendices. In other words, the Method section should consume as many pages as it takes you to describe the details that provide sufficient justification for your methods and allow replication. In our experience, Method sections may be 15 to 25 pages long for dissertations (shorter for publication-style dissertations); in theses they may be shorter, given that theses are often smaller in scope.

Results (Analysis Plan)

In your final thesis or dissertation document, the Results section will present the fruits of your data collection for the world to see. At the proposal stage, the "Analysis Plan" section is where you lay out the steps you'll take to turn your data into interpretable results. Ordinarily, this section describes (a) any preliminary analyses you plan to do (e.g., checking whether groups of participants are demographically equivalent, summarizing data on manipulation checks) and (b) analyses you will use to test your hypotheses or answer your research question. You might also include (c) supplemental analyses you plan to conduct (e.g., to explore the data further). Chapter 9 goes over these sections in more detail, along with the steps involved in selecting appropriate statistics for quantitative theses and dissertations.

Departments and committees vary on where they expect you to place the analysis plan and how extensive they expect it to be. Although we describe it as a separate section, some proposals include it as the final section of the Method section. Some departments and committees want it to be presented separately as the beginning of a Results chapter. Check with your chair and look at completed proposals to get an idea of the local norms for the content students typically include in their proposals at your institution.

References

Include a list of the references cited in your proposal. Prepare this list using the format suggested in the *Publication Manual of the American Psychological Association* (seventh ed.; APA, 2020), unless your school specifies otherwise. Be sure to include only those references you actually cited in the proposal. Some novice writers prepare a reference list that reflects every article they read. Although this may impress your committee and stand as a memorial to your extensive time in the library or on your computer, such a list is overly inclusive for a proposal. References you read but do not cite in the proposal should be deleted from the list. Continue to update your references, however, because you will want to consult the full list when you complete your study and are preparing the final version of your project.

Appendices

Appendices are the repository of extra detail that might be important to committee members to assure them that you approached your task in a competent way. Instructions to participants, consent forms, debriefing scripts, data collection instruments or treatment manuals that are not copyrighted, construction blueprints, and wiring diagrams for apparatus are examples of the kinds of entries one might expect to find in appendices that accompany the proposal. Ordinarily, materials copyrighted by others may not be included in an appendix; if you wish to include them, you must obtain written permission to do so from the copyright holder.

Another appendix item that is less standard but gaining popularity is an extended literature review. An important part of the thesis or dissertation is the student's demonstration to their committee that they have mastered the appropriate literature. Especially as more departments move to briefer publication-style or grant proposal–style theses and dissertations, the introduction section may not do this adequately. The literature review appendix can be in the form of a table, annotated bibliography, written narrative (i.e., traditional literature review), or another format that the chair deems appropriate. Chapter 6 provides an example of a literature review table. One benefit of this appendix, especially in table or annotated bibliography format, is that it provides a vehicle for you to store and organize your literature, identify patterns and gaps, guide your writing, and—importantly—get feedback from your committee on your process.

Place appendices in the order that readers encounter them in the proposal. For example, Appendix A could contain your extended literature review, Appendix B the advertisement placed in the local newspaper for participant recruitment, Appendix C the next piece of supplemental material, and so on.

Abstract

An abstract is not a universally required part of the proposal. However, it will be required for the final thesis or dissertation document, so we recommend adding it to the proposal as well. Writing a proposal-stage abstract is a great way to practice distilling your project down to its core by identifying the main research aims, rationale, methods, and hypotheses or expected findings. You'll probably be asked to describe your study to colleagues, potential data sources or funders, or relatives, so it will be handy to have a very brief and to-the-point spiel ready—your own personal elevator speech. Clearly, the abstract is not exactly that (abstracts tend to be more scholarly, sometimes referred to as "drier," than elevator speeches), but writing the abstract helps you pare the project down to its bones. Your committee will also appreciate the brief project overview that an abstract provides; it will help orient them to what to expect from the proposal and remind them of key study details as they go into your proposal meeting.

An abstract typically mirrors the major sections of a study—the introduction (study aims and rationale), Method, Results, and Discussion. Because you don't have results or a discussion yet, a proposal abstract can include your analysis plan, including anticipated findings and their implications. Abstracts for a thesis or dissertation are typically longer than publication-style abstracts, often extending to a full page or two. Check with your committee chair about your institution's expectations or requirements for the abstract.

Table of Contents

Once the rest of the proposal is complete, you can produce the table of contents, right? Actually, although it is not customary in all departments to prepare a table of contents for the proposal, it can be a good idea to do so, and to prepare it ahead of time in the form of an outline. This can help you organize your literature review and Method sections. It can also help you identify and avoid problems in conceptualizing your material. Preparing the table of contents ahead of time also provides a task analysis or checklist of what is required to complete the thesis or dissertation. A carefully prepared, three-level (I, II, etc.; A, B, etc.; 1, 2, etc.) outline or table of contents shows clearly what needs to be done. As you complete the different sections, you can obtain immense satisfaction from checking off your accomplishments.

Of course, the table of contents will not have page numbers until the entire proposal is complete. In fact, the contents should be regarded as a tentative outline that can be revised as your writing proceeds. When you are ready to insert page numbers (i.e., just before submitting your proposal to your committee), be sure to assign titles to the appendices as well. Thus, the entry "Appendix A: Instructions to Participants. . . . p. 86" tells readers exactly where to go to find what the participants were told. (Some theses and dissertations indicate merely that Appendix A begins on p. 86, without indicating what the appendix contains—unnecessarily shabby scholarship.) Word-processing programs often have a function that allows you to create a table of contents that is linked to the document sections so that the table will auto-populate with section headings and page numbers. Using this function lets you check your use of heading levels by seeing whether they show up correctly in the table of contents. It also removes any worry about adding something to the text that will throw off page numbers—the contents page is updated automatically. Another nice touch is to give the actual page numbers of the appendices when referring to them in the text. Thus, "Participants were told they would receive relaxation training for 10 minutes at the start of each session (see Appendix A, p. 86)" is more helpful to readers than ". . . (see Appendix A)."

Figure 5.1 presents the proposal table of contents for a thesis one of us chaired. Studying the tables of contents of theses and dissertations that your chair recommends as models will show you alternative ways of organizing a proposal.

FIGURE 5.1. Sample Proposal Table of Contents for a Study of Positive Emotion Regulation Strategies and Reward Positivity

Contents

FIGURE 5.1. Sample Proposal Table of Contents for a Study of Positive Emotion Regulation Strategies and Reward Positivity (*Continued*)

Note. From *Association Between Positive Emotion Regulation Strategies and the Reward Positivity Effect* (unpublished master's thesis proposal), by K. Irvin, 2017, University of Missouri. Reprinted with permission.

INVESTIGATE THE GENERAL PROPOSAL PROCESS

The process that students follow in preparing a proposal varies from chair to chair and from institution to institution, but there are some general consistencies. The process usually starts when you have (a) nailed down both an idea and a chair (not necessarily in that order!), (b) gathered and read the relevant literature, and (c) arrived at a good idea of what you propose to do and how you propose to do it. You then write the proposal. Some students submit parts of the proposal for review by their chair (e.g., literature review, then Method section) as they write, whereas others wait until they have a complete draft to turn in. Your chair can advise you on the process they usually follow.

Identifying your committee members can happen anytime along the way—ask about your department's conventions. In some departments, it is customary to identify committee members early to allow them time to plan their committee service for the academic term or year and to allow you to seek consultation from them if indicated. In other departments, it is more typical to wait until your proposal is almost ready and then to ask faculty to serve on your committee.

Generally, your committee members will not provide much input on your study or read early drafts of your proposal unless they have serious interest and expertise in your area. Your chair should provide feedback on what you have written and have you continue to revise your document until they think it is suitable to give to your committee members. Usually, submitting it to the committee members signals that you are ready for a proposal meeting (see Chapter 13), where they will raise additional issues for you to consider and suggest revisions to the document. After the proposal meeting, you will make the revisions requested by your committee and submit the proposal for any additional required approval.

At some point in this process, you will also prepare and submit additional documents to allow you to complete your research. If you'll be collecting new data, you must secure the approval of the institutional review board (IRB) for the protection of human subjects, animal care and use committee, or whichever body oversees the ethics of data collection at your institution. These documents provide an overview of your procedures and how you will handle the ethical issues involved in any research (e.g., confidentiality, risks of the procedures) along with specific ethical issues pertaining to your study (e.g., use of deception). You may also need to secure approval of the agency or organization (e.g., school district, hospital, community organization) from which you are recruiting participants. If you are using archival data, you may still need to secure approval from whoever owns the data. If the data belong to your research adviser, that process probably already occurred when you first identified your research topic. If the data belong to another faculty member, a research group, or an outside organization, find out what their approval process is. Typically, they are interested in how you plan to use the data so they can ensure that your plan is ethical, scientifically sound, and consistent with their values or mission, and that your study does not overlap too extensively with other projects using the data.

The timing and nature of these procedures vary from department to department and chair to chair. For example, one of us worked in a program in which proposals did not receive final approval from the director of the graduate program until the students had secured IRB approval for their study. Another's requirements were the opposite: Students could not submit proposed dissertation research for IRB approval until the committee formally approved their proposal. Occasionally, requirements conflict with one another—as with the student whose committee wanted letters of support from the schools where data collection would occur, but the schools wanted committee approval before providing letters of support! Consulting with other students, checking thesis and dissertation requirements, and asking your chair for information and guidance can all help you inform yourself about the normal sequence and timing of key events in the proposal process.

One final prestudy step that is gaining popularity is preregistration (Nosek et al., 2018). Briefly, preregistration involves publicly describing your study protocol before you begin to examine any data. Sounds like your thesis or dissertation proposal, right? In fact, preregistration has many similarities to a thesis or dissertation proposal, although it is shared with a much larger audience. For instance, the Center for Open Science's Open Science Framework (https://osf.io) maintains an open-access registry of research across all areas of science, with nearly 300,000 searchable registrations as of the end of 2018 (https://osf.io/registries/). Preregistration is part of a multifaceted effort among scientists to improve the reproducibility of research findings (e.g., by reducing biases in how research findings are interpreted and which findings are published) and, consequently, the quality of our knowledge base (see Munafò et al., 2018, for discussion of this effort). By preregistering your study, you not only help promote the ideals of open, reproducible science but also may stand a better chance of having your work published.

A growing number of journals are encouraging authors to preregister their studies and even offering multistage peer reviews in which registered studies are initially reviewed on the basis of the importance of their research questions and rigor of their methodology. Papers that are provisionally accepted at this stage are later reviewed not for the specifics of their outcomes but for the quality of study execution and adherence to the registered protocol (Nosek et al., 2018). In essence, the focus shifts from specific (e.g., significant) outcomes to important questions and sound methods. Aside from being good science, this approach can be quite reassuring to budding researchers who have put a great deal of effort into study design and execution and are trying to build a research career, but fear that their results may not turn out as beautifully as hoped. And given the work you've already put into your proposal, preregistration may be a fairly easy next step.

In the end, all of your approvals and registrations will converge, and you'll be ready to start your study. In the chapters that follow, we delve more deeply into each piece of the project.

✓   **TO DO . . .**
WRITING THE PROPOSAL

☐ Understand the functions of the thesis or dissertation proposal.

  – Find out whether the proposal is binding and how binding it is.

  – Identify requirements of the department and school.

☐ Know the elements of a thesis or dissertation proposal.

  – Introduction (literature review)

  – Method

  – Results (analysis plan)

  – References

  – Appendices

  – Abstract

  – Table of contents

☐ Investigate the general proposal process.

  – Timetable

  – Involvement of committee members

  – Submission of the protocol for institutional review board approval

  – Department requirements

  – Preregistration

6

Reviewing the Literature

This chapter covers how to prepare your literature review section, including
- locating and critically reviewing the literature that lays the foundation for your study
- writing a literature review that presents a clear picture of the existing literature and a compelling case for your study

Read thoroughly if
- you are new to conducting the type of literature review required for your thesis or dissertation
- you want to learn or brush up on current methods of identifying relevant literature

Skim or skip if
- you have already identified the literature relevant to your project
- you are already experienced in writing literature reviews of the sort your thesis or dissertation will involve

After you find a topic, you must learn more about it. This involves finding, reading, and summarizing (in written form) the relevant professional literature. Reading and thinking about what others have done and said teaches you about key conceptual and methodological issues in the field. This process also allows you to see whether another enterprising individual has already done

https://doi.org/10.1037/0000161-006
Dissertations and Theses From Start to Finish: Psychology and Related Fields, Third Edition,
by D. J. Bell, S. L. Foster, and J. D. Cone

your study. A related benefit is that you can spend hours avoiding writing anything at all by sitting in an armchair and reading!

LOCATE SOURCES OF RELEVANT LITERATURE

Literature relevant to your research comes from journal articles, books, book chapters, and occasionally the internet. You may also want to examine conference papers, theses, and dissertations. (Throughout this chapter, we refer to these types of work collectively as "papers.") Each source contains a large collection of information, however. What are the effective ways of sorting through them to extract the material most relevant to your particular topic? Several traditional and some more technologically sophisticated methods provide vehicles for locating relevant literature. Although none of these is perfect, using all of them together will ensure a reasonably comprehensive literature search.

Before starting your search, we have three important suggestions to help you avoid pitfalls and keep you on track as you plan your attack: Use primary sources, avoid the popular press, and lay out your search strategy.

Use Primary Sources

Always look up the primary sources (i.e., original papers) and read them yourself. Do not rely on descriptions of studies and their findings in other authors' work, referred to as "secondary sources." Authors of such papers too often describe studies erroneously, indicating that the original authors said something they did not say or did something they did not do. We know—our own work has been cited to support points that opposed the very stand we were taking in the article being cited! In addition, you may not agree with others' conclusions about the paper. Now is the time to stand on your own intellectual feet and draw your own conclusions. We are not saying there is no value in reading others' critiques of original papers. This is best done after reading the original work yourself, however, and then considering whether you agree with the secondary source's opinions.

What if you cannot find the original paper because it is in an obscure, difficult-to-obtain journal or was presented at a conference but not published? Do not cite the paper as though you actually read it. Instead, follow the guidelines in the *Publication Manual of the American Psychological Association* for citing a secondary source (e.g., "Bell & Foster, 2008, as cited in Cone, 2016"; American Psychological Association [APA], 2020).

Avoid the Popular Press

Articles published in the popular press, such as *Time* magazine, *Wired*, the *New York Times*, and similar publications, have little place in a scholarly literature review. Although these publications may be excellent ways of learning what is happening in the world, they are no substitute for articles from peer-reviewed journals and other scholarly works. The same is true of many internet sites, blogs, and podcasts, in which the origin and accuracy of information can be even more difficult to discern. Although the information in the popular press may be accurate, you cannot evaluate it as easily as you can a journal article in which the methodology is transparent and delineated clearly enough for all to critique.

In addition, the popular press is often used as a vehicle for sharing opinion, rather than for conveying scientific information with enough detail that allows evaluation and critique. So does this mean that popular press articles will never have a place in a thesis or dissertation? Not necessarily. Although you would never use them as a source of research findings, they are occasionally useful in conveying the importance of an issue to the public or in illustrating how something is portrayed in the media.

Deciding whether to use information on websites can be tricky because websites are so variable. At one extreme are sites created by individual hobbyists who have a point of view to express or who share information without sufficient expertise or fact-checking. At the other extreme are sites where bona fide scientific organizations provide information compiled by groups of scientists on the basis of current research. For example, the websites of government organizations (e.g., Centers for Disease Control and Prevention, Substance Abuse and Mental Health Services Administration, National Institute of Mental Health) and those maintained by APA and other major psychology organizations have reasonably trustworthy information. The Cochrane Library website (https://www.cochrane.org) is a source for sound, research-based information; this nonprofit, nongovernmental organization makes available systematic reviews of health-related research by experts from around the world. Thus, evaluating the quality and veracity of internet information is crucial. Is the information authored by experts and, therefore, similar to a book chapter or review of the literature? Or are the authors and origin of the information unclear? Stick closer to the former and stay away from the latter, at least as a source of reliable and valid information.

Lay Out Your Search Strategy

A multitude of excellent resources can help you locate the literature that will guide and support your study. Laying out your strategy for identifying these resources and using them effectively will go a long way toward an efficient and effective literature review process. Before you begin, it may be a good idea to consult with a research or reference librarian. These librarians do so much more than hand you books—they are trained to locate information. They know where to look and how to sift through the millions of pieces of literature to find the gems that are relevant to your study. Even those of us who have been doing literature reviews for decades (and think we have the process well in hand) have been surprised at what a good reference librarian can teach us. Check with your university library; most institutions have one or more reference librarians on staff and often have librarians with specific expertise in social sciences research. They can show you the best places to look for relevant information, explain how to set up database queries or search parameters to produce the results you need, and help you refine your search to avoid being buried under mountains of literature.

Next, lay out a strategy for how you intend to search. We cover details of *what* and *where* you might search later in this section, but a few words about *how* to search effectively are in order here. Although the specifics of how you execute your search may vary depending on what you are looking for and where, most searches have similar characteristics. We discuss online or computerized searches because these will form the bulk of your literature search strategy. You can use similar (albeit much less efficient) strategies if you are searching manually.

First, you must identify keywords or search terms, which are words or phrases that describe the contents of the papers you want to find. Start with keywords listed in the relevant papers you've already found; many journals include keywords or descriptors beneath the abstract. For articles that do not provide keywords, examine their abstracts; words that show up frequently are good candidates as keywords. Authors' names and journal titles can also be used as keywords.

Finding the right keywords is critical to success but is by no means easy. Not all authors use the same terminology to describe their studies. For example, a recent search by one of us using the term "trichotillomania" turned up different results from when "hair pulling" was substituted. In addition, some publishing programs have professional indexers select the terms by which works are indexed, but these indexers might not be familiar with the technical terms of a discipline. It is better to start your initial search using a variety of keywords and synonyms rather than limiting the search to specific technical terms.

One especially useful feature of many electronic databases is a thesaurus of terms (e.g., PsycINFO's *Thesaurus of Psychological Index Terms*) that allows you to look at terms related to the keywords you select and may give you ideas about other terms that relate to your project but that had not occurred to you. You can also consult the thesaurus for more inclusive or more specific categories associated with your keywords. As Rothstein (2012) noted, keywords may differ across, and sometimes even within, databases and search engines. Again, a good reference librarian can be immensely helpful in your keyword-based search.

Once you select your keywords, enter them in the databases or search engines you use and specify where to look for them, usually in the abstract, title, or body of the paper (where the computer looks for the keywords depends on the particular database). In addition, you can tell the computer to search for combinations of keywords; usually you list the ones you want, connected by the word "and," and the computer lists papers in which the abstract, title, or paper body contain all the words you have listed. Alternatively, you can instruct the computer to pick out papers that contain any one (not all) of the keywords; you list all the terms connected by "or." You can scan search results on the computer screen, print them, and (sometimes) download them to an electronic file or email them to yourself. Some search engines automatically email you when new information relevant to your interests appears on the web.

A trap with computerized searches is to believe you have done an exhaustive literature search this way. The problem is that the search is only as good as (a) your keywords; (b) the extent to which authors (and indexers) in the field use the same words in their titles, abstracts, and so forth; (c) the range of journals the database contains; and (d) the number of years covered by the database. Therefore, although the mechanics of an effective search are often guided by keywords, your search strategy should go beyond these. Think about the objectives of your search. Is your objective to learn everything you can about your topic in order to develop research questions that build on the literature? Probably not; by the time you get to this stage of your thesis or dissertation, you should be at least somewhat familiar with the literature and should have potential research questions and hypotheses in mind. Thus, the goal of your search is to identify the literature that sets the stage for your questions and hypotheses. Of course, this is an iterative process, and your questions and hypotheses may evolve as you dig into the literature. But this can be a great strategy for ensuring that you keep your search focused on literature that is relevant to your study.

CONDUCT YOUR SEARCH

Now that you have done the preliminary work to set up your search, where should you look to locate as much relevant literature as possible?

Identify Key Authors and Journals

A good initial step in compiling relevant literature is to locate key players in your research area and their favorite publication outlets. Who are the big names? What journals regularly publish their work? Others who know the area better than you do are good sources of this information (e.g., your chair and committee members).

A second excellent source is the bibliography or reference section of a recent book, chapter, or article on your topic. Scan the references to locate relevant articles and to find out who's working in the area. Read the book, chapter, or article to orient you to key issues and concepts in the field.

A third effective strategy is to conduct an internet search of the key players in your field (e.g., "Google" them). Go to https://www.google.com, https://www.scholar.google.com, or the search engine of your choice and type in a name to be searched. This can be a very efficient way to obtain up-to-date information on what these people are doing currently in the area, much of which might not yet be published. For example, you might easily find this information in their curriculum vitae on a university website. Additionally, you may uncover information about recent presentations or workshops they have given on relevant topics. We say more about internet searches later in this section.

Use Bibliographic Reference Sources

Bibliographic reference sources are designed specifically to collate and organize published literature, and these sources will likely provide the bulk of the literature for your review. In the "old days," students visited the reference section of the library and spent hours poring over large bound volumes; today, most of these sources are available online in searchable databases. The PsycINFO database, for example, contains abbreviated abstracts from psychological journals that it indexes by topic and author (see the Supplemental Resources at the end of this chapter for URLs for the bibliographic reference sources mentioned in this section). This online resource is maintained by APA and is available online through most major university libraries. Dissertation Abstracts International is a similar reference source for dissertations.

The Education Resources Information Center (ERIC) is a major clearinghouse for information related to education. Broader databases include PsycNET (APA) and Current Contents Connect (Web of Science). PsycNET is an online platform that provides access not just to abstracts but also to many full-text articles, chapters, reference books, and conference papers. Current Contents Connect is updated weekly and includes abstracts and bibliographic information on articles from major journals and websites.

One additional type of reference source—citation indexes—bears special mention. Citation indexes allow you to look up every article that has cited a particular article since its publication, which is very useful when you wish to ascertain what has been done since the article was published. You can track the influence of the article through time and may find papers that other literature searches did not locate.

The Social Sciences Citation Index (SSCI) indexes every article from more than 1,500 professional journals representing 50 different disciplines in the social sciences. SSCI is also helpful for locating research containing information about the psychometric properties of measurement tools you might decide to use; most authors cite the original or seminal article on the tools they use. SSCI is available electronically by subscription, so check with your institution for availability. Read the instructions carefully and ask a reference librarian to help you the first time you use this source; many people find it hard to master SSCI without instructions.

Another citation index, Google Scholar, is also a search engine (see the next section). This website allows you both to search for articles using keywords and, once you have located an interesting article, to identify other papers that have cited the articles since publication. One word of warning: We have not checked the convergence between SSCI and Google Scholar, nor do we know the extent to which errors in the reference lists of articles influence the results of either of these indexes. It is generally advisable to use multiple sources and cast a broad net, especially early in your search process.

Use Online Search Engines

Online search engines enable you to search the literature quickly. Google Scholar, designed specifically for the academic literature, allows you to search the vast majority of peer-reviewed English-language journals, as well as documents that are not published commercially (often called "gray literature")—theses, dissertations, technical reports, government reports, and conference presentations (see the Supplemental Resources at the end of this chapter for URLs for the online search engines mentioned in this section). Some studies indicate that Google Scholar does a good job of uncovering all material available on the web (almost 90%, as estimated by Khabsa & Giles, 2014), and the free access to this search tool can make it more accessible than subscription-based services such as Scopus and Web of Science.

However, Google Scholar is not perfect, and like gas mileage, your results may vary. Depending on your specific research area and search strategy and the location of the research you're looking for (e.g., books, non-English-language literature, institutional repositories), you may miss a fair amount of relevant literature (see Fagan, 2017, for a discussion of Google Scholar and similar search engines). In addition, Google Scholar has been criticized for favoring breadth of coverage over selectivity and for including predatory journals (i.e., journals that charge for publication and do not include adequate quality review) and other low-quality sources. As with any internet-based information, it is wise to use this type of search tool as one part of a thoughtful literature review and to seek consultation from a research librarian or others familiar with cutting-edge literature review resources.

Several other sites are worth examining. PubMed is a free online search engine operated by the National Institutes of Health (NIH) and the National Library of Medicine. NIH requires recipients of federal grants to provide the full text of published articles based on NIH-funded research in the PubMed database. Microsoft Academic, introduced in 2016 after an extensive overhaul of prior tools (e.g., Windows Live Academic, Microsoft Academic Search), may evolve into a search engine comparable to Google Scholar.

ResearchGate is an increasingly popular research-focused social networking site that allows researchers to share and follow each others' work, follow a topic, blog about research topics or articles, and post questions. One of our students was recently looking for a brief, free, and psychometrically sound measure of a construct that was slightly outside of our primary research area. After searching the literature with limited success (the most widely used measures were all either lengthy or beyond the student's budget), she posted a question on ResearchGate. Within a day, she had a wealth of information and was able to use convergence of opinions from many well-known research labs to identify just what she was looking for.

Look at Literature From Other Disciplines

PsycINFO, PsycNET, and other resources are limited by the journals they include. Even a Google search may be limited by the search terms you use. Disciplines such as medicine, communications, education, social work, sociology, and business all have journals that publish articles relevant to some areas of psychology. Your research area may overlap with these other disciplines, so be sure to consider this when selecting your search terms, bibliographic reference sources, and search engines. Many disciplines have abstract services or databases you should consult if your research area is addressed by more than one discipline.

Scan the Tables of Contents of Key Journals

As you become familiar with your topic area, you will identify the journals in which most articles in your area have been published. You can supplement your review by examining their tables of contents (or the index in the last issue of each volume) for the past 10 years. This will help you find articles that may be too recent to appear in reference and bibliographic materials, and it will serve as a double check on the results provided by your other search methods. Tables of contents are included in Current Contents Connect, and most journals make them readily available on their websites.

Use Reference Lists

As you scan relevant articles, look at their reference lists and bibliographies and note relevant references. This is an invaluable source of papers that you may not find through other means. Rothstein (2012) provided examples in which online searches identified different groups of articles depending on the specific database platform and missed articles identified by manual searches of journals.

Cooper (1998) pointed out a trap with both the key journals and the reference list scanning approaches. Most researchers in a particular area, Cooper noted, have informal interpersonal and journal networks. Thus, they tend to publish in and cite articles from their journal network, leading to over-representation of articles in journals inside the network and undercitation of articles in those outside the network. This is yet another reason for using multiple methods to conduct a comprehensive literature search in your area.

Your search is over when you have done all of the above and keep turning up the same articles repeatedly as you look at others' reference lists and bibliographic sources. This may not mean you have collected everything ever written on a topic, but you have probably found the major articles produced in the area.

COLLECT AND ORGANIZE RELEVANT INFORMATION

Your literature search will generate a lot of information, including the list of citations you will consider including in your review and the actual papers you will review. So how can you organize this information?

Keep Track of Citations

As we scan published reference lists for relevant articles, we like to copy complete citations (in APA Style; APA, 2020) into a computer file or some other permanent record (e.g., a notecard). If you have a laptop or tablet that you carry to the library with you or use to do home-based searches, get in the habit of typing your citations into a file; you will be glad you did this later when you create your reference list and can cut and paste your citations rather than having to look them up a second time.

Take the time to learn APA Style for the kinds of references you will use in your ultimate reference lists. Be aware that sources may claim to provide reference citations in APA Style that you can cut and paste, but these citations sometimes contain APA Style errors or omissions. We cannot tell you how many hours we have spent in our careers trying to track down page numbers of chapters, author initials, digital object identifiers (DOIs), and the like that we failed to note when we first wrote down the reference.

Some colleagues swear by EndNote (https://endnote.com/), a reference manager software program that allows you to organize citations and format them in many different styles, including APA Style. Keeping pace with contemporary development in research support tools, EndNote also allows you to locate PDFs and share your resources and citations with colleagues. Check at software publishers' websites and with your institution—some offer reference management software to students either free or at reduced cost.

Think about the best way to organize your citations. Although some people still prefer old-school methods like hardcopy lists on which they can make handwritten notes, most students manage their citations electronically. For example, you can create an electronic file system with separate folders and subfolders for different categories of references (e.g., references to track down, references found and awaiting review, references relevant to the various topics you will cover, references that may be relevant later or somewhere else but not for this project). This way, you can move citations easily from one stage of the review process to the next, store them alongside full-text downloaded documents, and keep them organized and easily accessible any time and place you can access your computer files. Whatever referencing system you choose, be sure to check the accuracy of each entry as you look up the original work, and make corrections to your citation document as needed; as noted earlier, not all citations in articles, chapters, and online databases are accurate.

Plan Your Document Storage System

You will end the literature review process with pages and pages of down-loaded (or, if you prefer, photocopied) articles and chapters and with pages of notes. As you collect and store the papers you have found, think about what storage system will be most helpful to you now and in the future. People differ in their preferred methods. Consider whether you prefer a small number of folders each containing many articles or a larger number of folders that contain fewer articles sorted into finer grained categories. In addition, think about how to name the files containing the documents: by author? journal or book? year? Create a system that will help you find things easily, and use it consistently—you will be glad you did months later when you go back to the literature to write your Discussion section.

Another important consideration is your ability to take notes on important aspects of an article or chapter. Many of us like to make margin notes or highlight notable passages in a document. This "on the spot" method of note-taking has advantages beyond the active, engaged reading it encourages. In addition to being able to record your responses at the time of reading, noting the location within the document of a point you found important makes it much easier to go back to it later. Clearly, you can do this on hard copies, but the expense and hassle of making, organizing, and storing these physical documents may outweigh the ease of putting pen to paper for your margin notes. Many free versions of PDF reader software include functions that allow you to highlight text or insert comments into the electronic documents.

CRITICALLY READ WHAT YOU FOUND

After you collect your literature, read it critically. Remember, you are going to synthesize this information into a coherent review that highlights the main themes, strengths, and weaknesses of the work. To do that, you need to get a sense of the forest as well as the trees. Start thinking about how you will orga-nize this literature in a literature review. A good idea is first to scan the papers you have collected (Galvan & Galvan, 2017). Look for themes and commonal-ities in the methodologies and conceptual frameworks the authors used. You probably will not cite every paper you read, and you will not read every paper in the same depth. Which material is most relevant to your study, and which is tangential? Which topics will you really need to cover, and which can you skim?

Pay attention to unanswered questions and methodological strengths and weaknesses of the studies you peruse, and keep notes. These notes will come in handy as you write the review. Exhibit 6.1 provides a list of questions you can use in evaluating the empirical studies most relevant to your review. See Galvan and Galvan (2017) for other ways of doing this.

EXHIBIT 6.1

Guidelines for Evaluating Empirical Studies

Introduction

1. Does the introduction provide a strong rationale for why the study is needed?

2. Are the research questions and hypotheses clearly articulated? (Research questions are often presented implicitly within a description of the purpose of the study.)

Method

1. Is the method described so that replication is possible without further information?

2. Participants

   a. Are participant recruitment and selection methods described?

   b. Were participants randomly selected? Are there any probable biases in sampling?

   c. Is the sample appropriate in terms of the population to which the authors wished to generalize?

   d. Are characteristics of the sample described adequately?

   e. If two or more groups were compared, are they shown to be comparable on potentially confounding variables (e.g., demographics)? If they are not comparable, was this handled appropriately?

   f. Was informed consent obtained?

   g. Was the size of the sample large enough for the number of measures and for the effect being sought?

3. Design

   a. If appropriate, was a control group used?

   b. Was the control condition appropriate?

   c. What was being controlled for?

   d. If an experimental study, were participants randomly assigned to groups?

4. Measures

   a. For all scores (e.g., data from measures used to classify participants, dependent variables), do the authors provide evidence of reliability and validity, either by summarizing data or by referring readers to an available paper that provides the information?

   b. Do the reliability and validity data justify the use of each score? Specific evidence is particularly important if a measure was created just for this study.

   c. Do the measures match the research questions and hypotheses being addressed?

   d. If different tasks or measures were used, was their order counterbalanced? Did the authors analyze for potential order effects?

   e. Were multiple measures used, particularly those that sample the same domains or constructs but with different methods (e.g., self-report, ratings by others, self-monitoring, direct observation)?

   f. If human observers, judges, or raters were involved, was interobserver or inter-rater agreement (reliability) assessed? Was it obtained for a representative sample of the data? Did the raters do their ratings independently? Was their reliability satisfactory?

(continues)

EXHIBIT 6.1

Guidelines for Evaluating Empirical Studies (*Continued*)

5. Bias and Artifacts

   a. Were administration and scoring of the measures done blindly (i.e., by someone who was unaware of the experimental hypotheses)?

   b. If a quasi-experimental study, do the authors describe appropriate steps to rule out competing explanations of the findings?

   c. Were procedures constant across participants in all groups? Were any confounds introduced as the result of using different procedures? How troublesome are these?

6. Independent variables

   a. If an experimental study, was there a check that the independent variable was manipulated as described?

   b. If an intervention study, did a sufficient sample of therapists or change agents implement the intervention (i.e., to enhance generalizability)?

   c. If multiple treatments or conditions were being compared, do the authors document that these conditions differed in ways they were supposed to differ? Were they the same in every other way (e.g., length, qualifications of therapists or change agents)? If not, is this confound likely to influence the conclusions seriously?

   d. What aspects of the procedures and independent variables limit the external validity of the study?

Results

1. Do the data fulfill the assumptions and requirements of the statistics (e.g., linearity for regression)?

2. Were large amounts of data missing, and if so, did the authors handle this appropriately?

3. Were tests of significance used and reported appropriately (i.e., with sufficient detail to understand what analysis was being conducted)?

4. In correlational studies, did the authors interpret low but significant correlations as though they indicated a great deal of shared variance between the measures? Are the correlations limited by restricted ranges on one or more measures? Do the authors provide means and standard deviations so that you can determine this?

5. If many statistical tests were performed, did the authors adjust the alpha level or use appropriate multivariate techniques to reduce the probability of Type I error that could be due to the large number of tests performed?

6. Do the authors report means, standard deviations (if relevant), effect sizes, and confidence intervals so that readers can examine whether statistically significant differences are large enough to be meaningful?

7. For multivariate statistics, is there an appropriately large ratio of participants to variables?

EXHIBIT 6.1

Guidelines for Evaluating Empirical Studies (*Continued*)

Discussion

1. Do the authors discuss marginally significant or nonsignificant results as though they were significant?

2. Do the authors overinterpret the data (e.g., use causal language to explain correlational findings or interpret self-report of behavior as equivalent to direct observation)?

3. Do the authors consider alternative explanations for the findings?

4. Do the authors include a "humility" section that mentions the limitations of the research (including methodological problems)? Do the authors point out aspects of participant selection, procedures, and dependent variables that limit the generalizability of the findings?

5. Do the authors "accept" the null hypothesis?

Note. Adapted from "A Reader's, Writer's, and Reviewer's Guide to Assessing Research Reports in Clinical Psychology," by B. A. Maher, 1978, *Journal of Consulting and Clinical Psychology*, *46*(4), pp. 835–838. Copyright 1978 by the American Psychological Association.

With empirical papers, read the rationale for the study (usually in the paragraphs just before the Method section), the Method section, and the Results section most carefully—not the conclusions. You should be able to figure out the conclusions for yourself; you can then check whether you agree with the authors about what they said they found. Don't be surprised if you think the findings have implications the authors did not discuss or if you think the authors overplayed some of their findings.

Record your observations, either in separate notes or in the margins, to keep a record of them. If similar observations characterize much of the literature, they may lead you to some major insights about your topic. Group the papers into categories as you scan your collection. Be aware that one disadvantage of making margin notes is that it can be more difficult to keep track of your notes, especially across studies. For this reason, we often keep two sets of notes: (a) margin notes to highlight specific points within a paper and (b) a separate document with brief summaries of each paper and themes or points we want to track across papers. This second document can be organized as a running list of important points, in a table (e.g., with a row for each paper you review and columns for your notes on specific aspects of the paper you want to remember), or using any format you find useful. If you write a one- to two-sentence summary of each paper as you read it, you may find that by the time you are ready to write your introduction or Discussion section, you have several sentences already written!

If you go the route of making a notes document as a supplement to or substitute for margin-marked documents, be sure to include complete details on the methodology in your notes; details that do not seem important now may become important later as you try to reconcile discrepant findings and search out potential confounds in others' procedures. One idea is to develop a list of information that you will note about every paper you read (e.g., number and characteristics of participants, independent variables). As noted earlier, this can be helpful even if you have physical or electronic copies of the papers. You can even systematize this into a prepared coding sheet on which to record specific details from each study. An example of a coding sheet used by one of us in keeping track of literature he was reviewing in behavioral parent training is presented in Figure 6.1. This kind of systematic approach makes it less likely that you will forget to record certain details of a particular paper that you need later. You can also use the Preferred Reporting Items for Systematic Reviews and Meta-Analyses, or PRISMA, system (Moher et al., 2009). Developed primarily to facilitate systematic reporting of reviews of clinical trials, this system includes guidelines and supports (e.g., checklist, flow diagram) that can be useful for any systematic review. Engaging in a systematic review now can make it easier to publish your work later.

Technology can once again be your friend. You can use a word-processing (e.g., OpenOffice, Microsoft Word) or spreadsheet program (e.g., Microsoft Excel) to create a coding sheet you can complete on your tablet or laptop as you encounter particularly relevant papers. You can also do this with a database program such as FileMaker or Microsoft Access. Although you will need to take some time up front to develop your form or database, a real time-saving feature of using this type of technology is the ease with which you can search for particular information (e.g., that study that used remote auditory prompting, all studies using children under age 6) from among the dozens you unearthed in your library and internet sleuthing.

It is essential, if you copy someone's words into your notes, that you put them in quotation marks and write down the page numbers where they appear. It is easy to forget later which notes you wrote in your own words and which were quotes or close paraphrases. Even if you do it by accident, using others' words without appropriate citation is plagiarism. We discuss this topic again at the end of this chapter.

Finally, avoid the trap of overreading, a popular procrastination strategy. Memorizing details of or taking copious notes on every article published in your area is not necessary before starting to write your review. Experience suggests that you may need to read the literature at least twice, but in different ways. Scan it the first time to learn about the key issues in the field and to decide which material is relevant and how to organize it—to get a sense of the forest or big picture. Consult the papers you have selected again and in more detail as you write the review and realize that you need to know more about what particular authors did and found—that is, as you write about the contribution of specific trees to the big picture. Expect to engage in this focused rereading once you begin to put your ideas in writing.

FIGURE 6.1. Coding Sheet for Recording Information From Research Articles on Behavioral Parent Training

Circle relevant study characteristics.

Author(s):				
Title:				
Source:				
Availability:	on file	requested	unavailable	
Type of study:	single family	multiple family		
Problem behavior(s):				
Number of children directly involved:				
Type of dependent measure and on whom taken:				
Observation of behavior by experimenter:	yes	no		
Locus of observation by experimenter:	home	clinic	lab	residential facility	school

(continues)

FIGURE 6.1. Coding Sheet for Recording Information From Research Articles on Behavioral Parent Training (*Continued*)

Number of therapy (training) sessions:			
Design:			
Case study, no measurement			
Case study with measurement:	pre	during	post
Time series (O O O X O O O)			
Equivalent time samples:	A-B	A-B-A	B-A-B	other
Multiple baseline (sequential) design			
Single group, no measurement			
Single group with measurement:	pre	during	post
Single group time series (O O O X O O O)			

FIGURE 6.1. Coding Sheet for Recording Information From Research Articles on Behavioral Parent Training (*Continued*)

	A-B	A-B-A	A-B-A-B	A-B$_1$-A-B$_2$	B-A-B	other
Single group, equivalent time samples:						
Two-group classic (experimental vs. control)						
More than two groups (control, treatment, and other treatment comparisons)						
Two or more groups (other treatment comparisons, no untreated controls)						
Factorial design						
Other:						
Follow-up:	yes		no			
Amount of time since termination mode:						
Comments:						

PREPARE TO WRITE YOUR LITERATURE REVIEW

Before you start to write, keep two features of your thesis or dissertation clearly in mind. First, you are not writing for yourself. You are writing for an audience. You know what you know, but your committee members cannot see directly into your brain. Nor do most of them know the literature as well as you do; some may be completely unfamiliar with your topic. Thus, your job in writing the literature review is to educate your committee about the topic. In so doing, you can also convince them that you are a competent researcher by showing them that you have integrated the material you read and that you have evaluated the quality of the information.

After finishing your literature review, committee members should understand the research questions, procedures, and findings that characterize the field. They should also know the weaknesses of past studies, gaps in the literature, and what needs to be done to move the field forward. By the time they read your final sections, the rationale for your research question should be obvious, as should ways you are attempting to improve on past methods, designs, and procedures. If you have organized the review skillfully, you will have led readers to the conclusion that the absolutely best next study to be done in the area is the one you are proposing.

Second, you are not writing a detective story. Most of us enjoy a good detective novel now and then, sifting through the clues, dead ends, and twists and turns that ultimately lead the novel's protagonist to a solution. And your literature review may certainly have felt like this! You likely read papers that turned out to be dead ends (at least as far as your study is concerned), papers that sent your literature review and perhaps your study in a new direction, and papers that proved critical to your ultimate research questions and methods. However, whereas a good novel takes readers through these twists and turns, a scientific paper follows a more linear path. At each step of your literature review, your readers should be nodding "yes, that makes sense" rather than being surprised at a turn you take or having to backtrack to get to your study.

Thus, as you sit down to write, don't think about your own path of discovery that led you to your proposed study. Instead, think about your study as the end point of the review, the broad research question or need that drives your study as the starting point, and the literature review as the theoretical and empirical path that takes readers on a fairly direct route from beginning to end. To jump back to our funnel metaphor from Chapter 5, this means that although you will start broadly and end with a specific study, you will spare your readers all of the "mis-pours": the pieces of information that are so tangential they don't actually funnel down to your study. A skillful literature review leads readers to expect exactly your study as the logical next step in this line of research. We now turn to the details of how to accomplish this.

Investigate Length and Format Parameters

Before you put pen to paper or fingers to keyboard, find out the local norms for reviews of the literature in projects like yours. These vary widely across schools, and it is important to know the parameters of what you are writing before you begin. Chapter 5 described differences between the one- and two-chapter organizational models and variability in portfolio-style literature reviews, important format distinctions that will influence how you organize your material.

Literature reviews vary considerably in length as well as format. Ask your chair how long and how comprehensive the literature review is expected to be; this determines how you define the scope of what you cover. Note that we tell you to ask your chair rather than to look at others' literature reviews; this is because, paradoxical as it may seem, it is easier to write an excessively long review than to limit its scope and be concise. Thus, faculty often complain in private about 40- to 50-page (and longer!) literature reviews but let students keep producing them, when as few as 10 to 15 pages would suffice to demonstrate the students' skill at synthesizing a body of literature. Personally, we prefer brief (e.g., 10 pages) or moderate (e.g., 20–25 pages) and more focused reviews over lengthy treatises that try to cover everything and do so poorly. An added advantage of shorter reviews lies in their potential for publication: Many journals do not accept more than 20 to 25 total pages of text (which often translates to only four to five pages for the literature review!), so you might as well get used to being succinct.

Write a Preliminary Outline

To get an idea of what you want to cover and how, make an outline or a list of the major headings you plan to use in your literature review. Next to each, indicate the approximate number of pages you plan to allocate to each section. Exhibit 6.2 shows one student's working outline for a literature review for a thesis on the relationship between self-reported dampening of positive affect and physiological measures of reward processing, both of which have been related to depressive symptoms; the thesis investigated the idea that they are simply different methods of assessing a similar underlying construct. This outline is typical in terms of the section page allocations that we recommend for a one-chapter literature review of about 15 pages. Because norms and preferences vary so widely, be sure to ask your chair for feedback about your organization and page allocations.

The outline in Exhibit 6.2 follows the funnel approach we described in Chapter 5. It begins with the general context and gradually becomes more specific, ultimately focusing on the integration of two largely separate research areas and leading to the specific rationale for the study being proposed.

A preliminary outline lets you see how long your chapter will be if you write it as planned, whether you need to limit or expand your scope, and

---

EXHIBIT 6.2

Literature Review Outline With Page Allocations for a Thesis on Positive Emotional Regulation Strategies and Reward Positivity

Outline

I. Introduction (1 page)

II. Depression as a Disorder of Affective Experience and Regulation (2–3 pages)

   A. Experience and Regulation of Negative Affect

   B. Experience and Regulation of Positive Affect

   C. Specific Emotion Regulation Strategies—Savoring and Dampening Strategies

   D. Role of Anhedonia in Understanding Depression as an Affect Regulation Disorder

   E. Conceptual and Measurement Issues, Gaps, and Unanswered Questions

III. Physiological Measures to Assess and Understand Emotional Experience and Regulation (3–4 pages)

   A. Reward Processing as Emotion Regulation

   B. Physiological Assessment of Reward Processing

   C. Conceptual and Measurement Issues, Gaps, and Unanswered Questions

IV. Integrating Dampening Constructs and Measurement Methods (1–2 pages)

   A. How Dampening and Reward Processing May Overlap

   B. Measurement of Dampening and Reward Processing in the Same Study

V. Current Study (2–3 pages)

   A. Preliminary Hypotheses

   B. Primary Hypotheses

   C. Supplementary Hypotheses

Note. From thesis outline for *Association Between Positive Emotion Regulation Strategies and the Reward Positivity Effect* (unpublished master's thesis proposal outline), by K. Irvin, 2017, University of Missouri. Copyright 2017 by K. Irvin. Adapted with permission.

whether the flow follows the direct path we have recommended. Even if you hate outlines or find they have never worked for you, use one now! In our experience, even people who have always been great writers benefit from an outline for the sort of comprehensive, complex literature review required for a thesis or dissertation. At a minimum, make a list of what you think you need to cover and about how many pages you will devote to each area so that you can see whether your scope is too broad or too narrow. You can also get feedback from peers and your chair about whether your logic and organization seem clear.

For many literature reviews, you could introduce material in a variety of different orders. For example, you might cover the literature relevant to your independent variables, dependent variables, or moderators first. Any of these orders might be appropriate, but that is not to say that order doesn't matter. Indeed, it does—the order in which you organize your review and the logic you use to link separate literatures or points to one another tell readers something about how you are conceptualizing your study. A logically tight organization is much more likely to compel your readers to the desired outcome we mentioned earlier of responding to your proposed study with "yes, of course!" as opposed to something like "but what about . . . ?"

An added advantage of an outline or list is that having a concrete list often reduces the anxiety and procrastination associated with the seemingly amorphous and enormous task of writing a literature review. Look at your page allocations, and remember that all you are really doing is writing a series of two- to 10-page papers (the subsections of your review) with a lot of transitions to connect them. How many two- to 10-page papers have you knocked off in graduate school? These are just more of the same.

Don't be surprised if your outline changes as you write the review. For example, you may decide to cut a section if you realize that it raises an issue that, although interesting, is tangential to the study. Many of our students reorganize their review once they think through the details of the argument they are making for their study. Think of your outline as a way of helping you get started and organize your material, but be flexible about altering it as you begin to write.

This is an area in which a low-tech approach might actually be helpful. Using a bulletin board and notecards can allow you to approach your literature review sections, subsections, and even articles or points as puzzle pieces to be assembled into a coherent whole. You can try out different orders without cutting and pasting your entire document. One of our students used a variation of this approach, with sticky notes all over her dining room table. Fortunately, the table was not a popular eating spot!

Limit the Scope of Your Review

After putting page numbers on your outline, you may wonder, "How can I get all that information into only 10 to 20 pages?" If this is your problem, chances are you are making two mistakes. First, you may think you must cite everything you read and cover everything related to the topic: history, theory, old research, new research, speculations, anecdotal evidence, and so on. Wrong! A more functional approach is to examine the literature that guides the rationale and methods of your study. You need to know all that background information and be able to answer questions about it, but you do not need to demonstrate that knowledge in writing for the committee. An evaluation of the current state of the field should suffice.

Incidentally, students often ask how far back their review should cover, sometimes hoping they can ignore anything that was published more than 10 years ago. We reply that they should read relevant empirical information, regardless of its age, to get a broad view of the development of the field. Their review, however, is likely to emphasize recent literature (usually the most recent 5–10 years), because this will describe the current state of the field.

Earlier work that is seminal or highly important should also be included, of course.

If you still are wondering how to cram everything into 10 to 20 pages, you may be making a second mistake. Perhaps you are not limiting explicitly the scope of what you will write about. Although you do not need to cite every article you read, you do need decision rules for what you include and what you leave out. "I like this study" and "I didn't understand the statistics in this one" are not good reasons to include or leave out a paper. Limiting the literature to a particular group of participants (e.g., by age, race, gender, or other characteristic relevant to the study you are proposing), a type or quality of design (e.g., only controlled studies), or specific independent or dependent variables may be appropriate depending on the literature you are reviewing. Articulate your criteria for inclusion very specifically and as far in advance of writing as you can to avoid allowing personal biases (e.g., "This one doesn't really support my ideas") to sneak into your selections (Cooper, 1998). Be sure to write these criteria into the introduction to your literature review, too.

As an example, Julie planned a study to evaluate a program to teach children to deal effectively with peer provocation. She amassed huge literatures on peer rejection and its correlates, social skills training programs, and generalization of behavior change from skill-training programs to the natural environment. After some thought and discussion, she realized that (a) very few social skills studies addressed peer provocation problems directly, (b) much of the literature on correlates of rejection was tangential to her project, and (c) the conclusions of the literature on generalization should be incorporated into her review of why certain studies failed, rather than being reviewed study by study. Most of her pages would be devoted to reviewing studies that attempted to teach social skills to intellectually normal children with identified excesses in negative behavior. The rest of the literature would be mentioned in passing, if at all. By limiting the populations and the topics she would cover, writing the review became far more manageable.

Lisa, another student, encountered a different problem. She was interested in the effects of therapist self-disclosure on adolescent involvement in therapy. She found large literatures on self-disclosure in therapy with adults, on self-disclosure in personal relationships (by adults and adolescents), and on the effects of different kinds of therapy for adolescents, as well as theoretical writings on the effects of self-disclosure in personal relationships. She found very little, however, that was specific to her topic. What should she include in her literature review? Lisa decided to review the literature on self-disclosure in adult therapy to justify her independent variable and highlight the innovations in her methodology. She also reviewed the role of self-disclosure in adolescents' personal relationships to make a case for why self-disclosure might play a useful role in therapy. She did not need to review the theoretical literature, adolescent treatment outcome studies, or the adult interpersonal relationships literature, although she might integrate key points from these literatures as they contributed to her analysis of the two areas of research she would cover in depth.

Organize the Literature You Will Cover

Writing the preliminary outline required you to organize and synthesize material from all those articles, chapters, and books—something you should also have been thinking about as you read those materials. Now, as you finalize your preliminary outline, add detail by fleshing out what literature you will cover in each of your sections. You can group the literature into manageable, coherent subgroupings in several ways. The following are some of the most common:

- Cover studies that examine *related independent variables* together. If, for example, you are reviewing different strategies for enhancing organizational effectiveness, grouping them by types of strategy may provide a good, easy-to-follow framework.

- Organize your studies by examining *related dependent variables* together. If you are looking at the characteristics of adult children of alcoholics, for example, you could review studies examining personality, then those examining drinking patterns, then those examining relationship skills, and so on. Alternatively, you could group findings on this population by *assessment method*: self-report, ratings by others, direct observation, and so on.

- Organize by *type of design*. Ordinarily, this kind of coverage begins with weaker and progresses to stronger designs. Thus, uncontrolled case studies are presented before controlled designs, relational studies before experimental, and cross-sectional before longitudinal. Paul's (1969) classic chapter describing research on systematic desensitization exemplifies this organizational strategy.

- Organize around *theoretical premises*. This method is useful if your study tests competing explanations of a phenomenon or if different theoretical threads all lead to the formulation of your research question. Our example in Exhibit 6.2 used this approach. Irvin (2017) was interested in two areas of research that both have something to say about the role of positive affect in the experience of and risk for depression. Several studies have demonstrated that dampening of positive affect (e.g., by suppressing or distracting from positive feelings) is related to higher depression. Largely unrelated research has shown that a blunted physiological response to reward is also related to depression symptoms and risk. Although these research areas arise from different theoretical perspectives and use different methods, Irvin theorized that they are simply different ways of getting at a similar underlying process. Thus, she organized her literature review around the central tenets and findings of each research area, then considered their potential overlap and proposed a study to examine this issue.

These strategies are only a few of the many ways of organizing a literature review. Select an organizational framework that highlights important aspects of the literature, particularly ones you wish to address or improve on in your study. For example, suppose your study improves over past research by using direct observation instead of self-report methods. By presenting findings and studies according to the methods used to assess the dependent variables, you clearly show readers the absence of research using direct observation. Remember the funnel: Work from the general (existing literature) to the specific (your proposed study).

It is also a good idea to use subheadings liberally. These show you have thought carefully about the major sections of your review, and they help readers understand the logic of your organization. Another good practice is to provide summaries as you go along. Although these may be unnecessary for very short literature reviews, they can be especially useful after especially long or complex sections. Remember, your goal is to educate your readers and establish good arguments for why your study is an important next step in your area.

START WRITING

You are now ready to put pen to paper or fingers to keyboard. Organize your notes or photocopies, pull out your outline, and write individual sections of the review.

Beware of Writer's Block at This Point

Writer's block affects many students, even those who regularly produce literature reviews with little difficulty for class assignments. Sometimes this block results from the mistaken assumption that your review must be perfect, that you must cite all relevant studies and produce consistently brilliant insights before you dare hand a draft of your review to your chair. This is unrealistic self-talk.

Why unrealistic? Virtually all students hand in and revise several drafts of their literature review before they are finished. No matter how polished your prose, your chair will have suggestions and will expect the first draft to need work. Everyone's first draft needs work. Because it is impossible for your draft to be perfect, give yourself permission for your work to be improvable. Remember, this is a learning experience. If your manuscript was flawless on the first try, there would be nothing left for you to learn. And even if your initial drafts aren't bad, remember that it's not uncommon for the outline and pieces of your review to evolve as you write. There are many ways to write a literature review that are perfectly fine, but there are fewer ways to write reviews that are outstanding. You probably didn't get into graduate school by being fine, so why settle for that now? An outstanding review will be more likely to wow your committee, as well as potential journal reviewers or funding agencies. Use your rewrites as opportunities to develop the skills to write for these audiences as well as your committee.

Another difficulty that students sometimes encounter when they begin to write comes from the mistaken assumption that they must start at the beginning, write the introduction, and then proceed sequentially. This is the "linear way is the only way" fallacy. They then sit before the page or the computer for hours as the words to begin the document elude them. Several of our students have told us that they didn't write the introduction until after they wrote the bulk of the review—that way, they had a good sense of the general thrust and organization of the review and could provide a much better overview. Other students have found it helpful to begin with their proposed study's specific aims and hypotheses. Assuming that the aims and design of your study are based on your knowledge of the literature (even if you haven't written that knowledge down in paper form yet), knowing where you want your literature review to end—at your proposed study—can make it easier to create the literature review path that leads to that point.

Several wise mentors (e.g., Bolker, 1998; Miller, 2009; and us, of course!) have suggested that most people should think of writing as a messy process, one that is not necessarily linear but that is characterized by consistently putting words on paper, even if those words get shuffled around and some of the paper sees only the recycle bin. Remember, the end product should be clean and generally linear, but that doesn't mean the process is!

If you find it hard to start with the introduction, start with a section that comes more easily. If paragraphs don't come easily, work on expanding from your outline. Write the ideas or points you want to cover within each section, and then build paragraphs around them. If you can't figure out good transitions between studies, describe the studies first and write the transitions later. The key is to write whatever you can, because tasks that seem impossible one day may be much easier the next. Getting started is more important than completing sections one by one in a specified order. It is also well to remember that revising your words is easier than writing the words in the first place. Write something—anything—then sequence, integrate, and polish it later.

In addition, several of the ideas we mentioned in Chapter 3 may be useful here. If you encounter problems getting started, set very small goals. Set product rather than process goals. A *product goal* indicates what you must accomplish: "Write one page" or "summarize and critique one key article." A *process goal* indicates what you must do, not the end product: "Work on dissertation for 2 hours." To accomplish the latter goal, all you have to do is stare at your computer, not actually produce anything! Small product goals help you see progress and work more efficiently.

You can also allow yourself small rewards for accomplishing small product goals. Remember the Premack principle mentioned in Chapter 3? Any behavior that is higher in probability than writing your dissertation or thesis can serve as a reward. For many writers, that's almost anything! In writing this book, for example, we often said to ourselves, "I'll get a cup of coffee after I finish three pages," or "I'll take a break and check Facebook after I type this table," or "I'll call my friend after I edit this chapter." These examples show that rewards need not be expensive or time consuming to be motivating.

Write the Introduction to Your Review

Begin your literature review with a brief introduction. The introduction should do just that—introduce and make a brief pitch for the topic, introduce key concepts and terms, and describe the scope and organization of the review. A brief introduction might occupy about three pages in a 25-page literature review, or one to two pages in a 10- to 15-page review.

A good way to end the introduction is with a paragraph that lays out the scope of the literature review. Sometimes referred to as an "advance organizer," this material should describe both the literature you will cover and the sequence readers can expect to follow. In addition, if you omit studies to keep the length of your review manageable, let readers know your criteria for inclusion or exclusion and why you selected them. For example, suppose a whole group of studies on your topic area was later found to have a particular methodological problem, and you do not have the space to cover these studies. The final paragraph of your introduction could say,

> The remainder of the section critically reviews contemporary literature regarding [topic area]. Early studies in the area (e.g., [citations]) generally concluded that _____. As [citation] pointed out, however, these studies all failed to distinguish between _____ and _____, and thus their conclusions are suspect. Later studies corrected this flaw, and these will be the focus of the review that follows. Initial sections discuss _____. The review concludes with a summary and critique of existing literature, followed by a discussion of the specific research question and hypotheses suggested by the review and examined in this [thesis or dissertation].

Write the Subsections of the Review

After the introduction, write subsections that describe and synthesize portions of the literature. These subsections should be consistent with whichever overall organizational approach (e.g., by independent variable, by dependent variable, by design type) you selected earlier. In a longer review, perhaps the easiest approach is to introduce the section, then describe relevant studies one by one, grouping related studies together. Some writers follow a chronological sequence, citing earlier research first. Provide comparable information for each study: participants, independent variables, dependent variables, design, and findings. Mention noteworthy details (e.g., methodological problems, ethnicity or gender of participants) that will form the basis for themes in your analysis. Then go on to the next. Use parallel organization, describing the aspects of each study in the same way. As Bem (1995) noted, "repetition and parallel construction are among the most effective servants of clarity. Don't be creative; be clear" (p. 174). Pull the material together with a summary and overall critique at the end of the subsection.

Describing studies one by one requires considerable skill to keep the review from being incredibly boring and reading like a series of index cards typed up one after the other. Liberal use of transitions helps. Identifying and developing important themes as you go along help, too. For example, brief comparisons of methods and findings help link studies together and highlight their similarities and differences.

A second method of organizing subsections of a literature review groups weaker studies or studies that share similar methods, reviews them only briefly, and devotes greater attention to seminal, prototypical, or stronger studies. With this method, a section might begin with a few paragraphs that provide an overview of a large number of studies, their findings, and the strengths and weaknesses they share as a group. Later paragraphs then devote greater individual attention to more important studies.

A third and increasingly popular way of organizing subsections of a literature review is to discuss studies in the context of their findings. In this approach, the literature review is much more like one you would see in the introduction of a journal article—the author organizes the literature review around the logical series of points that build the rationale for the study and uses relevant literature to support those points. This type of review contains less description of individual studies than the first two types, because rather than describing each study one by one, the author synthesizes across studies that are relevant to specific points. However, for this same reason, a point-based (vs. study-based) review is the most difficult type to write. You must develop your points logically, integrate across the specific literature relevant to each point (specific studies will likely be relevant to multiple points), and use the literature in an even-handed way to consider the support (pro and con) for your ideas. This multifaceted and integrative consideration of the literature may be most appropriate when your study will pit different theoretical explanations against one another, when your selection of variables is guided more by theory than by atheoretical empirical findings, or when you are writing a briefer, journal-format introduction to your study.

One advantage of this point-based approach is that it is closer to being journal submission ready and will help you later in the game when you want to write up your study for publication. However, committee members may want to see a fuller demonstration of your mastery of the relevant literature, especially if you are in the earlier stages of research skill development. Thus, as noted in Chapter 5, some programs or departments require an extended literature review, sometimes in the main body of the document and sometimes separate from it. For example, the first author's program requires an in-depth literature review as part of the master's thesis proposal. The student and chair can choose among several options for documenting the student's review and understanding of relevant literature (e.g., traditional extended literature review, annotated bibliography, table of studies). Table 6.1 includes excerpts from a thesis appendix that used an annotated bibliography table format. Writing an annotated bibliography can follow fairly easily from the coding sheets you used to organize your literature.

TABLE 6.1. Excerpts From an Annotated Bibliography to Supplement a Narrative Literature Review for a Thesis on Positive Emotion Regulation Strategies and Reward Positivity

Dampening and savoring research

Citation	Constructs covered	Constructs defined	Relevant findings	Issues and potential problems
Feldman et al., 2007	☐ Depression ☐ Anhedonia ☑ Positive affect ☐ Negative affect	Dampening: using cognitive or behavioral strategies to decrease positive moods Savoring: using cognitive or behavioral strategies to increase positive moods	Development of a self-report measure of ruminative and dampening responses to positive affect	
Werner-Seidler et al., 2013	☑ Depression ☑ Anhedonia ☑ Positive affect ☑ Negative affect		Study 1: In undergrads, dampening was associated with dysphoria and anhedonic symptoms. Study 3: Depressed community sample dampened more than never-depressed sample but didn't differ from recovered sample. Dampening again was associated with anhedonic symptoms.	Did not assess comorbidity

Foundational reward processing literature and behavioral studies: Reviews

Citation	Constructs defined	Relevant findings	Issues and potential problems
Admon and Pizzagalli, 2015	Reward processing components: motivation, reinforcement, and hedonic capacity	Depression and subclinical anhedonia were associated with reduced reward sensitivity rather than impaired learning. Depressed individuals were less likely to expend effort for reward. Anhedonia in depression is not necessarily expressed by reduction in pleasure, but by an impaired ability to modify behavior as a function of positive reinforcement.	
Forbes and Goodman, 2014		Dysfunctional reward processing may be an endophenotype of depression because it has been shown in individuals before the onset of depression in those at risk for depression. Severity of maternal depression was associated with youths' neural response to rewards.	

Foundational reward processing literature and behavioral studies: Empirical studies

Citation	Constructs defined	Relevant findings	Issues and potential problems
Treadway et al., 2012	Anhedonia: reduced motivation and enjoyment of positive life experiences	Depressed and nondepressed participants completed an Effort Expenditure for Rewards Task that assessed how much effort they were willing to expend for various rewards. Participants with major depressive disorder (MDD) were less willing to expend effort for rewards and showed less reward learning (i.e., use of magnitude and probability of rewards to guide behaviors).	

Neurological reward processing studies (EEG and fMRI)

Citation	Study methods	Constructs defined	Relevant findings	Issues and potential problems
Bress et al., 2015	☑ EEG ☐ fMRI	Error-related negativity (ERN) Feedback negativity (FN)	Twenty-five 11- to 13-year-olds completed EEG tasks designed to elicit ERN (Flanker Task) and FN (Doors Task). Anxiety symptoms were related to greater ERN. Depressive symptoms were related to lesser FN.	Small cross-sectional sample
Foti et al., 2014	☑ EEG ☑ fMRI		Depressed and nondepressed participants completed gambling tasks in a dual event-related potential and fMRI study. FN amplitude was reduced in the MDD group, driven by an MDD subgroup characterized by impaired mood reactivity to positive events. Reduced ventral striatal activation was found in the same MDD subgroup. Results suggest that not all MDD is characterized by reward dysfunction.	Small sample of MDD subgroups Mood reactivity assessed with single item from the Structured Clinical Interview for *DSM*, limiting reliability Impaired mood reactivity not assessed in nonclinical sample

The various methods of writing a literature review just described involve qualitative analysis and synthesis of the literature. Another, quantitative alternative involves systematically scoring studies for particular characteristics and conducting a meta-analysis. With a meta-analysis, results of studies that investigated the same issue are grouped with statistical procedures to evaluate the findings of the group of studies as a whole. Thus, studies using direct observation dependent measures can be compared with those using informant ratings or self-report in terms of the overall significance (effect size) of their findings. Comparison of treatment outcomes across different types of treatment or treatment recipients is another common application of meta-analysis. Although technically a literature review, meta-analyses are rarely used in thesis and dissertation literature reviews; rather, a meta-analysis would constitute the thesis or dissertation study itself, with journal articles and data sets as "participants." Thus, we do not cover meta-analyses in this book (see Cooper et al., 2009, for more on conducting meta-analyses).

SYNTHESIZE AND CRITICALLY ANALYZE THE LITERATURE

One of the most frequent complaints we hear from faculty colleagues is that graduate students do not analyze and synthesize the literature they review. Novice literature reviewers often provide excessive description but inadequate critical analysis. Do not simply describe what you read. Instead, synthesize the literature. What patterns do you see in investigators' findings? Are the findings consistent? If not, why not? Consider potential explanations, including methodological, design, and population differences among studies and assumptions that may be erroneous about how the independent variables operate or relate to the dependent variables. By the end of your literature review, readers should have a good idea of the patterns of findings and methods that characterize your area.

In addition, evaluate the literature critically. Which studies are best, and why? Which studies are worst, and why? Consider methodological as well as conceptual strengths and weaknesses—they are the lenses through which you must interpret each study's conclusions and impact. Use the checklist in Exhibit 6.1. Just because something is published does not mean it is free of methodological problems. Help readers see the methodological issues that future studies in your area should address. Highlight topics that merit further study. If you kept a record of problems and issues as you read the literature, consult it for ideas about what to say.

Use a Professional Tone in Commenting on Others' Work

Obviously, you do not want to trash your chair's work (although your chair will likely be the first to agree that limitations in the lab's prior work warrant acknowledgment). Less obvious is the fact that you should not overstate your criticisms of others who think differently than you. Ad hominem criticisms (i.e., of the person rather than the work) are never appropriate. Be even-handed, and remember that all research has strengths as well as weaknesses. Also remember that research builds and evolves over time: Methods that are expected or normative in current research (e.g., nuanced consideration of racial, ethnic, or gender identity; power analyses) may have been rare or even unheard of even a few years earlier.

Your analysis of the literature should pave the way for your study. By the time readers finish the bulk of your literature review, the rationale for what you propose (your questions) and why you propose to do it a certain way (your method) should be obvious. Thus, your synthesis should highlight important unanswered questions (i.e., the ones you are proposing to examine). Similarly, your critiques should emphasize methodological problems with past studies that you plan to correct with your study. Think of this as developing your argument. Think like a good lawyer: You want to point out to the jury (your readers) how pieces of evidence are relevant to the case you are trying to make as you proceed.

You can integrate statements that synthesize and evaluate the literature into the review in several ways. First, use integrative transition sentences and phrases to help readers see patterns as they read the document. Note how the following paragraph ties a group of studies together and highlights major similarities and differences with the study about to be discussed:

> Although most studies described thus far used correlational designs, Smith and Jones (2001) explored the issue of _____ with an experimental design. Their findings were remarkably similar to those of previous relational studies.

Second, use comparative and evaluative phrases. Some evaluative comments, such as the following critique of an underpowered study, are unique to a particular study. These fit best when you describe the study:

> The authors failed to replicate others' findings. Unfortunately, the small *n* in some of their groups (as low as 8) may have seriously limited their power to detect significant effects.

Other comments pertain to a whole group of studies but not to the area as a whole, and you can cover them as you end a particular section of the review:

> Most of these studies share similar strengths and weaknesses. [Elaborate these.] Despite their methodological problems, most tentatively point to similar conclusions. [Tell what they are.]

In addition to analyzing and integrating the literature throughout the review, you may wish to include a final Summary and Critique subsection. This subsection can specify unexplored topics worthy of future study as well as strengths and weaknesses of the existing literature. Go beyond a summary of what you have already said. Instead, weave together the threads you have been developing in the rest of the review. Most importantly, use this section as a logical precursor to your statement of the problem and hypotheses sections. Alternatively, if you have been weaving your threads together throughout the literature review, your Proposed Study section can begin with a brief synopsis of the strengths, limitations, and gaps in the literature as a lead-in to a description of your study's aims and hypotheses.

If you need examples of how to conclude a literature review, peruse journals that publish literature reviews, such as *Psychological Bulletin*, *Clinical Psychology Review*, and *Developmental Review*, and book chapters that provide integrative overviews of the literature. Ask your chair for particularly good examples of literature reviews from theses or dissertations they have chaired. Examine the structure and organization of different reviews and see how different writers integrated and analyzed the literature. Studying others' writing may give you ideas for how to write your own review.

Introduce Your Study and Hypotheses

The introduction to your specific study (or studies, in the case of a portfolio-style project) will appear in subsections such as Statement of the Problem, Proposed Study, or Research Questions and Hypotheses. Placement of these sections will vary depending on what format your literature review section takes:

- If you write a one-chapter literature review, these subsections will follow your Summary and Critique of the literature.

- If you write a two-chapter version, these subsections will usually follow a general introduction to the problem area and to your specific topic in Chapter 1, and your literature review will appear in Chapter 2.

- If you are writing a portfolio-style dissertation with an integrated literature review, you may include your Statement of the Problem section as part of the general introduction (similar to the two-chapter format) and separate Proposed Study and Research Questions sections as the introductions to each specific study.

Pay attention to how the order of these sections will affect readers' understanding of the material. If the introduction to your specific topic (problem area, proposed study) will precede your literature review, make sure the material covered in the introduction is clear enough to stand by itself.

Regardless of the format you use, your Statement of the Problem subsection should provide the rationale for your study, including how the study will make a novel contribution to the field. You should also include a brief overview of your population, design, independent variables, and dependent variables. This overview will help readers understand the specific research questions and hypotheses that follow.

Chapter 4 described how to state research questions and derivative hypotheses, and your written presentation should reflect those suggestions. In addition, if the rationale for a particular hypothesis is not obvious, briefly give the reason for your prediction by saying something such as, "This hypothesis is based on Smith's (2016) findings that ___." Ideally, by the end of your literature review, the rationale for every hypothesis should be clear, so at most you will provide your readers with a reminder about why you are predicting certain outcomes. If you find yourself having to explain one or more hypotheses, consider adding the relevant information to the literature review. Otherwise, the hypotheses read like an afterthought . . . and perhaps they were! But now that you've thought of them, you must determine how to go back and weave them into the rationale and supporting literature for your study.

As Chapter 4 suggested, you should be able to form hypotheses related to your major research questions. You may, however, have certain secondary comparisons for which deriving hypotheses may be difficult (e.g., if the area is very new, if previous findings conflict). If you truly have no basis in research or in theory for making a prediction, you have several options. First, you can simply state that this is the case and offer no directional hypotheses. Second, you can subdivide your research questions into those that address the primary purposes of your study (for which you offer hypotheses) and those that are secondary (for which you offer no hypotheses). Third, you could drop the particular question as part of the formal study. We prefer the first or second of these, provided, of course, that the question is worth asking in the first place. Check with your chair on their preference.

Write Additional Required Subsections

Many schools require that theses and dissertations include the subsections we have just covered. In addition, some programs or committee chairs require additional material such as definitions of terms, descriptions of limitations of the study you propose, and discussion of the theoretical orientation underlying the study. Check your local requirements for any additional material you must cover as you prepare your literature review.

Be Careful Not to Plagiarize

Earlier we mentioned plagiarism. Its definition bears repeating here. To *plagiarize*, according to Merriam-Webster (n.d.-b), is "to steal and pass off (the ideas or words of another) as one's own: use (another's production) without crediting the source." Lifting someone's words without enclosing them in quotation marks is obviously plagiarism. So, however, is closely paraphrasing another's sentences. So is presenting another's ideas as though they were original to you. Copying paragraph organization—or a general way of organizing a topic—is also plagiarism. Even presenting your own prior published work without appropriate acknowledgment (often called "duplicate publication" or "self-plagiarism") is plagiarism!

Find your own way of organizing ideas in your own words. This is easier if you've read a variety of papers that cover the topics or points you are writing about; because authors vary in how they present information and ideas, every paper you read will describe the topic a little differently. As you pull together key points from several papers, the voice that emerges from these varied writing styles is more likely to be your own. Limit direct quotes, and acknowledge others' ideas and organizational frameworks when you use or borrow them. Many academic websites now give examples of what constitutes plagiarism—search "plagiarism examples" and take a look. If you are still in doubt, ask a colleague or your chair for feedback.

Revise and Rewrite

Be prepared to revise and rewrite your initial material. Do this after rereading it yourself, and later, after receiving feedback from your chair. New ideas will occur to you, and you will find holes in your own logic. In addition, your chair (and sometimes peers, if you ask for their comments) can give you feedback to improve the paper. A word of caution about soliciting peer input: Choose peer reviewers carefully. Your closest grad school friends may be great sources of support, but they may not be critical readers. Unconditionally positive (and often vague) comments like "nice job" may make you feel good in the short term, but honest critiques such as "you are hypothesizing gender effects, but the strongest studies you cite didn't find these effects" or "I cannot tell what you are talking about here!" will be much more helpful in guiding rewrites. Likewise, lab mates may be too close to your topic to notice the gaps that will trip up readers not familiar with your topic area. Select peer reviewers who are logical, who pay great attention to detail, and ideally who are good writers themselves.

Then, be open to the feedback you receive; these critics are on your side! Your readers will see ambiguities that are perfectly clear to you, but remember that you are writing for them, not for yourself. In addition, your goal is to have a solid document that can stand up to examination by the academic community. Look at this as a chance to improve your writing, sharpen up your thinking, master an area of literature, and produce a first-rate document, rather than as an evaluation of your personal worth or a chance for your writing to serve as someone's punching bag. The thinking and writing skills you hone as you develop your thesis or dissertation will benefit you no matter what career path you choose.

Finally, remember that pulling together the information you found in your literature search into a coherent, focused review does more than just help you get a major writing task out of the way. It also should sharpen your thinking about your topic and help you see conceptual and methodological themes in the literature. In addition, the process should lead you to identify methodological issues and possible procedures for your study. In fact, writing your literature review and working out your methodology go hand in hand: As you work out the methods, you think about the literature differently, and vice versa. Your Method section will describe the choices you make about how to conduct your research. Chapters 7 and 8 assist you in articulating those choices in writing as you prepare that part of your thesis or dissertation.

✓   **TO DO . . .**
REVIEWING THE LITERATURE

☐ Locate sources of relevant literature.

  – Use primary sources.

  – Avoid the popular press.

  – Evaluate the quality of internet information.

  – Lay out your search strategy.

☐ Conduct your search.

  – Identify key authors and journals.

  – Use bibliographic reference sources.

  – Use online search engines.

  – Look at literature from other disciplines.

  – Scan the tables of contents of key journals.

  – Use reference lists from articles, chapters, and books.

☐ Collect and organize relevant information.

  – Keep track of citations in APA Style.

  – Collect and organize downloaded or photocopied full-text documents.

  – Plan your document storage system.

☐ Critically read what you found.

  – Identify themes.

  – Identify strengths and weaknesses of individual papers.

  – Identify strengths and weaknesses of the literature as a whole.

  – Make notes about the literature, including study specifics and your own observations and conclusions.

☐ Prepare to write your literature review.

  – Consider the audience and purpose of a literature review.

  – Investigate length and format parameters.

  – Write a preliminary outline.

  – Limit the scope of your review.

  – Organize the literature you will cover.

☐ Start writing.

  – Address potential sources of writer's block.

  – Write the introduction to your review.

  – Write the subsections of the review.

  – Synthesize and critically analyze the literature.

  – Use a professional tone in commenting on others' work.

  – Introduce your study and hypotheses.

  – Write additional required subsections.

  – Be careful not to plagiarize.

  – Revise and rewrite.

SUPPLEMENTAL RESOURCES

Cooper, H. (Ed.). (2012). *APA handbook of research methods in psychology: Vol. 1. Foundations, planning, measures, and psychometrics.* American Psychological Association.

Cooper, H., Hedges, I. V., & Valentine, J. C. (Eds.). (2009). *The handbook of research synthesis and meta-analysis* (2nd ed.). Russell Sage Foundation.

Galvan, J. L., & Galvan, M. C. (2017). *Writing literature reviews: A guide for students of the social and behavioral sciences* (7th ed.). Routledge.

Heppner, P. P., & Heppner, M. J. (2004). *Writing and publishing your thesis, dissertation, and research.* Thomson Brooks/Cole.

On Plagiarism

Plagiarism.org (https://www.plagiarism.org/)—Information and resources about plagiarism, including what it is and how to teach about and prevent it, as well as news articles and blogs.

On the Writing Process

Bolker, J. (1998). *Writing your dissertation in 15 minutes a day.* Henry Holt and Co.

Overviews the author's ideas about how to write generally and provides strategies for writing a dissertation.

Miller, A. B. (2009). *Finish your dissertation once and for all! How to overcome psychological barriers, get results, and move on with your life.* American Psychological Association.

Discusses how to identify and overcome cognitive, emotional, behavioral, and logistical challenges to dissertation progress.

Vernoff, J. (2015). Writing. In K. E. Rudestam & R. R. Newton (Eds.), *Surviving your dissertation* (4th ed.). Sage.

Speculates on causes of problems with writing and provides suggestions for writing a dissertation.

Bibliographic Reference Sources and Online Search Engines

Current Contents Connect—https://clarivate.libguides.com/webofscienceplatform/ccc
Dissertation Abstracts International—https://www.proquest.com/products-services/dissertations/Dissertations-Abstract-International.html
Education Resources Information Center—https://eric.ed.gov/
Google Scholar—https://scholar.google.com/
Microsoft Academic—https://academic.microsoft.com
PsycINFO—https://www.apa.org/pubs/databases/psycinfo/
PsycNET—https://psycnet.apa.org/
PubMed—https://www.ncbi.nlm.nih.gov/pubmed/
ResearchGate—www.researchgate.net
Scopus–https://www.elsevier.com/solutions/scopus
Social Sciences Citation Index—http://mjl.clarivate.com/cgi-bin/jrnlst/jloptions.cgi?PC=SS
Web of Science—https://clarivate.com/products/web-of-science/

7

Research Methodology and Ethics

This chapter provides a detailed look at how to conduct methodologically sound and ethical research by addressing
- typical elements of a Method section
- ethics codes and regulations that guide research with human and nonhuman animal participants
- steps involved in implementing ethical standards in your research

Read thoroughly if
- you could use a refresher on methodological considerations for your research
- you want to ensure you know what elements to include in your Method section
- you are not familiar with how to work with research ethics or regulatory bodies

Skim or skip if
- you have already established your research methods
- you are already familiar with ethical issues relevant to your study
- you are not using human or nonhuman animal research participants

https://doi.org/10.1037/0000161-007
Dissertations and Theses From Start to Finish: Psychology and Related Fields, Third Edition,
by D. J. Bell, S. L. Foster, and J. D. Cone

In this chapter, we elaborate on the elements of the Method section, which we introduced in Chapter 5, to help you organize your thinking about how to conduct your study. Then, we discuss ethical principles governing research in psychology and examine the process involved in designing and conducting studies in accord with these principles. We also cover navigating the requirements for the protection of humans and nonhuman animal research participants.

Be aware that this chapter is not an instruction book on research design, procedures, or ethics. It will not tell you, for example, whether it is better to use a correlational or a group design for your research or whether you have thought of all the appropriate controls. If your background in research methodology is rusty, scanty, or otherwise lacking, the Supplemental Resources list at the end of this chapter will point you toward information that will help you bone up on material you never learned or cannot remember.

Planning, implementing, and then writing about your methods is a process that will continue throughout your entire thesis or dissertation project. You will consider what you are going to do and describe your plans in the proposal. Once you complete your study, the final thesis or dissertation document will describe what you actually did. Ideally, if you plan your methods well and things go according to plan, the main content of the Method section in your proposal and the final document will not differ much beyond changing future to past tense. Thus, throughout this chapter, we focus on the "meat" of your methods, with examples sometimes referring to the proposal and sometimes to the final document. In either case, it is the elements and content of the Method section that matter most.

KNOW THE ELEMENTS OF A METHOD SECTION

The American Psychological Association's (APA's) recently updated journal article reporting standards (JARS) for quantitative (Appelbaum et al., 2018) and qualitative and mixed methods (Levitt et al., 2018) research provide recommendations for the content and organization of the Method section. These standards offer guidance for researchers in psychology and other social sciences on what information to include, at a minimum, in journal articles (for more information, visit https://www.apastyle.org/jars). Although these standards are designed for journal articles, they can also be quite helpful as you prepare a thesis or dissertation, as they describe details that will eventually be needed for publication. However, you may also need additional elements to fully describe your methods.

In this section, we describe aspects of methodology you should consider in planning your study and include in a complete Method section. Not all aspects are relevant to all studies, of course. Similarly, the order that we suggest may work for your Method section; if not, use an order that fits your study.

Design

It may be most appropriate to locate your first specific reference to design elements before the Method section. Possibly, you gave an overview of your design when you wrote the statement of the problem early in the literature review or in your Current Study subsection at the end of your review. We prefer to describe the general design before the Method section because the nature of the design you are using will influence all of the Method section elements, and this placement will help readers understand the choices you describe. However, you may need a Study Design subsection somewhere in the Method section as well, particularly if your design is complex or needs more explanation than an overview can provide. Be flexible about placement, and put the design information where it makes most sense for your project.

What should you include in describing your design? First, make clear whether it is of the within- or between-subjects variety. If the variation needed to identify the relationships involved in your study comes from changes in the same participants over time or across situations, you are using a within-subjects approach. If the variation comes from differences between participants at a single point in time, you are using a between-subjects approach. Another important point to elaborate is the general class of your design. Major classes include quantitative approaches (e.g., experimental and quasi-experimental, correlational, epidemiological, longitudinal, N-of-1), as well as newer but increasingly mainstream qualitative approaches (e.g., thematic, narrative) and mixed methods approaches (i.e., use of both a quantitative and a qualitative approach). If you are fuzzy about these distinctions, see texts such as Shadish et al. (2002) or Cooper (2012). Shadish et al. provided a classic treatment of the differences among major quantitative design approaches. In an extensive three-volume handbook, Cooper detailed both major design approaches and more specialized designs (e.g., genetic epidemiology, statistical and mathematical modeling).

Once you have clarified the basic nature of your approach, you are ready to present the details of your particular design. In describing your design, it is useful to provide both labels (e.g., two-group, true experimental design; A-B-A-B withdrawal design; Solomon four-group design; correlational design; survey research) and descriptions of what you plan to do. Avoid confusing design and statistics in this subsection: "A one-way ANOVA will test the differences between the groups" is a statement of the statistical test used, not the design. Think of it this way: Design is what you do with your participants, and analyses (statistics; described in Chapter 9) are what you do with your data. Thus, the following are appropriate design statements:

- "Children will be assigned randomly to high- and low-reward conditions and math facts of high and low difficulty in a 2×2 factorial design."

- "A multiple-baseline design will be used in which Family 1 will be instructed in and implement positive household rules initially, then Family 2, and finally Family 3."

If you plan to administer multiple measures, make a plan for their order (e.g., will you administer them in the same order, a counterbalanced order, or a random order?) and describe this as part of your design. If participants will be assigned to specific groups, specify whether you will use random or some nonrandom assignment. If groups will be matched for certain participant characteristics (e.g., gender, IQ, problem severity), describe how this will be accomplished. If you have forgotten why administration order, group assignment, and matching may be important, dust off your old research design text and reacquaint yourself with these concepts.

A diagram or chart can help you describe designs that are complex or hard to follow. The research methods texts mentioned previously provide good examples of these (Cooper, 2012; Shadish et al., 2002).

Participants

In the participants subsection, you should answer three questions: (a) Who will participate? (b) How will they be selected? and (c) How many will participate?

Who Will Participate?

Describing your study participants is a two-part process: First, name the general participant category or categories (e.g., youth, adults, patients, students, parents, teachers, employers), and second, describe your actual (or anticipated) participants in more detail. Novice researchers sometimes get confused about who the participants are when different groups of people are used at different times in the research. For example, in constructing a scale to assess problem spending, one of our students used consumer credit experts to judge the adequacy of responses to specified problem situations involving how people handle money. She used these judgments to weight the responses of individuals completing the instrument in order to establish preliminary norms. Because the primary thrust of the research was to develop a reliable and valid instrument for identifying problem spending, the individuals who provided the data relevant to reliability and validity (i.e., the people who completed the instrument) were considered the participants. The experts who coded response adequacy were referred to as "judges."

Another common example involves studies of children in which parents and teachers provide data about the children's behavior. One of our students examined adjustment correlates of youths' emotion regulation and included youth, parent, and teacher reports of the youths' emotional and behavioral adjustment, as well as trained observers' ratings of youth behavior during an experimental task. Were the parents, teachers, and observers also study participants? Parents and teachers yes, but observers no.

In general, participants are those who provide the data to test the specific study hypotheses. You should collect data on all participants, although only the primary targets of your study (i.e., the children in the previous example) need to be described fully, as outlined in the next paragraph. You probably don't need to provide as much detail about other reporters unless their characteristics are important to your study. You may not care about whether the children's teachers are men or women or how old they are, but you probably do care about how well or in what context the teachers know the children (e.g., are they homeroom teachers who see the children for most of each day? specialty subject teachers who interact with the children less often?). In a study of children's ethnic identity and school achievement, you may care about the ethnicity of the teachers. You likely also care whether a caregiver reporter is the mother or the father and is a biological, step-, adoptive, or foster parent, and you may also care about caregivers' educational attainment, which is relevant to family socioeconomic status (SES). In contrast, individuals involved in producing instruments or coding data (e.g., expert or trained coders or observers) are not considered participants, so you would describe only their relevant characteristics, such as their qualifications and roles, in the Measures or Procedures subsection.

Study reports vary considerably in the details they include about participants. Remember that your participants represent a subset of some larger population to which you wish to generalize your findings. You should select and describe them in ways that reassure readers that they do, indeed, represent this population. For example, it is a good idea to provide information on major demographic characteristics such as gender, age (mean and range), race and ethnicity, geographic area represented, SES, source (e.g., university under-graduate classes, mental health clinics), and basis for participation (e.g., voluntary, paid, course credit). Depending on the nature of your study, you may want to include other information, such as school placement (e.g., regular or special education placement), intellectual functioning (mean and range on a standard IQ measure), scores on any selection variable (e.g., depression, anxiety, percent overweight), disability status, medical or psychiatric diagnosis, or sexual orientation.

If a participant characteristic is an independent variable, you should describe it completely, including how you will determine that participants have or lack this characteristic. Additionally, you should describe characteristics that will disqualify individuals from participating (i.e., your exclusion criteria and how you operationalize them). If participants will be sorted into groups on the basis of some characteristic (e.g., age, diagnostic classification, performance on a specific task) rather than randomly assigned, and that characteristic is an independent variable, indicate how this classification will be made.

How Will Participants Be Selected?

Describe your sampling strategy and how you plan to recruit participants. Will you advertise in the local paper? put up notices around campus? sample birth registers? recruit online participants (e.g., using Amazon's Mechanical Turk or Facebook)? Describe exactly what you will do. Put copies of your proposed wording for inviting participants to participate in an appendix. If you will be recruiting online participants, you should be aware of the issues involved in this relatively new recruitment method. An emerging literature on its methodology describes the uses and limitations of online recruitment (e.g., Buhrmester et al., 2011; Crump et al., 2013).

If nonhuman animals will be your subjects, you'll need to report the number of animals you use; their genus, species, and strain number or other specific identifier, such as the name and location of the supplier and the stock designation, if available; and their sex, age, weight, and physical condition. Information on the source of animals is also useful (e.g., supplier, stock designation). A description of any essential details of their history, care, and handling should also be included (APA, 2020).

Be sure to keep track of the number of potential participants you contact as well as the number who actually participate, including the number screened out because they did not meet your inclusion criteria. The representativeness of your participants is crucial to the external validity of the study. Therefore, in your final document, report not only these figures but also any information you can obtain related to differences between volunteering and nonvolunteering individuals, especially if such differences are likely related to the independent variables of your study. If participants drop out prematurely, report the number and the reasons they dropped out.

As when deciding whom to select as participants, a good rule of thumb when deciding how to select them is the representativeness rule: Consider the larger population of individuals you want your participants to represent. To whom do you wish to generalize? When you are clear about this, then develop procedures to attract those people. To check your success, gather supplemental information to see how closely your participants match the characteristics of that population. Likewise, there may be populations to whom you do not wish to generalize. For example, if you are studying elementary-age children, you would not necessarily care whether your results apply to older children. To use your time and other resources efficiently, include procedures and measures that will allow you to screen out individuals who are not members of your population of interest.

The specific nature of your design will also have implications for decisions about whom to include and exclude. In general, a more homogeneous population is likely as a group to have less variable scores on your measures than a heterogeneous population. This is because extraneous participant characteristics that are related to scores on your measures are more likely to occur in a heterogeneous population. Variability in independent and dependent variable scores is generally prized in purely correlational designs in which r and its variants (e.g., multiple regression statistics, factor analysis) will be used. This is because restricted ranges on variables being correlated limit the values correlations can obtain (Urbina, 2014).

Alternatively, you may be comparing discrete groups in your study using ANOVA and related statistics. Extraneous and variable participant characteristics, unless they are controlled, will inflate your error variance. This will require you to have a more potent independent variable to detect significant findings than if extraneous variance is limited. In this case, it makes sense to limit your population. Identify a characteristic that may not be of immediate importance in generalizing your findings—say, SES—but that has been shown to correlate with your major dependent variable—say, intelligence. You can then restrict your participants to a certain subpopulation that has this characteristic—for example, all persons within a relatively narrow socio-economic range. In this example, it is important to acknowledge that SES is ultimately an important variable to include in order to understand broader relationships between your independent and dependent variable. But it is also important to realize that you cannot do everything in one study, especially as a graduate student who likely does not have extensive time or grant funding. Designing a more circumscribed (and potentially less generalizable) study that minimizes sources of error variance will increase your chances of obtaining interesting and useful results.

Variability in participant characteristics can also be handled in two other ways in group designs. First, you can control some of this variability by adding one or more participant characteristics as independent variables in your design. For example, if you are concerned about SES in your study of the effects of watching *Sesame Street* on preschool reading test scores, you could add SES as an independent variable. Of course, this would add to the total number of participants you need. A second way to handle this problem is statistical: Measure SES and see whether it correlates with your dependent variable after your data are collected. If it does, you might control for SES as a covariate in subsequent analyses.

From this material, it should be obvious that you will need to collect information on your participants not only to exclude those you decide not to study and to provide adequate descriptions of those you include but also to provide alternative explanations for your anticipated results and identify inadvertent confounds with your independent variables. Pick potential confounds by consulting the literature: What participant variables have correlated with your dependent variables in previous research? These are good nominees as potential confounding variables. You should measure and later analyze them to see whether they can be ruled out as explanations for your findings. In our earlier example, you might decide that instead of restricting your sample to a narrow socioeconomic range, you want to measure and control for SES. This could help you avoid the errors of previous studies that identified variables that were presumably related to intelligence but were really just markers for (or confounded with) SES or vice versa.

You will also need to indicate how you will measure the participant characteristics you plan to assess. If you use a noncopyrighted demographic data sheet or questionnaire to gather participant information, state this and refer readers to an appendix containing the instrument. You will also describe these measures and their psychometric properties, either here in the Participants subsection or later in a Measures subsection. Chapter 8 describes measurement procedures in more detail.

How Many Participants Will You Have?

You must address the question of how many participants you will have before beginning your research. Your thesis or dissertation committee will expect to see a carefully formulated answer as part of your research proposal. There are different ways to figure this out, with some clearly better than others. First, the not-so-good ways: One is to look at the literature and see what the norm is. This is the easy way and, unfortunately, except for individual organism designs, not a very good one. Repeated reviews of even the most prestigious journals show that published studies in many areas of psychology shot themselves in the foot before they got started because they used too few participants to have the statistical power needed to detect all but the most powerful effects (Abraham & Russell, 2008). Even studies that have sufficient power may be different enough from your study that they do not provide the best guidance. Another option uses general rules of thumb such as using 10 to 20 participants per group or setting minimum participants-to-variables ratios. If you are thinking these rules of thumb seem arbitrary and imprecise, you have company. Statistics experts criticize this approach as being too simplistic and argue that the all-important numbers decision really should take advantage of the precision of power analysis.

Power is a concept referring to the likelihood that the statistics you use can detect the effects of your independent variable. Power is a function of three things: (a) your sample size, (b) the magnitude of the effects of your independent variable, and (c) the alpha level you select. Power analyses allow you to estimate how many participants you will need to detect small, medium, and large effects. Given a fixed number of participants and alpha level (ordinarily $p < .05$), the larger the effect you expect from your independent variable, the fewer participants you will need to detect it. Your Method section should include a description of the power analysis that supports your sample size. Depending on the complexity of this analysis, you will describe it in a paragraph within the Participants subsection or create a separate subsection for it.

So, what is the smallest effect you care to detect? You will learn quickly that detecting tiny effects can mean that you will need thousands of participants (see Abraham & Russell, 2008; Cohen, 1992). A good way to approach this issue is to ask, What is the minimum effect that would be meaningful in this area? In psychological research, this is often a moderate effect: Large effects are rare in explaining psychological phenomena, and small effects may be too small to be of any practical significance. The importance of small effects can depend on your field of study, however. In fields in which we know a great deal about factors that affect the dependent variable (e.g., some aspects of medicine), documenting a small effect can be very important.

To do your power analysis, you need to have various pieces of information. First, you need to select the level of power you wish to have in your study; .80 is often considered a reasonable value. This level of power indicates that you have an 80% chance of detecting an effect (of whatever size you determine—we discuss this next) of your independent or predictor variable at your specified alpha level. Second, you also need to know the analyses you will be conducting (e.g., ANOVA, regression, correlation, structural equation modeling). Furthermore, you need to have a precise idea of where to look in your analysis to find data to support the prediction. For example, it's not enough to know that you will do a 2×2 ANOVA. You also need to know whether your hypotheses predict main effects or interactions. Similarly, with regression, you need to know whether you expect that all of your variables together will predict an outcome (i.e., the overall R^2 will be significant) or whether each will add significant unique variance (i.e., its β will be significant). You will judge the adequacy of your power on the basis of the parameter of the statistic you use to assess whether your findings are significant.

Third, power calculations require estimates of actual numbers that are based on guesses about what your data will look like when they are collected. For example, if you are using parametric statistics, you may need to come up with means, standard deviations, and effect sizes (e.g., ds). If you are using correlational statistics, you may need to provide values for the correlations you anticipate. If you are wondering how you will get these numbers before doing the research, the answer is that you cannot, of course, at least not precisely. But you can estimate what these might be on the basis of the pilot data you collect or published studies that used similar dependent variables and related independent variables. You then use these in formulas that allow you to calculate the number of participants to recruit.

Several available resources can help you conduct power analyses. The classic text by Cohen (1988) provides a brief, very readable discussion of power analysis and tables you can use to estimate the number of participants you will need to detect small ($d = 0.20$), medium ($d = 0.50$), or large ($d = 0.80$) effect sizes at the $p < .01$, $.05$, and $.10$ levels. The tables cover t tests, correlations, tests of proportions, chi-square, ANOVA, and multiple regression statistics. Several other sources (e.g., Lipsey & Wilson, 2000; Liu, 2014; Murphy, Myors, & Wolach, 2014) provide formulas for calculating d (or d equivalents) from a wide range of statistics you might find in the published literature, describe power analysis for complex designs and analyses (e.g., meta-analysis, multilevel modeling, latent growth curve analysis, structural equation modeling), and provide several sources for simulation-based approaches to power analysis (e.g., Monte Carlo studies). Finally, you can also use several software programs, websites, and online calculators, some free and some available for purchase, for studies of various designs (e.g., PASS [NCSS Statistical Software, 2005], G*Power 3 [Faul et al., 2007]). If you're not sure how to approach your power analysis, consult the statistical literature on your specific design and analysis plan, and find an expert who can advise you.

Setting and Apparatus

Describe the general context in which your research will take place. If the setting and apparatus are commonly used in research in your area, you need not describe them in detail and can simply include this information in a general Procedures subsection. In a controlled experiment, however, give the general dimensions and furnishings of any experimental room and indicate the position of the experimenter and the participant (e.g., "The study took place in a 9 ft. × 12 ft. experimental room, with the participant and experimenter seated and facing each other across a 4-ft.-wide table"). Such details would generally not be necessary for studies involving data collected from groups of participants in college or elementary school classrooms, however. Also, because journal space is more limited than thesis or dissertation space, you would omit these details when preparing your study for publication. If you use a particular piece of apparatus to present stimuli or to afford participants a way of responding that is unique to your study, describe it in detail and include construction plans (in either the text or an appendix). If the apparatus is commercially available, include the brand and model number.

Experimental Condition or Manipulation

If your study involves some sort of experimental manipulation, provide details about how the conditions are set up and delivered. Where you provide these details depends on their complexity. Fairly straightforward conditions can be described in the Design or Procedures subsection. However, more complex conditions, such as those involved in an intervention project or exposure to a specific set of stimuli, may require a separate subsection or even an appendix (e.g., with the treatment manual) that describes the independent variable in enough detail that someone else can replicate your manipulation.

Regardless of where you place this information, certain details are essential. First, you must describe what the manipulation is intended to accomplish. Then, specify how you will operationalize the independent variable that your manipulation represents. Next, describe how you will implement the manipulation, including enough detail that it can be replicated.

Be sure to explain who will serve as the experimenter. An abundance of literature shows that any experimenter or data gatherer who will interact with participants should be unaware of the experimental hypotheses, so this person should not be you unless you can keep yourself unaware of who is in which condition. If you cannot remain unaware of your participants' status on factors that might bias your interactions with them, and you cannot afford to hire an experimentally naïve person to collect your data, several options are available to you. If you are in a university setting, perhaps you can give independent study credit to an undergraduate for serving as your experimenter. Perhaps you and an equally poor colleague can trade services: Your friend will be your experimenter, and you will be theirs (be aware, however, that you cannot then discuss your project in detail with this person for social support!). A final and least preferred option is to act as the experimenter yourself, using some procedure to ensure that you do not treat participants in different conditions differently. This might include administering a questionnaire that participants in all conditions complete about the experimenter or video recording experimental sessions. The questionnaire or recordings can be rated for adherence to standardized methods by assistants who are unaware of your hypotheses.

If implementing the experimental manipulation requires skill or elaborate procedures, indicate how you will train your experimenter and ensure their competence before and during the study. This is particularly important with studies that involve interventions, animal surgery, and use of experimental confederates who have to act out scripts.

Include information on the control procedures you institute to prevent confounds. For example, if participants will view a series of video recorded stimuli, indicate how you will control for possible order effects. If different experimenters implement different levels of the manipulation (i.e., different conditions), how will you ensure that levels of this variable, and not experimenter differences, influence the results? Provide the information necessary to convince readers that your conditions differ only on the independent variable and nothing else. To do this, of course, will require that you figure out potential confounds in advance and eliminate them or assess the effects of their presence.

Finally, you must indicate how you will ensure the integrity of the manipulation and the independent variable(s) it represents, sometimes referred to as "treatment fidelity" (Cooper, 2018). In other words, describe how you will determine that the variables are manipulated consistently and as planned. This may involve manipulation checks by judges (e.g., ratings of therapist or experimenter behavior to ensure that they did what they were supposed to do) and precautions taken by the experimenter (e.g., observing sessions through a one-way mirror). If your study involves instructional manipulations (e.g., to make your participants think they are winning a game played single-handedly against a two-person team in another room), include some way of assessing whether they really believed these manipulations.

Manipulation checks can be complex. One of our students, for example, was interested in whether fourth-grade girls would be rated as more socially competent by peers if they engaged in higher frequencies of certain behaviors thought important to the peers (Hoier, 1984; see Hoier & Cone, 1987, for a published version). Increases in these social behaviors were the independent variable and ratings of competence the dependent variable. To make sure the social behaviors actually were increased, Hoier (1984) made videotapes of the experimental sessions, and trained observers then scored the videotapes. It was important to describe the reliability of this scoring system in the Method section. Whether information about manipulation checks such as this one would be placed in the Independent Variables subsection or Measures subsection depends on where the material will be clearest for readers.

Measures

The Measures subsection provides details about the data collection devices you will use to measure your dependent variables and any independent variables that were not described as part of an experimental manipulation. Chapter 8 describes what to look for in measures adequate for use in your study. Here, we mention the information to provide about them once you have selected them.

General Considerations

You may want to put your measures in subsections of the Measures subsection. You can use a separate subsection for each individual measure, labeled with the measure name, or you can group measures by the construct they are used to measure (e.g., a Measures of Anxiety subsection can include separate paragraphs for your measures of general anxiety and social anxiety). You can also group measures by their type (e.g., self-report, rating by other, direct observation).

First, describe each instrument by name, author, and year of publication (or creation if unpublished). When possible, include a copy of each measure in an appendix to your document. You are legally required to obtain written permission both to use and to reproduce copyrighted measures. For some copyrighted measures, the copyright holder may grant you permission to use the measure in your study but not to reproduce it in your thesis or dissertation. If you do not include the measures in your document, you may wish to bring your own personal copies of all measures to your proposal and defense meetings so that committee members can review them if they wish.

Next, describe what the measure looks like (i.e., its topography). That is, paraphrase or quote the instructions to participants, describe representative test stimuli or items, and state the response format (e.g., yes–no, 4-point rating scale). You might want to include representative items in a table or in the main text to make them readily available to readers, even if the entire instrument is reproduced in an appendix. If you are using a well-known instrument such as the Minnesota Multiphasic Personality Inventory, you generally won't need to go into detail because most readers will be familiar with it. Ask your chair for advice if you are unsure whether your measures are considered well known. Note that items from some tests (e.g., Wechsler Adult Intelligence Scale–Revised) cannot be reproduced in publicly available documents as this would compromise the security of the test items and invalidate test results for anyone who takes one of these tests after having seen the items.

Finally, describe how each measure is scored. If it yields more than one score, describe the scores you intend to use. For many measures, scoring is simply a matter of summing or averaging ratings or other numeric data across items. However, some measures (or manipulations) require complex procedures to transform the data into scores, such as may be the case with coding of direct observation or physiological data. We describe some of the special issues involved in describing more complex coding systems and procedures in the sections that follow. Finally, include information about each measure's psychometric properties, including reliability and validity of the scores you plan to use (see Chapter 8, this volume, for more on this topic).

Describing Newly Developed Measures

If you develop a measure de novo for your study, you may not have information on the psychometric properties of its scores. In this case, we highly recommend a pilot study. If you cannot collect pilot data, be sure to describe how you plan to obtain reliability and validity information during the course of your research. In most cases, this should be done before collecting the data needed to answer the main research questions. The reason for this is simple. Suppose that you collect reliability and validity data on your instrument at the same time you are collecting data to answer the main research questions. If your data show that your measure is poor, how will you then interpret your primary research data? If the data do not turn out the way you hypothesized, the fault may lie in your instrumentation, not in the logic underlying your hypothesis. In other words, your measure will not be sufficiently reliable or valid to answer your research question. Cone (1992) provided a detailed discussion of this issue.

Describing Data From Direct Observation and Other Complex Measures

As we noted, some measures involve several steps to get from the raw data collected to usable data. If you plan to use observers or judges to score or code your data, you need to describe both the observation or coding system and the people using it. Provide a complete description of the system (e.g., definitions of coding categories, rating scale anchors) and procedures (e.g., data collection forms) the coders will use. Include the coding manual or guidelines and scoring forms in an appendix. Indicate who the coders will be (e.g., undergraduates, supervisors, content experts); how they will be recruited, selected, and trained; and how you will know that they are ready to be let loose on the real data (e.g., have demonstrated acceptable accuracy). Indicate the procedures you will use to check interobserver or interjudge agreement as data coding progresses, including how and how often you will check (e.g., Will observers know when you're checking agreement? Will you use the common standard of checking a minimum of 20% of the data?) and how you will calculate agreement. Resources are available to help you determine these details (e.g., Hallgren, 2012).

If you are collecting physiological or neurological data, you will need to provide similar details. Describe the equipment you will use to collect data (e.g., EEG equipment, eye movement tracker, heart rate monitor, MRI machine) and how the equipment will obtain the data (e.g., number and location of electronic sensors, duration and frequency of scan). Describe any procedures you will use to train participants in equipment use or to obtain baseline or resting data. Finally, indicate how you will transform your raw data, typically in the form of waveforms or images, to quantitative data you can use in your analyses. If these transformations involve specific computer software, be sure to indicate which programs and versions you use.

Procedure

In the Procedure subsection, describe the steps you will take to obtain data from participants. Walk readers through the process just as a participant will experience it. Start at the beginning: For studies with human participants, this is the recruitment and consent process; for studies with nonhuman animals, you can skip this step, but be sure to describe how you acquired the nonhuman animals in the Participants section. If a research assistant will telephone or screen participants from a list of volunteers, indicate this and state exactly how potential participants will be identified and what they will be told on the phone; it is a good idea to have a script for the caller to follow. If your study involves recruiting online or through posted fliers, describe how and where these recruitment efforts will appear. If you'll be visiting schools to recruit school-age children, describe your script for what you will say to the children and how you will obtain parents' consent for their children's participation. If your study includes multiple linked participants, such as multiple family members or children and their teachers, describe how each type of participant will be recruited. Include copies of your fliers, scripts, and other recruitment materials in appendices. You will have to submit these later with your institutional review board (IRB) application anyway, so develop them at the proposal stage and get the benefit of committee feedback.

Describe the timing of consent in the overall recruitment process. Will it happen at the same time as recruitment (e.g., if potential participants are recruited online or via a mailed survey and simply indicate consent to proceed to the study), or will it occur at a subsequent contact (e.g., if participant eligibility is determined with a phone screen and then followed by an appointment for consent and data collection)? Your proposal doesn't need to include the level of detail on the consent process that your IRB application will require; just make sure to include enough detail so that readers understand how participants will learn of and opt in or out of the study. Place a copy of all informed consent forms (and, if applicable, youth assent forms) in an appendix.

What if you're using a preexisting data set and do not actually have to recruit or obtain consent from participants? In the case of large national data sets that have been used extensively (e.g., National Longitudinal Study of Adolescent to Adult Health, https://www.cpc.unc.edu/projects/addhealth), cite the source of the data, if you haven't already done so in your Participants section, and indicate how participants were recruited, consented, and so on in the original study. If you're using preexisting data from your adviser's lab, include a brief description of participant recruitment, noting that this occurred as part of a larger or preexisting study. If you were not personally involved in this stage of the study, get these details from your adviser or lab mates. These details are important to include because they help readers understand the participants' experience.

Next, describe the procedures you will use when data collection begins for the participants. For some studies, such as online studies or mailed surveys, data collection may be triggered automatically once someone agrees to participate. Describe how this happens: Is a questionnaire packet included with mailed paper copies of a recruitment and consent letter? Do consenting participants follow a link to the online study? If data are collected in person, describe what happens once participants arrive at the data collection site, including who is responsible for each of the procedures. If participants are assigned randomly to an experimental or control group, state how. Be alert to the need to protect against potential participant reactivity to experimental conditions and other forms of participant bias, such as the infamous Hawthorne effect in which participants change their behavior when they are aware of being observed (cf. Ray, 2011). Tell participants only what they need for informed participation. Implement double-blind procedures to minimize experimenter bias whenever possible.

Provide word-for-word instructions to be used with each participant. If different groups will receive different instructions, indicate how the instructions differ, and put copies of all instructions in an appendix. Making an audio recording of instructions and playing it for participants ensures standardization and helps avoid experimenter burnout, communication of boredom or impatience, or any of a number of normal (but idiosyncratic) experimenter reactions that might inadvertently affect the outcome of the study. (Recall our earlier recommendations concerning integrity checks.)

Describe the process you will use to debrief participants after they have participated. Compose a script for this, and place it in an appendix. You may want to offer participants a chance to obtain a summary of the research findings. A good way to do this is to provide a box for them to check on the consent form if they are interested in receiving such a summary (include a place for their mailing or email address as well). In studies that involve sensitive topics or enroll potentially at-risk participants (e.g., studies that explore traumatic experiences), it is often beneficial to provide resources as part of the debriefing process. Create a list of websites, books, and local support groups or mental health providers that you can distribute to every participant.

Finally, if your design calls for repeated data collection, as with post-treatment assessment, follow-up, or other longitudinal design, be sure to describe these subsequent data collection procedures. When will they occur? Will participants be brought back? Will they be telephoned, contacted only by mail, and so on? Make sure to describe how you will maximize retention (see Cotter et al., 2002, for several useful procedures).

BE PREPARED TO CONDUCT ETHICAL RESEARCH

This section highlights the ethical principles governing research in psychology, as well as our practical suggestions for implementing the principles, in order to help you conduct your own research in as ethically sensitive a manner as possible.

Be Familiar With Research Ethics

APA Ethics Code

The professional conduct of psychologists—whether practitioner or researcher, whether student or seasoned veteran—is governed by the *Ethical Principles of Psychologists and Code of Conduct* promulgated by the American Psychological Association (APA Ethics Code; 2017b). The current code, including amendments and updates, is available at http://www.apa.org/ethics/code/index. We encourage you to pay particular attention to Standards 2.05, 3.04, 3.08, 3.10, 4.01, 4.02, 4.04, 4.05, 4.07, 5.01, 6.01, 6.02, and 8.01–8.15, the sections most directly relevant for research. The essence of the principles and conduct code is that, when psychologists conduct research, they do so competently and with the welfare of participants as a paramount concern. If you are one of our readers from a discipline outside of psychology (e.g., education, social work, human development, biology, neuroscience), you may have other ethics codes that govern your discipline (e.g., American Educational Research Association, 2011; National Association of Social Workers, 2017). If your discipline does not have a specific ethics code, following a combination of these standards and your IRB's regulations will ensure that you are acting in an ethically responsible way.

Institutional Ethics Guidelines

Researchers' behavior, regardless of discipline or whether they work with human or nonhuman animal participants, is also governed by institutional ethics guidelines, which in turn are governed by U.S. federal regulations. These regulations cover many of the same areas as the APA Ethics Code. Your institution has one or more committees (e.g., Institutional Review Board for the Protection of Human Subjects, Animal Care and Use Committee [ACUC]) that manage required training for researchers, review proposals for any research to be conducted at the institution, and handle research ethics complaints. Many universities require that all researchers complete specific training in research ethics (e.g., Collaborative Institutional Training Initiative Program, https://about.citiprogram.org/en/homepage/) before beginning any research.

Implement Ethical Standards in Your Research

In this section, we offer suggestions for implementing ethically responsible research. We describe some of the more common issues that arise for developing researchers, discuss logistics, and provide examples. We focus here on research using human participants; if your research involves nonhuman animals, be sure to contact your institution's relevant committee for guidance. Exhibit 7.1 summarizes our informal recommendations for ethically responsible research with both human and nonhuman animal participants based on our interpretation of the APA Ethics Code, together with our years of responding to the requirements of IRBs and our understanding of ACUCs. You can find more details in several publications devoted to the topic, such as *Ethics in*

EXHIBIT 7.1

Suggestions for Conducting Ethically Responsible Research

Research With Human Participants

- Evaluate the ethical acceptability of your research.

- Assess the degree of risk involved for participants, and make sure the benefits of the research outweigh the risks.

- Oversee research assistants and others involved in your project to ensure that they conduct the research in an ethically sensitive way.

- Obtain a clear, fair, informed, and voluntary agreement by participants to participate.

- Avoid deception and concealment unless absolutely necessary and justifiable.

- Respect participants' right to decline or withdraw from participation at any time without penalty.

- Protect participants from any physical harm, danger, or discomfort possibly associated with the research procedures.

- Protect participants from any emotional harm, danger, or discomfort possibly associated with the research procedures.

- Debrief participants after data collection has been completed.

- Correct any undesirable consequences to participants that result from participating in the study.

- Maintain strict confidentiality of any information collected about participants during the research in accord with agreements reached with participants while obtaining informed consent.

Research With Nonhuman Animals

- Conform with all laws and professional standards pertaining to acquiring, caring for, and disposing of the animals.

- Ensure that a psychologist trained in research methods and experienced in animal care supervises the use of the animals and is ultimately responsible for their health, comfort, and humane treatment.

- Ensure that all individuals involved in the research have been specifically trained in research methods and ways of caring for, maintaining, and handling the particular animals being used.

- Minimize any discomfort, infection, pain, or illness in the animals.

- Use procedures involving stress, pain, or privation only if alternatives are unavailable and the research goal is justified by the practical, educational, or scientific value expected.

- Perform any surgery while the animals are under appropriate anesthesia, and use procedures to prevent infection and minimize pain both during and after surgery.

- Proceed rapidly, using appropriate procedures and minimizing pain, and apply life-terminating procedures when it is appropriate to terminate an animal's life.

Research With Human Participants (Sales & Folkman, 2000) or *Introduction to the Responsible Conduct of Research* (Steneck, 2007). Steneck's book, as well as Chapter 8 of Nagy's (2005) *Ethics in Plain English: An Illustrative Casebook for Psychologists* and Emanuel et al.'s (2016) chapter "Research Ethics: How to Treat People Who Participate in Research," include interesting vignettes that bring to life the ethics codes and IRB regulations.

Know the operation of your local IRB or ACUC. Although such committees are governed by federal requirements and national standards, the implementation of these requirements and standards is likely to vary across institutions. Thus, you should be familiar with your institution's policies and procedures. These are typically published, so get a copy and read them. They include the steps you must follow to have your research approved before you begin to collect data.

Because IRB procedures usually cover pilot testing as well as formal studies, it is important to examine these procedures early in your planning. Pay particular attention to the dates of IRB meetings and the deadlines and rules for submitting proposals. If the meetings occur monthly, missing one could mean a delay of as much as a month in getting started. Look also at the different categories of research to make sure exactly what the requirements are in your particular case. Perhaps the research you plan is exempt from IRB review or can receive an expedited review. If you are obtaining data only from archival sources or are using relatively benign surveys, observing public behavior, or evaluating normal educational practice, it is usually the case that full IRB review will not be necessary.

Rely on the experience of your chair or other committee members. No doubt, they will be knowledgeable concerning the process and politics of the local IRB and will have sage advice for navigating the process successfully.

In addition, it is important to know the timing of IRB approval relative to your proposal meeting. Some schools require students to obtain approval before holding a proposal meeting because sometimes substantial changes are necessary to respond satisfactorily to IRB concerns. These changes can have implications for fundamental aspects of the research, including the basic question and hypotheses, and the committee will not want to have to convene again to consider such changes. Other schools require students to submit the IR application after the proposal meeting because they expect the proposal meeting to result in significant changes to the planned project that would affect IRB approval.

Whether you seek IRB approval before or after the proposal meeting, anticipate difficult steerage through the IRB process if the research you are planning is the least bit controversial. An interesting example comes from some research in the area of children's social skills that Sharon Foster attempted to conduct some years ago. The procedure involved having children nominate their three most- and three least-liked peers. One member of the IRB was especially insistent that such a procedure was potentially harmful, arguing that the process would call attention to disliked children and that peers might respond to these children even more negatively than usual as a result of the nominations. Foster decided to recruit the concerned IRB member's assistance in designing a study to test this very concern. She argued that no data showed the procedure to be harmful. To reassure the IRB, however, Foster offered to conduct a study that would examine whether children were negatively affected by the nomination procedure. Surely the IRB member would have to give permission for such a test, at least. He did, and Debora Bell, then a student of Foster's, designed and conducted the study as a master's thesis. Incidentally, no negative effects emerged, and the paper has been helpful to many other researchers planning to use peer nomination procedures (Bell-Dolan et al., 1989).

Determine Ethical Acceptability

The first requirement of the research you plan to undertake is that it be ethically acceptable. How do you find out if it is? A simple test is to examine the principles articulated in Exhibit 7.1. Can your research be done if you adhere to each of them? If it can, it is probably ethically acceptable. If it cannot, it still may be ethically acceptable, but you will have to take some extra steps to determine this and to assure yourself and others that it is.

Deception and concealment in research raise particular concerns about ethical acceptability because they can be used only when absolutely necessary and justifiable (see APA Ethics Code Standard 8.07, Deception in Research). To illustrate, imagine a study that involves a task in which the participant competes against other people. However, to exercise precise control over the other "people's" performance and the outcome of the competition, the experimenter might program a computer to compete against the real participant and win or lose at some predetermined rate. Clearly, the participant is being deceived in this experiment. Is this inconsistent with the prohibition against deception, or can the experimenter establish that the research is important and that it cannot be done without the deception?

Frequently you can avoid deception altogether with a little ingenuity and/or statistical sophistication on your part (Kazdin, 2016c). For example, pilot testing in the above example might reveal that groups told they were competing against a computer performed comparably to those told they were competing against real people. If the research question involves whether competition is critical, showing that computer and people competitors are equivalent eliminates the need for deception about the competitor. The experimenter can simply tell participants they are competing against a computer.

However, the experimenter might draw a different conclusion about the necessity of deception about the nature of the competition. One of our students completed an experimental study in which he examined families' affective responses to success and failure. The experimental paradigm involved families playing a game together and (ostensibly) winning or losing money on the basis of their performance. In reality, the families were assigned to predetermined success and failure conditions, and all families received equal compensation at the end of the study. Imagine how difficult it would be to induce positive or negative affect (or effort) if families knew from the outset that their performance didn't matter. It would also be hard to ensure that all families experienced comparable levels of both success and failure if the task were not standardized. At the same time, imagine the effects of actually paying families on the basis of their performance, including paying nothing to families who lost the game. The disappointment felt by the latter participants would be an undesirable consequence of participating in the study. In this case, the deception was considered necessary for the required task standardization, minor in comparison to everyday life (a standard often set by IRBs), and offset by the debriefing and standard payment amount that equaled the high end of possible "winnings."

As these examples illustrate, doing a thorough job of ensuring that controversial research methods are ethical can be time consuming and is often beyond the resources of fledgling researchers. Performing a pilot study as Kazdin (2016c) suggested may not be realistic if you want to finish your project and receive your degree while you are still young enough to walk across the stage at graduation.

The challenge of showing that your research is ethical is another reason to plan a study within the context of a research area that is currently viable in the literature. If you have a body of research to draw on, chances are that most of those studies have been done in ways consistent with the APA Ethics Code. You can refer to precedents in the established literature to assure yourself, your IRB, your committee members, and others that you are conducting your research ethically. Of course, it is not enough simply to refer to the existing literature to prove that yours is ethical. You need to address each of the principles and be able to assure your committee and your institution's IRB that you are proceeding ethically.

Examine Risk to Participants

Thinking about potential risk to participants is a crucial part of planning ethical research and seeking IRB approval. You must assess the extent of any risk posed to people, whether physical, emotional, or other, by participation in your project. Potential risk can generally be ascertained from the existing literature if other researchers used procedures comparable to those you plan to use. In a few cases, the potentially harmful nature of research procedures has been studied directly (cf. Bell-Dolan et al., 1989). You can refer to the results of such studies in designing your voluntary consent form. In most cases, however, potential risks have not been studied directly and must be inferred from the literature. In this event, you should refer to the body of literature and indicate whether there have been any reported instances of physical, emotional, or other types of harm to participants in the "dozens of studies reported in the literature using these procedures," or words to that effect.

In our experience, novice researchers sometimes underestimate risks, but a more common problem is that they overestimate the likelihood that people will become distressed as a result of participating in their research. For example, we have seen draft IRB proposals that talk about concerns that participants might become upset answering completely innocuous question-naires simply because they include questions about bad habits, negative moods, or the like. It is important to remember that the benchmark for "minimal risk" is the degree of risk a participant would encounter in a routine physical or psychological examination. People are routinely asked for personal information when they sign up for social media or talk to a psychologist, so researchers can assume that reporting normal, everyday information will not be unduly distressing. After all, would you be significantly distressed if asked to report how often you have negative thoughts about yourself? Is there really much chance that your participants will become upset? At the same time, asking for highly sensitive information (e.g., about sexual habits, suicide attempts, or use of illegal drugs) might be more problematic or pose greater risk. When in doubt, reread the APA Ethics Code and consult with your adviser and others in the profession about likely risks.

Plan Informed Consent Procedures

Informed consent is a process that includes both informing prospective participants of what their participation in the research will likely entail and obtaining their written agreement to participate. One part of this key element in ethical research involves giving the participant (or the participant's parent or guardian) an informed consent agreement or form. The exact contents that must be included in consent forms vary from place to place in keeping with institutional variations in IRB procedures. In general, the minimum essential elements of any consent form include a description of the study (e.g., its pur-pose, what the participant will be asked to do, how long it will take), potential risks and benefits to individual participants, a statement that participation is voluntary and that the participant can withdraw at any time without penalty, reassurance that all data will be confidential (and a description of any limits to confidentiality), information on any compensation or incentive provided to the participant, contact information for the researcher and the IRB in case the participant has questions or concerns, and places for the participant and researcher to sign the form indicating consent. Be sure to check with your committee chair and your IRB about the content your consent forms should include.

If you are working with children or other individuals who are not legally able to give informed consent, a parent or legal guardian must sign the consent form. Participants themselves should also be given an opportunity to assent or refuse participation—the researcher should describe the study in simple terms and ask them directly whether they agree to participate. Children can be asked to sign an assent form, similar to a consent form but in simpler language. From our perspective, if either the legal guardian or the potential participant declines, the individual is excluded from the study.

Other populations besides children need special protections to ensure that their consent is voluntary. These include individuals with intellectual disabilities, prisoners, homeless people, individuals in the military, employees, and students. With some of these populations, limited competency to understand what they are agreeing to is an issue, as it is with children. With others, indirect coercion may be a concern. For example, employees may think that their superiors expect participation and that their job security is at risk if they decline.

Requiring college students to involve themselves in research in order to satisfy the criteria of a particular course is also considered coercive. At many universities, it is common practice to give students enrolled in an introductory psychology course class assignment credit for participating in research. It is considered potentially educational because, after all, these students are learning about psychological research and its results, and this is an opportunity to experience research firsthand. However, IRBs at such institutions typically require that (a) the research participation is in fact educational (e.g., with a more in-depth educational debriefing) and (b) there are alternative methods to earn that class assignment credit (e.g., with a paper or other assignment estimated to require a comparable amount of time) to avoid coercion. Seek assistance in ethically recruiting people from special populations from your chair and your school's IRB.

In addition, special ethical considerations may arise when you involve ethnic minority populations in your research. Indeed, given our pluralistic society and researchers' increasing awareness of the need to expand the scientific knowledge base to include diverse populations, you quite likely will have members of several racial and ethnic groups in your research unless you purposely design the research to study particular groups. Numerous concerns can be important here, such as how you categorize your groups and the applicability of your constructs and measures to diverse groups. You should be sure to avoid inappropriate generalizations when members of minority groups form only a small part of your sample and it is impossible to test whether the results hold equally well for different groups. When ethnic minority groups are a primary focus of your research, additional special considerations apply. APA's (2017c) *Multicultural Guidelines: An Ecological Approach to Context, Identity, and Intersectionality* (see also Leong, 2014) provides extensive discussion of issues involved in culturally informed and respectful research, including consent and confidentiality procedures.

It is important to attend to the reading level of any consent form you use. Be sure that it does not exceed the level of the participants with the lowest reading proficiency you are willing to include in your research. Research evidence suggests that many consent forms are written at a level much higher than the reading level of participants. For example, in medical settings it has been noted that the average consent form requires reading proficiency that is five to six grade levels above that of the average patient (Hochhauser, 1999). One of our IRBs actually checks the reading level of consent forms and requires that they not be above the eighth-grade level.

It is easy to get estimates of the reading level of your consent form. Many word processing programs have reading level calculators built into them. For example, Microsoft Word provided a Flesch-Kincaid Grade Level estimate of 8.7 for the two sentences immediately preceding this one. Helpful hint: Reading level is influenced by the length and complexity of both words and sentences. Some multisyllabic words are hard to replace (e.g., "psychology"!), but you can influence the reading level of your consent form by choosing the shortest, simplest words possible to convey the information and by using short, direct sentences. Here is an example of a rewrite of the sentences we checked above: "It is easy to check the reading level of your consent form. Most word processing programs have an option to do this." The reading level is now 7.4, consistent with our IRB's requirements.

As a procedural matter, signing the informed consent form occurs as the first order of business when the participant appears for the initial experimental session, if this has not happened already. If the research is particularly sensitive or if perceived pressure or coercion could be an issue, your IRB may require that you use procedures to ensure that participants have time to fully consider their option to participate or decline—without an experimenter staring at them! Allowing a time lapse between informing participants about the study, obtaining a signed consent form, and beginning data collection may accomplish this. If you are recruiting therapy clients, you might leave recruitment fliers in the waiting room or have an experimenter (not the therapist) available to describe the study, and then schedule the consent and data collection procedures at a separate time. If schoolchildren are participating, it is common to send the form home with the children to be returned with their parent's signature. Ask the parents to return the form regardless of whether they assent or decline so you can be sure they received the form.

Monitor Research Ethics Continually

The job of ensuring ethical conduct of your research does not end with approval from the IRB and your committee. In fact, it is just beginning. When you start to collect data, be sure that all people involved behave ethically at all times. Develop procedures for monitoring this, and describe them in your document. We come back to this topic in Chapter 10 when we talk about the actual implementation of your research.

✓   **TO DO . . .**

PLANNING YOUR METHODOLOGY AND WRITING THE METHOD SECTION

☐ Plan all aspects of your study methodology and write the subsections of the Method section:

- Design

- Participants

- Setting and apparatus

- Experimental condition or manipulation

- Measures

- Procedure

☐ Prepare to conduct ethical research.

- Read ethics guidelines and regulations and complete any required training.

- Work with the institutional review board or animal care and use committee to ensure you implement ethical standards in your research.

- Write recruiting scripts and letters, and follow informed consent procedures, using carefully worded consent and assent forms.

- Monitor the conduct of your study continually to ensure that ethical practices are maintained throughout.

SUPPLEMENTAL RESOURCES

Research Design

Hayes, S. C., Barlow, D. H., & Nelson-Gray, R. O. (1999). *The scientist practitioner: Research and accountability in the age of managed care* (2nd ed.). Allyn & Bacon.

Kazdin, A. E. (2016). *Research design in clinical psychology* (4th ed.). Pearson.

Kerlinger, F. N. (2000). *Foundations of behavioral research* (4th ed.). Harcourt Brace.

Kratochwill, T. R., & Levin, J. R. (Eds.). (2014). *Single-case intervention research: Methodologies and statistical advances.* American Psychological Association. https://doi.org/10.1037/14376-000

Miller, D. C. (2002). *Handbook of research design and social measurement* (6th ed.). Sage. https://doi.org/10.4135/9781412984386

Ray, W. J. (2011). *Methods: Toward a science of behavior and experience* (10th ed.). Cengage Learning.

Shadish, W. R., Cook, T. D., & Campbell, D. T. (2002). *Experimental and quasi-experimental designs for generalized causal inference.* Houghton Mifflin.

Smith, J. D. (2012). Single-case experimental designs: A systematic review of published research and current standards. *Psychological Methods, 17*(4), 510–550. https://doi.org/10.1037/a0029312

Solso, R. L., & MacLin, M. (2002). *Experimental psychology: A case approach* (7th ed.). Allyn & Bacon.

Weisberg, H. F., Krosnick, J. A., & Bowen, B. D. (1996). *An introduction to survey research, polling, and data analysis* (3rd ed.). Sage.

White, T. L., & McBurney, D. H. (2013). *Research methods* (9th ed.). Wadsworth Cengage.

Power Analysis

Cohen, J. (1988). *Statistical power analysis for the behavioral sciences* (2nd ed.). Erlbaum.

Heinrich-Heine-Universität Düsseldorf. (2018). *G*Power: Statistical power analyses for Windows and Mac.* http://www.psychologie.hhu.de/arbeitsgruppen/allgemeine-psychologie-und-arbeitspsychologie/gpower.html

Kabacoff, R. I. (2017). *Quick-R: Power analysis.* https://www.statmethods.net/stats/power.html

Liu, X. S. (2014). *Statistical power analysis for the social and behavioral sciences: Basic and advanced techniques.* Routledge.

Murphy, K. R, Myors, B., & Wolach, A. (2014). *Statistical power analysis* (4th ed.). Routledge.

Research Ethics

Cone, J. D., & Dalenberg, C. J. (2004). Ethics concerns in outcomes assessment. In M. E. Maruish (Ed.), *The use of psychological testing for treatment planning and outcomes assessment* (3rd ed., Vol. 1, pp. 307–334). Erlbaum.

Knapp, S. J. (Ed.). (2012). *APA handbook of ethics in psychology.* American Psychological Association.

National Institutes of Health. (2018). *Office of Laboratory Animal Welfare.* https://olaw.nih.gov/

U.S. Department of Health and Human Services. (2017). *Office for Human Research Protections: Regulations.* https://www.hhs.gov/ohrp/regulations-and-policy/regulations/index.html

8

Measuring Study Variables

This chapter covers basic issues in operationalizing dependent and independent variables, including
- types of measures to use in operationalizing the variables you will study
- important psychometric qualities they must have
- where to find and how to select instruments
- what to do if there are no existing measures for the variables you plan to study

Read thoroughly if
- you have taken no courses in the measurement of human behavior
- you have no idea where to find instruments for your study or how to select the best ones

Skim or skip if
- you have taken courses in measurement (psychometrics) and are comfortable with concepts such as reliability, validity, and generalizability theory
- you have experience selecting objective instruments in past research with human participants

https://doi.org/10.1037/0000161-008
Dissertations and Theses From Start to Finish: Psychology and Related Fields, Third Edition,
by D. J. Bell, S. L. Foster, and J. D. Cone

This chapter addresses how to measure your dependent and independent variables. We discuss the characteristics of good measures and suggest places to find them and information about them. Further, we suggest what to do when the psychometric adequacy of your measures is not yet known. We focus mostly on measurement of more traditional psychological constructs, such as personality, behavior, thoughts, and feelings. However, our discussion of the importance of operationalizing variables, selecting measurement approaches, and evaluating psychometric properties is also relevant to other types of measurement, such as assessment of biological processes or genetic makeup. If your research focuses primarily on these types of methods, be sure to consult other sources for information specific to relevant measures.

OPERATIONALIZE YOUR VARIABLES

If you are at the point of planning a thesis or dissertation, you probably know what operational definitions are. If not, avail yourself of a good text in research design (e.g., Ray, 2011; White & McBurney, 2013; see the Supplemental Resources list at the end of Chapter 7, this volume, for additional suggestions) and review the relevant sections.

The Measures subsection of your Method section, introduced in Chapter 7, describes how you plan to operationalize all your variables, both dependent and independent. For example,

- Suppose you expect to examine the differences among families with high, middle, and low socioeconomic status (SES) in time spent on social media. How will you establish SES? How will you measure time spent on social media? How will you measure each of the differences you plan to study?

- Or suppose you want to look at differences in brain activity during a specific cognitive task between youth with autism spectrum disorder and neurotypical youth. What measures of brain activity will you use? How will you determine the diagnostic status of your participants?

- If you are going to expose participants high and low in appraisal anxiety to high-, medium-, and low-stress public speaking situations, how will you manipulate stress? Just as important, how will you determine the success of your manipulation? What differences do you predict your stress alteration will produce? How will they be measured?

- If you are going to document whether obese patrons eat more carbohydrates in fast casual dining establishments than nonobese patrons, how will you make your observations?

The answer to most of these questions is that you will use an objective instrument of some type. The instrument may be a short, rather gross categorization of participants into SES levels or immigrant groups; a lengthy, rather specific index of appraisal anxiety or some other personality characteristic;

imaging of brain activity using an MRI scan; or direct observation of specific behaviors. Whatever its nature, your operational index will need to have certain psychometric qualities for your findings to be acceptable to the scientific community.

To conduct your thesis or dissertation research to answer substantive questions about your topic of interest, you will require measures with certain qualities. Assessing the adequacy of measures in the social sciences has traditionally relied on concepts from classical test theory (CTT). At this point in your graduate studies, you recognize these qualities as reflected in the reliability and validity of measures. More recently, item response theory (IRT) has taken its place alongside CTT in the development and evaluation of measures in the behavioral sciences (DeMars, 2010; Embretson & Riese, 2000; Faulkner-Bond & Wells, 2016). IRT involves the construction and evaluation of instruments on the basis of analysis at the level of their individual items. This level of analysis contrasts with CTT's analysis at the level of total scale scores. IRT can be traced to the early work of psychometrician L. L. Thurstone with the Stanford-Binet, a measure of children's intelligence (see Bock, 1997), and to that of educational psychometrician Frederic M. Lord (1952) more than 25 years later. It took another half century for IRT to gain a substantial foothold in the behavior sciences. Interested readers are referred to Faulkner-Bond and Wells (2016) for more on the origins of IRT and its development. As they noted, the availability of rapidly increasing computing power together with the appearance of better programming languages have played a significant role in its greater use.

If you focus on a substantive question in your thesis or dissertation research, you will likely use existing measures with established reliability and validity rather than developing new ones. If you find yourself drawn to a project that includes measure construction, however, you should become knowledgeable about IRT. The Supplemental Resources at the end of this chapter provide references to get you started in this endeavor. Be forewarned, though, of the extensive work required to construct a measure from scratch. Doing this competently takes great preparation followed by a substantial commitment to data collection and analysis. And all of this is needed just to get ready to use the newly constructed measure to answer the substantive questions of your research. Then you must conduct what amounts to another complete study to gather these data. Incidentally, the availability of online measure construction and administration services (e.g., Mechanical Turk, SurveyMonkey, Qualtrics), although helpful in developing a self-report measure and administering it to large numbers of people, does not eliminate the need to show the measurement adequacy (e.g., accuracy, reliability, validity) of that measure. In sum, our recommendation is to avoid what are essentially two thesis or dissertation undertakings and find measures already established and, ideally, used by others in your area of interest.

Assuming that more substantive concerns provide the basis for your research, let us turn to some of the CTT concepts that will be important in selecting measures to pursue these concerns.

KNOW THE IMPORTANT ASPECTS OF POTENTIAL INSTRUMENTS

Any measure used in scientific research should (a) be chosen wisely, (b) have certain psychometric characteristics (i.e., reliability and validity) for the population you intend to study and the scores you plan to use, and (c) be adequately direct. These features can be ensured by considering the following questions.

What Is Your Subject Matter?

Wisely chosen measures fit the variables that interest you. If you are concerned with conflict in marital relationships, for example, your measure should reflect this. It will if you define such conflict precisely before selecting the measure to use. "Conflict" is a general term that could refer to numerous behaviors. These behaviors might involve observable interactions with one's spouse or partner, or they might not; a person could be having private conflicting thoughts about staying in the relationship, for example. If conflict as you view it concerns interaction between spouses, is this conflict verbal, physical, or both?

It will be easier to choose the right measure if you know precisely what it is you want to assess than if you do not. This is true of any of the constructs you plan to study, whether they are independent or dependent variables. Anxiety can be viewed in a variety of ways, for example. Immigrant status, race, and gender are similarly open to different definitions. Furthermore, you cannot rely merely on the name a measure has been given by its developer. You must examine its content to see if it fits the construct as you define it for your study. We have all been delighted to discover a new measure in the literature, with a name suggesting that it measures exactly what we needed, only to have our hopes dashed when we examined the measure's items and found that only a few (and certainly not the psychometrically validated scale scores) even came close to what we wanted to examine.

You should also be clear about whether your study will be about observable behavior in its own right (e.g., motor actions, verbal description of thoughts, physiological reactions) or behavior as an index of some hypothetical construct. This distinction has important implications for how you evaluate the measure's adequacy (Foster & Cone, 1995). If your concern is measuring differences in participants' actual behavior, your instruments should accurately reflect the participants' actions in the real world. If constructs are your interest, the fact that your measure accurately reflects "reality" is less important than that it correlates with other measures in the same theoretical net as your constructs. Because assessment of behavior is less familiar to most students than assessment of hypothetical constructs, in the paragraphs that follow we spend a bit more time on issues involved in assessing observable actions than on issues involved in assessing constructs.

If actual behavior is your interest, you will want a measure that reflects it directly. A direct measure assesses the behavior of interest at the time and place the behavior occurs naturally (Cone, 1978). In the marital conflict example discussed earlier, you might have chosen to focus on verbal forms of conflict. If so, you will identify specific vocal responses that constitute conflict as you view it.

What Assessment Method Will You Use?

One method to assess the occurrence of specific vocal responses that indicate conflict would be to ask your participants about them in an interview. Other assessment methods include administering an appropriate self-report measure, having others who know the couple well rate each member on verbal conflict, having the couple self-monitor (i.e., observe and record their conflict at home), and having trained observers directly observe the couple and record all instances of verbal conflict.

We can place these assessment methods on a continuum showing how close they are—that is, their degree of fidelity—to the specific behavior of interest (e.g., vocal responses defined as conflict). A measure has higher fidelity if it taps the actual behavior at the time and place of its natural occurrence. Normally, you will be interested in participant responses that occur in the natural environment; this is because you want your data to have real-world implications. In other words, you want your study to have as much external validity as possible. Direct (high-fidelity) measures enhance external validity. In contrast, asking someone to tell you about something they did at some other time and some other place is likely to produce lower quality data than observing their behavior as it occurs naturally.

Unfortunately, fidelity often correlates positively with cost. To have trained observers watch people in their natural environments is difficult. Direct observation involves spending hours developing and standardizing an observation code, finding and training observers, gaining access to participants' natural settings, observing them unobtrusively in those settings, and reducing observers' data to usable form (Cone, 1999). Compare this to developing a structured interview in a few hours and meeting with and administering it to someone. Even if you train interviewers, audio record the interviews, and produce transcripts from the tapes, you will still invest much less effort than if you had chosen the direct observation approach.

Even less cost is involved if you use a self-report measure. Rather than training interviewers, transcribing tape recordings, and scoring the transcriptions, why not merely ask your participants to respond to a limited set of items describing their behavior? Many a researcher, novice and otherwise, has seen virtue in this form of economy, particularly when considering limited budgets and the increased opportunity to administer surveys online (e.g., with free online survey software) to large samples (e.g., via Mechanical Turk). In fact, self-report measures are so common that they are generally the first form of assessment we think of when launching the search for objective measures. In our marital conflict example, we could ask our couple to respond "true" or "false" to statements asking whether they "argue about money," "raise their voices in front of others," and so on. When we do this, we make the important assumption that what the couple says corresponds to some degree with other important forms of behavior. Unfortunately, research looking at correspondence between reports of what people say they do and what they really do indicates that this assumption is often false (Bellack & Hersen, 1977; Fallon et al., 2017; Ramírez-Esparza et al., 2009; Shiffman, 2000).

Furthermore, it is now very clear that retrospective self-report is subject to a whole host of biasing factors, many of which are the product of normal cognitive processing (Stone et al., 2000). That is not to say that self-report measures do not relate to other measures. They often do, especially to reports on other self-report measures. We merely emphasize that the widespread practice of using self-reports as substitutes for more direct forms of assessment does not receive much support in the research literature. Indeed, many researchers openly acknowledge that self-reporting may not mirror other behavior. Unfortunately, only a few take the next step to determine whether it does.

We encourage you to consider alternatives to sole reliance on self-report measures. Informant ratings offer an improvement in objectivity, for example, because the data are provided by individuals with less personal investment in how their ratings are to be used. They are still indirect, however, as they rely on reports about behavior that occurred at other times and places. In addition, they have well-documented difficulties, some of which mirror those of self-reports, including inaccurate recollection, halo effect, generosity bias, and different interpretations of what is being measured, to name a few (e.g., Cairns & Green, 1979).

Self-observations (also sometimes called "self-monitoring," "ambulatory assessment," or "ecological momentary assessment") provide yet another alternative (Trull & Ebner-Priemer, 2014). These are more direct than interviews, self-reports, and ratings by others because they require participants to observe and record the occurrence of the behavior of interest and to do so at the time and place of its occurrence. To be sure, the objectivity of self-observation is hindered by the assessor and assessee being one and the same person. You can mitigate this problem by having participants focus on specific, very well defined responses. In addition, you can sometimes determine the accuracy of self-observation just as you can determine the accuracy of observation by others (see Johnston & Pennypacker, 1993, and Vazire & Mehl, 2008, for descriptions of how). Self-observations via cellphone are becoming quite common in sampling daily activities, interactions, moods, and the like (Harari et al., 2016; Mehl, 2017; Miller, 2012; Sandstrom et al., 2016; Smyth & Stone, 2003). Recent use of camera glasses in assessing adolescent aggression is a further example of technology-assisted observational methods (Wettstein & Scherzinger, 2015). Trull and Ebner-Priemer (2014) addressed many of the decisions and issues to consider in planning to use self-observation approaches.

Finally, we recommend you consider direct observation (Thompson & Borrero, 2011) as a way of assessing your variables. True, it can be costly, as we mentioned earlier. There are ways of using direct observations that are less costly than others, however. For example, rather than having trained observers travel to natural contexts and station themselves unobtrusively to collect data, you could use video cameras or cellphones to digitally record video or audio segments of the behavior for later analysis. For some field studies, the data might already be available via the ubiquitous presence of closed-circuit cameras. Observers can also watch participants in research rooms from behind one-way mirrors. Although such an approach removes the behavior from its natural context, it is still likely to yield higher quality data about actual performance than some of the less-direct methods just described. Digital records of the behavior provide a relatively permanent record that can be reviewed frequently to produce highly objective data. The recent use of digital devices such as the electronically activated recorder (Mehl, 2017) shows promise for observations made directly in natural contexts. Ecological momentary sampling using cellphones is seeing increased use (Kuntsche & Labhart, 2013), and smartphones and wearable devices are also appearing more often in the collection of naturally occurring behaviors of all sorts (e.g., Alisic et al., 2016). Mehl (2017) provided a helpful table summarizing the differences among these major technological advances for tapping behavior at the time and place of its natural occurrence.

As this discussion indicates, you can measure the constructs in your study in several ways. In the next section, we describe some sources you can consult to find existing measures. If you are lucky enough to find existing measures of your variables in the literature, you can avoid the work of developing and validating your own. You must ensure, of course, that each measure you locate is psychometrically sound and that its soundness generalizes to your planned use.

We said earlier that good measures are ones you choose wisely, are adequately direct, and produce scores that demonstrate appropriate psychometric qualities (e.g., reliability, validity) for your purposes and for the population you wish to assess. Note that we say "for your purposes" and "for the population you wish to assess." This underscores an important principle: Reliability and validity are conditional; they depend on the nature of the construct you wish to assess, your purpose, and your population. Test–retest reliability of .60 over 2 weeks may be fine for a state measure like mood but not for a measure of a presumably stable trait like intelligence. A measure of depression may have content validity that is adequate as a screening measure but inadequate if its purpose is diagnosis or treatment monitoring. A measure shown to have good predictive validity for assessing satisfaction in straight couples may not do as well for gay couples.

Next, we review important psychometric characteristics and offer suggestions and minimum criteria for evaluating measures you might be considering. We assume that you have some familiarity with test construction and measurement theory, although you might not have thought about them in the context of your thesis or dissertation project. The literature provides many excellent treatments of these issues (Clark & Watson, 2016; Cooper et al., 2012; Furr, 2018; Urbina, 2014).

What Is the Reliability of Scores From Potential Instruments?

Regardless of one's measurement perspective, the essential criterion for any measuring instrument, whether in the physical or behavioral sciences, is that its data should be reliable (i.e., reproducible). Over the years, measurement scholars have defined different forms of reliability (Furr, 2018; Peters, 2014; Urbina, 2014). You have heard of these before: interrater (scoring) reliability, test—retest (temporal) reliability, alternate form reliability, internal consistency, and so on. In 1972, Cronbach and colleagues proposed consolidating various forms of reliability under the rubric of generalizability theory. Essentially, they argued that different types of reliability all have to do with the diverse ways in which one may generalize the data from a measuring device. Although there have been surprisingly few appearances of generalizability theory applications in the literature since Cronbach et al.'s classic 1972 paper, more recent treatments by Gao and Harris (2012), Wiley et al. (2013), and Clauser and Clauser (2016) illustrate its continued importance and utility for a thorough understanding of the measurement issues in serious research.

The diverse ways of viewing the reliability of scores from measuring instruments differ from one another conceptually and practically. As a result, it is not informative to say in your Method section that you chose a particular instrument because it is reliable. Indeed, it is not technically correct to say so, because it is the scores on a measure, rather than the measure itself, that have certain psychometric properties (Thompson, 2003). The statement to make is that you chose the instrument because its scores have the psychometric characteristics necessary for your own research. To make this assessment is not easy, if it is done correctly. It requires a clear understanding of your subject matter and of just how you plan to study it. For example, if you are studying a psychological construct, different psychometric issues will come up than if you are studying behavior from a natural science perspective (Foster & Cone, 1995; Johnston & Pennypacker, 1993).

If you are studying a psychological construct, what are your assumptions about it? Is it supposed to be relatively consistent across time? across situations? Is it a relatively unitary construct or one made up of multiple dimensions? Is it best revealed in the verbal behavior of the participant or in motor or physiological responses? Your answers to these and other questions will bear on the types of psychometric information to examine when selecting among possible measures. Ideally, you will be able to identify the information you need in advance, select a measure whose scores provide this information, and present the information to support your choice in your Method section. At the very least, you should say more than that the measure has adequate evidence supporting the reliability and validity of its scores for your population and purpose. It is good to say first that, for your purposes, "the following types of reliability data are needed." Then state what these types are and document their existence for your measure. Finally, repeat the process for validity, a subject to which we now turn.

What Is the Validity of Your Prospective Instruments?

In addition to producing scores on your variables in consistent ways, you want these scores to mean something. Whether they do turns on the evidence for their validity. An instrument may produce highly reliable data that do not relate to anything. In other words, you may have a measure with reliable scores that are not meaningful. Incidentally, contrary to what you might occasionally see in textbooks, the reverse is not possible within the context of classical measurement theory. To be valid, scores must be reliable. What we mean by "validity" is the extent to which scores on a measure relate to scores on other measures. This is more general than the hackneyed definition that scores on a measure are valid if they measure what they are supposed to measure. They may not do this at all well and still have a great deal of validity in the larger sense meant here.

As with reliability, scores may show diverse types of validity. A measure has *face validity* if it looks to participants like it is appropriate for the purposes at hand. *Content validity* refers to how well the measure samples the universe of content relevant to the construct or behavior being assessed, omits irrelevant content, and contains a balance of indicators of the construct (Haynes et al., 1995). Thus, item selection, category definitions, and so on are key issues. Content validity is often assessed formally by expert judgments.

Scores have *construct validity* if they enter relationships required by the theory underlying the construct they presumably reflect. They have *convergent validity* if they relate to other ways of assessing the same behavior or construct. They have *discriminant validity* if they do not relate to measures from which theory would require them to be independent. They have *discriminative validity* if they produce expected mean differences between groups.

Criterion-related validity refers to the extent to which scores can be used for their intended purposes. Scores on a measure have criterion-related validity if they allow prediction of scores on other measures, usually of a practical variety. If scores on the criterion are available at the same time as scores we are validating, we refer to *concurrent validity*. If the scores are obtained at a future date, we refer to *predictive validity*.

Which of these types of validity will be necessary for the scores on your measures? Why are these particularly appropriate?

As with reliability, the types of validity you need to show depend on the nature of your subject matter, your population, and the specific research questions you are pursuing. If you are studying a psychological construct (e.g., hostility, narcissism, bigotry, altruism), you need evidence of content and construct validity, at a minimum. For example, if your study deals with bigotry, it will examine relationships between bigotry and some other variables. What is the source of these anticipated relationships? The correct answer is, someone's theory concerning bigotry. To test the relationships properly requires use of a measure of bigotry that meaningfully taps the construct as it is understood in the relevant theoretical writings. This meaningfulness resides in the research literature dealing with the measure's construct validity.

If your subject matter is behavior, especially as studied from a natural science perspective, you may not be especially concerned with construct validity as we describe it here. Instead, you will be more likely to focus on the content of the measure. You will want to be satisfied that it contains stimuli likely to set the occasion for samples of behavior that are representative of larger populations of that behavior that are not feasible for you to study directly. Moreover, you will want to know the extent to which the behavior produced by the instrument is representative of what you might expect to see at other times or in other places. We discussed how well data generalize to other assessment occasions as *temporal stability*. How well data might represent behavior in other contexts deals with their generalizability across settings (Cone, 1978). For example, if you observe positive verbal interchanges between spouses in the laboratory, are they representative of similar observations made in the home? As with our prior discussion of reliability, different forms of validity can be conceptualized in terms of generalizability theory. Clauser and Clauser (2016) provided excellent examples of generalizability theory in educational measurement that have broader application in research involving any form of behavior assessment.

As with reliability, it is not enough to state in your Method section that your measure is valid. Instead, state the types of validity or facets of generalizability that are important for your purposes and then provide evidence that they exist for your particular scores. You will most certainly do this if your research involves a validity study itself. This is because to make the case for doing the research, you will have provided an extensive review of the validity evidence for scores on the device you plan to use. Any study needs this scrutiny, however. You always need to know whether a measure assesses the variable of interest and whether it does so consistently for populations like the one you intend to study. If this vital information is lacking, it is extremely hard to interpret your research findings. For example, if your study involves young Black adolescents but your proposed measures have been validated only for White adults, it will be impossible to determine whether any unexpected findings (or lack of findings) are due to unexpected or no relationships among your constructs of interest or simply to idiosyncrasies of what may turn out to be an invalid measure for your study.

You will find information about the psychometric properties of scores produced by a measure in four places: (a) manuals describing the measure, (b) chapters or review papers evaluating the measure, (c) papers specifically evaluating the psychometric properties of the measure, and (d) papers using the measure. Be aware that the last of these may not mention in the abstract or introduction that psychometric data are presented; because this is not the principal focus of the study, these data are likely to be hiding in the Method section. In addition, some studies that do not even mention psychometric issues may provide findings relevant to validity. For example, repeated findings that self-report measures of anxiety and depression correlate highly have cast doubt on the discriminant validity of scores on these measures and have contributed to theoretical reconceptualization of these constructs (see Barlow, 2000; Barlow et al., 2004).

LOOK BROADLY FOR APPROPRIATE MEASURES

We have described the basic assessment methods you can use to operationalize the variables in your research. We have also discussed important characteristics that good instruments have. Where do you look for such instruments? If you are working in an active research area, you will probably use measures that are common to it, and often measures that your mentor or lab are already using. If you are braving new frontiers, the existing literature may not make clear just what the best measures are.

Several published compendiums provide valuable information about assessment instruments. The Buros Center for Testing at the University of Nebraska (https://buros.org/) houses perhaps the longest running and most extensive collection of measure descriptions and reviews. Its best-known publication is the triennial *Mental Measurements Yearbook*, which has been around since 1938 (Carlson et al., 2017). The latest volume describes hundreds of tests of various types, and more than 10,000 test reviews provide commentary on their psychometric adequacy. *Tests in Print*, also produced at the Buros Center, includes listings of all commercially available tests and is good for locating addresses and journal articles relevant to a measure (Anderson et al., 2016). In addition, it includes information about a test's purpose, individuals for whom it is appropriate, and administration times. The *Mental Measurements Yearbook With Tests in Print Internacional* combines into a single database the *Yearbook*, *Tests in Print*, and *Pruebas Publicadas en Español*, which contains descriptions of more than 600 Spanish-language tests (Schlueter et al., 2018). Test Reviews Online is a fee-based service that provides the monthly updates and reviews appearing in the *Yearbook* and allows users to download reviews and descriptive details of more than 2,800 tests. For a brief video describing these resources, see https://www.ebscohost.com/academic/mental-measurements-yearbook.

Many other sources also provide detailed information about a range of assessment methods and measures. We provide several examples here, but be aware that new measures are being developed and validated all the time. Even the classic instruments that are still in use may have revised items or scoring criteria. These sources are useful starting points, but be sure you consult with the current literature, your mentor, and other experts in the area in order to select the most appropriate measures for your needs.

If you are working with a clinical population or variables common to such populations, the *Handbook of Clinical Rating Scales and Assessment in Psychiatry and Mental Health* (Baer & Blais, 2010) might be worth consulting. This volume includes information about the most commonly used measures for psychiatric conditions, including measure descriptions, psychometric information, and recommendations for use, along with scoring instructions and photocopy-ready versions or links to online versions of many measures. Likewise, the two-volume *Measures for Clinical Practice and Research* (Corcoran & Fischer, 2013) provides information on hundreds of measures for use with adults, couples, families, and children. The volume editors describe and review each measure, provide recommendations for use, and include complete copies of the measures. Additional books provide information about measures specific to problem areas, such as anxiety (e.g., Antony et al., 2001), depression (e.g., Nezu et al., 2000), anger (e.g., Ronan et al., 2014), or children's social skills or behavior at school (e.g., Kelley et al., 2003; Nangle et al., 2010).

If you are planning to use a more behaviorally focused measure, Haynes and Heiby's (2004) *Behavioral Assessment* (Volume 3 of the *Comprehensive Handbook of Psychological Assessment*) can help. Additionally, although now a bit dated, Hersen and Bellack's (1988) *Dictionary of Behavioral Assessment Techniques* gives descriptions and includes reviews and references to papers in which an original instrument can be found. Do not be put off by reference to "behavioral" in the books' titles. They include many instruments that would hardly be considered any different from traditional, trait-oriented forms of assessment long familiar to social scientists everywhere.

An excellent database available in many academic libraries is PsycTESTS, an extensive collection of information about instruments appearing originally in the scholarly literature. The measures are taken from journals that are included in the PsycINFO database. PsycTESTS currently includes approximately 40,000 unique tests, organized into 15 instrument types and 30 categories. It is easy to use. When you enter the name of the variable you are studying—for example, "compassion fatigue"—a list of articles appears showing examples of research involving assessment devices that include your construct. You can also search PsycINFO and/or Google Scholar for the same construct. These entries will deal with compassion fatigue broadly, including research on and treatment for it, as well as other relevant information. If you enter "compassion fatigue assessment," you get a narrower array of citations, all of which refer to some aspect of assessing the construct. As described in Chapter 6, PsycINFO can be especially useful in locating current literature on the variables relevant to your project and may even alert you to free measures you can use.

A particularly useful source, if you are doing research in the health fields and related disciplines (e.g., psychosocial sciences, behavioral medicine, social work, occupational therapy, physical therapy, speech-language therapy), is the Health and Psychosocial Instruments (HaPI) database. HaPI includes information on unpublished instruments, has entries for more than 8,000 measures, and is updated quarterly. HaPI is available in many libraries that subscribe to the service. Most of the measures are relevant to behavioral medicine and assess such variables as pain, quality of life, and medication efficacy. Although the database does not provide copies of the measures themselves, it does provide a bibliography of instruments you can order. Note that you will need copyright permission to use any of the instruments found in HaPI.

Another useful source of information on tests that are not commercially available is the Educational Testing Service (ETS) database. The ETS Test Collection (https://www.ets.org/test_link/about) is said to be the largest in the world, including 25,000 tests and other measurement instruments developed from the early 1900s to the present. Although many of these assess cognitive and other school-related variables, others (e.g., Achenbach–Lewis Symptom Checklist) are included as well.

KNOW WHAT TO DO IF VITAL PSYCHOMETRIC INFORMATION IS UNAVAILABLE

Suppose you have selected your measure and searched high and low for evidence to support its psychometric adequacy with your population. You have not found any. Suppose further that no alternative measures exist that you can use. If you have understood the material presented earlier, you know the types of psychometric qualities that your measure needs to show. What do you do if information about them is not available? There are several choices: (a) ignore their absence and proceed anyway, (b) develop the needed information yourself before starting your project, (c) start your project and pilot test the measures as a first order of business, or (d) embed checks for reliability and validity within your larger study.

We do not advise the first of these. If what is missing would be relatively easy to provide yourself (e.g., scoring reliability for transcripts of structured interviews, temporal stability over short periods of time, discriminant validity from major pervasive constructs [e.g., SES, academic achievement, social desirability]), you could obtain the relevant data in a preliminary study involving participants like the ones you plan to use in your actual study. This could be done before starting the main study or as a first order of business after starting it. If you find that your measures hold up, great—you can push ahead to study your substantive research questions. If there are deficiencies, depending on what they are, you may be able to mitigate their influence by using a larger number of participants, averaging data across multiple observers rather than a single one, and so on. Finally, you may be able to tweak your design to examine whether the missing information is really that critical. For example, if you are doing a treatment study and lack data on the stability of your measures, you might include an untreated control group that gets assessed with these measures over a pre- to posttreatment interval comparable to that of your treated participants.

Previously we discussed the important psychometric characteristics that good measures have. We did not go into the details of how to establish these if they are not already known for the instruments you use. In the next few sections, we review these briefly. Space does not permit the in-depth treatment you have been (or will be) exposed to in measurement courses. To review these concepts more thoroughly, you may consult the texts used in such a course (see the Supplemental Resources at this chapter's end).

Reliability

Scoring Reliability

A reliably scored instrument is essential to any research. Even if the literature shows that your measure was reliably scored in other research, you should provide evidence that it is reliably scored in your study as well. If you are using a self-report method, have a second person independently score some portion—say, a randomly selected 25%—of the answer sheets. If the two sets of scores don't agree, identify the problem and correct it. If you are using structured interviews, you should have coders independently score tapes or transcripts of sample interviews selected specifically for training. Once the coders reach satisfactory levels of agreement, they are ready to score interviews obtained in the study itself. All of these should be recorded, if possible. As mentioned in Chapter 7, at least 20% should be scored by a second coder. If there are problems with the 20% to 25% that you check, retraining or increased incentives for accuracy might be needed.

If you are using rating-by-other or direct observation methods, the logic just covered with interviews applies to the scoring reliability of these data as well. You will have to compare scores obtained from independent raters or observers before and during the formal data collection process to assure yourself of the scientific adequacy of your instruments. There is an extensive literature dealing with methods for doing this. Be sure to review treatments such as those listed in the Supplemental Resources at the end of this chapter before you embark on a project involving rating-by-other or direct observation procedures. Although we do not go into the details here, we do call your attention to an important point to consider when checking scoring reliability. Use a level of precision in your reliability checking that is at least as precise as the scores you will use in your analyses. For example, if you are using total scores on a measure of social cues awareness to assign participants to groups, it is important to show that independent scorers produced comparable total scores. They may not agree at the individual item level, but their scores should lead to the same assignments.

If you are using a direct observation coding system, consider supplementing it with video or audio recordings to produce permanent records of the participants' behavior. This is becoming easier with the increasing use of smartphones in behavioral research (cf. Harari et al., 2016). With apps such as Behavior Connect, multiple observers working independently can code behavior and compare their data. Again, it is important to select some percent-age of the observations randomly and calculate agreement.

If you obtain data from an archival source (e.g., patient files in a hospital, records from a county courthouse, personnel records of teacher performance), do not assume you can ignore scoring reliability. You might think it is a routine matter, for example, to determine chronicity of schizophrenia by sub-tracting a person's date of first hospitalization from the current date. The file might have different dates of initial hospitalization depending on where you look in it, however. Or you or your assistants may not reliably perform the simple tasks of recording such a date or subtracting one date from another. Always check the accuracy of all steps in the production of data.

Temporal Stability

There are several steps you can take if temporal stability data for scores on your measure are necessary but not available. This is especially the case if your study involves pre- and postintervention comparisons. You have to control for the possibility of change occurring merely with the passage of time. One way to do this is to perform repeat administrations of the measure with a group of persons comparable to those selected for your research. Do this before beginning the study proper, using an interval (e.g., pre–post) equal to the interval that your participants will experience. Alternatively, you could include an untreated, assessment-only control group in your research design or use a more sophisticated design that includes such a group and others (e.g., Solomon four group). Another possibility involves repeated assessment before and after introducing your independent variable so that each participant serves as their own control for score changes that might occur merely with the passage of time.

Internal Consistency

A measure should tap a single variable (construct) consistently throughout the measures. For example, for a measure assessing depression, each of the measure's components should reflect depression and not anxiety, narcissism, or some other variable. If it does this, it can be considered homogeneous or unitary; in other words, its components (items) relate to one another (i.e., are correlated). Most instruments you find will have addressed this already. If the instrument was developed using item response theory, data will be available documenting its internal consistency.

In the not-too-distant past, internal consistency was represented by coefficient alphas (Cronbach, 1951) or one of the formulas (KR-20, KR-21) earlier identified by Kuder and Richardson (1937). Unfortunately, measures such as these reflect the intercorrelation among components while relying on both that correlation and the number of items (components) in the scale (Cortina, 1993). As Clark and Watson (2016) pointed out, internal consistency conceptually reflects correlations among the items. The number of items is irrelevant. It would be possible to obtain a high value for alpha or KR estimates by merely using a large number of items. In such a case, nothing can be said about the homogeneity of the instrument. The problem comes from thinking of traditional measures of internal consistency (i.e., alpha, KRs) as synonymous with homogeneity. Because their resulting values confound interitem relationships with the number of items involved, they are not suitable as homogeneity measures. A measure may be adequately reliable (e.g., alpha of at least .80) without uniformly tapping a construct at all points within it. The uniformity question has to be answered in other ways. You still need to show that your measure is internally consistent. Given that it is, however, you will need additional analysis to attribute this to the measure's homogeneity rather than to the artifact of its length.

Setting aside the issue of homogeneity and returning to the scale's internal reliability, you will be happy to know that traditional reliability estimates are among the easiest characteristics to establish for new instruments. For this reason, the measure you choose is likely already to have this vital information. However, if it does not and you want to proceed with your chosen measure anyway, here is what we suggest: Use a sample of participants that is large enough to permit you to factor analyze the scale after the fact. You could then develop scores for your participants on each of the emerging factors. The factors that are most conceptually consistent with your theoretical and practical understanding of your constructs would then be your dependent variables. Of course, there would be no norms or reliability or validity information for these newly developed scales. Moreover, a reasonable factor analysis requires a good-sized sample, as mentioned in Chapter 7. Depending on the number of items in your scale, this could mean 100 participants minimum, or double that if you want to replicate your factor structure. Of course, this number increases if your analysis involves more items or measures. For samples that are difficult or costly to collect, this may be a very impractical prelude to your thesis or dissertation! A better solution may be to collect pilot data on a smaller number of participants and check out your internal consistency using classical KR procedures before you begin, with the caveat that the homogeneity of your measure awaits further examination.

This discussion applies largely to the use of self-report and informant rating methods, but it is applicable to all assessment methods, at least on a conceptual level. Space does not permit us to wander into this interesting arena in any detail. Suffice it to say that reliability and homogeneity can be important regardless of method and of whether your subject matter is a psychological construct or actual behavior. For example, imagine you are performing direct observations of the predatory behavior of free-ranging tarantulas. You will be assuming the several specific responses you code are all members of the class of predatory behavior. If some deal with nesting, some with foraging, and some with reproduction, how will a single score be meaningful, and how will you show that it is?

Discriminant and Convergent Validity

We mentioned discriminant and convergent validity earlier but did not discuss them in detail. These types of validity are especially relevant when self-report measures are used to tap psychological constructs.

New self-report measures often lack discriminant validity. That is, they correlate substantially with already existing measures of pervasive individual difference variables. We cited research showing that some measures of anxiety and depression correlate too highly to be considered discriminably different phenomena. Additional pervasive variables include intelligence, SES, years of education, and the tendency to say socially desirable things about oneself. Purveyors of new measures must show that they are not simply additional ways of measuring these variables (Campbell, 1960). Because of the pervasiveness of the tendency to respond in socially desirable ways, for example, new self-report measures must be shown to be independent of this characteristic (Edwards, 1970). There are already plenty of good measures of social desirability in the literature, and we do not need another one. Make sure your scale has been correlated with this attribute and shown to be unrelated to it or at least to have only a modest relationship. In doing this, be alert to the fact that the different measures purported to assess social desirability (e.g., Crowne & Marlowe, 1960; Edwards, 1957; Wiggins, 1959) are not interchangeable (Edwards, 1990; Helmes & Holden, 2003).

If your instrument has not been shown to be independent of the tendency to present one's self in a positive light, you should address this in your research. The first way to do this is to reduce demand characteristics that may increase the likelihood of at least some kinds of biased self-presentation (e.g., make responding anonymous; see Paulhus, 1991, for additional suggestions). Another would be to include a measure of social desirability along with your other measures and compute the correlation between them yourself. If the correlation is nonsignificant, social desirability can be eliminated from the interpretation of your results. If there is a correlation, however, you first should consider what degree of relationship between social desirability and your measure you would expect on the basis of previous literature and theory. For example, depressed individuals are known to distort information in a negative direction (Beck et al., 1979), and therefore a negative correlation between self-reports of depression and social desirability might be expected and even tolerated. Of course, a very high correlation would make your measure suspect. If social desirability is not supposed to correlate with your measure, you may want to control for the effects of social desirability statistically using partial correlation or analysis of covariance procedures. You might also consider filtering out those participants with social desirability scores that are high enough to make the rest of their data problematic. Incidentally, although we are discussing social desirability in some detail, the requirement for independence applies just as importantly to the other pervasive characteristics (e.g., age, SES, years of education) we have mentioned.

Convergent validity is also important. Campbell and Fiske (1959) articulated the requirement for convergence across measures many years ago. Noting that scores on any instrument are, in part, a function of the characteristics of the instrument itself, these authors suggested using multitrait-multimethod (MTMM) matrices to sort out this method variance, establishing both convergent and discriminant validity in the process. Statistical approaches to analyzing MTMM matrices are available (e.g., Saris & Andrews, 2004), as are examples of its use (e.g., Crego & Widiger, 2016).

As with discriminant validity, the importance of convergent validity for measures of constructs cannot be emphasized enough. The structure of our language builds in relationships between concepts automatically. When we use language-based assessment instruments, constructs will likely relate to one another at least partially because of this shared structure. For this reason, the validity evidence for a measure should involve more than correlations resulting from the fortuitous use of common assessment methods. If there really is a construct underlying the scores on a given instrument, logic requires it to be assessable in more than one way. The reason for this is that if a single measure completely operationalizes a concept, the concept is no longer hypothetical. Because being hypothetical is a cardinal characteristic of psychological traits, without it one is not dealing with a trait. This is the basis for saying that relationships between assessment alternatives establish the convergent validity of the alternatives and extend the construct validity of the underlying psychological variable at the same time.

If convergent validity has not been established for your scores or with your population, you will have to address this in your own research. The simplest way to do this would be to provide alternative ways of assessing your variables and to compare these after you collect the data. If different methods correlate (i.e., if their data converge), you can use them interchangeably or in some combination in your data analyses. If they do not, the data from each may have to be treated separately, leading to some interesting material for your Discussion section.

Incidentally, by "alternative ways of assessing your variables," we are not referring to a second self-report measure, a second informant rating, and so on. Self-report data require supplementation with data from other assessment methods—for example, independent informants or direct observation. Sometimes collateral data sources can be used effectively. If, for example, self-reports of drinking are one of your measures, you might compare these with reports from an informant such as a spouse, roommate, or friend (Allen & Wilson, 2003). Or you might use an unobtrusive measure such as a transdermal sensor (Leffingwell et al., 2013) or the number of empty beer cans or liquor bottles in the trash (Webb et al., 1966). Some behaviors have direct products or traces that can be used for corroboration. Self-reported homework completions or time spent working on one's dissertation are obvious examples. Look at problems completed correctly or pages written to support the verbal measure. Wearable digital instruments are a good source of collateral data to support self-reports of exercise and time spent in different locations (e.g., library, theater, classroom).

Generalizability Across Settings

If you are assessing a person's performance (e.g., homework completion, marijuana smoking), you will be especially concerned about whether data collected with your anticipated measure in one setting can be safely generalized to others. Most likely, you will have to examine this issue yourself. Alternatively, you could rely on one of the most used caveats among researchers that "caution should be exercised in interpreting these results, because it is not known whether participants would have performed similarly in their home [classroom, neighborhood, and so forth]." If your study is an applied one, you are probably doing it in the setting of eventual interest anyway. In such a case, if the act of assessing itself is nonreactive, setting generalizability is irrelevant. If you are dealing with psychological constructs, their cross-setting generality is often assumed and rarely tested. This is an issue worth pondering, especially if you are concerned with the ecological validity of your research.

ADAPT OTHERS' MEASURES WITH CAUTION

What if you wish to adapt others' measures for your own purpose? For example, you may find a potentially promising scale for assessing compassion for people living on the streets that was developed using college students in a course on introductory sociology. You want to use it in your master's thesis research in your criminology program to assess compassion in police officers interacting with such people. Moreover, you want to relate this variable to other characteristics of the officers, including their time on the force, education level, and attitudes toward community policing.

Will the measure's original psychometric properties still be relevant? You cannot be sure. Police officers represent a different population from college undergraduates. How much will variables such as social desirability and item reading level affect the internal consistency and convergent validity of the measure? Logically, the less you change the variables involved in the development of an instrument, the more you should be able to assume its properties will remain robust across subsequent applications.

As another example, suppose that, in the interest of minimizing participant effort in your study, you decide to save time by administering only certain subscales (facets) from the factors of the Big Five Inventory (John & Srivastava, 1999). There are numerous facets within each of the five dimensions of the inventory. In other words, they are not homogeneous. For example, within the extroversion–introversion dimension, one finds positive emotions and warmth. Could you reasonably expect your subscale scores to be a faithful representation of scores for the larger dimension? If you are lucky, data from participants who are like yours will already be available on this question. If not, you can gather some data to assess whether this is so. One way to do this would be to conduct a pilot study. You could test whether scores on the shortened and full versions of extroversion—introversion are correlated (as when assessing alternate form reliability). And, as indicated previously, you could build the use of other measures to assess the validity of the altered instrument into your research project. Dodeen and Al-Darmaki (2016) provided an example of the use of item response theory to create a shorter form of a longer marital satisfaction measure. IRT provides an alternative for you to consider should you need to develop an alternate form of a measure or compare it with scores on the larger one from which it was extracted.

AVOID COMMON ERRORS IN EVALUATING AND SELECTING MEASURES

Several common errors pervade descriptions of measuring devices. Avoid these. First, do not assume that the name of an instrument captures what it measures. Many fledgling and even some experienced researchers fall into the trap of assuming the name of a measure indicates what it assesses. This is not necessarily the case, as we discussed earlier in this chapter. Examine the content of the measure carefully; it may be misnamed, at least as you understand the construct being assessed. This is an error in logic long known in psychology as the "jingle fallacy" (Kelley, 1927).

To assume that a name mirrors a measure's content is especially a problem with questionnaires that have subscales derived using factor analysis. Putting it simply, a factor analysis looks at the data, sorts out what is most closely associated with what, and shows the investigator what these relationships are mathematically. The investigator determines which items hang together closely enough to be considered a factor. Item content has nothing to do with the mathematics of factor analysis; items that load on the same factor may (or may not) tap widely different content. The investigator then must inductively figure out a name that seems to fit the items. Unless the original creator of the measure used confirmatory factor analysis to test whether a group of conceptually related items hang together, the name is the investigator's a posteriori creation, often influenced by their a priori ideas about what was important. Do not assume the name reflects scale content adequately (i.e., in the same way others would name it) or that the scale captures the construct adequately.

Second, do not assume that a significant correlation is a high correlation. Many researchers make this and other mistakes when describing their findings. A significant correlation between two measures of the same construct may or may not support the validity of the measure being investigated. The magnitude of the correlation, not its statistical significance, is important. For example, if the correlation between a self-report measure of work productivity and a mechanical count of the number of objects actually assembled is .20 and is significant at $p < .05$, the measures have only 4% of their variance in common. Does this really indicate that one can be substituted for the other?

Third, do not assume that a self-report measure assesses behavior because it correlates with other self-report measures. As we indicated earlier, Campbell and Fiske (1959) long ago pointed out the fallacy of assuming that correlations between measures that used the same method to assess the same construct prove the validity of a new measure. Method variance could explain the results. When two self-report measures involve the same method, their scores may be related because of this shared approach to assessment. The true test of an indirect measure of behavior (e.g., self-report) is whether it correlates with a more direct assessment of the same phenomenon (e.g., counts of positive self-statements or compliments). In general, correlations between different methods for assessing the same thing should exceed those between different things assessed with the same method.

Fourth and finally, avoid single-item measures. For this suggestion, we stop short of our "do not" admonition, although this is still our preference. Single-item measures of any construct or behavior are notoriously unreliable. Nonetheless, beginning researchers (and sometimes even experienced researchers) often persist in assuming that a participant's affirmative answer to the question "Was either of your parents an alcoholic?" is an effective way to classify the individual as one who grew up in an alcoholic family! Single-item measures are especially a problem when measuring participants' characteristics either for descriptive or classification purposes (e.g., as an independent variable). Happily, this is easy to avoid when designing your own study—you simply select the best measures for your constructs and population of interest. However, if you will be using an existing data set, an increasingly common practice that allows researchers to share resources to amass very large samples, you may have to rely on a single item for one or more of your variables. Proceed with great caution. Again, single-item measures are unreliable, are unlikely to have demonstrated validity for your purposes, and may end up negating any benefits of being able to use preexisting data (see Chapter 4 for additional discussion of archival data).

GET COPIES OF INSTRUMENTS

To examine the content of an instrument you are considering using, first obtain a copy of the measure. This often turns out to be surprisingly difficult. Journal articles rarely publish copies of measures, and although some are available from commercial publishers, many are not. To obtain a copy of a measure that interests you and that is not commercially available, contact the creator of the instrument and request one. Make sure to find out the person's current address. Professional directories and member listings of other professional organizations (e.g., Society for Research in Child Development,

Association for Psychological Science, American Speech-Language-Hearing Association) are updated regularly and should help you locate the individual. Often, the easiest way to find someone quickly is merely to do a Google search. When you find the person, request a copy of the instrument, and inquire whether it is copyrighted and by whom. If it is copyrighted, you must obtain permission in writing from the copyright owner to use the measure.

If you cannot find the measure's creator, if the creator fails to respond to your request, or if you just want to hedge your bets, find someone else who has used the measure in published research. This person must have found a copy of the measure, right? Ask your chair, too, about colleagues who might have used the instrument. Then track down the users and ask for a copy. Use your adviser's name (with permission) to enhance the chances that the person will respond to your request. Remember, however, that if you are having this much trouble locating a copy of the instrument, it is likely to be relatively unknown. This can mean there is little information about the critical psychometric characteristics we have discussed in this chapter.

Once you have the measure in hand, you will do well to consider whether it is really the best you can find for your study. As you examine it, assess whether it really seems to get at the variables as you view them. Briefly revisit the discussion of psychometric characteristics in this chapter, and be sure they are adequately represented in the instrument. This won't take long, because it is very likely its measurement qualities are adequate, or you wouldn't have chosen it in the first place. In addition to psychometric sufficiency, take time to address the practicality of using the instrument in your study. Put yourself in the role of participants for a moment: Are you being realistic about the participation load they'll experience? How long will participants have to be available? How much of that time will involve completing data collection instruments? Is the instrument's content likely to be interesting, boring, challenging, or threatening? Will you run any risk of scaring participants off so that they quit prematurely or fail to return for additional sessions?

If this review leads to "go for it" optimism on your part, great—get going! Collect some data! If your appraisal suggests that obvious or incipient problems may be lurking, deal with them now. Ask others (your adviser, committee members) for their input. Do they have similar concerns? Do they bring up ones you hadn't considered? You want to move ahead with the knowledge that you've silenced any obvious warning bells and can communicate competence and confidence to others who will be critical to the success of your project.

Selecting satisfactory instruments to use in collecting your data is a major step in advancing your research. The next consideration is what to do with the data when you have them. What statistical procedures will you use to establish whether your hypotheses are supported? Chapter 9 will help you answer this important question.

✓   **TO DO . . .**

SELECTING THE APPROPRIATE MEASURES

☐ Operationalize your variables.

☐ Know important aspects of potential instruments.

- Subject matter

- Assessment method

☐ Identify the forms of reliability prospective instruments will need for your study, and make sure the instruments you select have them:

- Interrater (scoring) reliability

- Test–retest (temporal) reliability

- Alternate form reliability

- Internal consistency (item) reliability

☐ Identify the forms of validity prospective instruments will need for your study, and make sure the instruments you select have them:

- Face validity

- Content validity

- Construct validity

- Convergent validity

- Discriminant validity

- Discriminative validity

- Criterion-related validity

- Concurrent validity

- Predictive validity

☐ Look broadly for appropriate measures, using the following sources:

- Measurement compendiums

- Computer-based databases

- Published literature

☐ Know what to do if vital psychometric information is unavailable:

- Scoring reliability (interrater reliability)

- Temporal stability

- Internal consistency (item reliability)

- Discriminant and convergent validity

- Generalizability across settings

☐ Adapt others' measures with caution.

☐ Avoid common errors in evaluating and selecting measures.

☐ Get copies of instruments, and comply with all copyright requirements.

SUPPLEMENTAL RESOURCES

General Measurement Textbooks and Articles

Butcher, J. N., Graham, J. R., Haynes, S. N., & Nelson, L. D. (Eds.). (1995). Special issue: Methodological issues in psychological assessment research. *Psychological Assessment, 7*(3).

Campbell, D. T., & Fiske, D. (1959). Convergent and discriminant validation by the multitrait-multimethod matrix. *Psychological Bulletin, 56*(2), 81–105. https://doi.org/10.1037/h0046016

Cronbach, L. J. (1990). *Essentials of psychological testing* (5th ed.). HarperCollins.

Furr, R. M. (2018). *Psychometrics: An introduction* (3rd ed.). Sage.

Nunnally, N. C., & Bernstein, I. H. (1994). *Psychometric theory* (3rd ed.). McGraw-Hill.

Thompson, B. (Ed.). (2003). *Score reliability: Contemporary thinking on reliability issues.* Sage. https://doi.org/10.4135/9781412985789

Urbina, S. (2014). *Essentials of psychological testing* (2nd ed.). Wiley.

Item Response Theory

DeMars, C. (2010). *Item response theory.* Oxford University Press. https://doi.org/10.1093/acprof:oso/9780195377033.001.0001

Dodeen, H., & Al-Darmaki, F. (2016). The application of item response theory in developing and validating a shortened version of the Emirate Marital Satisfaction Scale. *Psychological Assessment, 28*(12), 1625–1633. https://doi.org/10.1037/pas0000296

Embretson, S. E., & Riese, S. P. (2000). *Item response theory for psychologists.* Erlbaum.

Faulkner-Bond, M., & Wells, C. S. (2016). A brief history of and introduction to item response theory. In C. S. Wells & M. Faulkner-Bond (Eds.). *Educational measurement: From foundations to future* (pp. 107–125). Guilford Press.

van der Linden, W. J. (Ed.). (2016). *Handbook of modern item response theory: Three volume set.* CRC Press.

Questionnaire Methods (Self-Report, Ratings by Others)

DeVellis, R. F. (2003). *Scale development: Theories and applications* (2nd ed.). Sage.

Fink, A. G. (Series Ed.). (2003). *The survey kit* (2nd ed.). Sage.

Paulhus, D. L. (1991). Measurement and control of response bias. In J. P. Robinson, P. Shaver, & L. S. Wrightsman (Eds.), *Measures of personality and social psychological attitudes* (pp. 17–59). Academic Press. https://doi.org/10.1016/B978-0-12-590241-0.50006-X

Schwarz, N., & Oyserman, D. (2001). Asking questions about behavior: Cognition, communication, and questionnaire construction. *American Journal of Evaluation, 22*(2), 127–160. https://doi.org/10.1177/109821400102200202

Stone, A. A., Turkan, J. S., Bachrach, C. A., Jobe, J. B., Kurtzman, H. S., & Cain, V. S. (Eds.). (2000). *The science of self-report: Implications for research and practice.* Erlbaum.

Direct Observation

Bakeman, R., & Quera, V. (2011). *Sequential analysis and observational methods for the behavioral sciences.* Cambridge University Press. https://doi.org/10.1017/CBO9781139017343

Cone, J. D. (1999). Observational assessment: Measure development and research issues. In P. C. Kendall, J. N. Butcher, & G. N. Holmbeck (Eds.), *Handbook of research methods in clinical psychology* (2nd ed., pp. 183–223). Wiley.

Suen, H. K., & Ary, D. (2014). *Analyzing quantitative behavioral observation data*. Erlbaum. https://doi.org/10.4324/9781315801827

von Eye, A., & Mun, E. Y. (2005). *Analyzing rater agreement: Manifest variable methods*. Erlbaum.

Yoder, P. J., & Symons, F. (2010). *Observational measurement of behavior*. Springer.

Unobtrusive Measures

Webb, E. J., Campbell, D. T., Schwartz, R. D., & Sechrest, L. (1966). *Unobtrusive measures: Nonreactive research in the social sciences*. Rand McNally.

Self-Observation

Christensen, T. C., Barrett, L. F., Bliss-Moreau, E., Lebo, K., & Kaschub, C. (2003). A practical guide to experience-sampling procedures. *Journal of Happiness Studies, 4*(1), 53–78. https://doi.org/10.1023/A:1023609306024

Mehl, M. R. (2017). The electronically activated recorder (EAR): A method for the naturalistic observation of daily social behavior. *Current Directions in Psychological Science, 26*(2), 184–190. https://doi.org/10.1177/0963721416680611

Trull, T. J., & Ebner-Priemer, U. (2013). Ambulatory assessment. *Annual Review of Clinical Psychology, 9*, 151–176. https://www.annualreviews.org/doi/10.1146/annurev-clinpsy-050212-185510

Selecting the Appropriate Data Analysis Approaches

This chapter
- covers issues involved in selecting and planning data analyses
- provides guidelines for selecting appropriate statistics

Read thoroughly if
- statistics terrify you or your background in statistics is weak
- you have limited practice in matching the appropriate statistic to the research question

Skim or skip if
- you understand basic statistics very well and have conducted analyses using the statistics you plan to use
- you have consultation and reference sources lined up in case you get stuck

Nothing strikes terror into the heart of many beginning researchers like the word "statistics." Even students who breezed through required graduate statistics courses in rigorous training programs sometimes claim total ignorance of all things numerical when asked to select suitable statistics for their own research.

Why do even the best students sometimes have difficulty with this topic? Sometimes stats classes do not provide sufficient practice with the nuts and

https://doi.org/10.1037/0000161-009
Dissertations and Theses From Start to Finish: Psychology and Related Fields, Third Edition,
by D. J. Bell, S. L. Foster, and J. D. Cone

bolts of data analysis to build confidence. In addition, in less research intensive programs, a good deal of time may elapse between taking statistics classes and having primary responsibility for one's own analyses. Another problem is math anxiety, often fostered by early disparagement of one's math ability or failure experiences in mathematics classes (which may well have resulted from poor teaching and not poor student skill). Math anxiety, in turn, can lead students to avoid opportunities to use numbers and thus miss the chance to develop self-confidence in this area. Avoidance and a resulting lack of practice lead students to depend on others to select statistics for their projects. As a result, they never learn to become independent in this area.

This chapter helps nervous students sort out which analytic techniques are most suitable for their research design. We focus here on quantitative analytic methods; if your study calls for qualitative methods, we recommend that you review texts that cover the analytic methods that match the type of qualitative study you plan to conduct (e.g., Cooper, 2012). If your study is quantitative (or a mixed methods study, using a combination of qualitative and quantitative methods), we strongly recommend that you read this chapter and follow its suggestions *before* you complete your proposal instead of putting off the dreaded statistics questions until after you collect your data. That is why we place this chapter before the chapter on collecting the data, rather than after it. We have been faced too often with the unpleasant task of advising students who have already collected data that they have a statistical nightmare on their hands because they did not think about their analyses when they selected their measures and designed their study.

We assume that you would like to avoid this unfortunate situation. We also assume that you have taken the usual statistics courses and are at least generally familiar with different statistical techniques. Thus, in this chapter, we do not go into how to calculate, derive, or program specific analyses. Rather, we focus on a broad overview of several of the more common analytic approaches and what to consider when evaluating whether they are appropriate for your purposes. Moreover, we cover mainly statistics designed to examine either (a) differences between two or more discrete groups of individuals or (b) relationships among variables within a single group of individuals. For most of the strategies we discuss, we assume that your study involves independent (or predictor) and dependent (or criterion) variables that you are able to identify. The chapter also includes a brief discussion of model-testing analyses. Model-testing statistics may be appropriate if your study explores the underlying structure of a set of variables or examines a set of relationships among variables considered simultaneously.

We do not cover every one of the hundreds of statistical tests available or specialized approaches used in subdisciplines. Among the more common procedures we omit are contemporary psychometric techniques (e.g., item response theory, Rasch analysis), survival analysis, sequential analysis and other time-series procedures, meta-analytic techniques and specific statistics for calculating effect sizes, complex longitudinal analyses, and person-centered approaches (e.g., cluster analyses, growth mixture modeling). Nor do we cover all the controversies involved in using particular statistics. Instead, we survey widely used statistics and their potential role in your analytic plan. To the statistical sophisticate, our coverage will likely seem too simple. To the less experienced, it may seem quite complex, and the chapter will be just a glimpse of what you'll need to learn much more about.

Our goal in this chapter is to help you get some idea of potentially suitable statistics for your research—to provide enough information to put you on the right track. Once you select what might be right for your study, you will need to supplement the material here to make sure you understand the statistics you have selected and to ensure that they are the most appropriate for the analyses you plan. We start by looking at how you can prepare to deal with the statistical analyses you will be conducting.

BEEF UP YOUR STATISTICAL KNOWLEDGE EARLY

You will be able to select and conduct your analyses with less angst if this is not the first time you are working with statistics. If you are at an early stage in your graduate career, get involved in research and volunteer to take some responsibility for data analyses. Then, work closely with the faculty member or research director. Ask questions about why particular analyses are more suitable than others. Taking responsibility for handling the statistics of a study will force you to learn about parameters and options relevant to the statistics you use. It will also have the related practical benefit of serving as a starting point for your systematic desensitization—a common and effective treatment for statistics anxiety!

Another step to take is to start looking for statistics books and online resources that speak your language. Dozens of books cover every conceivable statistical topic. Some manuals and online instructions for major computer programs also provide good statistical information. In addition, many professors put descriptions of statistical methods online for students to use. Books, websites, and YouTube videos vary in complexity, focus, balance between mathematical and explanatory material, depth of coverage, and (sometimes) terminology and symbol systems. Consequently, different material will be more or less user friendly to you. Throughout this chapter, we refer to statistics books that we find useful (although even the three of us sometimes disagree about which statistics books we find most comprehensible!). We provide more suggestions at the end of this chapter. The key is finding resources that explain what you need in ways that you understand.

EXAMINE YOUR RESEARCH QUESTIONS AND CREATE YOUR ANALYSIS PLAN

The ultimate goal is to create an analysis plan with appropriate statistics matched to your specific research questions and goals of the analyses. As a first step in choosing suitable statistics, itemize the purposes you want your analyses to serve. Initially, you should specify clearly the various questions you want your statistics to answer. The logical place to start is with your research question and hypotheses. You need to go beyond these, however, because you will probably use statistics for more than just testing your hypotheses. For example, you may wish to do some preliminary analyses, such as examining the relationships among various dependent variables or checking that your experimental groups do not differ in demographic characteristics. You may also want to plan for some supplemental or follow-up analyses that will help you dig further into findings that emerge from your primary hypothesis testing. You may not be able to predict exactly what follow-up analyses you'll do, but you can start thinking about them. In the paragraphs that follow, we describe a series of steps for figuring out what kinds of analyses may meet your needs. We suggest that you proceed through the steps listed for each analysis you plan.

After you make a list of the questions or objectives you wish your analyses to address, make a list of each variable you plan to analyze to answer each research question and test each hypothesis you've listed. For example, if your question is, "What are the demographic characteristics of my sample?" list each piece of demographic data you plan to examine. Now, determine how you will score your measures to get a number for each participant on each variable. Do the same thing for your dependent and independent variables. You should wind up with a list of questions. Under each question will be a list of scores that will be involved in the analysis. Note that we said "scores," not "measures." It is not enough to say "Minnesota Multiphasic Personality Inventory," for example. The MMPI produces dozens of scores. Surely you won't look at every single one, so list the specific scores you plan to analyze.

Don't be surprised if you get confused. Confusion can be a signal that you need to clarify how each measure will generate numerical data. If so, pull out a copy of each instrument, make up mock data for a few participants, score the data, and examine the results. How many scores does each instrument produce? Which will you use in your analyses to address your hypotheses and research questions? Add these to your list. At the end of this process, you should have one list of questions you intend to answer with statistics and a second list of variables and associated scores that those statistics will use in one way or another.

As with our recommendation in Chapter 4 to chunk research questions into preliminary, primary, and sometimes supplemental hypotheses, it is also a good idea to separate analysis plans into two or three sections. At a minimum, we recommend a Preliminary Analyses section and a Primary Hypothesis-Testing Analyses section. You can also add a third Exploratory or Supplemental Analyses section if you know what these are likely to entail. Preliminary analyses are those you do to (a) examine the characteristics of your data, (b) examine the properties of your measures (e.g., reliability, validity), (c) check for potential confounding variables, (d) test the assumptions of the statistics you plan to use for testing your hypotheses, and (e) examine missing data. Hypothesis-testing statistics are just that: the statistics that allow you to examine whether your data support your main predictions. For the moment, just list the questions and hypotheses you wish to examine, along with the specific variables and scores you will use for each. Later, you can fill in the name of the specific analysis you will use to answer the question or test the hypothesis. Figure 9.1 shows portions of an analysis plan Bryan (2017) developed for her dissertation study looking at how gay and straight men responded to different types of body image–related talk expressed by other men.

Next, choose one of the questions you intend to answer with statistics. Indicate the specific independent and dependent variables (scores) involved in answering this question. For example, if your question is, "Do girls and boys with attention-deficit/hyperactivity disorder (ADHD) differ from those without ADHD in their recall of social material?" you would list diagnosis (ADHD vs. non-ADHD) and gender (scored as boy or girl) as the independent variables and the recall score as the dependent variable. Then, ask yourself, will this question be answered by comparing scores for groups of participants? Or will it be answered by relating scores on the different variables to one another in a single group of participants? With the example just given, the answer would be "yes" to the first question: You want to compare boys and girls, ADHD and non-ADHD groups, and so on. This comparison will require some sort of statistic that compares the scores the different groups obtain. Statistics that compare groups are typical of between-groups, within-groups, and mixed experimental and quasi-experimental designs.

Designs that require group comparison statistics use independent variables that the researcher defines in ways that require participants to fit into discrete groups—in this case, ADHD versus non-ADHD and girls versus boys. If you want to treat your participants as a single group and examine associations among scores, a correlational design might be most appropriate. This would be the case, for example, if the research question was, "Do health beliefs (assessed by a single score on a multi-item questionnaire) and social support relate to adherence to a medication regimen?" This research question treats all participants as a single group. They are not sorted into separate discrete groups. Participants' scores on social support and health belief measures will be related to their adherence scores. In correlational designs, variables can be continuous or discrete, although they are most often continuous. Correlational statistics (e.g., correlation, regression) are required to answer association or relationship types of questions.

Other research questions ask about the conditions under which certain phenomena operate. These are typically moderation questions: Does the presence of one condition or circumstance change how or whether another variable relates to, predicts, or causes an outcome? For example, Bryan (2017) hypothesized that gay men would react differently to body talk than straight men—in other words, that sexual orientation would moderate the relationship between exposure to comments about other men's bodies and self-reported state self-esteem. Moderation hypotheses most often involve looking at

FIGURE 9.1. Example Data Analysis Plan for a Dissertation on the Psychological Effects of Body Talk Between Gay and Heterosexual Men

I. Preliminary analyses

  A. Determine group differences between participants who pass versus do not pass the final manipulation check.

    1. Variables: Passing/not passing check, sexual orientation (heterosexual, gay). Statistic: Chi-square

    2. Variables: Passing/not passing check, assignment to experimental groups (muscle talk, fat talk, control). Statistic: Chi-square

  B. Determine internal consistency reliability of scales.

    1. Variables: State Self-Esteem Scale (SSES)—Appearance subscale, Body Image States Scale (BISS)—Total, Sociocultural Attitudes Towards Appearance Questionnaire (SATAQ–4)—Peer Societal Pressure subscale

    2. Statistic: Coefficient alpha

  C. Calculate descriptive statistics for dependent variables.

    1. Variables: SSES—Appearance subscale, BISS—Total, SATAQ–4— Peer Societal Pressure subscale, Linguistic Inquiry and Word Count (LIWC2015) body words, positive affect words, negative affect words

    2. Statistics: Means, standard deviations (*SD*s), frequency distributions

      a. Calculate for sample as a whole.

      b. Calculate for each experimental group.

  D. Calculate descriptive statistics for categorical demographic variables.

    1. Sex/gender, sexual orientation, gender reassignment, English speaking, handedness, vision, race/ethnicity, education level, occupation

    2. Statistic: Frequencies

  E. Calculate descriptive statistics for continuous demographic variables.

    1. Age, body mass index (BMI), years speaking English, years writing English

    2. Statistics: Means, *SD*s

  F. Assess correlations between DVs.

    1. Variables: SSES—Appearance subscale; BISS—Total; SATAQ–4— Peer Societal Pressure subscale; LIWC2015 body words, positive affect words, negative affect words

    2. Statistic: Pearson *r*

FIGURE 9.1. Example Data Analysis Plan for a Dissertation on the Psychological Effects of Body Talk Between Gay and Heterosexual Men (*Continued*)

G. Identify covariates.

   1. Calculate group equivalence of sexual orientation and experimental groups on potential confounds.

      a. Continuous variables

         i. Age, BMI

         ii. Statistic: 2 (Sexual Orientation) × 3 (Experimental Condition) ANOVA

      b. Categorical variables

         i. Ethnicity, education level

         ii. Statistic: Chi-square

            • Experimental Condition × Ethnicity, Experimental Condition × Education Level

            • Sexual Orientation × Ethnicity, Sexual Orientation × Education Level

   2. Calculate correlations between DVs and continuous demographic variables.

      a. Variables: SSES—Appearance subscale, SATAQ–4—Peer Societal Pressure subscale, BISS—Total, LIWC2015 body words, positive affect words, negative affect words correlated with BMI, age, other identified potential confounds

      b. Statistic: Pearson *r*

   3. Examine relationship between DVs and categorical demographic variables.

      a. Variables: SSES—Appearance subscale, BISS—Total, SATAQ–4—Peer Societal Pressure subscale, LIWC2015 body words, positive affect words, negative affect words, education, ethnicity

      b. Statistics: One-way ANOVAs with education as IV, each study dependent variable as DV; one-way ANOVAs with ethnicity as IV, each study dependent variable as DV

H. Check whether data meet assumptions of ANCOVA.

   1. Normality: Examine histograms

   2. Homogeneity of variance: Levene's test for equality of variance

   3. Reliability of covariates: Coefficient alphas (calculated above)

   4. Correlations among covariates: Scatterplots, Pearson *r*

   5. Linear relationship between covariates and DVs: Scatterplots

   6. Homogeneity of regression slopes: Scatterplots within cells

   7. Correlations between DV and identified covariates (see above)

(*continues*)

FIGURE 9.1. Example Data Analysis Plan for a Dissertation on the Psychological Effects of Body Talk Between Gay and Heterosexual Men (*Continued*)

II. Tests of hypotheses

    A. Hypothesis 1: Participants in appearance conversation conditions (muscle talk and fat talk) will report significantly higher rates of state body dissatisfaction (BISS) and significantly lower rates of appearance state self-esteem (SSES) than control participants (main effect of condition).

    B. Hypothesis 2: Significant results will be moderated by sexual orientation, with significant differences being larger among gay men than among heterosexual men.

        1. For BISS: IVs = sexual orientation, talk condition; DV = state body dissatisfaction (BISS—Total), covariates to be determined. Analysis = 2 (heterosexual vs. gay) × 3 (muscle talk, fat talk, neutral talk) ANCOVA

        2. For SSES: IVs = sexual orientation, talk condition; DVs = state self-esteem (SSES—Appearance subscale), covariates to be determined. Analysis = 2 (heterosexual vs. gay) × 3 (muscle talk, fat talk, neutral talk) ANCOVA

    C. Hypothesis 3: Participants in appearance conversation conditions (muscle talk and fat talk) will use more negative affect and more body-related words than control participants.

        1. For negative affect: IVs = sexual orientation, talk condition; DV = negative affect words, covariates to be determined. Analysis: 2 (heterosexual vs. gay) × 3 (muscle talk, fat talk, neutral talk) ANCOVAs

        2. For LIWC2015 body words: IVs = sexual orientation, talk condition; DV = body words, covariates to be determined. Analysis: 2 (heterosexual vs. gay) × 3 (muscle talk, fat talk, neutral talk) ANCOVAs

    D. Exploratory question: What is the relationship between internalization of peer pressure, state body dissatisfaction, and state self-esteem when gay and heterosexual men are exposed to body talk–related conditions (muscle talk, fat talk)?

        1. Analyses: correlations (*r*s) of peer SATAQ with BMI, BISS, and SSES.

        2. Use participants in muscle and fat talk conditions combined.

        3. Calculate for gay and straight groups separately.

Note. Portions of this figure were excerpted from the analysis plan created by Sophie Bryan (2017) for her dissertation proposal. Bryan examined gay and straight men's responses to experimental conditions in which they reviewed hypothetical advertisements and alleged chat room comments that involved talk about male models' (a) muscles or (b) body weight or (c) neutral comments not related to physique, then responded in writing to the comments and rated their own body satisfaction and self-esteem. The actual analysis plan listed details for scoring variables, examining missing data, and cleaning data; critical values and other information to examine for tests of assumptions; and references Bryan had consulted (with page numbers) for specifics on how to interpret analyses. From *The Psychological Effects of Body Talk Between Gay and Heterosexual Men* (unpublished doctoral dissertation proposal), by S. Bryan, 2017, California School of Professional Psychology. Copyright 2017 by S. Bryan. Adapted with permission.

interaction effects, so they require analyses that provide these. In essence, these hypotheses combine questions about relationships between variables (i.e., body talk and self-esteem) and questions about differences between groups (i.e., gay and straight men) in these relationships.

What if you are interested in questions that explore whether the relationship between two or more variables is explained by a third variable? These are mediation questions. Mediation effects are also sometimes called "indirect effects" (Tabachnick & Fidell, 2013). For example, suppose you propose that low academic achievement is related to high school dropout and that this relationship is explained by—that is, mediated by—students' poor attitudes toward school and by lack of connection to teachers and school activities. You will need an analysis that allows you to estimate both direct effects (e.g., academic achievement predicting dropout) and indirect effects (e.g., via attitudes and connectedness) of your variables. These typically involve more complex correlational statistics (e.g., hierarchical regression, path analyses) or model-testing analyses.

Model-testing analyses do just what they say they do—they test how well a researcher's model fits the obtained data. Structural equation modeling (SEM), confirmatory factor analysis, and mixture modeling are examples of model-testing statistical approaches. One principal way in which these techniques differ from other types of statistical analyses is in how they test hypotheses. In many group comparison and correlational statistics, the most common approach involves seeing whether you can reject the null hypothesis and looking for results that indicate that the test statistic differs significantly from zero. Model testing, in contrast, tests how well the model (theory) that you believe describes the relationships between variables actually fits the relationships between variables in your data set. The statistics reveal the extent to which your data are compatible with your theory or the model you designed.

Many students have trouble at this point because they have not completely worked out their design. Some research topics can be approached with either a group comparison or a correlational design. Suppose, for example, you are interested in whether children with high IQs experience more problems with their peers than do children with lower IQs. You could study this in two ways: (a) collect IQ scores and peer interaction scores and examine the relationship between them (i.e., correlate them), or (b) sort children into two or more discrete IQ groups (e.g., high IQ and average IQ) and look at differences between the groups in their peer interactions using a group comparison statistic.

If you are not certain which you are doing, look again at the design section of your proposal (see Chapter 7) and clarify what you intend to do. Correlational designs are often most appropriate when you conceptualize your independent variables as natural continua (e.g., intelligence) or if you wish to examine the best combinations of independent variables to predict a single dependent variable. Some researchers also hold that correlational designs are more appropriate than group comparisons when you do not manipulate your independent variables. In addition, creating groups by dichotomizing or trichotomizing continuous measures and then using group comparison instead of correlational statistics results in loss of statistical power when relationships between variables are linear (Kraemer, 2013). Group comparison designs are more appropriate than correlational designs when the independent variables are natural categories (e.g., ethnicity, gender) or are based on variables combined in a nonlinear fashion (e.g., psychiatric diagnosis, which is usually based on the presence or absence of several symptoms). Group comparisons are also generally more appropriate when you manipulate the independent variable, as with an experimental or treatment outcome study.

Some researchers find it helpful to make a drawing or graph showing what they expect to find as an aid in selecting statistics. Suppose your research question is, "Do school dropouts differ from students who graduate in their experience of connection with their teachers, and does this vary for male and female students?" You might make a graph like that in Figure 9.2 hypothesizing one relationship you expect. This graph clearly shows that you have discrete groups and you expect them to differ in scores assessing relationships with teachers. This also shows a moderator relationship—you expect that gender moderates the association between dropout and relationships with teachers.

Now let's change the question slightly. Suppose you want to study the relationship between academic achievement and relationships with teachers. You think that the relationship will vary depending on how much the youth have been a victim of bullying and that a positive relationship with teachers will protect victimized youth from declines in academic achievement.

FIGURE 9.2. Figure Depicting Hypothesized Mean Differences Between High School Dropouts and Completers

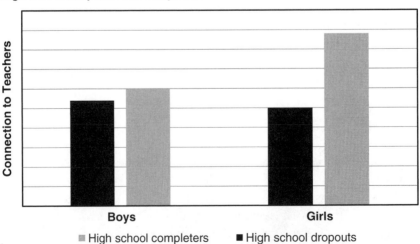

Note. The figure shows that the student proposes that the difference between high school dropouts and completers depends on gender. The most likely analysis for this graph is an analysis of variance.

FIGURE 9.3. Figure Depicting Hypothesized Relationship Between Connection to Teachers and Academic Achievement of Youth Who Have and Have Not Been Victims of Bullying

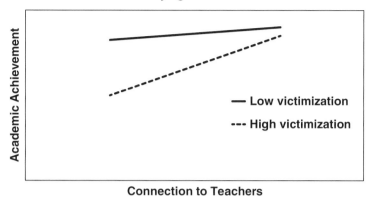

Note. The figure shows that connection to teachers is more strongly related to achievement for youth who have been bullied than for those who have not. The most likely analysis for this figure is multiple regression, with the interaction between victimization and connection to teachers included as a predictor.

Here, you are testing moderation: The strength of the relationship between achievement and teacher connection depends on how much the youth have been bullied. To show this, you might draw something like Figure 9.3. Like Figure 9.2, this figure shows a moderation relationship, but all the variables are continuous. Because it is difficult to depict a relationship among three continuous variables in a two-dimensional space, you look at what you might expect at high and low levels of the moderator variable (in this case, bullying).

Let's change the scenario yet again. Suppose you want to ask whether lack of connection to teachers and poor attitudes toward school are related to low academic achievement. You might draw something like Figure 9.4. As this figure illustrates, you do have multiple predictors but are not proposing moderation.

FIGURE 9.4. Figure Depicting Hypothesized Contribution of Connection to Teachers and Attitudes Toward School as Predictors of Achievement

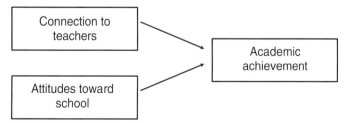

Note. The figure shows that both connection to teachers and attitudes toward school are expected to make independent contributions to achievement. The most likely analysis for this figure is multiple regression.

One final example: Let's suppose you want to look at some of the same variables, but in a more complex way. You propose that low academic achievement is related to whether a youth drops out of or completes high school, and that this relationship is partially but not completely explained (or mediated) by students' lack of connection to teachers. You would draw a model of how these variables relate. Figure 9.5 shows a diagram of this mediation model.

Figures can be simple, like those here, or much more complex. Visually oriented students often find them very helpful in clarifying their thinking. In addition, very complex diagrams of relationships can be a clue that you are trying to do too much in one study. It's wonderful that you can see how the big picture might operate, but consider whether this is a manageable dissertation for you. If not, you may need to focus on more circumscribed elements of the picture.

Another thing to figure out is which of your dependent variables are suitable for parametric statistics. Parametric statistics involve the assumption that the underlying distribution of scores in the population you are sampling is normal (particular parametric tests have additional requirements). Examples of parametric statistics are analysis of variance (ANOVA), multiple regression, Pearson r product–moment correlations, and t tests. A common rule of thumb is that ordinal and categorical dependent variables cannot meet these assumptions and should be analyzed using a nonparametric approach. When dealing with continuous data, look at parametric analyses first. If the characteristics of your data violate the assumptions of the parametric analysis, you may need to consider nonparametric alternatives (e.g., logistic regression instead of linear multiple regression). This is especially true if the analysis is not robust (i.e., does not react well) to your particular violations of its assumptions and if you cannot minimize the impact of these violations (e.g., by data transformations).

The choice between parametric and nonparametric analyses is usually determined by the nature of your dependent variable. Examine each dependent variable one by one. Not all variables have the same characteristics. A common error, for example, is to assume that you can use the same analysis to test whether two or more experimental groups are equivalent on age,

FIGURE 9.5. Figure Depicting Connection to Teachers as a Partial Mediator of the Relationship Between Academic Achievement and Dropping Out of School

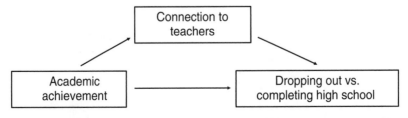

Note. The most likely analysis for this figure is path analysis or structural equation modeling.

ethnicity, gender, years of education, and other demographic variables. Age and years of education are usually analyzed with parametric statistics because they are continuous dependent variables. Gender and ethnicity are usually examined with nonparametric statistics because they are categorical dependent variables. Similarly, you may use entirely different statistics to answer different questions in your study. Don't assume one test will do it all.

At this point, you should have a list of questions you will use statistics to answer. You should also have a list of independent and dependent variables for each question and the scores from the measures you want to analyze. For each dependent variable, indicate whether a parametric or nonparametric test is more appropriate. Finally, indicate whether the question involves grouping the participants and comparing the groups (group comparison statistic), relating scores on one or more measures in a single group (correlational statistic), or testing a specific model that involves multiple independent and dependent variables considered simultaneously. In the sections that follow, we consider each of these options in turn.

CONSIDER GROUP COMPARISON STATISTICS

Parametric Statistics

Analysis of Variance and *t* Test

ANOVA and the *t* test are widely used parametric statistics for examining differences between groups. If you decide one of them is appropriate for your analysis, you must then select among their numerous variations.

To assist in this process, first ask yourself how many independent variables will be involved in answering your particular research question. Next, ask yourself how many levels (conditions or groups) will be included with each independent variable. To do this, break each independent variable into the discrete groups it includes (e.g., condition: priming for recall, priming for recognition, no priming [three levels]; time: pre, post, follow-up [three levels]). Finally, for each independent variable, ask yourself whether the levels involve *different* groups of people being compared with each other (as with the "condition" independent variable above) or the *same* group being compared with itself on the same variable under different conditions (e.g., at different points in time after exposure to different experimental stimuli, as with the "time" independent variable above). Once you have answered these questions, you can use the flowchart in Figure 9.6 to identify the most appropriate statistic for your analysis.

Following this flowchart leads you to the most suitable initial choice and then instructs you to examine whether your data meet the assumptions of the statistic. If not, you must ascertain whether the statistic is robust to any violations of its assumptions you might be making or whether there is some way of transforming the data or adjusting the statistic to alleviate the problem. Many students approach data transformation warily. However, using

FIGURE 9.6. Flowchart for Selecting Appropriate Parametric Statistics for Group Comparison Studies (Assuming Analysis of a Single Dependent Variable)

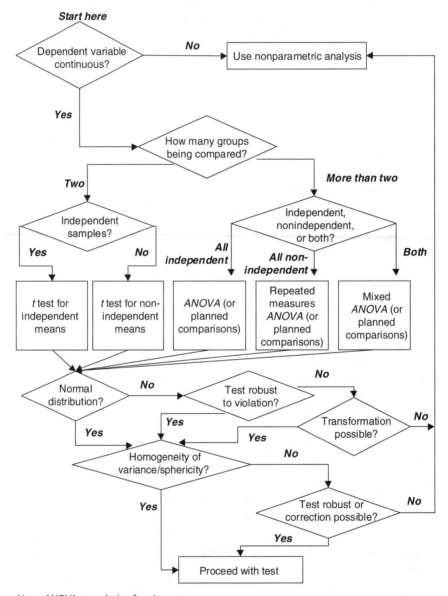

Note. ANOVA = analysis of variance.

a transformation to meet the assumptions of a nonrobust statistic is not cheating. In fact, it may help guard against Type I or Type II errors. Furthermore, the operations involved are completely objective, and the original data are recoverable at any point.

If you cannot figure out a way to compensate for assumptions that you violate (and if you cannot find literature showing that the results will be robust even in the face of such violations), the flowchart directs you to seek an alternative statistic with fewer assumptions. Of course, along with fewer assumptions may come lower power. Usually, parametric statistics are more powerful than nonparametric ones, so you generally should use a parametric test if possible. Maxwell and colleagues (2018a) pointed out, however, that this—like most rules of thumb—is an oversimplification: In some cases, a nonparametric approach can be more powerful than its parametric alternative. Which test is more powerful will depend on the characteristics of your data set. If it's truly a toss-up and if you are a statistical novice, let pragmatic considerations prevail: Pick the one that you or your statistics consultant knows better.

Let's work through the steps listed so far in this chapter with an example. Suppose you are interested in the effects of individual therapy on couple relationships. Your research will involve testing whether insight-oriented individual therapy leads to better couple satisfaction than problem-solving individual therapy. Your dependent variable is the score on a couple satisfaction scale. The two independent variables are type of treatment (two levels: insight-oriented vs. problem-solving therapy) and time (three levels: pre- vs. posttreatment vs. follow-up). The first independent variable involves comparing different groups of participants; the second involves comparing a group with itself at different points in time. If you follow the flowchart in Figure 9.6, you'll find yourself at the "mixed ANOVA" box: one between-subjects factor (treatment) and one within-subjects factor (time). Your likely analysis is a 2 (Treatment) × 3 (Time) mixed ANOVA.

The next step is to consider the assumptions of this analysis. ANOVA assumes homogeneity of variance. Although it is generally robust to violations of this assumption, this is not necessarily the case with repeated measures, very unequal ns, or outliers (Field, 2018; Tabachnick & Fidell, 2013). Your best guess might be that the results of the treatment are likely to be robust to violations of the assumptions of homogeneity of variance, but analyses involving the time factor would not be. Thus, you need to examine your variances for homogeneity. You can do this by using one of several tests described in most statistics books (e.g., Field, 2018; Maxwell et al., 2018b; see also the Supplemental Resources list at the end of this chapter). Standard statistical software such as SAS and SPSS will calculate most of these tests.

If group variances are not homogeneous, data transformations might help. You can also consider whether methods for dealing with outliers will correct your problem (Judd et al., 1995; Tabachnick & Fidell, 2013; see Chapter 10, this volume, for more on this topic). An alternative is to adjust your degrees of freedom to accommodate this problem using one of several procedures (see Maxwell et al., 2018b). The result of the latter option is that the statistic often becomes more conservative (i.e., decreases the probability of a Type I error) as a way of protecting against the bias introduced by heterogeneity of variances. This means you need to have greater differences between your groups to achieve the same level of statistical significance you would have had if the assumptions had not been violated. In addition, the F^* and W tests (Maxwell et al., 2018a) are alternatives if you have no repeated measures. These variations of the F test produce unbiased results when variances are unequal, with both equal- and unequal-n cells.

Bootstrapping is another approach to consider (Erceg-Hurn & Mirosevich, 2008; Field, 2018; Wright et al., 2011). Bootstrapping creates new "resamples" from the data you collect, then basically recalculates your ANOVA or t test with these many different samples created on the basis of your data. Through the magic of complex statistical computations, this process provides robust estimators of the statistical effects you wish to estimate—in other words, statistical values less likely to be influenced by whatever violation of assumptions you encountered. Many statistical programs now have bootstrapping options or modules that can be used with more common analyses, so using ANOVA or t test with bootstrapping is worth considering if no alternative analysis fits the bill for you.

Planned Comparisons

But wait! The box in the flowchart also says that "planned comparisons" are an option. As an alternative to the standard ANOVA approach, you can select a certain set of comparisons that you wish to make among pairs of means. You do this in advance, before you collect the data. In effect, you state that you expect certain means to differ in certain directions and wish to test only these differences. No other comparisons are important to you. This advance selection permits the option of doing planned comparisons in place of an omnibus or overall ANOVA. This option has the advantage of giving you more statistical power, because you restrict in advance the number of tests you will do. It has the disadvantage of making it more difficult to snoop through the data later on for something interesting that did not involve an a priori hypothesis, however. There is no free lunch! True, you get more powerful tests to use for your planned comparisons, but the trade-off is that later snooping requires you to use more stringent tests.

In general, planned comparisons make sense if you have well-defined hypotheses with good support in the literature. They may also make sense if you have a complex design in which only a few means are expected to differ and most are not (e.g., if you are running a lot of control conditions) or if you are testing a well-defined moderation hypothesis involving categorical independent variables and are reasonably sure about how your groups should differ. In this case, you predict not only that your interaction will be significant but also which specific means will differ. If your study is more exploratory, however, you may prefer not to restrict yourself in exchange for greater power. Most statistics books that discuss ANOVA also discuss how to do planned comparisons. Note that several different ways of doing planned comparisons exist, depending on how you select among groups you wish to compare.

Post Hoc Tests

What if you elect not to do planned comparisons? Don't put away your statistics books yet! You need to select a post hoc test. Post-hoc testing allows you to see which mean differences are contributing to any significant effects you find. For example, suppose you find a significant main effect for time and an interaction between time and mode of treatment. You will need post hoc tests to see which difference in group means contributed to your interaction effect (you do not need to interpret the main effect of time, because that variable is included in your significant interaction).

Many post hoc tests exist. You can evaluate them in terms of their power, their robustness to violations of their assumptions, and the situations in which each is most appropriate from a conceptual point of view. Maxwell et al. (2018b) and Kirk (2013) provide good overviews of different options and compared and contrasted these options. If you are using either a within-subjects or unequal-n design, be aware that these are not robust to violations of homogeneity of variance and normality assumptions. Look for a post hoc test appropriate for these designs.

ANCOVA and MANOVA

What about ANCOVA, you might say? Or MANOVA? Should I be using them? Analysis of covariance (ANCOVA), multivariate analysis of variance (MANOVA), and multivariate analysis of covariance (MANCOVA) all provide alternatives to t test and ANOVA statistics. We consider each below.

Essentially, an ANCOVA is an analysis of variance with the statistical influence of one or more variables (i.e., covariates) removed from the dependent variable. In theory, an ANCOVA is what you would get if you could do the ANOVA with the level of the covariates controlled by randomization (in practice, this situation is more complex, as we shall see). When such control is not possible, ANCOVA may be a suitable alternative to ANOVA. This is true when there is a strong relationship between your dependent variable and another variable that is related to your independent variable. Remember, you want to say something about the effect of a particular independent variable on your dependent variable. You do not want this relationship to be the result of some other variable that you failed to hold constant. Because ANCOVA decreases your error variance by extracting variance that is due to the relationship between the covariate and the dependent variable (Tabachnick & Fidell, 2013), your independent variable may be more likely to show a significant effect. For example, suppose you investigate the effects of three different reading programs on reading scores. You know, however, that IQ correlates highly with reading scores and that unless you control for it in some way, this relationship will prevent you from seeing any differences between your three interventions. In essence, doing an ANCOVA with IQ as a covariate will allow you to extract the relationship between IQ and reading from your analyses, making an effect of your independent variable easier to detect.

Researchers sometimes use ANCOVA when some variable emerges after the fact as a potential confound and they want to remove its influence statistically. In fact, one strategy commonly used in thesis and dissertation proposals is to state that you intend to do an ANOVA unless preliminary analyses reveal the need to control for additional variables. Consider the outcome study comparing insight-oriented and problem-solving therapy. Suppose you found that despite random assignment, the insight-oriented group had significantly more years of education than the problem-solving group. Suppose further that education level correlated with therapy outcome. In this situation, any differences favoring the insight-oriented group could be due to education and not therapy. To protect against this, you could use years of education as a covariate. Theoretically this removes the potential impact education may have on, say, marital satisfaction, so you can see the effects of your treatment independent of the effects of education. There is some dispute as to when this procedure is appropriate, however, because ANCOVA can produce hard-to-interpret or even misleading results in certain cases, as we discuss later in this section.

There are several other things you should know about ANCOVA. First, using ANCOVA to control for potential confounds makes sense only if there is a significant correlation between the covariate and the dependent variable. If there is no correlation, the suspected confounding variable really isn't one. It thus offers no viable alternative explanation for any differences between your treatment groups. Furthermore, the results of the ANCOVA will not differ much from the ANOVA results (but you will lose a degree of freedom—i.e., a bit of power—by including the covariate).

Second, ANCOVA controls only for a linear relationship between the covariate and the dependent variable—a confound could still exist if there is a curvilinear relationship between the covariate and your dependent variable. Third, ideally all the covariates should be uncorrelated with each other (Tabachnick & Fidell, 2013). Fourth, using ANCOVA when your covariate may be related to or caused by differences in your independent variable poses major interpretive problems (see Field, 2018, and Miller & Chapman, 2001, for a discussion). For example, suppose you are testing differences between therapy dropouts and completers and are thinking about covarying how much the clients expected to benefit from treatment before starting. Client beliefs may in fact have contributed to dropout, making this ANCOVA a poor choice. Related interpretive problems also emerge if you use ANCOVA and your groupings do not involve random assignment (i.e., your study is not a true experiment; Miller & Chapman, 2001). The argument goes something like this: By extracting variance due to the covariate, you may wind up removing meaningful parts of your independent variable, and therefore your independent variable no longer represents what you want it to represent.

Thus, although ANCOVA can be a useful procedure, interpreting its results can sometimes be less than straightforward for the reasons just described. If ANCOVA seems like a possible analysis to you, examine what it can and cannot do. If you are considering ANCOVA—especially in a study that does not involve random assignment—carefully think through how your covariate and your independent variables are likely to be related and whether using ANCOVA will land you in an interpretive muddle. If so, consider redesigning your study to avoid these issues (e.g., matching groups on the covariate; Field, 2018).

What about MANOVA? A MANOVA also resembles an ANOVA, except that multiple dependent variables are examined all at once. A MANOVA for the insight-oriented versus problem-solving study, for example, might examine participants' reported satisfaction with communication, sexual interaction, and instrumental tasks (three dependent variables). A MANOVA basically asks, Do the various factors (independent variables) make a difference for this group of dependent variables? Conceptually, MANOVA procedures create a synthetic variable that combines the information in all the dependent variables that are included in the analysis, then analyzes the synthetic variable, and finally tells you about the significance of main effects and interactions for that synthetic variable. This means you will know whether your independent variable affected the synthetic variable but not whether it affected any one of the individual variables making up the synthetic one.

Some investigators attempt to control Type I error rates by doing a MANOVA. The risk of Type I error increases when you do many statistical tests on numerous separate dependent variables by increasing the likelihood that at least one will be significant solely as a function of doing so many tests. Because MANOVA treats the dependent variables as a group, the investigators conduct fewer analyses and thus reduce the likelihood of experiment-wise Type I error. If the MANOVA is significant (so the logic goes), the investigators can then proceed to do a series of individual ANOVAs on each of the dependent variables to see what produced the significance, much as one can do a post hoc test comparing specific groups following a significant ANOVA. Alternatively, the investigators can use a step-down procedure, eliminating variables one by one to see which accounted for the effect (Tabachnick & Fidell, 2013).

We do not recommend this approach for several reasons. First, this use of MANOVA does not uniformly protect against experiment-wise Type I error and in some cases may even inflate it (Bird & Hadzi-Pavlovic, 2014). Second, MANOVA answers questions about a synthetic dependent variable (not the individual variables) and is most appropriate when the investigator is interested in the dependent variables as a system or when the dependent variables are conceptually related and assess the same or similar underlying constructs (Huberty & Morris, 1989). Multiple ANOVAs may be preferable when dependent variables are conceptually independent, when doing exploratory research, when previous studies have used separate univariate analyses (so your data will be comparable to those of previous investigators), and when examining whether groups are equivalent (e.g., on possible confounding variables).

So, what is our recommendation? If your dependent variables are conceptually related, a MANOVA may make sense if you can meet its assumptions or if the particular type of MANOVA (e.g., repeated measures) is robust with regard to violations of its assumptions. If your dependent variables are not conceptually related, think about correcting your experiment-wise alpha level as a way of protecting against Type I error (more on this later in this chapter). If you decide to use MANOVA, you can control for potential covariates with MANCOVA.

Nonparametric Statistics

Let's suppose your data do not fulfill the assumptions required for an ANOVA. What do you do now? Nonparametric statistics may sometimes come to your rescue.

If you were planning to use a between-subjects ANOVA but your ordinal data are not suitable for one, the Kruskal–Wallis test is a nonparametric alternative. Appropriate for ordinal data, it is equivalent to the Wilcoxon rank-sum and Mann–Whitney U tests when only two groups are being compared (Maxwell et al., 2018b). Although the Kruskal–Wallis statistic makes no assumptions about underlying distributions, it does implicitly assume homogeneity of variance. For this reason, Maxwell et al. (2018b) recommended the F^* and W tests when variances are not homogeneous, particularly with unequal cell sizes. Joint ranking or pairwise ranking tests (Maxwell et al., 2018b) can be used to compare pairs of cells, in the same way that post hoc mean comparisons are used with ANOVAs.

If your design involves repeated measures and only one (repeated) independent variable, Friedman's test (Maxwell et al., 2018b) may be appropriate. Like the Kruskal–Wallis test, it analyzes rank orders of participants' scores and so requires ordinal data. For more complex designs, nonparametric alternatives may not be available (Field, 2018), and you may need to use a bootstrapping approach, as described earlier in this chapter.

With categorical data, the most appropriate analysis is often a chi-square (χ^2) test or cross-classification analysis (Rodgers, 1995). When there are several levels of an independent variable or when you have more than one independent variable, you may wish to do the equivalent of a post hoc test if your chi-square is significant. This can be done using z tests for proportions. Alternatively, the more complex nonparametric equivalents of ANOVA strategies (logit or log-linear analysis; Field, 2018) may be appropriate.

CONSIDER CORRELATIONAL STATISTICS

If your design involves looking at relationships among variables in a single group of individuals rather than comparing discrete groups, the first step in selecting a statistic is to decide what is being related to what. If you have two variables that you wish to relate, a bivariate (i.e., two-variable) correlation will be appropriate. If you have a set of variables (i.e., more than one) that you wish to associate with one or more different variables, a regression strategy or model-testing approach may be the best choice. If your dependent variable is categorical, perhaps you should use discriminant function analysis or logistic regression.

Bivariate Correlations (Parametric and Nonparametric)

The simplest measures of association are bivariate correlations. If your data on both variables can be considered interval or ratio, a Pearson product–moment correlation (r) may be suitable. If measuring one of your variables produces ordinal data and measuring the other yields ordinal, interval, or ratio data, a Spearman rank order procedure would be more suitable than a Pearson correlation. If one of the variables is dichotomous, a point biserial correlation will be appropriate. If both are dichotomous, the correlation between them is called the *phi* (Φ) coefficient. Note that the formula for r produces the point biserial and phi coefficients (as special cases), so telling a computer to give you an r statistic with dichotomous data will produce a correct point biserial or phi coefficient (Cohen et al., 2003).

Keep in mind that correlations involve rank ordering and do not take into account systematic mean differences in the two sets of data. Such differences may be important. For example, suppose you wish to correlate the data of two people who independently observed the same individuals' head-banging frequency. You would be interested not only in whether the observers saw the same individuals as higher or lower in head banging but also in whether both observers reported similar frequencies of head banging for each individual jointly observed. In such a case, you might prefer a correlation that takes into account mean differences (e.g., the intraclass correlation coefficient, von Eye & Mun, 2005).

Regression Strategies

Regression analyses basically select one variable as the criterion variable (also sometimes termed the "dependent" or "outcome" variable) and one or more predictor ("independent") variables. When two or more predictors are used, regression procedures develop an equation that describes the best way of combining the predictors to predict a person's score on the criterion variable. Regression might be appropriate, for example, if you wish to analyze whether rates of particular therapist behaviors are associated with treatment outcome; whether age, social competence, Graduate Record Exam scores, and undergraduate grade point average (GPA) are associated with graduate school GPA or professional licensing exam scores; whether various demographic and cognitive measures are related to rate of recovery from cancer surgery, and so on. Regression can also be used to test moderation hypotheses and is especially useful when one or more of the moderator variables is continuous (as depicted in Figure 9.3). Although it can be used with a single predictor, regression more commonly involves multiple predictors. Thus, this parametric version of regression is called "multiple regression."

Multiple Regression

Parametric versions of multiple regression analysis basically produce a list of those variables that enhance your ability to predict the criterion over your best guess if you knew nothing about your participants' scores on the predictors (this best guess, by the way, would be the mean of the criterion variable). The analysis procedures take into account the fact that some of the predictors may correlate with each other and are therefore redundant. Thus, each significant predictor variable contributes unique (nonredundant) information (i.e., information that goes beyond that added by the other predictors in the equation). Dichotomous and continuous variables can be used as predictors, but for parametric versions of multiple regression procedures, the criterion must be a continuous variable (we mention nonparametric versions of regression [logit analysis and logistic regression] later in this chapter). Categorical variables that have more than two levels can also be used as predictors, but these must be treated specially by dummy coding (see Cohen et al., 2003). You can also use regression to assess the effects of interactions between predictor variables (e.g., whether one variable moderates the relationship between a second, and even third, variable and the criterion variable). Aiken and West (1996) described how to create, analyze, and interpret interactions in regression analyses.

Many forms of regression exist. Most have to do with how you enter your predictor variables into the regression equation—in what order, and one by one or in one or more groups. Different forms of regression also vary in the ways the analysis tests each variable to see whether it contributes any new information (above and beyond the information contained by other variables in the equation) in predicting the criterion variable. A crucial point here is that regression analyses can be performed in many different ways. Examine the options and their pros and cons in light of the purposes of your analyses and then make an informed decision.

One popular approach to regression analysis is hierarchical multiple regression, in which you specify the order in which the variables go into the equation in advance on theoretical or methodological grounds. The analysis extracts the amount of variance associated with the first variable, then does the same with the second, and so on. You can either specify the order in which each and every individual variable is entered or group variables into subsets and then enter the subsets, letting the analysis sort out the order within each set. In either case, one benefit of hierarchical approaches is that they offer a way to test hypotheses about the additive influence of your variables—in other words, what the variables added at a later step in the analysis add to what you already know about the criterion or outcome variable on the basis of variables entered in prior steps. This can be a great way to test the value added by a new construct or measure.

For example, one of our students wanted to predict in-law satisfaction on the basis of parental marital satisfaction and the quality of the relationship (cohesion) between parent and child. In-law satisfaction was his criterion variable. He first entered several demographic variables (as a set) in a hierarchical multiple regression analysis. Then, he entered a single measure of social desirability. Finally, he entered the marital satisfaction and cohesion measures (as a set). He chose this order of entry because he wished to control for demographic characteristics and the tendency to respond to self-report measures in a socially desirable way. He also wanted to look at the relationship among marital satisfaction, cohesion, and in-law satisfaction, holding demographic and social desirability variables constant. He wanted his results to tell him whether knowing the marital satisfaction and cohesion scores gave him any new information over and above that provided by the demographic and social desirability measures. He had no reason for ordering his variables within sets.

However, let's say this student did want to test marital satisfaction and cohesion separately. For example, perhaps existing literature suggested that general measures of marital satisfaction tended to predict in-law satisfaction but had not examined cohesion specifically. He might enter marital satisfaction as Step 3 (after Step 1, demographics, and Step 2, social desirability) and then cohesion as Step 4. These results could provide information about whether a separate cohesion measure added anything to his ability to predict in-law satisfaction.

Hierarchical multiple regression is also sometimes used to test mediation hypotheses. Let's go back to the earlier example (Figure 9.5) in which you propose that low academic achievement is related to whether youth drop out of or complete high school, and that this relationship is partially but not completely explained (or mediated) by students' lack of connection to teachers. Baron and Kenny (1986) and Holmbeck (1997) described regression analytic approaches that have been widely used to test these kinds of mediation hypotheses, although most researchers now eschew these approaches because of lack of power (MacKinnon et al., 2007). Many alternative approaches to testing mediation, including path analysis, also make use of regression strategies to test mediation (Field, 2018; Meyers et al., 2017).[1]

An alternative to hierarchical multiple regression is stepwise regression. In this procedure, purely computational decision rules identify which variable predicts the criterion variable best, then which variable adds significantly after that, and so on. Variations in stepwise regression include forward entry procedures, forward stepwise procedures, and backward deletion procedures. Whereas with hierarchical multiple regression you specify the order in advance, with stepwise regression the computer does the ordering. If the student

---

[1]Path analysis can also be done using model-testing strategies; see Meyers et al., 2017, for a description of both ways of approaching mediation.

studying in-law satisfaction used a stepwise procedure, he would enter all of his variables and let the computer tell him the order in which they predicted in-law satisfaction.

Cohen et al. (2003) pointed out several disadvantages of using stepwise procedures. First, when large numbers of predictors are used, the approach seriously capitalizes on chance. Second, the results using these procedures may not replicate in another sample. Third, depending on the rules used to enter and remove predictor variables, results may be quite misleading. Finally, using stepwise procedures means you can avoid having to think through the logical relationships among your predictors and criterion variable. This is a bit like using ANOVAs and post hoc comparisons to snoop through your data rather than making the effort to preplan and specify exactly what you want to examine in advance. All of these issues mean that you run the risk of obtaining results that aren't generalizable or theoretically meaningful.

You may justify stepwise procedures more readily under certain conditions: (a) when the sample is large, (b) when replication is possible (either with a second sample or by randomly splitting the sample in two), and (c) when the research goal is not based in theory (as in some applied research, when the goal may be simply to predict a phenomenon and not explain it; Cohen et al., 2003). For example, you may not know which factors should be most influential in predicting students' success in an internship program. In this case, it may make sense to let the analysis tell you which variables are important. Tabachnick and Fidell (2013) characterized stepwise procedures as model-building techniques; early atheoretical studies in an area might use them. Tabachnick and Fidell viewed hierarchical procedures as hypothesis-testing techniques[2]; investigators would use these when a research area matures enough to allow reasonable predictions.

Regression procedures, like all parametric tests, have certain conditions that can cause problems if you fail to meet them. Some of these can be anticipated and are worth considering as you plan your analyses. First, multiple regression procedures assume the absence of multicollinearity. Multicollinearity occurs when two or more of the predictor variables are highly intercorrelated, a situation that produces an unstable regression equation (i.e., the weights associated with each of the predictor variables are unlikely to be replicated in a new population).[3] Look at correlations between your predictors in

---

[2]You can combine stepwise and hierarchical procedures. That is, you can enter a series of subsets of variables hierarchically but use stepwise procedures to figure out the order of variables within each subset.

[3]One common guideline is that bivariate correlations above .70 (some say .80) may suggest a multicollinearity problem (e.g., Field, 2018; Tabachnick & Fidell, 2013). Note that a bivariate *r* below .70 does not guarantee the absence of multicollinearity, however: Two predictor variables might be only moderately correlated with a third predictor when looked at individually but might be more highly correlated when combined. SPSS and other programs can calculate indexes (e.g., tolerance levels) to test combinations of variables for multicollinearity; Cohen et al. (2003) discussed these issues as well.

the literature. If you suspect you may have a multicollinearity problem, you could select the most important predictor from among the correlated variables or explore whether you can legitimately combine the correlated variables into a single score.

A second condition you must satisfy in using multiple regression is that predictor variables cannot be combinations of other predictor variables (this is termed "singularity"). In other words, you cannot use scores for hitting, swearing, punching, and total aggression as predictors; the last is a combination of the first three. Third, regression assumes linear relationships between each predictor and the criterion.

Two other assumptions of multiple regression are worth thinking about as you plan your analyses. First, regression assumes that you have included all theoretically relevant predictors and that none of the predictors is irrelevant (Licht, 1995). In addition, multiple regression procedures assume that variables are measured without error. These two assumptions seem impossible to meet—if you knew everything that was and was not related to the criterion variable, why do the research? And how many variables can be measured without error? The truth is, researchers use regressions in spite of the fact that no one can meet these assumptions fully. But this doesn't mean you should ignore them. Instead, follow several practical recommendations for dealing with them: Think about the degree to which they are met, use theory and past data to select appropriate predictors, select the most reliable and valid measures available to minimize measurement error (Klem, 1995; Licht, 1995), and consider how these limitations will affect your results (e.g., reduce the total variance you are able to explain).

Robust and Other Versions of Regression

Ordinary least squares (OLS) regression (the full name of the types of regression we've been discussing so far) has another important assumption: that residuals (the difference between what you predict each participant's score on the criterion variable will be and what the score actually is) are normally distributed—in other words, that your regression equation predicts equally well (or poorly) regardless of whether the person has a low or high score on the criterion variable you are predicting. You won't be able to test this assumption until you obtain your data. You also won't be able to look for outliers (i.e., extreme values on your variables) until after you collect your data. OLS regression can produce misleading results when errors are not normally distributed, when the data set contains influential outliers, or both. If you suspect you may have problems in either of these areas (e.g., based on past studies or the type of data you are collecting), you may need to look for a more specialized variant of regression.

As with ANOVA, other regression methods are available for dealing with violations of assumptions that bias the results of OLS regression. Robust regression methods (Wilcox, 2017) reduce the influence of outliers. Poisson regression and negative binomial regression (Coxe et al., 2009) counteract some of the problems with using OLS regression when data are counts of discrete events (e.g., number of cigarettes smoked per day, number of criminal arrests) and the mean of the count variable is relatively low (Coxe et al., 2009, indicated < 10).

Nonparametric Regression

Logistic regression resembles multiple regression in that a number of predictors are related to a single dichotomous criterion variable. Predictors can be continuous or not, but unlike multiple regression, the criterion variable is categorical. For example, you may wish to predict diagnostic status (presence or absence of a diagnosis of major depressive disorder) or voting behavior (did or did not vote). In addition, the mathematics underlying logistic regression are more closely aligned with nonparametric than parametric statistics and differ greatly from those underlying parametric versions of multiple regression. Nonparametric regression statistics tell you about how well obtained frequencies in a particular cell fit the expected frequencies, rather than about how much of the variance each predictor variable accounts for in the criterion. A similar procedure, logit analysis (a version of log-linear analysis), is more restrictive than logistic regression in that all variables (predictors and criterion) must be categorical. Multinomial logistic regression can be used when the outcome consists of multiple discrete categories (e.g., different diagnoses, which of several television programs a viewer watches). With this analysis, you must designate one of the groups as a reference group. The analysis compares whether each of the predictor variables significantly enhances or reduces the likelihood a participant belongs to each of the remaining categories relative to their chance of being in the reference group (Feingold et al., 2014).

Discriminant Function Analysis

Discriminant function analysis (DFA; also called "discriminant analysis"; see Meyers et al., 2017, for a description and SPSS example) has many of the same uses as logistic regression but involves parametric statistics. DFA is most useful when you want to predict discrete group membership (considered the dependent variable) from a set of variables (considered the independent variables or predictors).[4] For example, you may wish to assess how well several MMPI scores predict psychiatric diagnosis or whether you can derive a way to combine demographic data with scores assessing attitudes toward work and the company to predict which prospective employees will and will not quit during the first year on the job. As with group comparison questions, you divide your sample into two or more discrete groups to form your dependent variable (e.g., antisocial personality disorder vs. control, those who leave the company vs. those who stay). And as with regression questions, you want to

---

[4]DFA can also be used to help understand the results of a significant MANOVA (see Field, 2018, for a discussion and example).

examine whether a combination of variables will allow you to separate the groups. A DFA can be useful in these situations if you meet its assumptions; otherwise, logistic regression or multinomial logistic regression may be a more viable alternative.

Essentially, DFA examines the predictors (independent variables) and formulates an equation that weights each one to maximize the correct classification of participants into groups (the dependent variable). As with regression, variations of DFA exist. Mathematically, DFA is closely related to MANOVA. One important consideration involves whether you want the computer to test certain variables before others (hierarchical DFA) or to order the variables statistically (step-down DFA or direct ["standard"] DFA; see Tabachnick & Fidell, 2013).

Factor Analysis

We assumed in the previous sections that you have designated some variables as independent variables and some as dependent variables and you are interested in how the independent variables and dependent variables relate to one another. Maybe you do not view your data in terms of independent and dependent variables, however. Perhaps you are interested in numerous variables without specifying causal or predictive relationships among them. If so, another set of correlation-based statistics might be more suitable.

Factor analysis and its sibling, principal components analysis, summarize patterns of correlations among a set of variables. Investigators often use these to reduce a large set of variables or items to a smaller number or to test hypotheses about the underlying structure among variables. For example, an investigator developing a new questionnaire may wish to reduce the 50 items to a few homogeneous subscales before looking at differences between groups. As with regression analyses, factor analyses can be set up to test hypothesized structures (i.e., confirmatory factor analysis [CFA]) or can be more exploratory in nature (i.e., exploratory factor analysis [EFA]). Issues involved in using factor analysis are too numerous and complex to cover here (see Beavers et al., 2013; Fabrigar et al., 1999; Floyd & Widaman, 1995; and Preacher & MacCallum, 2003, for excellent overviews of some these issues).

One issue does warrant mentioning, however: sample size. We are reluctant to endorse rules of thumb (e.g., a minimum of 5–10 participants per item [variable] or 100 participants in total, whichever is higher) because these rules are not consistent (Beavers et al., 2013) and have been widely criticized by factor analysis experts (e.g., MacCallum et al., 1999). MacCallum et al. (1999) showed that the number of participants required depends on the degree to which the factor structure accounts for variance in the items and on the extent to which each factor is measured by a reasonable number of items. If the analysis accounts for a reasonable amount of variance (i.e., communalities [the statistic that tells you how much variance all the factors account for] around .50) and there are at least six or seven items for each factor, a sample of 100 to 200 may be sufficient, according to MacCallum et al. With fewer numbers of items per factor, more participants will be needed. In addition, many investigators recommend replicating a factor analysis to be sure of the findings.

The bottom line: You will need a lot of participants to make sure you obtain a stable solution. Are you willing to recruit enough participants to do the analysis right? If not, do not promise to solve the problem of too many variables by conducting a factor analysis to create a more manageable number of scores. A better solution is to think through whether all those measures are necessary, especially given the very great likelihood that they do not measure different constructs.

A second important consideration is whether to use exploratory factor analysis or confirmatory factor analysis. Your particular research questions will guide your selection of which approach to use. EFA allows the computer to determine the best-fitting organization of variables; this may or may not make conceptual sense. Principal components and principal axis factor analyses are both examples of exploratory factor analysis. In contrast, CFA is a model-testing technique in which you specify which variables load on which factors, then test your theoretical model against the actual data. In general, EFA is most appropriate in the initial stages of measure development, whereas CFA is more appropriate for testing clear theories of how items or scores are organized with well-developed measures.

CONSIDER MODEL-TESTING APPROACHES

As mentioned earlier, model-testing approaches differ from the other statistical approaches covered in this chapter in that they test whether the actual data fit a theoretical model proposed by the investigator. Possibly the best-known model-testing analysis in psychology is structural equation modeling. Confirmatory factor analysis is one application of SEM. With CFA, you might tell the computer which items from a questionnaire are supposed to make up different subscales. The analysis tells you about the extent to which they do.

SEM can also be used as an alternative to multiple regression–based path analysis to test mediation hypotheses and is often used (a) to test multiple or complex relationships among predictors, (b) to examine multiple dependent variables in the same model, or (c) when multiple measures are used to examine one or more of the constructs included in the model. To illustrate, consider the mediation example in which you propose that feeling connected to teachers mediates the relationship between low academic achievement and dropping out of high school. Suppose you also expect that association with deviant peers predicts both lack of connection with teachers and school dropout but is not a mediator of the relationship. You are hypothesizing a rather complex set of relationships here. SEM permits you to test all of these relationships in one analysis and could be diagrammed by a figure like Figure 9.7.

FIGURE 9.7. Diagram of Hypothesized Structural Equation Model for Predictors of Dropping Out Versus Completing High School

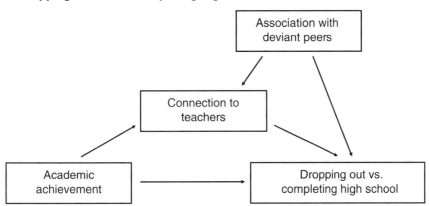

Note. By convention, measured variables are depicted inside rectangles and latent variables inside ovals. This example assumes that each variable is measured using a single score as its indicator.

Path analysis looks at direct and indirect relationships between predictors and criterion variables. A typical simple path model might speculate that A (e.g., achievement) leads to B (e.g., poor attitudes and lack of connections), which leads to C (e.g., dropout). The model might also suggest that A also leads to C directly (i.e., that B plays no role in this part of the A–C connection). Mediation analyses can be considered subsets of path analytic strategies. Complex path models are possible, too. For example, A could lead to B, which leads to C, which leads to D (e.g., lower lifetime earnings). In the past, researchers typically used regression to calculate direct and indirect path coefficients that showed the relationships among variables, but SEM is more often used in contemporary research to test this kind of model if sample sizes are sufficient.

Many investigators also use SEM when they use multiple measures of the same constructs and wish to estimate relationships among the constructs (sometimes called "latent variables") rather than the actual measured variables (also known as "observed" or "manifest" variables or "indicators"). This is because, conceptually speaking, SEM combines features of factor analysis (creating a synthetic or latent variable that is based on the observed scores) with features of regression analysis (examining the extent to which one variable or set of variables predicts another). With this sort of model, you tell the computer (a) which variables measure which latent construct and (b) how you expect the constructs to be related. How well the model fits depends on how well you got both (a) and (b) right.

Model-testing approaches all share the requirement that you tell the computer in advance how you expect variables to relate to one another. The analytic strategies then test the extent to which the relationships you predict fit the covariation pattern existing in the data. The test statistic is chi-square, but a significant chi-square means that your predictions deviated significantly from the actual data. In fact, this is one of those rare times that you will be hoping for a nonsignificant result from your statistics!

The problem with this approach, however, is that whether the chi-square is significant depends both on how much difference there is between your model and the actual data and on your sample size. The larger the sample, the smaller the difference the chi-square test will be able to detect. A cruel twist of fate here is that statisticians generally recommend large samples for SEM. This increases the chances of finding that your model doesn't fit, even though the lack of fit may be by a rather trivial amount. If you paid attention solely to the chi-square result, you might discard your model prematurely. Fortunately, statisticians are aware of this conundrum and have devised some ways around the large sample–significant chi-square issue. The solution is a boatload of different "goodness of fit" indicators (Iacobucci, 2010; Kline, 2015). And yes, this means you have to choose the fit indicators you will use. Many recommend using more than one. Each has its own recommended cutoff scores, although as with most rules of thumb, these have been criticized and so should be taken with a grain of salt (see Chapter 1 of Raykov & Marcoulides, 2006, for a discussion of some of the more common indicators and rules of thumb for their interpretation, and Kline, 2015, for alternative methods of looking at overall model fit).

Structural equation modeling has several advantages. A big one is that it permits you to test many relationships simultaneously in a single analysis rather than running many individual ones. This reduces Type I error. Another is that it forces you to articulate a theory or model you wish to test in advance—a step that helps ensure that your findings will have theoretical, and not just statistical, significance. Finally, if you use multiple indicators of the same construct (some recommend a minimum of three indicators per construct), SEM tests relationships between the construct score and other variables. In so doing, it removes some of the measurement error from your model, which should result in greater statistical power.

SEM is not for every data set, however. First and foremost, sample size is an issue, and what constitutes an adequate sample depends on several factors (Wolf et al., 2013). In general, the more complex the model, the smaller the effect sizes you expect, the more missing data you have, and the more skewed the data, the larger your required sample will be. In our experience, published studies using SEM rarely have fewer than 100 to 150 participants. Second, novices may fall in love with the idea of testing very complex models with SEM. Not only do these demand large samples, they also are prone to a variety of problems. The result can be a computer printout with ominous messages like "the model cannot be identified" and output that either is missing key statistics or looks screwy in some other way. We strongly recommend that you take a course that includes a large dose of SEM, get some experience doing SEM, start collecting and reading articles and books on the approach (e.g., Kline, 2015; Schumacker & Lomax, 2016), and line up some good consultation on SEM if you are new to it and are likely to use it in your thesis or dissertation.

SET YOUR ALPHA LEVELS

Now that you have selected an analysis plan, you are ready to begin, right? Not quite! Take a look at the plan to see how many analyses it will take to test your hypotheses. Will you have to run three analyses or 30? If you are closer to the latter than the former, remember that running lots of statistical tests increases the chances of Type I error, a problem called "experiment-wise error."

There are several solutions to this problem. First, you can see whether you really need to conduct all those statistical tests: Is there another viable analytic approach that will permit you to test the hypotheses with fewer analyses? Perhaps you can use SEM in place of several regression equations or use regression in place of lots of correlations. Second, you can reexamine your hypotheses to see whether you are trying to do too much in one study. If so, pare down your hypotheses to those that are most important and viable (see Wilkinson, 1999, for a related discussion).

A third common method is to adjust your *p* value downward on the basis of the number of tests you want to run, using the Bonferroni method or a related variation for controlling experiment-wise error (see Keppel & Wickens, 2004). A related alternative is to use a method that is based on the false discovery rate, which is the percentage of times the researcher rejects the null hypothesis in error, related to the total number of times the researcher rejects the null (Keselman, 2015). In everyday language, this can be thought of as the percentage of times you are wrong about concluding you have a significant finding. In general, false discovery rate procedures are more powerful than Bonferroni and related methods for controlling against Type I error (Keselman, 2015). Regardless of the method you select, your adjustment comes at a price. That price is statistical power—if your *p* is more conservative, your power goes down. So, go back and redo those sample size calculations with the new *p* value. Don't be surprised if the number of participants you need increases dramatically.

Another solution that Keppel and Wickens (2004) suggested is to consider your hypotheses carefully. If each hypothesis truly tests something separate from the other hypotheses, they suggest you retain an alpha level of .05 for all analyses. If, however, your hypotheses fall into families (e.g., you have five hypotheses, two of which seem logically related and the other three of which fit together as a separate family), you should adjust your alpha levels by family.

What counts as an analysis for purposes of examining experiment-wise error? Most students do three sets of analyses: preliminary analyses, hypothesis-testing analyses, and supplemental analyses. In considering Type I error, we focus primarily on hypothesis testing. We generally recommend setting alpha at .05 for preliminary analyses, because the purpose of these analyses is usually to look for confounds or problems; here Type II error is more important than Type I (we don't want to conclude there are no covariates that warrant control when in fact there are a few potential confounds). In fact, one could argue that *p* values should be increased, not decreased, in these circumstances. With supplemental analyses, you could adjust your *p* value or not, depending on your philosophy. If you are truly on a fishing expedition and want to be cautious, adjust your alpha downward to be more conservative. If you are afraid of missing something important, though, keep your alpha at .05. If you do the latter, however, do not overinterpret isolated findings with small or medium effects—there is a good chance they are spurious. Instead, look for consistencies across related supplemental analyses and large effects, which are less likely to be the result of chance.

We should point out that most of this discussion is based on the assumption that your analyses will rely at least in part on traditional null hypothesis significance testing (NHST). This approach has received a great deal of criticism for placing too much emphasis on *p* values and not enough on effect sizes and confidence intervals (e.g., Cumming, 2014). To our knowledge, however, none of the critics of NHST have addressed the issue of multiple analyses, so until alternative approaches become the norm, we recommend considering this issue in a thoughtful way. As you can see, you have a number of options. Think through the approach you wish to take, and incorporate that approach into your analysis plan.

BE CAREFUL WITH NONINDEPENDENT DATA

Although appropriate statistics exist for most questions and types of data, be wary about special circumstances that can complicate your statistical life. The first and most important comes from a basic assumption of many parametric and nonparametric statistics: independence of observations. Keppel and Wickens (2004) defined this clearly: "This assumption says that what one subject does has no effect on any other subject's performance" (p. 134). This assumption is important because violating it biases the results by leading to underestimates of standard errors of the statistics. This in turn increases the likelihood of Type I error.

You may remember from your introductory statistics courses that one common violation of this assumption occurs when the dependent variable comes from the same participants being tested more than once in within-subjects designs. A common example involves a treatment and a control group who are pretested on the dependent variable of interest, receive either an experimental or a control manipulation, and then are posttested on the same dependent variable. Well-developed methods exist for handling this issue when making group comparisons (e.g., *t* tests for nonindependent samples, repeated-measures ANOVAs). Regression analyses can handle longitudinal data from two time points, usually by using data from Time 2 as the dependent variable and data from Time 1 as a predictor or control variable.

Researchers may be less likely to think about nonindependence in studies that do not involve assessing the same participants repeatedly over time. Recall Keppel and Wickens's (2004) definition of independence: One participant's performance on the dependent variable has no effect on another participant's performance. In some between-subjects designs, even though each participant contributes only one dependent variable, independence is not a viable assumption. These circumstances occur when the participants come from the same group and something about the nature of the group may cause participants' performance to be affected by that of others. For example, consider studies in which researchers observe interactions between dating couples or among small groups of individuals. Clearly what one person does affects another's performance; the data from people who are dating each other or interacting together cannot be assumed to be independent. When classrooms or groups of individuals receive interventions as a group, how one person responds to treatment likely influences how others respond.

Situations in which several family members participate, people interact in groups, and interventions address groups of individuals who are likely to influence one another are the most frequent situations in which data are not independent. Fortunately, multilevel analytic procedures (i.e., multilevel modeling, hierarchical linear modeling; Bickel, 2007; Hox, 2010; Raudenbush & Bryk, 2002; Singer & Willett, 2003) can be used to deal with nonindependent data of this sort and can be thought of as the regression-based counterpart of repeated-measures ANOVA. Actor–partner interdependence models (e.g., Kenny et al., 2006; Raudenbush & Bryk, 2002) deal with nonindependence in dyadic data (e.g., from two friends, romantic partners). Multilevel analysis can be used with either continuous or categorical dependent variables. Multilevel modeling can also handle longitudinal data collected at multiple time points.

In essence, multilevel models build differ layers or "levels" of analysis, each of which contains predictors appropriate to that level. Suppose, for example, that you want to predict how well employees' admiration of their boss contributes to work satisfaction. Furthermore, you want to examine whether the age of the participant and the gender of the boss affects this relationship. To examine this, the multilevel model would examine two levels. Level 1 would be the employees you assess, who would provide data on their work satisfaction (the criterion variable), age, and admiration of their boss. These employees would be nested with bosses (e.g., the first 10 employees all have Boss A, the next 12 have Boss B, and so on), so Level 2 would be the boss level and contain data on the gender of each boss. To run the analysis, you would specify the predictors at each level. In this example, employee age and admiration of their boss would be Level 1 predictors and gender of the boss a Level 2 predictor.

Multilevel analysis has many of the same issues as regression, plus a few more. First, be aware that not all data that seem nonindependent will turn out to be. For example, you may think that clients seen by the same therapists will have related outcomes because some therapists are more talented than others, but this might not actually be the case. Therefore, your first step in data analysis will be to test whether the criterion variables are statistically nonindependent using a variation of the intraclass correlation coefficient, which tells you how much variance the nesting variable accounts for. If the nesting variable doesn't account for much (cutoffs vary), you will likely be able to use regression or SEM rather than multilevel modeling to examine your data. The second issue involves determining the number of participants you will need at each level. In the previous example, this would require that you consider both the number of employees and the number of bosses you will need. Finally, there are a number of tricky statistical issues you have to handle, such as deciding whether effects are fixed or random and how to center data in higher level groups. If the previous sentence looks like gobbledygook to you, you probably have limited experience with multilevel analysis and will need some additional help in planning and conducting your analyses.

What is our take-home message here? Although approaches to non-independent data have become more generally available in the past 2 decades, they are still not as plentiful and well developed as statistics that are based on the assumption of independent data. Virtually all statisticians seem to agree that the assumption of independence must be taken seriously, however. Therefore, make sure you have worked out how to deal with nonindependence problems from the outset. If the problems are quite complex, you may need to redesign your study to ensure independence of observation. As with SEM, if you know you will be dealing with nonindependent data, we advise you to seek out opportunities to learn how to use multilevel approaches and to line up consultation from someone familiar with the approach who can help you. We learned these analyses after obtaining our PhDs and have taught our students to use them, and there is definitely a learning curve in both setting up the analyses and interpreting the output.

BEWARE OF CAUSAL TERMINOLOGY

Be careful about allowing the name or nature of the statistic to dictate your reasoning about causality. For example, some students mistakenly believe that significant ANOVAs mean that the independent variable caused the changes in the dependent variable. Not so. Yes, differences in levels of the independent variable relate to differences in the dependent variable. Whether you can say the independent variable caused the differences, however, depends on your design, not the statistics you use to test relationships between variables. If you didn't manipulate the independent variable, you cannot legitimately ascribe causal status to it.

In this vein, some still refer to structural equation modeling as "causal modeling," an unfortunate moniker that produces droves of inappropriate inferences. Many SEM models are based on data collected at a single point in time. Similarly, path and mediation analyses with cross-sectional data are simply fancy correlational analyses. Ditto for regression in which one or more variables "predict" an outcome and all the variables are measured concurrently. No matter the lingo used to describe the statistic, a correlation is just a correlation. Your design, not your statistic, determines whether you can say that your independent variable caused changes in your dependent variable. Be aware of this when writing your Results and Discussion sections! Overstatement or misstatement of causal connections is an error that not only influences your defense meeting but can also lead to incorrect conclusions that get passed along in the literature.

USE CONSULTATION PRUDENTLY

At this point, you may have some idea of which statistics are suitable for your study. If so, you may wonder whether you have selected correctly. Go to the library or to good internet sites and read about some of your potential statistics in more detail. Check out your selections with other students or faculty members to see if they agree with your choices.

What should you do if you still feel clueless and need additional help? Are you allowed to get help or consultation on statistics, and if so, for what purposes? The answers to these questions depend on the degree of consultation involved. Consultation can range from asking your chair, another graduate student, or your statistics professor a few isolated questions about particular aspects of your analyses to hiring someone to select, program, and run the analyses for you. These extremes are very different in how much of the work is done by the consultant versus by you, the one who is earning the degree.

Consultation is healthy. Most faculty members consult colleagues with more knowledge about a particular statistical procedure than their own and learn from the experience. Seasoned researchers frequently write statistical consultation into the budgets of their grants. We consulted with colleagues in writing this chapter. Consultation with faculty and graduate students to point you in the right direction about the ins and outs of particular analyses generally falls within the boundaries of accepted professional practice. In fact, figuring out what you do not know and then finding the answer by reading and consulting are an important part of the professional repertoire. Most students seek consultation in selecting their statistics or in verifying their choices.

But what about more than this level of consultation? This is a complex question. Ideally, students do all of the work themselves, with occasional advice. Unfortunately, at some schools, the statistics classes may not have taught the students well or covered all of the analyses their research will require. Similarly, students may embark on a project before having had a chance to take all of the relevant classes and so may need to do some independent learning. In addition, some students have had a great deal of difficulty with the material covered in stats classes, their chair may be as frightened of statistics as they are, or the software resources and consultation needed for complex analyses may not be available. In these cases, expecting students to figure out what to do with the data and then conduct the analyses without extensive assistance may be unrealistic.

If you use consultation, remember that you ultimately must be responsible for the statistics in your project, regardless of how much you need to lean on your consultant for advice. This means that you must know why one particular statistic and not another is suitable, what computer program you used and what choices you made in analyzing your data, how you handled things such as missing data, what the computer output means, whether the analyses were done correctly, and how to interpret the findings. In other words, whether you actually perform the analyses or not, you must know what was done, inside and out, and be responsible for understanding the decisions made along the way, the accuracy of the results, and their interpretation. It's not your consultant who will be on the hot seat during your proposal meeting and oral defense!

What should you do if you need more than occasional advice? First, we recommend that you do as many of the analyses as you can yourself. If you have appropriate computer resources but no understanding of the particular statistic, you might consult with someone regarding choosing the statistic, programming the analysis, and reading the output. You would score, reduce, and enter the data yourself and run the analyses (perhaps with the assistance of a computer consultant who can help you find errors in your program statements). Second, we recommend that you obtain consultation specifically aimed at teaching the skills you lack. This might be more appropriately termed "tutoring" than "consultation." At the end of this tutoring, you should be prepared to pass an examination on what you did, why you did it, the assumptions and characteristics of the statistics you used, and what you found.

In fact, just such an examination may occur in your oral defense! "Well, I really am not sure about exactly what was done; I'll have to ask the person who ran the statistics" or "because my stats consultant said so" are *not* good ways to answer statistics questions in your final orals. You and you alone—not the person who assisted you—must defend your thesis or dissertation before your committee. It is your competence to do research, not your consultant's, that your committee assesses, and you are the one earning the degree. Therefore, get the assistance you need to learn and understand what you are doing, but do as much as you can on your own, and take full responsibility for ensuring that the statistics have been selected and calculated correctly.

Even if someone will assist you with all of your analyses, prepare your data yourself. Enter the data into the computer after talking with your consultant about how to do it. If your data come to you already entered, do your own data cleaning (see Chapter 10 for details). This will help you understand what the raw data look like. It will also prompt you to think about important issues, such as how to handle missing values. You can identify outliers—extreme scores that can distort your results and that you might want to handle carefully. We also recommend that you do preliminary analyses yourself, looking at means, standard deviations, frequency distributions, and so on. We will say more about preliminary analyses in Chapter 10.

SEEK ADDITIONAL ASSISTANCE IF YOU ARE STILL CONFUSED

Still confused about what statistics you should use after reading this chapter? You probably are not alone. Books, professors, and disciplines have different language systems for talking about analyses. Not only is the notation different, but sometimes people use different names for the same analysis. We could not cover every statistic or even every variation on the basic ones we mentioned. Like many students, you may need additional assistance at this point.

An additional tool in decision making is the decision tree, like the one in Figure 9.6, which is based on information compiled from statistics texts and other decision-making aids. Andrews et al. (1998) provided extensive decision trees for selecting appropriate statistics. They covered repeated measures (within-subjects) statistics only minimally, however. Tabachnick and Fidell (2013, pp. 29–31) provided a decision tree for multivariate techniques, including correlational strategies. Various additional resources for selecting statistics are available online; among the most comprehensive (though not free) are those from Laerd Statistics (https://statistics.laerd.com/).

Another idea is to examine recent articles in well-respected journals that present studies like the one you are proposing and see what kinds of analyses they used. Be sure to look for examples that have variables and types of measures (e.g., suitable for parametric analyses or not) that resemble yours. They should also have a similar design.

We recommend that you use these tools like you use this chapter—as a way to get ideas that you later confirm or reject through appropriate reading and consultation. Your chair, statistics professor, graduate student colleagues, and local consultants may provide further assistance to ensure you've selected the best statistical tools to use in your research.

WRITE YOUR ANALYSIS SECTION

As we noted in Chapter 7, planning, implementing, and then writing about your methods is a process that will continue throughout your entire thesis or dissertation project. The same is true of your analyses. You will consider what analyses you plan to conduct and describe the analyses in the proposal.

Once you complete your study, the final thesis or dissertation document will describe what analyses you conducted and their results. In this chapter, we concentrate on the proposal. Chapter 11 covers how to describe your analyses and findings in the final thesis or dissertation document.

Recall that you may have up to three main subsections for the analysis plan in a proposal—preliminary, primary, and (if needed) supplemental analyses. Your Preliminary Analysis section should include your data cleaning procedures (e.g., handling missing data and invalid responses, examining score distributions to identify outliers) and any preliminary analyses you will conduct, such as checking the reliability of your measures, conducting validity analyses, and presenting descriptive statistics for your final sample (e.g., means, standard deviations, ranges, often presented separately by specific variables of interest). You may also plan to include a general examination of relations among study variables—that is, a correlation table—in this section. Even if some of your hypotheses (presented in the Primary Analyses section) call for correlations, you are almost certainly not examining all such relations among your study variables. A general correlation table provides detail that others who peruse your work might be interested in, and a thesis or dissertation is often used to archive such detail.

Next, your Primary Analyses section describes the statistical procedures you will use to test your hypotheses and address your research question. You will make statements such as "A 2×2 ANCOVA will be used to analyze the effects of anxiety and task complexity on errors, with GPA serving as the covariate." If you have not already done so in your Preliminary Analysis section, indicate that you will provide appropriate tables of means and standard deviations for each of your groups on each dependent variable.

Be sure to provide details regarding exactly how you plan to enter variables into your analyses. For example, if you use ANOVAs or ANCOVAs, you might include a summary (source) table indicating the main effects, interactions, error terms, and degrees of freedom you will use. Similarly, if you use regression-based analyses, you might include a table indicating steps of entry (e.g., for hierarchical multiple regression) for individual predictors and interaction terms; if you use structural equation modeling, you might include a figure depicting your manifest and latent variables and the expected associations among them that you will test. Make sure you indicate which statistical test you will use for every piece of data (e.g., variable, score) that you plan to analyze. Your readers should also know exactly how each variable is to be scored, a topic you covered in the Method section when you described your measures.

Finally, you may have a Supplemental Analysis section that covers research questions that are not the primary focus of your study but that you still want to explore. These may be questions that are interesting but tangential to your primary research aims, or questions that you want to explore but that are "weaker" or very preliminary in nature because of an underdeveloped literature base, your small sample, or other reason. Including these supplemental analyses in your proposal allows you to present the ideas to your committee for feedback while communicating that you recognize that they are not your top priority. It will also protect you from being accused of data snooping after the fact and of taking advantage of surprises as though they were anticipated. This section contains information similar to that presented in your Primary Analyses section—a statement and description of the analysis you propose for each question.

It is possible to be more extensive than this, however. One way to clarify your analysis plan for yourself (and your committee) is to create a mock Results section. For example, you could provide appropriate tables of expected means and standard deviations for each of your groups on each dependent measure. Or you could present figures to show graphically the effects you might find. For example, if doing an ANOVA, you might present figures to illustrate the main effects and interactions that you expect to find if the study turns out exactly as you predict. Figuring this out ahead of time will help you get clear about what you are really doing and will permit you to check computer printouts later for errors. Show your results in the ideal form. That is, show how they will look if the study turns out exactly as your hypotheses predict. Then, show how they will look if the study is a total bust. Finally, show the most likely case, namely, a mixture of positive, negative, and confusing results.

You may wonder why we would include a mock Results section in our suggestions for your thesis or dissertation proposal. After all, almost no one requires this, so why do something you don't have to do? In addition, after all, you are proposing to do the research. You haven't done it yet, so where are the results to include in this section?

It might help you appreciate our suggestions if you consider this section a "Hypothesized Results" section. Although not everyone would agree with the need for a Results section in a proposal, such a section forces you to think about exactly how you are going to analyze and present your data. A mock Results section requires you to identify in advance the statistical procedures you will use. This will help you discover whether your data are likely to meet the assumptions of the various statistics, whether your data can even be analyzed to answer the questions you have posed, and what type of consultative or other resources you will need. Looking at different ways the data could turn out may also help identify design weaknesses that you can correct before you run the study. Doing this should also help you learn more about your statistics in advance of running the study, which will save you lots of time later. When your data are collected, you can begin your analyses immediately and will not have to stop and decide just what you are going to do and how. Keeping the momentum going on complex, drawn-out research projects is extremely important. In addition, mock results provide just the level of detail needed for busy committee members to understand exactly what you are planning to do. Then they can identify potential snags and help you steer around them before you run into problems.

A word of caution if you plan to present mock data—make sure you label all of it clearly and correctly! That includes the tables and figures in your proposal, as well as the data and analysis files you store on your computer. It can be incredibly frustrating to go back to old tables, figures, or files and not be able to remember whether they are hypothetical or real; the only thing worse might be misremembering and accidentally presenting mock data as real. We have heard horror stories of individuals losing jobs and having doctorates revoked on the basis of these types of "irregularities" in dissertation data discovered after they graduated. The distinction between accident and data faking may be lost on your committee and institution or the journal in which you publish your results. The consequences of falsifying data (even inadvertently) range from embarrassing to career ending. Good organizational skills now will help you avoid this pitfall.

Students often write their Analysis section as the final step in writing the proposal. If this is the case for you, finishing this section means you have reached a major milestone in your thesis or dissertation journey—you have completed a draft of your proposal! Take time to consider everything you have done. You found a topic, came to understand it thoroughly, developed a plan for a study that will contribute new knowledge relevant to your topic, and figured out how to collect and analyze your data. Kudos to you—celebrate at least a little before you move forward to your proposal meeting and data collection!

✓ **TO DO . . .**

SELECTING APPROPRIATE STATISTICS FOR QUANTITATIVE ANALYSES

☐ Beef up your statistical knowledge early.

 - Find comprehensible statistics books, websites, YouTube presentations, and articles.

 - Get experience doing statistical analyses.

☐ Examine your research questions and create an analysis plan.

 - List your research questions and hypotheses and identify questions you want statistics to answer.

 - Identify preliminary analyses you want to do.

 - Identify hypothesis-testing analyses you want to do.

 - Identify whether your questions and hypotheses are about differences between groups, relationships among variables in a single group, or a model that involves multiple independent and dependent variables.

 - Make a list of independent and dependent variables you plan to analyze.

 - Identify scores used to operationalize the variables.

- Identify the nature of each score (e.g., continuous, categorical).
- Identify whether dependent variables are suitable for parametric or nonparametric analyses.

☐ Match analytic methods to research questions, hypotheses, and scores.

- Select among group comparison statistics.
- Select among correlational statistics.
- Select among model-testing approaches.
- Select other statistics or analytic approaches (e.g., cluster analysis, growth mixture modeling, visual analysis) if appropriate.

☐ Set your alpha levels.

☐ Be careful with nonindependent data.

☐ Beware of causal terminology.

☐ Use consultation prudently.

☐ Seek additional assistance if you are still confused.

- Look at decision trees.
- Read stats books.
- Check out websites.
- Look at articles about studies that used designs like yours.
- Talk to your mentor, stats professor, or knowledgeable students.

☐ Write your Analysis section.

- Preliminary analyses
- Hypothesis-testing analyses
- Supplemental (exploratory) analyses

SUPPLEMENTAL RESOURCES

Comprehensive Statistics Textbooks

Field, A. (2018). *Discovering multivariate statistics using IBM SPSS Statistics* (5th ed.). Sage.

Keppel, G., & Wickens, T. D. (2004). *Design and analysis: A researcher's handbook* (4th ed.). Pearson Prentice-Hall.

Kirk, R. E. (2013). *Experimental design: Procedures for the behavioral sciences* (4th ed.). Brooks/Cole Wadsworth. https://doi.org/10.4135/9781483384733

Maxwell, S. E., Delaney, H. D., & Kelley, K. (2018). *Designing experiments and analyzing data: A model comparison approach* (3rd ed.). Routledge.

Mertler, C. A., & Vannatta, R. A. (2016). *Advanced and multivariate statistical methods* (6th ed.). Routledge.

Meyers, L. S., Gamst, G., & Guarino, A. J. (2017). *Applied multivariate research: Design and interpretation* (3rd ed.). Sage.

Pedazhur, E. J. (1997). *Multiple regression in behavioral research: Explanation and prediction* (3rd ed.). Harcourt Brace.

Siegel, S. (1956). *Nonparametric statistics for the behavioral sciences.* McGraw-Hill.

Tabachnick, B. F., & Fidell, L. S. (2013). *Using multivariate statistics* (6th ed.). Pearson.

Specialized References

Aiken, L. S., & West, S. G. (1996). *Multiple regression: Testing and interpreting interactions.* Sage.

Aiken, L. S., West, S. G., & Taylor, A. B. (2007). Correlation methods/regression models. In D. McKay (Ed.), *Handbook of research methods in abnormal and clinical psychology* (pp. 79–106). Sage.

Brown, T. A. (2015). *Confirmatory factor analysis for applied research* (2nd ed.). Guilford Press.

Bruning, J. L., & Kintz, B. L. (1997). *Computational handbook of statistics* (4th ed.). Pearson.

Cohen, P., Cohen, J., West, S. G., & Aiken, L. S. (2003). *Applied multiple regression/correlation analysis for the behavioral sciences* (3rd ed.). Erlbaum.

Coxe, S., West, S. G., & Aiken, L. S. (2009). The analysis of count data: A gentle introduction to Poisson regression and its alternatives. *Journal of Personality Assessment, 91*(2), 121–136. https://doi.org/10.1080/00223890802634175

Fabrigar, L. R., Wegener, D. T., MacCallum, R. C., & Strahan, E. J. (1999). Evaluating the use of exploratory factor analysis in psychological research. *Psychological Methods, 4*(3), 272–299. https://doi.org/10.1037/1082-989X.4.3.272

Field, A. P., & Wilcox, R. R. (2017). Robust statistical methods: A primer for clinical psychology and experimental psychopathology researchers. *Behaviour Research and Therapy, 98*, 19–38. https://doi.org/10.1016/j.brat.2017.05.013

Floyd, F., & Widaman, K. F. (1995). Factor analysis in the development and refinement of clinical assessment instruments. *Psychological Assessment, 7*(3), 286–299. https://doi.org/10.1037/1040-3590.7.3.286

Gorsuch, R. L. (2015). *Factor analysis* (classic ed.). Routledge.

Hayes, A. F. (2013). *Introduction to mediation, moderation, and conditional process analysis: A regression-based approach.* Guilford Press.

Hox, J. J. (2010). *Multilevel analysis: Techniques and applications* (2nd ed.). Routledge. https://doi.org/10.4324/9780203852279

Kenny, D. A., Kashy, D. A., Cook, W. L., & Simpson, J. A. (2006). *Dyadic data analysis.* Guilford Press.

Kline, R. B. (2015). *Principles and practice of structural equation modeling* (4th ed.) Guilford Press.

MacCallum, R. C., Widamon, K. F., Zhang, S., & Hong, S. (1999). Sample size in factor analysis. *Psychological Methods, 4*(1), 84–99.

MacKinnon, D. P., Fairchild, A. J., & Fritz, M. S. (2007). Mediation analysis. *Annual Review of Psychology, 58*, 593–614. https://doi.org/10.1146/annurev.psych.58.110405.085542

Newton, R. R., & Rudestam, K. E. (2013). *Your statistical consultant: Answers to your data analysis questions* (2nd ed.). Sage. https://doi.org/10.4135/9781506374673

Preacher, K. J., & MacCallum, R. C. (2003). Repairing Tom Swift's electric factor analysis machine. *Understanding Statistics, 2*(1), 13–43. https://doi.org/10.1207/S15328031US0201_02

Raudenbush, S. W., & Bryk, A. S. (2002). *Hierarchical linear models: Applications and data analysis methods* (2nd ed.). Sage.

Raykov, T., & Marcoulides, G. M. (2006). *A first course in structural equation modeling* (2nd ed.). Erlbaum.

Schumacker, R. E., & Lomax, R. G. (2016). *A beginner's guide to structural equation modeling* (4th ed.). Routledge.

Singer, J. D., & Willett, J. S. (2003). *Applied longitudinal data analysis: Modeling change and event occurrence.* Oxford University Press. https://doi.org/10.1093/acprof:oso/9780195152968.001.0001

Thompson, B. (2004). *Exploratory and confirmatory factor analysis: Understanding concepts and applications.* American Psychological Association. https://doi.org/10.1037/10694-000

Wilcox, R. R. (2017). *Introduction to robust estimation and hypothesis testing* (4th ed.). Academic Press.

Wilkinson, L., & Task Force on Statistical Inference. (1999). Statistical methods in psychology journals: Guidelines and explanations. *American Psychologist, 54*(8), 594–604. https://doi.org/10.1037/0003-066X.54.8.594

Internet Resources

Kenny, D. A. (2013, December 5). *Webinars and powerpoints entry page.* http://davidakenny.net/webinars/intro.htm

Kenny, D. A. (2014, January 12). *Structural equation modeling.* http://davidakenny.net/cm/causalm.htm

David A. Kenny provides a variety of materials related to dyadic analyses and structural equation modeling; access to webinars currently requires a very small fee.

Laerd Statistics. (n.d.). https://statistics.laerd.com

Laerd Statistics offers guidance in breaking down what your study is doing in much the same way this chapter does, then guides you to recommended statistics. This information is not free but seems priced with graduate student budgets in mind. Other guidance addresses running analyses in SPSS, reading the output, and writing up findings.

10

Collecting, Managing, and Analyzing the Data

This chapter
- covers the nuts and bolts of running your study
- describes steps in preparing data for analyses

Read thoroughly if
- you have not had primary responsibility for conducting research
- you want to see how experienced researchers approach these tasks

Skim or skip if
- you have extensive experience in managing data sets
- you are using archival data already in analyzable form

You've finished the proposal, your committee has approved it, and now it's time to collect the data—to do what you promised to do in your Method section. The promises may have been easier to make than to keep, however. How much difficulty you have keeping them will depend in part on careful planning to minimize potential hassles. Chapter 3 described planning steps you could take early in your project. Here, we provide more advice for avoiding and coping with common problems that fledgling researchers encounter as they put their plans into practice.

https://doi.org/10.1037/0000161-010
Dissertations and Theses From Start to Finish: Psychology and Related Fields, Third Edition,
by D. J. Bell, S. L. Foster, and J. D. Cone

Before you rush out to recruit participants, take time to pilot test and fine-tune your procedures, train any research assistants (RAs) you have working with you, develop a data storage and management plan, and arrange for equipment and facilities. In this chapter, we discuss each of these steps in detail. In addition, make sure you obtain written approval from your institutional review board (IRB) for the protection of human or nonhuman animal participants for the procedures you plan to use before you even advertise for or recruit participants.

PILOT TEST YOUR PROCEDURES

If you have not already pilot tested your procedures, now is the time to do it. The specific purposes of pilot testing are (a) to ensure that participants will respond in accord with instructions, (b) to uncover and decide how to handle unanticipated problems, (c) to gauge how long participants will take to finish their tasks, and (d) to learn how to use and check the adequacy of your equipment.

Pilot work is important because what you plan to do may look good on paper but not work well when you try it out with real participants. For example, the procedure you thought would take 15 minutes may take an hour for some participants. Your computer-administered questionnaires may not screen out participants as intended. The equipment may not work the way you thought it would, or participants may not understand your carefully crafted instructions. Even if your procedures run smoothly, pilot work will alert you to issues that you need to train your RAs to handle. It is hard to train someone to use procedures that you do not know intimately yourself.

Initially you will want to try out procedures yourself. This is especially true if you have computer-administered procedures, such as computerized experiments or online survey software (e.g., Qualtrics, SurveyMonkey), and have questions that involve branching (i.e., some participants see certain questions on the basis of their responses to previous ones). Make sure you try out each of your branches to ensure that they are set up as planned. If the software is randomly assigning participants or randomly ordering materials, make sure you test out those procedures as well. You do not want to discover midway through your study that—oops!—all of your first 20 participants were assigned to the same experimental condition.

Once you are sure all of your materials are ready to go, try out the study on a few individuals besides yourself and get their feedback. Who should serve as pilot participants? If you will have no problem recruiting a sufficient sample for the research, designate the first few participants you recruit as pilot participants. Do not include their data in the study, because normally you will treat them differently than later participants. If participants who meet your criteria are likely to be scarce, use individuals who have characteristics that match your target population as closely as possible but who would not qualify as participants in your actual study. For example, in our work with children, we often recruit children of colleagues or of graduate students to serve as pilot participants. Other graduate students, undergraduate RAs, and friends may be willing to serve as pilot participants for some or all of your procedures.

Now is the time to fine-tune your procedures and work out the bugs. To facilitate this, ask your pilot participants to give you feedback, something that usually does not occur during the study proper. Ask your participants whether the instructions were clear, what difficulties they had following the instructions, whether anything about the environment or the experimenter's behavior interfered with their performance of the task, and so on. In addition, watch your participants as they complete the procedures. Do they perform as you instructed? Make suitable changes based on their feedback and your observations and run the next pilot participants. Again, ask for feedback. Keep adjusting your procedures until you are satisfied the study will run smoothly. Keep written notes to use in training any assistants you might involve.

If you use human judges or observers to rate or record participants' responses, collect pilot data to use when you train them. For example, videotape the kinds of interactions observers will be recording on the playground, bar, grocery store, or other location, or collect samples of written open-ended responses that raters will later code. Having pilot data will allow your assistants to practice during training on real data. This step is important because real data often pose difficulties you may not anticipate when you make up training materials. Perhaps this is why interobserver agreement often drops when observers begin to observe real participants after training (e.g., Taplin & Reid, 1973). Train assistants to deal with these problems *before* you start collecting the data needed for your thesis or dissertation.

Pilot testing occasionally turns up a problem that requires a major change in design or procedures. Your clever use of an experimental confederate, for example, may be blatantly transparent to the pilot participants. Your experimental manipulation of participants' motivation may not motivate them, and so on. Remember, your chair must approve all changes in procedures and design. If you propose a major change, you may need to meet again with your entire committee. At a minimum, you should circulate a memorandum outlining the changes you propose and asking committee members to agree to the changes in writing. In addition, changes in procedures may require you to alter your consent form. In most cases, you will need to apply to your IRB for approval of any changes to your initial protocol.

If you are collecting your data using software to record participants' responses, download your pilot participants' responses and look at those data as well. Qualtrics, for example, will download data in SPSS or Excel formats. This is worth doing with some pilot data to see how the program sets up the file. Check to make sure the program will download all of the data you need. Look at the format in which the data are presented. Is everything there? You will also get some idea about steps you will need to take later to clean the data and get your file into analyzable shape—a topic we cover later in this chapter.

Similarly, if you are using mechanical devices or pieces of equipment to collect data (e.g., when collecting physiological data, when experience sampling using cellphones), make sure you know how to use them, how to detect whether they are working correctly, and how to prepare the data they produce for analyses. Many of these approaches produce data that require a great deal of cleaning, which we address later in this chapter. Students who work in research labs that use these methods typically get hands-on training in the ins and outs of these procedures, which may or may not be codified in written form in the literature. If this is your maiden voyage into a measurement or research method that requires complex cleaning and data reduction, find good sources to help you learn state-of-the-science procedures before you collect your own data. Make sure you have access to any specialized software needed to help with these tasks, and learn to use it. Be aware that cleaning and reducing some types of data can be very time consuming, so make sure to factor this time into your planning, particularly if you are concerned about deadlines for completing your project.

RECRUIT AND TRAIN ASSISTANTS

Thesis and dissertation studies are big undertakings. Ordinarily they require assistants of one sort or another. For example, you may need others to serve as experimenters, raters, observers, confederates, and the like. These individuals may be undergraduate students working for credit, paid assistants, other graduate students, or friends and relatives who have a perverse interest in your being indebted to them in a major way.

These assistants should first be told—preferably in the form of a written agreement that you and they sign—exactly what you will require of them and what they will get from participating in the project. This information should include the full nature of their duties; the times you will ask them to work; the duration of their involvement; compensation for services (if any); and if they are students working for credit, how you will evaluate them. We also recommend full disclosure of things that can get them "fired" from the project.

Be honest, direct, and realistic with prospective assistants. Remember that collecting data may take longer than you plan, that participants may not show up, and that training takes time. Leading prospective assistants to believe that their duties will be minimal and later dumping extra work on them can create resentment. If some applicants do not have enough time to meet your requirements, including the possibility of extending beyond the original time, let those people opt out in the beginning. This is better than spending considerable time training them only to have them quit because the project is more work than they initially expected.

Timing is important. A common error involves recruiting assistants too early. They then have nothing to do for several weeks or months. When the project is finally ready to go, typically several can no longer participate. A good rule of thumb is to begin recruiting assistants after (a) your committee approves your proposal, (b) you have arranged a source of participants, (c) your training materials are ready, (d) you have received approval in writing from the university IRB or animal care and use committee, and (e) your initial pilot testing is complete. An approved proposal ensures that your procedures will not change much on the basis of a committee member's suggestions. Having a source of participants usually means that you can begin collecting data as soon as you train your assistants.

Your proposal may dictate certain types of assistants—for example, a female confederate, a graduate-student therapist, or a child model. In addition to screening for qualities that relate to your design, select assistants who are dependable. You want RAs to be on time and to keep their commitments. With undergraduates, we sometimes assess this by asking about their job experience, on the assumption that individuals who have held part-time or full-time jobs have had to learn and demonstrate reliable performance. Another quality to look for is good judgment. Ideally, your RAs should do what you would do when an unanticipated problem occurs. For example, if RAs will be observing in the school setting, they will need to dress appropriately, interact professionally with the school office staff and teachers, and refrain from complaining if a teacher asks them to leave the classroom because it is time for a test they forgot to mention earlier. Finally, a reasonably high grade point average may indicate that a prospective RA learns quickly, is conscientious enough to consistently do well in classes, or both. Avoid the trap of looking only for good grades, however. Although high-level general intellectual functioning is a wonderful quality in an RA, dependability, social skills, and good judgment may be more important.

After you recruit your RAs, train them well. A large body of research has shown that instruction, modeling, rehearsal, and feedback contribute to skill acquisition and performance. Explain tasks to your RAs, show them (though role-playing, video, or other means) how to do them, and have them practice as you give feedback. If your RAs must perform complex duties, break the tasks down and have them learn and practice small steps that cumulate in mastery of the complete task.

As an example, Sharon Foster and her colleague Debra Kawahara (Cunningham et al., 2019) trained graduate students to conduct semistructured interviews of therapists and supervisors involved in delivering two different evidence-based interventions to youth and their families. Interviewers had to learn about the two interventions so they would understand the vocabulary used by the participants. The first step was for interviewers to read articles on the two approaches and listen to presentations given by experts on each therapy. They then practiced the interview with one of the investigators, who provided feedback. After that, the interviewers completed practice interviews with pilot participants and reviewed audiotapes of these interviews with one of the investigators. They were deemed ready to interview actual participants when they completed two different mock interviews that required minimal correction.

Because knowledge of experimental hypotheses has long been known to increase the chances of biased data (e.g., Rosenthal, 1969), keep your RAs as unaware as possible of the different conditions of your study. If this is not possible, at least make sure they don't know your hypotheses. At the same time, tell them enough so they can perform their duties adequately. To figure out whether a piece of information is inappropriate to share, ask yourself, Could this information conceivably alter the way this assistant interacts with participants or scores the data? If the answer is "yes," do not give the assistant the information.

It is also important to avoid experimenter–condition confounds. This occurs when different experimenters are exclusively responsible for different conditions. When this happens, you cannot be sure your findings are the result of your independent variable or of differences in experimenters.

When students are working for credit, make the experience an educational one. You can do this by teaching the fundamentals of research design and procedures (without revealing your hypotheses, of course!). Students can learn about the importance of standardized procedures, the concept of experimental control, why and how data on interobserver agreement are important, and so on. You may also be able to help undergraduate students learn the ins and outs of graduate school life, application procedures, and the like or to mentor other graduate students who are not as advanced as you are. As much as possible, we like to give students a variety of duties as RAs so that they can observe and experience many aspects of the research process.

BUILD IN ETHICAL SAFEGUARDS

You probably thought through a number of ethical issues when planning your study and obtaining IRB approval. Now is the time to make sure your RAs understand research ethics and how they apply to your study. Review the material on research ethics in Chapter 7, and have RAs complete any training required by your IRB. Remember to inform your assistants about the importance of confidentiality. They should not talk about participants' data or behavior with others outside the project. Be sure to tell them not to chat about participants with fellow assistants in public places; current or prospective participants may overhear their comments. Provide guidelines about where and how RAs should use cellphones to speak to participants about scheduling or to collect data.

Instructing yourself and others is only part of this process, however. Having procedures in place to ensure ethical conduct is also important. Think about how you will store the data, make sure no names are on data forms or included in computerized data files, and so on. Where will you store your information, and how safe is it? If RAs will keep data files on a computer or in the cloud, how will you ensure that these files are safe from theft or sharing? If you are working with children in school settings, how will you collect consent forms from teachers? How will you make sure you don't accidentally include a participant who does not have parental consent? How will you obtain assent and make sure that children have the opportunity to ask questions and demur if they decide they do not wish to participate?

In addition to developing procedures that ensure confidentiality and informed consent, make sure to monitor the way you and others conduct the research. If you are using assistants, you might sit in on or listen to tape recordings of their interviews with participants. This provides a check that they really are obtaining informed consent and explaining participants' rights in language the participants can understand. Likewise, sit in on or listen to tapes of debriefing sessions to make sure your assistants tell participants the essential details of the experiment in which they have just participated. If you are running participants yourself, ask your best RA to observe you and provide feedback on these aspects as well.

Make sure you have procedures to follow in case of emergency situations. If your study involves greater than minimal risk, you probably already had to think about how you would handle the risk in order to obtain IRB approval for your research, and now is the time to make sure you have those procedures in place. Even if your study involves minimal risk, think about accidents or other unexpected events that could happen, and be prepared. What should you or your RAs do if a participant seems distressed during the study? if a participant unexpectedly discloses ongoing abuse or suicidal ideation? if some unexpected emergency arises? If you are not clinically trained and are dealing with sensitive populations, it will be helpful to have a committee member or other faculty member with clinical or counseling skills who agrees to consult with you in these circumstances. Make sure you know how to contact your on-call resources and your chair for assistance should an unexpected emergency arise. You will need to report any adverse events (usually defined as negative events that exceed the sorts covered in the initial IRB protocol) to your IRB using the procedures in place at your institution.

A final note related to ethics: If your study involves minimal or greater than minimal risk (i.e., received an expedited or full board review), you will need to renew your IRB approval if your study extends more than a year beyond the initial approval date. Some IRBs require that the approval be extended until any additional data coding or analysis is complete, others only until contact with human participants ends. In our experience, most IRBs notify investigators that they will need to renew their approvals, but some do not—so make sure to keep track of your IRB's requirements and due dates for annual renewals.

SCHEDULE SETTINGS AND ARRANGE MATERIALS

After you finalize your procedures and establish a timetable for starting the project, work out the final logistical details. This section prompts you to think about how you are going to keep the project running smoothly from week to week and to plan accordingly. Such planning involves ensuring that you have a physical location to run participants at appropriate times. If you are running animals in a long series of trials over a specific time period, make sure someone will be available to run the animals during weekends and vacations.

If you are purchasing measures or other copyrighted materials, order these in advance (be sure to ask about discounts or freebies for starving students working on theses or dissertations). Get permission in writing to use the measures from the individuals who hold the copyrights. Similarly, if you need equipment, make sure it will be available when you need it, and have a backup plan in case equipment suddenly fails or disappears. If several people will take equipment to different sites, make rules for checking out and returning it to a central spot in a timely fashion so that you can locate missing tape recorders, electric cords, and so on. Have a plan for preventive maintenance, such as replenishing batteries, keeping extra supplies on hand, and making sure laptops are fully charged.

If you are administering measures to participants via computer, make sure the computer files are prepared, your internet access is working, and so forth—and make sure you have backup paper-and-pencil versions on hand in case your technology fails during the session. If you are using paper-and-pencil forms, prepare them. Write the participant's code number on all pieces of data in case the pieces get separated later on. If your procedures are complex, include a checklist (e.g., in computerized form, stapled to the inside of the participant's folder) listing the tasks and measures to be completed. As the participant completes each task, the experimenter can check the appropriate item on the checklist. Create a method of checking for missing data as participants or RAs turn in forms. For example, in studies using paper questionnaires, we scan through the items when the participant turns in the forms. When we see a blank item, we ask the person whether they accidentally or intentionally left the answer blank (in the latter case, we say, "That's fine; you don't have to answer anything you don't want to").

Arrange a place to store the data as they come in. To ensure confidentiality, keep physical data and consent forms in a locked room (at a minimum), and preferably in a locked filing cabinet. Make sure RAs know the rules and procedures for filing data (e.g., all data must be filed immediately after running a participant, not carried around in a car; no raw data may leave the building). The same applies for computerized data—have a secure central place to store the files. Check periodically to make sure you have forms on file for all participants. If there is a key that codes their names with identifying numbers, make sure it is up to date and kept in a separate, locked place or a secure computer file. Incidentally, consider the possibility of natural disaster (e.g., fire, flood) and major computer crash and plan how to make sure key data are not lost in the event of unexpected catastrophe.

Think, too, about easy ways of keeping track of how many participants have been run as the study progresses (a publicly posted cumulative graph of accomplishments motivates everyone) and of informing others involved in the project about what is happening that week. For example, one of us often conducts research involving individual sessions with children in school settings. Sometimes schedules must change from week to week because of teacher requests, RA availability, student absence, and the school schedule. When we cannot create a master schedule to follow every week, we check with the school office administrator every Thursday or Friday about field trips, teacher conference days, and other times when the children will not be available. We then schedule RAs for the following week and email tentative schedules to the teachers for approval, and we send final approved versions to the teachers, the principal, the school's administrative assistant, and the RAs. The RAs also get a list of children who have parental permission with notes about who has and has not participated at that point. RAs update a master list once they have finished data collection for the day.

Another detail to think about involves transferring paper-and-pencil data to computer-usable form. Unless you are doing a single-organism study with no statistics involved, eventually you will need to do this. Although some researchers like to wait until all data are collected, we prefer to get data ready for and into the computer as they come in. That way, individuals running participants can also be responsible for recording and inputting their own data, and the process is not as tedious as it is when all data are input at once. We discuss methods for recording data later.

One exception to our "do it as you go" advice arises if observers or raters code videotapes or written responses. Observer (i.e., rater or coder) drift (Cooper et al., 2007) can distort data if a coding scheme is not implemented carefully. When only one observer deviates or drifts in how they apply a coding scheme, you will be able to detect this when you calculate interobserver agreement (which you should do frequently during data collection). However, this won't be the case when two or more observers drift consensually in how they use a coding system over time. This can happen if they discuss problems using the coding scheme and evolve implicit decision rules among themselves that do not appear in the original coding manual. If everyone drifts as a group (i.e., consensually), interrater or interobserver agreement figures will be high, and it will not be apparent that drift has occurred. Most important, data that come in later in the project will be coded differently than early data, creating a potential confound for longitudinal, time-series, and pre–post designs. Thus, assembling all the data first and coding tapes or responses in random order later ensure that drift and time of data collection are not confounded. Another way to combat drift is to recalibrate by having observers score criterion tapes periodically throughout the data collection process (Croasdale, 2016). Recalibration is important for any project involving human judges, and it is crucial when data must be coded as they come in rather than randomly at some later time.

PLAN FOR THE UNEXPECTED

No matter how carefully you plan, things will go wrong. An important step is to identify the most probable areas in which unexpected events might occur. In our experience, there are three: participants, personnel, and equipment. What unexpecteds can you expect for each of these?

With respect to participants, we have already considered negative events that have ethical ramifications. Two additional potential sources of problems involve recruitment and appointment keeping. Remember the rule of threes here: Allow three times as much time as you think it will take to recruit enough participants.

You might be saying this doesn't apply in your case because you already have the permission of the instructors of three college classes that will provide more than enough participants for your administration of the XYZ Scales. Perhaps so, but what if the class is canceled one day because the instructor is ill, and the very next class cannot be used because an exam is scheduled? Or what if a lower percentage of class members volunteer to participate than you expected? Maybe you plan to do your recruiting by advertising online. Do you know the positive response rate to different ways of doing this? Do you have any pilot information to indicate what kind of positive response rate you can expect with your own study?

If you schedule participants for in-person appointments, do you have any way of ensuring they show up? Will it help to reimburse them for getting to and from the session (e.g., via bus, Uber, Lyft)? What is the typical no-show rate for studies such as yours? What will you do if someone fails to keep an appointment? Will you schedule a makeup or decide not to run the risk of a repeat offense? Take a clue from physicians and dentists. They give you a card with the exact day and time of your appointment, then email, text, or call you to remind you of the appointment a day or two before it occurs. Have you made arrangements to do this?

Despite your best efforts, some participants will not keep their appointments. How will you use this unexpected time? If you are thinking it will be a good time to get caught up on your sleeping or recreational pursuits or to study for a class, consider another possibility. This is time set aside for working on your research. If a participant fails to appear, this is not really "free" time. It only looks that way. You will have to make up this session some time later if you plan to keep the project on schedule. Anticipate the occasional no-show and plan to do some research-related work during that time. Start updating your Method section now that you have had experience running the study. Input your latest data into the computer. Chase down that final elusive refer-ence at the library. If you keep to the task this way, you will minimize the time wasted by no-shows, and you will not be derailed from accomplishing your goal.

Incidentally, it is a good idea to keep track of no-shows. You may have some objective data (e.g., pretest scores, demographics) from these individuals that you can use to compare them with participants who keep their agreement to participate fully in the study. Are there differences? Will these slant the out-comes of your research in particular ways? For example, what if your study of therapy outcomes finds dropouts to be worse off on pretest measures? Could your excitement at finding pre–post improvement in your treated par-ticipants be dulled by finding out they were healthier at the outset? No-shows or study dropouts can lead to missing data, which you should examine as part of your analyses.

RAs or other project personnel are a second source of unexpected events. Being human, they get sick, fail to keep *their* appointments, or forget to collect or enter an important piece of data. How will you handle these little oversights?

Standard personnel management practices are the best advice here. Start with the selection of the very best people you can get. Who they are may depend on how you will compensate them. If you can pay them a reasonable amount in money or academic credit, you can select more skilled or experi-enced people and expect more from them. If you cannot pay, consider non-monetary rewards. The barter system sometimes works well. You agree to help someone with their data analyses if they will run participants for you. Or, how about a home-cooked meal for every six participants run?

To avoid problems when an assistant calls in sick or takes a vacation, cross-train your RAs. Make sure each knows at least one other person's job so you can arrange substitutions when needed.

Plan time for frequent monitoring. In addition to monitoring for imple-mentation of research ethics procedures, check the data as they come in. Make sure your assistants are following research procedures to the letter. Even conscientious assistants make errors; spot-checking their performance can allow you to catch errors before they get out of control. In a similar vein, calculate interobserver agreement as you go if your study involves raters or coders; otherwise, you may be in the same position as one poor dissertation student who had to retrain her observers and recode all her data because she waited until the end of the study to calculate interobserver agreement, only to find out that it was unacceptably low. Conduct recalibration checks if direct observation data are involved.

Finally, expect surprises from your equipment. You can anticipate all of these. Some (e.g., internet going down, laptop running out of battery life, difficulty hooking the projector to the computer) are more likely than others (e.g., someone stealing the polygraph), but it is best to assume that break-downs will happen and to be prepared for them. In case you are thinking that you are doing low- or no-tech research and equipment is not involved, think again. What about the car that gets you back and forth to the research site?

What about the computer you are using for word processing and data analyses? A couple of years ago, one of us had three hard disk crashes on different computers in the same year. Do you have plans for backing up documents and data in the cloud or on different computers maintained in different locations?

The Department of Redundancy Department is a good place for dealing with all three of these sources of potential surprises. Cross-training RAs is an example of the redundancy principle. Have more participants, personnel, and equipment ready to do the job than you think you will need. Arrange in advance to borrow or rent equipment to use temporarily while yours is being repaired. Have a plan to notify your backup or on-call RAs in case the primary one gets sick. The National Aeronautics and Space Administration exemplifies the principle of redundancy in its crewed flights into outer space: When one system fails, a backup system immediately assumes its functions. Run your research this way. In fact, run your life this way, and you will suffer fewer unpleasant surprises!

COLLECT THE DATA

Finally, the first participant arrives or you run your first animal. The procedures go smoothly, the participant stays for the entire session, and everyone is where they should be at the right time, doing what they are supposed to do. Time to kick back and have some fun while the RAs take over, right? Well, not quite.

A key to keeping the process running smoothly is close supervision. This does not mean micromanaging your RAs. But you do need to make sure they are performing their duties correctly and in a timely fashion. This ordinarily means setting objectives and arranging a schedule for yourself and your assistants, then regularly assessing progress toward those objectives and compliance with the work schedule. Reward RAs with positive comments and other signs of appreciation for successful performance. Talk with RAs about any performance problems in a courteous but firm fashion early in the process. Encourage RAs to bring up any difficulties they encounter early on, and thank them when they do so. Problems in procedures, data coding, and other aspects are best handled as soon as you discover them. Regular meetings of project staff provide a good forum for discussing progress and logistics and for discovering ways of improving the overall research effort.

If your data will be processed extensively or handled by different people, consider how you will organize the data files. For example, suppose you will be collecting, transcribing, and scoring audio-recorded data that are based on interviews. Audio files will have to be downloaded as they are collected and later assigned for transcribing. Transcripts will need to be stored and then accessed later for scoring. How will you organize the files that multiple individuals will need to access? File-sharing sites like Dropbox provide one option for organizing files and are especially useful for deidentified data. If you use a file-sharing site, make sure your RAs install the application on their computer and troubleshoot their access to it. If you put original data files into a file-sharing site, keep a backup on your hard drive. Adjust the file settings to prevent people from writing over or resaving original data files. If computerized files will be altered and you will keep sequential versions of the same file (e.g., original transcripts, edited or verified versions of the originals), create naming conventions to distinguish them (e.g., transP01 for the original transcript, transP01ver for the verified version), and make sure your RAs use these correctly. Plan a system for regularly backing up your data (and in fact, all of your dissertation documents!) someplace where they cannot be destroyed or lost if the system crashes, your computer is stolen, and so forth.

You will also need a system for keeping track of who has done what. Think about how you will keep track of each step of data processing. Spreadsheet programs such as Excel and Numbers provide one way; lower-tech tools such as checklists are another.

If you collect data in an applied setting, check periodically with contact people in the setting to make sure everything is running smoothly. Doing so will enable you to catch potential difficulties early in the process. We cannot emphasize this enough: One RA who fails to attend to protocol may sour those in the setting on research and even get you tossed out! Apprise key personnel in the setting of changes in schedules, and thank them formally (we do it in writing as well as in person) when you complete your data collection. If you promised to show them the results, let them know when you expect to have the data analyzed, and be sure to go back and present your findings. Your performance as a researcher affects whether an applied setting will allow future students and faculty to use their facilities.

Finally, keep a research log of unusual things that happen during data collection, decisions you make, informal observations, and the like. Jot down ways you wish you had done the study differently. These may come in handy later when you write your Discussion section, particularly if you have unusual results. Looking back at observations you made as you were running the data may help you identify possible reasons for your unusual findings.

SCORE, CHECK, AND PREPARE TO ANALYZE THE DATA

As you get ready to start data collection, think through how you will score (i.e., record) your data and transfer them to computer-analyzable form. A good rule of thumb is that the fewer the steps between the raw data and the computer, the better. Consistent with this rule of thumb is to use a computer to directly record the data—for example, by using a camera and eye-tracking software to record eye movements, EEG or imaging software to record psycho-physiological activity, or a voice-activated smartphone app to audio record social interactions. You could also have your participants record questionnaire responses directly into a computer; this requires that you have access to computer equipment and programming for your measures, that your measures are suitable for this process, and that your participants are able to follow the procedures. In addition, if your measures are generally administered in paper-and-pencil form, ensure that responses to the computer-administered measures are at least as reliable and valid as those of the paper-and-pencil form.

If direct entry by participants is not appropriate for your study, you and your assistants will likely enter the data from questionnaires, transcripts, or scoring sheets into the computer. Before beginning to enter data, write out instructions to be followed in entering data in a codebook. The codebook should specify the name of each variable in "computerese" (i.e., the name you give the variable for statistical analyses), a description of the data to which the name refers, and how to score the variable. For example, your codebook might indicate that you should enter responses to an ethnicity question on the demographic form under the variable called "ethnic," entering the number 1 for African American, 2 for Asian American, and so on.

Consider the computer program you will use as you plan how to code your data in computer-readable form. Each program has different rules about how to arrange the data. If you administer the same measure repeatedly over time to each participant, be sure to check how your program handles repeated measures data. Some programs work better with repeated measures data in different rows and others with all data from the same participant in adjacent columns. Also consider whether assistants who enter data will have access to this program on a regular basis.

If you are an analysis neophyte or are unfamiliar with the program you plan to use, consult with someone more knowledgeable about your particular analyses for suggestions about how to set up your computer data files. How-to guidebooks are also available for some of the major programs (e.g., Pallant, 2013, for SPSS; Delwiche & Slaughter, 2012, for SAS). Most of these provide basic instruction in how to set up data files, manage data (e.g., do variable transformations), and interpret output, as well as reviewing some of the basics of statistics. YouTube videos are also available that show how to set up data files. In addition, some textbooks provide step-by-step instructions on setting up analyses, checking assumptions, and reading output (e.g., Field, 2018, and Meyers et al., 2017, for SPSS).

Similarly, if you intend to purchase software for yourself, shop carefully. Be aware of your analyses, and ask questions that pertain to them before purchasing anything. Some software companies such as SPSS have demonstration seminars you can attend online for free to see whether the analysis will accommodate your data. Checking in advance is particularly important if you are doing unusual or cutting-edge analyses; even large software packages may not offer the options you wish to use. Make sure to ask whether graduate students can purchase the software using educational discounts and whether you will get a full version of the program or a version with some restrictions (e.g., able to handle only a limited number of cases or variables).

Free software is sometimes available online. You may be tempted to download some of this instead of investing in more standard software packages. Some of this software was created by capable, high-minded professionals who make it freely available. For example, R is a free open-source software that does many of the same analyses as costly software such as SPSS and SAS (Weston & Yee, 2017). It consists of a base program and add-on packages that perform more specialized analyses. In our experience, many statistical freebies are quite specialized or intended for individuals who are familiar with computer programming and creating and solving the formulas involved in statistical analyses. In addition, because creators of this shareware generally contribute their time, rarely do these programs have the documentation and user support that commercially available statistical programs provide (but see Field et al., 2012, for an exception—they wrote an entire textbook that shows how to use R for a wide variety of common statistics). If you are an experienced stats or computer junkie and this doesn't scare you off, more power to you. If you are a novice, you might be better off sticking with a more widely used package.

Set Up a Computer File for Your Data

What data should you record in a computer file? We recommend putting in anything that you could conceivably want to analyze, whether you planned an analysis with the variable or not. For example, we always include the identity of the person who ran the participant or coded the data, although we rarely use this variable in analyses (but we just might, if the data looked strange and we wanted to find out if one particular experimenter was responsible). Code individual items of questionnaires if you want the computer to derive subscales, if you wish to compute internal consistency scores on your scales, or if you think you might want to group items in a different fashion later. If none of these situations is relevant, you may choose to record only summary scores. A good rule of thumb is to record data at as molecular a level as your resources will allow. You can always aggregate later, but you can't always disaggregate. A note is in order here about some of the more complex data files that you may need to manage if your study collects data such as neurological or physiological activity (e.g., from brain imaging studies) or ambulatory assessments that include large numbers of repeated assessments across days or weeks: The massive amounts of data generated by these methods will require reduction, typically with specialized software or other methods. If you will be working with these sorts of data, make sure you know how to handle data reduction, or have a plan to learn this skill.

Set up your data file early in the process, and pilot test entering paper data. This way you can make sure your file helps rather than hinders data entry. For example, we like to arrange the computer file so that RAs enter data in the same order in which they are filed and enter items in the same order as presented on the questionnaire. Thus, if the demographics questionnaire comes first and the first question is age, "age" would be the first item in the file after the participant's ID number and any other important information (e.g., experimental condition, date run).

Think about how you name your variables. Give them names you will remember 5 years from now. Labeling the levels of your independent variable "CONDA" and "CONDB" may make sense to you now, but you may not remember what "A" and "B" stand for next month. Name variables systematically to aid recall. For example, if mothers and fathers provide Child Behavior Checklist data at two different time points, you might call your variables "M1CBC001," "M2CBC002," "F1CBC001," and "F2CBC002"— the first character indicates the respondent, the second indicates the time point, the third set indicates the measure, and the final set indicates the item number. In addition, be aware that some specialty programs (e.g., MPlus, HLM) accept only variable names that have eight or fewer characters. If you plan to import your data into one of these programs from SPSS or another program that accepts longer names, your life will be easier if you keep your variable names short.

Take time to label the variables. Adding labels allows you to elaborate and is especially important if you have short variable names. Provide unique longer descriptors that will help you remember what each score represents. This takes time, but believe us, it will pay off later when you are trying to interpret your printouts. Similarly, provide value labels for categorical variables (e.g., 1 = male, 2 = female).

Finally, once you have set up your file, look at the stats package you are using and set any default values for data display. Default values are the choices the computer makes for you if you do not tell it to do otherwise. Changing these values can help you make your data and printouts easier to work with. For example, SPSS allows you to indicate whether you want variable and value labels to be printed with your output, and you can set this up so that SPSS includes these labels on a routine basis. This means that when you see your output, the variable you called "M1CBCagg" will also contain your label "Mother T1 CBCL aggression *t* score." Having these labels means that you have one less thing to remember as you look at your output. You can also set up how you want output tables to look in SPSS (we like adding blank lines to separate different rows of numbers). Be aware, however, that you will likely need to set these defaults for each computer you use for analyses—a particular issue if you are working in a computer lab that has many computers each with its own default settings.

Verify Your Data

As you begin data entry, start thinking about data verification, part of the general process of data cleaning. *You must verify data for accuracy every step along the way that involves human recording.* We routinely verify our data at the data entry stage by having someone else check to make sure values have been entered correctly. One easy and efficient way to do this involves working in pairs in which one person reads the data and the other enters the data, then the two change places to verify. Some statistical analysis programs permit duplicate entry of the same data and signal you if the original and duplicate entries do not match (similar to requests for double entry of passwords on websites). You can also run summary statistics on each variable (e.g., frequency tables) to look for *n*s that are not what you expect them to be and for out-of-range values (e.g., a value of 42 on a 1–5 scale!).

Verification does not stop with data entry. If you score your questionnaires by hand to get summary scores, someone should check the scoring. If you write a variable transformation program to compute subscale scores, calculate a few by hand to make sure you did not make an error in creating the transformation. Now is the time to be obsessive–compulsive. We personally have detected major errors in recording and calculations, even by some of our most competent students—errors sufficient to change the results and interpretation of the analyses. Remember, the computer cannot tell you whether you scored the data correctly. It will only analyze what you give it. As the saying goes, garbage in, garbage out.

Clean the Data

Data cleaning is an important part of preparing your data for analyses. It can involve several different procedures: (a) making sure data fall within the range of expected or acceptable values for the assessment device, (b) looking for patterns that would indicate scores on a measure should be considered invalid for some reason, (c) looking for outlier values on variables, and (d) examining missing data and determining what to do about cases with missing values.

Data cleaning methods vary to some extent depending on the measurement and data collection procedures you are using. Physiological data, for example, often require extensive data cleaning to look both for out-of-range values and for patterns that should emerge from the measurement method being used for the assessment to be considered valid. These procedures vary according the type of measure used (e.g., EEG, cortisol, heart rate data). Some personality tests provide validity scales that indicate that a respondent has engaged in random responding. Data cleaning in studies that use online data collection from participants recruited using a method such as Mechanical Turk may entail checks to eliminate data faking or duplicate participation.

Even archival data require cleaning, sometimes quite a lot, depending on the data source, how the data were collected and entered in the first place, and other factors. As a general rule of thumb, the less the data (and your variables) have been used for analyses, the more cleaning they will need. Try to acquire descriptions of how variables were scored and why data are missing. If you are able to do so, establish a cordial working relationship with the individuals who collected or entered the data (or, with many grant-funded projects, the data analyst)—you may need to contact this person with questions about the data as you begin to look at them closely.

Decide How to Handle Missing Data

As you enter data into the computer, you will undoubtedly notice that participants omitted a question here and there, and some may have missing data for entire measures. How should you deal with these missing data? This sounds like an easy question, but actually the answers are fairly complex and depend on the reasons the data are missing. Are your missing data related to (a) both the independent and dependent variables ("nonignorable missingness" or "missing not at random" [MNAR]), (b) the independent variables but not the dependent variable ("missing at random" [MAR]), or (c) neither the independent nor dependent variables ("missing completely at random" [MCAR])? Graham (2009) and Enders (2010) provided extensive overviews of options for understanding and dealing with missing data under different conditions.

Once you have figured out whether your data are MCAR, MAR, or MNAR in your preliminary analyses, you have several choices for how to handle them. One of the most common is listwise deletion: If any of a participant's data are missing, none of that person's data are used. The practical disadvantage of this approach (lowered N) will be particularly obvious if you worked and slaved to recruit every participant in your study. With a related method, pairwise deletion, participant data are disregarded for any pair of variables for which one has missing data. For example, if relaxation practice times were missing for two of 80 participants, correlations involving relaxation practice and other variables would be based on 78 rather than 80 participants. The participants' data would still be included in analyses involving variables other than relaxation practice, however. With both of these approaches, in addition to reducing statistical power, the results produce biased estimates of population parameters under most circumstances unless the data are missing completely at random (Enders, 2010; Schafer & Graham, 2002). If very few data are missing, however, these may be viable options (see Graham, 2009, for a discussion).

A second common method of dealing with missing data is used when responses to items on multi-item scales are missing. A common procedure is to substitute the average of other available indicators of a construct—for example, the mean of remaining scale item scores for that individual. Schafer and Graham (2002) reported that this can produce biased results, but the biases are relatively small when the remaining items are highly intercorrelated (i.e., have high internal consistency). A usual practice is to do this only when more than 50% of items are present; the threshold can be raised for scales with few items.

Substituting a value for the missing score on a variable is one method of imputation—that is, making a good guess as to what the missing data would have been. This can be done by substituting the arithmetic mean for the sample (a type of single imputation) or by using regression procedures to estimate what the missing value might have been (Enders, 2010). Experts agree that single imputation is not a great way to handle missing data (with the exception of creating summary scores on multi-item measures as just described; Enders, 2010; Graham, 2009). A better way involves multiple imputation methods, in which many plausible values are generated for each piece of missing data and the results averaged. Multiple imputation methods have been incorporated into some mainstream software, sometimes in the form of add-on modules that come at extra cost. Finally, maximum likelihood methods can be used; these are statistical techniques that use available data to make their best estimates of what the statistical parameters of the population might be. These methods are suitable when data are missing either partially or completely at random; MNAR data are trickier to handle (Graham, 2009). Some software packages—particularly those specialized for more complex analyses, such as MPlus—incorporate maximum likelihood methods.

Decide How to Handle Outliers

An *outlier* is a value that falls outside the expected values for a particular variable. Osborne and Overbay (2004) described several reasons for outliers, including data entry errors, errors in sampling (e.g., failure to use exclusion criteria that should have eliminated extreme values), intentional misreporting, and mistaken assumptions about the distribution of the variable in the population (e.g., that the variable is normally distributed when in fact it has a skewed distribution). With physiological data, outlier values can result from measurement artifacts and other procedural issues. It is also possible that an outlier value comes from a genuine member of the target population—you just sampled an extreme value. Unfortunately, outliers can sometimes lead to violation of assumptions of statistics, produce biased statistical estimates, and reduce statistical power, none of which is desirable.

You will most likely identify possible outliers on individual variables when you calculate your descriptive statistics as part of your preliminary analyses (see Meyers et al., 2017, for detailed descriptions of using SPSS to identify outliers). In addition, regression analyses can produce statistics that identify outliers (including cases with combinations of variables that are unusual, considered "multivariate outliers") with potentially disproportionate influence on the results.

Unfortunately, how to deal with outliers is not as straightforward as identifying them. Possibilities include eliminating the participant from analyses, transforming the data, truncating or otherwise manipulating the outlier value, and retaining the original value and using a statistical method robust to the problem the outliers create (Osborne, 2010). We also sometimes analyze the data with and without the possible outliers to see how much the outliers influenced the results. Which method to use depends on the likely reason for the outlier, the number of outliers in the sample, the nature of the data, the likely distribution of the variable, and research norms in your area.

Review Your Analysis Plan

After you record, verify, and clean your data, it is time to perform the analyses. Haul out your analysis plan, discussed in Chapter 9. If you skipped this step or did an abbreviated version, flesh it out, listing the specific variables you will include in each analysis. If you are confused, this usually means that you were not specific enough in your proposal or that it has been a while since you thought about your statistics and you've forgotten the details of your plan. In either case, reconstruct your logic or seek consultation to help you get clear on the specifics of what you plan to do, and note these in your analysis plan. This then becomes a checklist for what you need to do.

COMPLETE PRELIMINARY ANALYSES

Complete the preliminary analyses before you go on to test your hypotheses. As noted in Chapter 9, preliminary analyses generally involve such things as checking

- the assumptions of the analyses you plan to use to test hypotheses,
- the reliability and validity of your measures,
- unintended confounds,
- whether methodological details such as order or sequencing have posed problems that you need to solve,
- the distributions of your variables and potentially problematic outliers on each variable,
- whether individuals with missing data differ from those without missing data, and
- whether your data meet the assumptions of your analyses.

Start by spending some time looking at your data. Calculate descriptive statistics for your variables. Look at frequency distributions of variables. An excellent way to get a good overview of your data is to produce a pirate plot such as that presented in Figure 11.4 in the next chapter. If you are examining groups of participants, look at how each group scored on major variables, whether the distributions of different groups overlapped, and if so, by how much. Get scatterplots of correlations among variables. This kind of systematic early data exploration provides you with a good feel for the data and will probably help you interpret more complex statistical findings later. It may also help you identify potential violations of assumptions (e.g., normality) and outliers. It will also help you prepare comprehensive tables containing these descriptive statistics, which you will likely include in the Method or Results section or an appendix providing more detailed information.

With group designs, before diving into your main analyses you should check whether your groups are equivalent on demographic characteristics and other potentially confounding variables. In correlation studies, correlate demographic variables with your independent or predictor variables. If the demographic variables (or other potential confounding variables) are related to your independent variables, you can then correlate the potential confound with your dependent variables. If uncorrelated, the potential confound is not linearly related to the dependent variable and is unlikely to influence your analyses. A significant correlation indicates you might need to control for that variable, however, either through a design change (e.g., using the confounding variable as an additional independent variable) or statistically (e.g., using analysis of covariance; but see our discussion of this in Chapter 9).

If you had a lot of missing data, you should also look at whether participants with and without missing data differ significantly. Examine study dropouts (if you had them) as well.

Finally, check whether your data meet the assumptions of the statistics you plan to use. If not, check whether your proposed analysis is robust with regard to violation of the assumption. If not, take appropriate actions (e.g., transform the data or select an alternative analysis). Return to Chapter 9 for a discussion of the assumptions of various statistics.

TURN TO YOUR PRIMARY ANALYSES

Revisit Your Hypothesis-Testing Plan

The results of your preliminary analyses will help you decide whether to test your hypotheses as planned or whether you need to rethink your hypothesis-testing plan. If your preliminary analyses showed something unexpected, consult with your chair about whether to proceed with your original set of analyses or whether you would be better off altering them.

Modifying your analyses might be quite straightforward. For example, one of our students examined predictors of youth substance use and intended to use multiple regression with continuous substance use scores as the criterion variable. Many youth reported no substance use, however, and the student wound up with a highly skewed distribution. She decided to dichotomize the substance use variable to deal with the problem and therefore needed to use a logistic regression instead of a linear multiple regression analysis. The scores she intended to use as predictors and her hypotheses could remain unchanged. At other times the issues might be more complex, as when scores you plan to use turn out to be highly unreliable or measures you thought were independent of one another produce multicollinear scores. Regardless, it is generally preferable to work out changes to your planned analyses in advance of actually running the analyses. This keeps your decision making from being biased by your results: It is hard to discard significant findings after the fact, even if you know there might be a problem with them.

Learn to Use Your Software

Doing your analysis allows you to learn not only about statistics, but also about the ins and outs of the software you are using. If this is your initial journey into a program or type of analysis, be prepared for frustration. Some of the most powerful computer programs have user-unfriendly help menus loaded with technical jargon but are short on the details of how to handle common types of data. Expect to run into difficulties, and be pleasantly surprised if you do not. Remember, you are not alone. You are not stupid because you cannot get the machine to do what you want. We have had to learn many data analysis programs in our combined century-plus as faculty members and have discovered that it usually takes about seven tries the first time through a new analysis with a new program to get it right!

If you are not familiar with the statistics you will be using, find someone who knows the software *and* the analyses you plan to use and who will help you or at least give you an example of their programming statements. We also like to ask this person to walk us through sample output from analyses like the ones we will run; we take extensive notes about how to read the output and what the different numbers and terms mean. Preferably, this person will be your chair or another student in your program. Do your analyses when that person is available for help. In-person availability is best, because your consultant will probably want to see your output and any error messages you receive.

As you tell the computer what to do, take the time to tell it how to label your output and your variables. It takes some time and imagination, but programming the computer to label the top of each page with the name of the project and to give each independent and dependent variable a meaningful name will pay off later in the intelligibility of your printouts. You will already have arrived at this conclusion independently if you have spent time staring blankly at computer file names several years after you created them, trying to remember what they meant.

If your statistics program is of the point-and-click variety (e.g., SPSS), learn to use and save syntax and syntax files if you have not done so as part of your stats classes or earlier research. Computer syntax is the language used by the program to tell the computer what to do. Often this language is hidden from view in the interest of making the program easier to use. Learn how to get the syntax you use and to save it, recall it, and reuse it. With this knowledge, you can reconstruct your analyses with minimal effort.

Why is this important? Recall the "it takes seven times to get it right" observation. Suppose you create summary scores for all of your variables and then discover that some of these scores look odd. If you have syntax files saved, you can go back and check your work. If not, you have no way of checking for errors except by completely redoing the analyses. Suppose you discover very late in the process that someone failed to enter data for one of the participants and that you need to rerun all of your analyses. Or suppose you want to see whether your analyses produce similar results if you filter out possible problem participants or outliers. With syntax files, rerunning analyses takes minutes, not the hours it would take to re-create the analyses from scratch.

In addition, remember to investigate and check the default values your program uses for the analyses you conduct. For example, the two most common default ways that software like SPSS uses to deal with missing values are listwise and pairwise deletion. The more complex the analysis, the more the analysis is based on choices about how to calculate the results. Take factor analysis. Factor analysis involves many choices about how to extract factors, whether factors are allowed to be correlated, and so on. Different statistical analyses have different choices, so software for each analysis may have different default values built in. Computer programmers try to program in the most widely accepted or common defaults. Numerous statisticians have gotten tenure by debating the pros and cons of these alternatives, however, so the default value is not always the best choice for every situation. Remember that you, not the creators of SPSS or SAS, are responsible for the details of your statistics and for the values, default or not, that are appropriate for your data and purposes. Most programs allow you to overrule the defaults, so it's a good idea to figure out which options to select for the analyses you run.

Another important preparatory step is to create a filing system for the many files you will generate in your analyses, as well as conventions for naming the files. You will likely create many syntax and output files as you run your analyses and redo those that turned out to be incorrect or incomplete. You will need to retrieve files you have used, so it is important to be able to find what you need and to be sure that what you find is the correct and latest version of the analysis. One idea is to date each file so that you know which is the most recent. Another is to have three folders: a "working results" folder, a "final results" folder, and an "archive" folder. The working results folder contains what you are doing at the moment—that is, what you are currently working on. Files go into the archive folder when you have finished with them and want to retain them, although they are not final. Files go into the final results folder only when you are sure that these are the results you will report in your Results section.

After you examine your data and the results of your preliminary analyses, determine whether you need to modify your hypothesis-testing plan. If you have run into snags, now is a good time to talk with your chair about how to handle the statistical or methodological problems you have encountered. Again, it is important to do this *before* you test your hypotheses to prevent biased decision making. It's not a good idea to pick one statistic or approach over another just because one turns out the way you like and the other does not. Better to make the decision beforehand.

Conduct Hypothesis-Testing Analyses

As you run your hypothesis-testing analyses, figure out which sample sizes and degrees of freedom the computer should be using, and check the printout to see whether the computer's figures match your own. If not, do not take the easy "oh, well, that must be the way it is" approach. Instead, look for errors in programming or data entry. One of the most common errors we find in drafts of Results sections are ns that do not match. If this happens late in the game, you will have to rerun your analyses and possibly rewrite your Results and Discussion—not something you want to have to do either right before or, even worse, right after your defense! Ask your chair or someone else more knowledgeable than you are to check your printouts for possible errors, too. Keep notes on any unusual features of your data or any unusual decisions you make (e.g., excluding outliers, transforming variables) so that you will be able to reconstruct your thinking later.

Finally, don't forget to calculate effect sizes and confidence intervals (Appelbaum et al., 2018). For nonsignificant findings, examine your power as well. Most computer programs do this for you if you specify that you need this information. Effect sizes will help you interpret the magnitude of your findings further down the road. Many serious statisticians see these as far more important than whether your *p* values were less than your designated alpha (e.g., .05). Power will permit you to assess one reason for any nonsignificant results. Confidence intervals will help you compare your findings with those of others.

CONDUCT SUPPLEMENTAL EXPLORATORY ANALYSES

Don't be surprised if, as you analyze your data, you come up with additional questions and need to perform analyses beyond those you originally proposed. The results of a study rarely turn out exactly as predicted and often lead to questions about why. Additional analyses can help you answer such questions.

Additional analysis differs from data snooping. Data snooping can involve running whatever you can think of in the hopes that you will turn up some interesting significant additional finding. The problem with this approach is that spurious results can emerge—the greater the number of analyses, the greater the likelihood of Type I error. However, if you adjust your alpha level for a huge number of "everything and the kitchen sink" analyses, your power will be greatly reduced, and you risk missing something that really might help you explain your findings.

Instead, we recommend targeted supplemental analyses to help you understand your data more fully. These analyses are tied to the reasons you did the study in the first place, what you intended to explore, unexpected findings, holes in the literature, and the like. The results of these exploratory analyses may or may not wind up in the final version of your thesis or dissertation, depending on what they tell you and how they qualify the interpretation of the analyses you planned. You may wind up running additional analyses later, too, once you start writing the Results and Discussion—the topics of the next two chapters.

✓ **TO DO . . .**

COLLECTING, MANAGING, AND ANALYZING THE DATA

☐ Obtain institutional review board (IRB) approval in writing.

☐ Pilot test your procedures.

  - Finalize stimulus materials.

  - Create versions of measures you will use.

  - Complete preinvestigation manipulation checks.

  - Download and check computer-entered data.

  - Have changes in procedures approved by your chair, committee, and/or IRB.

☐ Recruit and train assistants.

  - Train in research ethics.

  - Train in research tasks.

  - Assess mastery of research tasks.

  - Limit RA knowledge of study hypotheses to minimize biases and confounds.

☐ Build in ethical safeguards.

  - Maintain confidentiality.

  - Monitor the conduct of the research.

  - Arrange for unexpected emergencies.

  - Manage risk to participants.

  - Renew IRB approval if the study has not concluded within a year.

☐ Schedule settings and arrange materials.

  - Obtain and schedule a location for the study.

  - Obtain equipment, measures, and materials for the study.

  - Obtain a computer and software for data analysis.

  - Make arrangements for running participants during vacations, weekends, and so on.

  - Obtain permissions to use copyrighted measures.

  - Develop a system for scheduling assistants, participants, rooms, equipment, and so forth.

  - Write and post rules for equipment and computer use, including signing out equipment and dealing with breakdowns.

  - Make a plan for storing data securely.

  - Develop a system for keeping track of participants.

  - Specify the timing of data coding and entry.

☐ Plan for the unexpected.

- Participants

- Personnel

- Equipment

☐ Collect the data.

- Schedule regular meetings with research assistants.

- Closely supervise assistants' performance.

- Establish procedures for organizing data files.

- Identify probable problems early.

☐ Score the data.

- Write up a system for entering data into the computer in a codebook.

- Set up a computer file for raw data and participant information.

- Develop and implement a plan to verify your data.

☐ Clean your data.

- Look for unusual values and missing data.

- Examine missing data and determine how to handle them.

- Decide how to handle outliers.

☐ Review your analysis plan.

☐ Complete preliminary analyses.

☐ Revisit your hypothesis-testing plan and modify as needed.

☐ Learn to use your software.

- Obtain help if you are unfamiliar with the statistical analysis programs.

- Investigate the defaults and alternatives your software uses for your particular analyses.

☐ Conduct hypothesis-testing analyses.

- Look for errors in computer printouts.

- Calculate effect sizes, power, and confidence intervals.

☐ Conduct supplemental exploratory analyses.

SUPPLEMENTAL RESOURCES

Guides to Statistical Software

These are guides for relative newcomers to SPSS and SAS. Good sources for more advanced guides are reviews and book lists contained on major book retailers' websites (e.g., Amazon.com, Barnesandnoble.com). Some statistics textbooks also cover how to check assumptions and clean data and provide sample syntax and printouts for the analyses and software they cover.

Delwiche, L. D., & Slaughter, S. J. (2012). *The little SAS book: A primer* (5th ed.). SAS.
Laerd Statistics. (n.d.). https://statistics.laerd.com/

Laerd Statistics is an online resource that provides instructions for a subscription fee on using SPSS to conduct analyses and check assumptions, interpreting printouts, and writing up results; it also covers how to handle violation of assumptions (see https://statistics.laerd.com/features-overview.php).

Pallant, J. (2013). *SPSS survival manual: A step-by-step guide to data analysis using SPSS* (5th ed.). Open University Press.
R Foundation. (n.d.). The R project for statistical computing. https://www.r-project.org/

R is a free, open-source programming language that can be used to analyze data in many of the same ways as more familiar commercially available software packages (e.g., SPSS, SAS).

UCLA Institute for Digital Research & Education. (n.d.). https://stats.idre.ucla.edu/

The Institute for Digital Research and Education at the University of California, Los Angeles, provides great information on SAS, SPSS, and STATA basics and annotated output for many analyses.

Data Cleaning and Dealing With Outliers

DiLalla, D. L., & Dollinger, S. J. (2006). Cleaning up data and running preliminary analyses. In F. T. L. Leong & J. T. Austin (Eds.), *The psychology research handbook: A guide for graduate students and research assistants* (2nd ed., pp. 241–253). Sage. https://doi.org/10.4135/9781412976626.n16
Osborne, J. W. (2010). Data cleaning basics: Best practices in dealing with extreme scores. *Newborn and Infant Nursing Reviews, 10*(1), 37–43. https://doi.org/10.1053/j.nainr.2009.12.009
Osborne, J. W. (2013). *Best practices in data cleaning.* Sage.

Missing Data

Enders, C. K. (2010). *Applied missing data analysis.* Guilford Press.
Graham, J. W. (2009). Missing data analysis: Making it work in the real world. *Annual Review of Psychology, 60,* 549–576. https://doi.org/10.1146/annurev.psych.58.110405.085530
Schafer, J. L., & Graham, J. W. (2002). Missing data: Our view of the state of the art. *Psychological Methods, 7*(2), 147–177. https://doi.org/10.1037/1082-989X.7.2.147

11

Presenting the Results

This chapter provides
- information on what to include in your Results section
- tips on how to write up results
- suggestions for creating tables and figures

Read thoroughly if
- you are not sure what to include in your Results section
- you have never written up statistics or created tables and figures

Skim or skip if
- you have written up data similar to yours for professional audiences
- you know how to create user-friendly tables and figures (but read more carefully if you are tempted to cut and paste your printouts into the text)

You have collected all your data, analyzed them (incorrectly, at first; correctly, at last!), and now you are ready to present them to the world. Well, maybe not the world just yet. For the time being, you will be happy to get them down on paper so that this section of your writing will be out of the way and you can move on to the Discussion section.

Now is when you can reap the rewards of prior planning. Remember the analysis plan described in Chapters 5 and 9? If you organized it well, your

https://doi.org/10.1037/0000161-011
Dissertations and Theses From Start to Finish: Psychology and Related Fields, Third Edition,
by D. J. Bell, S. L. Foster, and J. D. Cone

plan can provide an outline of what you will cover in your Results section. This is because the logical sequence of analytic steps in an analysis plan— preliminary analyses, hypothesis testing, supplemental analyses—shows how each step in the analyses built your understanding of the data and led to the next step. Following the same sequence in presenting your results makes sense.

If you went further and prepared a skeleton mock Results section for your proposal (see Chapter 9), writing your Results section should be even easier. The mock Results section should have been helpful in clarifying your design and planned analyses. Now, it can provide the framework for the real Results section. In fact, if you prepared complete mock results for your proposal, most of your work has already been done. Producing a Results section now should be mainly a job of erasing the imaginary data and filling in the real results. Let's look at the kinds of information you should include in your Results section and how you might organize it for maximum clarity.

Not all of the statistics you calculated belong in the Results section. Some of the results of your analyses should be presented in the Results section, some are more appropriate as additions to the Method section, some might be relegated to appendices, and some may not be reported at all. Remember that your Results section should describe only analyses related to the purposes of your study. Avoid the temptation to inject analyses that are interesting but tangential.

The results of certain data analyses will be presented in the Method section. You likely did some analyses relevant to the instrumentation needed to produce the data for your major hypotheses. For example, as part of ensuring the adequacy of your measures, you may have collected psychometric information of one type or another. (Chapter 8 discussed several instances in which you might address reliability and validity issues in your study.) If you used direct observation data or other scores involving human judgment, you likely calculated interobserver or interrater agreement statistics. If you used questionnaire data, you probably calculated internal consistency for the scores you used for your sample. The results of these analyses are important in showing how sound your methodology was. They are not directly relevant to your major hypotheses, however, unless your study was about interrater reliability or internal consistency for the particular measure you used. The best place for these data is in the Method section where you describe your dependent measures. If your data required extensive or complex data cleaning or reduction (e.g., as with many types of physiological data), you may cover those details in the Method section or in the Results, depending on the conventions of your research area. Similarly, we recommend placing data related to the characteristics of your sample and the demographic equivalence of any groups you compare in the Participants subsection of the Method section. Be aware, however, that some disagree with us on this point, so be sure to check with your chair.

In addition, you may have done some data snooping—for example, looking at whether a demographic variable correlated with some of the other scores in your data set. If the demographic variable and these correlations are not central to your research purposes or to supplemental analyses that you conducted to understand the data more fully, you probably will not report them. If these are supplemental analyses that were guided by your initial findings but that turned out to add little to your conclusions, they might be relegated to an appendix and mentioned briefly in the text. Appendices are also a good place to put material elaborating on your approach, preliminary analyses, and nonsignificant findings, particularly if you are writing a dissertation modeled on a journal article and need to keep the Results section relatively brief.

It may be helpful to review your list of analyses and decide where you will describe each set of findings. In addition, before writing, review any guidelines that are available for presenting your specific area of research, and make sure to find a place to cover statistical topics that they suggest are relevant to your analyses. As noted in Chapter 7, one general set of guidelines is contained in the American Psychological Association's (APA's) journal article reporting standards for quantitative research (JARS–Quant; Appelbaum et al., 2018; see also https://www.apastyle.org/jars). Although written primarily to help authors prepare manuscripts for publication, JARS–Quant also contains information about statistical details that generally should be reported in any psychological research.

FIRST, DO SOME BASIC HOUSEKEEPING

Once you have gotten planning issues out of the way, you are ready to focus on your primary data. It may help to think of writing your Results section as analogous to having guests for dinner. Think of the guests as your primary data—that is, the numbers you will present to examine tests of your initial hypotheses. To get ready for these guests, you need to do a bit of housekeeping. The first thing you do is confirm that you have everything you need for the evening. We call this the Preliminary Analyses portion of the Results section. This subsection is where you describe the initial analyses you did to examine whether you could conduct your main analyses as originally planned and where you address any complications, qualifications, or limitations these analyses revealed. For example, here is where you identify missing data, participant dropout, and any other issues that might affect the representativeness of your sample.

The Preliminary Analyses subsection is the place to mention whether and how many data are missing, what patterns of missingness are apparent (i.e., whether they fit specific statistical definitions of being missing not at random, at random, or completely at random), and how you have dealt with this problem. If participants dropped out, describe them and indicate whether they compromise the equivalence of any groups you are comparing. Such a compromise occurs when there are disproportionately more participants going AWOL from some groups than others. The Preliminary Analyses subsection is also the place to describe other inadvertent factors that might bias your outcomes (e.g., a hurricane that closed schools in the middle of your study on children's anxiety and peer relations). Finally, this is a good place to create and display a participant flowchart, also sometimes called a CONSORT chart (Appelbaum et al., 2018; Cooper, 2018; Schulz et al., 2010). This chart shows the number of participants at each stage of an experiment or quasi-experiment, from screening to completion, and is especially helpful for studies with complicated or multistage recruiting and participation processes (see Appelbaum et al., 2018, Figure 2).

Now that you know you have all the ingredients for a successful dinner party, take a moment to examine the quality of those items. Did you use real butter or margarine? Is the wine of high caliber? Take time to stand back and look at your data critically and point out any observations to your readers. Are there obvious problems? Did you need to correct these problems, and if so, how? For example, did you change the scores you initially planned to use (and wrote about in your proposal) because of some problem with the data? A problem with the distribution of scores may have alerted you that you needed to transform your scores to allow the use of planned statistical analyses appropriately.

The Preliminary Analyses section is also the place to describe whether your data meet the assumptions underlying the statistics you planned to use. Describe the steps you took to determine whether they met these assumptions, the results of related analyses, and any changes to your analysis plan that were based on the outcomes.

Somewhere in your Results section you should provide tables of means and standard deviations for all the scores used in your analyses, and the Preliminary Analyses subsection may be a good place to include that information. For correlational studies, include these for the sample as a whole, unless the sample was subdivided for analyses, in which case you should provide sample sizes, means, and standard deviations for each subsample. This information is useful for assessing both the nature of the sample and any problem you might have with range restriction or ceiling or basement effects on your scores. In addition, a table of correlations among scores is useful to provide an overview of relationships among your variables, as well as information on multicollinearity or its absence. Even if your primary analyses will include some correlations, we recommend putting the complete correlation table in the Preliminary Analyses section. That way, all of the correlations (both hypothesized and nonhypothesized) are in one place, and you can simply refer to the table presented earlier when you discuss specific hypothesized relationships.

PRESENT YOUR PRIMARY ANALYSES

Your dinner guests have arrived, you've served the hors d'oeuvres, and now everyone is eagerly anticipating the main course. The remainder of the Results section is where you present the major types of data related to the hypotheses you examined in your study. In addition, you will include the statistical treatments you used to make sense of your data. You will want to be complete, but think "lean and mean" at the same time. Confine information presented in the Results section to data and their statistical treatment. Reserve the implications of the results for the Discussion section.

Your brevity will improve if you present your results in an orderly, logical way. Avoid presenting individual scores or raw data, unless, of course, your study involves an *N*-of-1 design. Retain the raw data for later consultation if needed. Keeping your raw data available in easily analyzable form can be very important, especially for any subsequent analyses that might be requested by editors of journals to which you eventually submit your research for publication. As well, be aware that there are increasing efforts to make science as open and available as possible. This includes giving others access to your data so they can confirm your findings, satisfy any concerns they have, and conduct additional analyses to test hypotheses of their own. APA's journals program has begun awarding "open science badges" to authors who agree to share their data or materials or preregister their studies. Kidwell et al. (2016) showed that such badges result in greater willingness by scientists to make their data available to others.

Happily, there is nothing mysterious about presenting results. Once you have decided what to include and what to avoid, the rest is rather mechanical.

Sequence the Results

The process of organizing your Results section really started back at the hypothesis-formulation stage. Recall our strong statements concerning hypotheses in Chapter 4. Assuming that you produced some hypotheses before starting your research (as Chapter 4 recommended), you likely listed them in some logically determined order (e.g., order of importance, moving from replication to extension of existing literature). If so, you simultaneously produced the general organization of the rest of your write-up, especially the Results section, without even knowing it. When presenting your primary analyses, describe results in that same, logical order.

Some authorities suggest that you organize your Results by major dependent measure. This seems to us to be logically less suitable than by hypothesis because you are not studying the measures themselves. Rather, you are using them as a vehicle for testing your hypotheses. If, however, you have several measures related to each hypothesis (e.g., self-reported data, parent-reported data), you might want to organize them by subheading within the subsection for each hypotheses. Even if you do not use subheadings within subsections, decide on an order for presenting the results for each hypothesis and then stick with that order monotonously when you present the results for the rest of the hypotheses. This systematic ordering helps your readers keep track of all of your findings.

Sometimes the clearest way of organizing your Results is by analysis. For example, suppose you have three hypotheses, each of which predicts that a specific variable will account for a significant percentage of the variance in a multiple regression equation. You may wish to summarize all three hypotheses, then present the results of the one multiple regression. In this way, you avoid redundancy and still keep your results tied to your hypotheses. For example, one of our students completed a dissertation examining several hypotheses about how a specific type of emotion regulation—dampening of positive affect—predicted depression (Hausman, 2017). Because she used a single hierarchical multiple regression analysis to examine the unique contributions of different aspects of dampening (internal cognitive experience, behavioral expression) beyond those of more established depression correlates (e.g., gender, affect), it made sense to group the presentation of all of the relevant hypotheses into a single section.

Whatever your organization, start the Hypothesis Testing subsection with a brief introduction. Include an overview of your hypotheses, along with important information that pertains to your analyses and that you do not want to repeat for each analysis. This might include information on the computer program you used (e.g., SPSS Version 20.1, MPlus Version 6.2), any method of correcting for conducting multiple analyses to reduce the likelihood of Type I error (e.g., modified Bonferroni), type of follow-up analyses used, and so on. If you use analyses that are likely to be new or unfamiliar to most doctoral-level readers, you may also provide some background on each analysis (e.g., how and why it is used, a description of the test statistics and how to interpret them, references for further information). In some theses and dissertations, this section may be labeled with a subheading (e.g., Analysis Plan), or it may be a separate section placed prior to or at the beginning of the actual Results section. Check with your committee chair on recommended placement and level of detail for this information.

Include Relevant Information

Now it is time to begin describing the specific details of the analyses and their results. Begin by briefly reminding readers of the hypothesis you are addressing. Then indicate the statistic used to test the hypothesis, along with any details needed to understand exactly how you used the statistic. For each analysis you conduct, include the name of the statistic and any particulars not described earlier in the introduction to this section. Particulars for analysis of variance (ANOVA), for example, include the factors, how many levels of each, whether any factors involved repeated measures, and the name of any post hoc test you used. If you did a factor analysis, present the method of rotation, how you determined how many factors to retain, and so forth. For regression, indicate the scores you used, the order in which each score was entered, the regression method (e.g., hierarchical), and the like.

Include important statistical values (e.g., F, t, R^2, p, effect size, confidence intervals [CIs]) for all effects. If you used a traditional null hypothesis approach, indicate the p values you selected as cutoffs for determining statistical significance and state the basis for their selection. Be sure to present effect sizes for your analyses; this is because *p* values do not tell readers about the strength of a relationship or the magnitude or possible range of an effect (indeed, some authors recommend doing away with them altogether; see Cumming, 2014). In addition, provide confidence intervals in the text or in a table. Your chair may want you to include only information for significant findings in the text and possibly to place nonsignificant effects in an appendix.

If you compare groups of participants, you should present means and their confidence intervals, standard deviations, and sample sizes appropriate to each significant effect. For example, if a Gender × Grade ANOVA shows a main effect only for gender, present these types of data for gender (collapsed across grade). You may also wish to present the same data for each grade–gender cell in an appendix.

What information should you include in a table or figure, and what goes in the text? Place the names of statistical tests and their description in the text. In general, means and their confidence intervals and standard deviations most often go in tables, unless there are so few of them that they can be accommodated easily in the text. Statistical values (e.g., *F*s, *t*s, effect sizes) may go in the text or a table, depending on which is easier to follow. Think of text as the place to tell the story or describe the findings and tables as the place to illustrate and back up the story. In other words, text should be predominantly composed of words. If there are almost as many numbers as words in the text (except perhaps in some quantitative or mathematical psychology dissertations, in which numbers are the language of communication), it is time to consider a table.

Word Your Results Clearly

Remember, the Results section is the place for maximum clarity. This is not the time to be creative or to look for the most poetic way of saying things. A good rule to follow is, Be monotonously repetitive! Although monotony and repetition may sound like bad things (and in some contexts, they are), the more positive spin is that they provide consistency, clarity, and precision that help readers follow along. Think of the chaos that could erupt if your GPS decided to use varied, creative descriptions to give you driving directions ("Wait! Is *go left* the same as *turn left*?"). Similarly, changing word usage and sentence structure can lose your readers. Use the same words to describe each score and each variable that you used in analyses. For example, if "ethnicity" is a variable and you dummy coded it as "Black/not Black," choose one term or the other to present the findings and stick with it. If you analyzed Child Behavior Checklist Externalizing scores to assess whether youth problem behavior changed over time, use the same words to refer to this score each time you mention it. Consistency and symmetry will help your readers follow your presentation more easily. Moreover, they allow readers to return more easily to previously read sections to check for understanding or to compare those sections against later results.

We advise following one of two strategies in presenting findings. With the first, state your conclusions, and then follow immediately with the data and statistical analyses supporting your conclusions. For example, you might say,

> As hypothesized, boys spent more time in types of play involving large muscle activity. This can be seen in Table X, in which the means for boys for both games involving such activity are significantly higher than for girls (main effect for gender [1, 58] = 5.35, p = .02, η_p^2 = .08).

The second is to reverse the order and present the finding first and the conclusion at the end. With this approach, you might say,

> A 2 (gender) × 3 (game type) ANOVA showed a significant main effect for gender, $F(1, 58) = 5.35$, $p = .02$, $\eta_p^2 = .08$. Boys spent more time than girls in both activities involving large muscle activity (see Table X for means and confidence intervals). This finding partially supports Hypothesis 1.

Decide on a sequence of sentences that most clearly fits your data and analyses, then stick with that structure for all results that are similar. For example, if your study is correlational and involves predicting three different criterion variables that you analyze using hierarchical regression, present the results for each dependent variable in exactly the same way. Thus, if gender was entered first in each regression, you might present results for it first, followed by those for predictors entered in the second step, and so on. Stick with this order as you lay out the data for each of your dependent variables. Moreover, if you discuss data for female participants first for the first dependent variable, discuss them first for all the rest.

In addition to being monotonously repetitive, put your findings into everyday language. This will help both you and your readers build a cumulative understanding of your results. For example, compare these two sentences:

> Younger children were less likely to notice differences in facial expression than adolescents (M_{young} = 6.95, 95% CI [xx, xx]; $M_{adolescent}$ = 9.47, 95% CI [xx, xx]), $F(1, 38) = 7.83$, $p = .008$, $\eta_p^2 = .17$.
>
> The mean for the young children on the Test of Facial Cue Reading was 6.95, 95% CI [xx, xx], which the ANOVA, $F(1, 38) = 6.49$, $p = .008$, $\eta_p^2 = .17$, revealed to be significantly lower than the adolescents' mean of 9.47, 95% CI [xx, xx].

Which tells you more about what the data are saying? Remember, you're telling a story.

Notice in our previous example that we also talked about the dependent variable when comparing male and female participants, not the specific scores used to measure it. This is acceptable when you are speaking about the general construct that you are studying rather than the specific scores you used in analyses. When you use different measures to examine a construct, make sure to anchor your findings to the specific measure—for example, "With respect to differences in facial expression, boys were less likely to notice differences in facial expression than girls on the Test of Facial Cue Reading."

You could then follow this with the results on the second measure—for example, "However, there were no differences on the videotape measure of visual affect."

Follow Conventions Concerning the Presentation of Statistics

Generally accepted rules or conventions govern how you are supposed to present the results of statistical tests. Remember our rule about being monotonously repetitive to aid reader understanding? Adhering to conventions in presenting statistics is based on exactly the same logic. Readers should not be distracted from understanding your findings by having to figure out your creative way of presenting statistics. The *Publication Manual of the American Psychological Association* (seventh ed.; APA, 2020) provides a lot of information about how to present statistics (Chapter 6). It also provides examples of how to present some of the statistics used in psychology (and most of the social and behavioral sciences) in its sample papers (Chapter 2). We gave you some examples of statistical results presented according to APA Style in the preceding section.

One question that commonly arises is how numbers should be rounded—to whole numbers? to how many decimal points? Usually numbers are rounded to two decimal points, with the exception of p values, which may include either two or three numbers to the right of the decimal point. For ps with exact values of less than .001, use "$p < .001$" (APA, 2020).

Unfortunately, the *Publication Manual* does not provide much guidance on what details should be included for specific statistics. Instead, the manual states, "include sufficient information to allow readers to fully understand the analyses conducted" (p. 181), leaving it up to you to figure out what this means in practice. The general rule when presenting inferential statistical information in the text is to give the symbol of the statistic followed by the degrees of freedom (e.g., $F[1, 29]$), then the value of the statistic (e.g., 6.49), then the exact probability level (e.g., $p = .002$), and finally the effect size. Confidence intervals are placed after the numbers to which they pertain. Because conventions in what should be reported change over time, ask your chair or knowledgeable members of your committee for guidance, and look for recent articles reporting results using the analyses you used in well-respected psychological journals. For example, although APA Style supports the use of exact p values, many researchers present p values by category only—ns (not significant), < .05, < .01, or < .001. Textbooks that explain analyses in detail may contain information on what should be reported, as may articles overviewing a particular type of analysis or critiquing its use in the literature (e.g., Jackson et al., 2009, for confirmatory factor analysis and Clatworthy et al., 2005, for cluster analysis). Some statistics textbooks provide examples of write-ups as well. Be sure not to copy these verbatim and just drop in your own numbers; that would constitute plagiarism. Instead, use them to guide you in what should be included and to help you develop your own style for presenting results.

DESCRIBE SUPPLEMENTAL ANALYSES

You may have included plans for supplemental analyses as part of your proposal to address research questions that are more preliminary and exploratory in nature than your primary analyses. Alternatively, analyses related to your principal hypotheses may lead to further questions that are germane to the primary focus of your study and that you have the data to examine. Both of these types of analyses can be included in a Supplemental Analyses subsection at the end of your Results. This can be a very important addition to your thesis or dissertation. Often it is fertile ground for stimulating new theorizing that can lead to hypothesized relationships to explore more fully in further research. Do not allow your excitement about these new possibilities to divert you from the task of clearly and thoroughly addressing the primary questions posed in the present research, however. Remember, exploratory or serendipitous findings, although potentially important, should not displace your principal hypotheses, which have an ancestry in careful review and theorizing about existing research in the area and were examined in your thoughtfully designed study.

PREPARE APPROPRIATE TABLES

A well-crafted table can assist readers immeasurably in understanding your results, especially if the results are complex. Do not merely cut and paste a table (or figure) from the printout of your computer software into your thesis or dissertation, however. These are rarely generated in the precise format, size, and quality expected by your institution. It is too bad that this easy way is problematic, because skillfully constructing tables and figures takes a good deal of practice. And crafting tables and figures also has two additional advantages. First, this process may help you visualize or understand your data more fully. Especially if you didn't do a mock Results section, starting with tables might be helpful in organizing your thinking about how to describe your results in the text. Second, working on tables and figures can provide a break if you need respite from the intellectual heavy lifting of writing.

The best advice we can give you about preparing tables is found in the five Ps referred to in Chapter 3: Prior Planning Prevents Poor Performance. Think about the effect you want your table to have on readers. If you are presenting data on a dependent measure to show the impact of more than one independent variable, decide which variable you want to emphasize most. For example, suppose you are studying student attitudes toward payment of college athletes. The scant literature you find suggests that these attitudes might vary by race, so you decide to look at differences between Black and White students. Additionally, you want to know if it matters whether the argument is presented by a Black or White advocate. Let's say you use a 2 (race of advocate) × 2 (race of student) ANOVA to examine your data in this

TABLE 11.1. Agreement With Payment by Race of Student Following Exposure to a Same- or Different-Race Advocate

	Race of student					
	Black			White		
Race of advocate	*M*	*SD*	*95% CI*	*M*	*SD*	*95% CI*
Black	4.4	1.8	[3.9, 4.1]	2.2	1.3	[1.8, 2.6]
White	3.9	2.0	[3.3, 4.4]	2.8	1.5	[2.8, 3.2]

Note. n = 50 per group.

fictitious study. You might arrange your data the way we have in Table 11.1, or you might prefer the arrangement in Table 11.2. Both tables show data from scores on a five-item measure of attitude toward payment in which higher scores represent a more favorable view. Which of these two tables gives more emphasis to the race of the student? If you said Table 11.1, you would agree with most readers. In general, it is easier to make side-by-side than up–down comparisons.

This was a straightforward example. Suppose we complicate it a bit by adding an additional independent variable. For example, you might look at participants' agreement with payment of college athletes after they listen to an argument for or against it. You might have both types of advocate take pro and con positions on the issue. Now you have doubled the size of your study and have a 2 (race of student) × 2 (race of advocate) × 2 (position of advocate) ANOVA design that has gone from the original four groups to eight. How would you represent the data for all three independent variables? Table 11.3 shows one possibility. This table gives greatest emphasis to the new variable, advocate's position. This is because the pro and con position data are presented side by side. If you place the forefinger (index finger) of your left hand below the means of the pro payment columns, you can compare them with those marked by the same finger of your right hand placed below the means of the con payment columns. Some quick in-your-head math shows overall higher means for the pro side of the table. More finger-assisted snooping reveals the means to be higher for Black advocates. Further, running two forefingers across the Black and White student rows shows overall greater agreement for the former. The addition of asterisks and footnotes to the table could guard

TABLE 11.2. Agreement With Payment by Black and White Students Following Exposure to a Same- or Different-Race Advocate

	Race of advocate					
	Black			White		
Race of student	*M*	*SD*	*95% CI*	*M*	*SD*	*95% CI*
Black	4.4	1.8	[3.9, 4.9]	2.2	1.3	[1.8, 2.6]
White	3.9	2.0	[3.3, 4.4]	2.8	1.5	[2.8, 3.2]

Note. n = 50 per group.

TABLE 11.3. Mean Student Agreement With Payment of Athletes Following Pro or Con Arguments

	Advocate's position											
	Pro payment						Con payment					
	Race of advocate						Race of advocate					
	Black			White			Black			White		
Race of student	M	SD	95% CI	M	SD	95% CI	M	SD	95% CI	M	SD	95% CI
Black	4.6	1.8	[4.1, 5.0]	3.8	1.3	[3.4, 4.2]	3.9	1.9	[3.4, 4.4]	4.0	2.2	[3.4, 4.6]
White	3.9	2.0	[3.3, 4.4]	3.7	1.5	[3.3, 4.1]	2.2	2.1	[1.6, 2.8]	1.9	1.4	[1.5, 2.3]

Note. n = 50 per group.

against inappropriate weighting of unreliable differences. A different arrangement of the table could make the evaluation of student and advocate race easier, as well as interactions among all three variables.

In theses and dissertations, it is generally better to use more rather than fewer tables. Those that are central to interpreting your findings should be included in the Results section; less central ones should be placed in appendices. Refer to every table by its number in the text using a callout (e.g., "As shown in Table 1, participants . . ."). For publication-style manuscripts in APA Style, you may either embed tables within the text after the callout or display each table on a separate page after the reference list. When the paper is finalized by the publisher, tables appear close to where they are discussed in the text.

For theses and dissertations, the *Publication Manual* notes that academic institutions or departments have detailed guidelines on formatting, and the requirements and acceptable format vary by discipline and take precedence over APA Style. Some schools dictate a format (e.g., tables embedded within the text) or allow more latitude in table placement. Check with your committee chair because guidelines are quite varied. For two of us, our preference is for tables to appear in the text as near as possible to where they are being described, just as they would in a published article. This facilitates reading, as there is no need to be switching back and forth between the text and the end of a long thesis or dissertation to find the relevant table. One of us prefers to have tables at the end, all grouped together. For her, there is so much page flipping with a double-spaced, single-sided document that there is little difference between flipping across a few pages within a Results section and flipping to the end of the document. This placement also makes it easier to go back to a table later, knowing that it will be at the end of the document (in numeric order) rather than embedded somewhere in the middle of a long document.

Readability is key when constructing tables. Allow sufficient space between entries, line up columns of numbers on the decimal points, and avoid splitting tables across pages if possible. Before making any final decisions, check your institution's table formatting requirements. Although 12-point font, double spacing, vertical orientation, and 1-inch margins are standard requirements, some institutions allow exceptions to font, spacing, and orientation (but generally not margins) for tables. Tables presented vertically on the page (i.e., portrait orientation), like Tables 11.1 and 11.2, are less cumbersome to read than those presented in landscape orientation, like Table 11.3, which require readers to turn the page sideways; a single-page landscape table, however, is usually preferable to a vertical table that must be continued on the next page. Sometimes, the difference in vertical versus landscape presentation can turn on the need for precision in your data entries. In behavioral science, it is rarely necessary to present data beyond the second decimal place. Omitting extra digits saves space and avoids the appearance of pseudoscientific writing. If you do use landscape format, be sure the table's title is on the binding side of the page (i.e., the left-hand side).

Speaking of titles, they should be brief and explanatory at the same time. Avoid including information in the title that also appears in the headings of the table itself. As an illustration, compare the titles of Tables 11.1 and 11.2. These tables present the same information, just arranged differently. The title for Table 11.2 errs on the side of excess detail. In part, this is the result of duplicating information that occurs in the headings of the table itself. Brevity was purchased in the title of Table 11.3 by omitting reference to the two independent variables, which were already shown in Tables 11.1 and 11.2. Significant information is not lost because the table headings convey these variables. Also, words like "levels," "means," and "scores" generally can be omitted because they are easily inferred from a glance at the table. This also applies to statistics presented in the table. You will observe that the title of Table 11.3 is inconsistent with the recommendation to exclude the word "mean"; we have done this to emphasize the point. It is evident from a quick glance at the table headings that means are included. Note that we prefer to state the dependent variable first, followed by independent variables. Thus, "Student Agreement With Payment of Athletes Following Pro or Con Arguments" keeps the focus on what is supposed to change with the manipulation of the independent variable.

We have one caveat regarding the recommendation to avoid redundancy between title and headings. You will have a list of tables at the beginning of your document. Your committee and other readers can use this to find the tables most likely to contain some piece of information they care about, such as general descriptive statistics, correlations among all study variables, or relations among specific dependent and independent variables. As recommended in the *Publication Manual*, make sure that your table titles are brief, clear, and explanatory, with enough detail for readers to infer their content easily.

As we said at the beginning of this section, preparing effective tables takes practice. The *Publication Manual* (Chapter 7) provides details concerning tabular presentations as well as examples. It even includes a checklist specific to tables (see Section 7.20). Consult this valuable resource before beginning your initial drafts. Bailar and Mosteller (2009) and Sternberg and Sternberg (2010) provided other good sources of sample tables for a variety of analyses. It is also helpful to look at journals to see how others have constructed tables for analyses like yours. Use the clearest ones as models. You will also benefit from trying out different arrangements, showing them to others, and having them tell you whether they are easy to interpret.

Once you have decided on a particular layout, present all similar data in tables set up exactly the same way. Remember our advice to be monotonously repetitious in presenting your results? The same applies to tables. Do not tax readers or yourself with different formats when the first, painstakingly prepared one can serve nicely as the template for others. Also, remember to present only the most important data in tabular form. Save the data from individual participants and other detailed peripheral information for your appendices or your own files. When you finish constructing a table, it is a good idea to review the APA Style checklist for tables to make sure your table conforms to it.

PREPARE SUITABLE FIGURES

The other major type of illustration you should consider is the figure. Anything that is not text or a table will fall into this category, which includes graphs, charts, maps, photographs, and drawings. Because some figures are more difficult and costly to prepare than text or tables, you may want to use them sparingly. Certain types of information are difficult to convey any other way, however, and you will have to rely on figures for these. For example, one of us had a student who, for his master's thesis, evaluated approaches to teaching mealtime skills to children with intellectual disability. The professionally prepared drawings that appeared in the thesis as figures greatly facilitated communication of the topography of the utensil grip the participants learned (Nelson et al., 1975). Also, figures are often used to portray interactions among independent variables and trends over time or over dosage levels most effectively.

Ask yourself the following questions before you decide to use figures:

1. What do you want the figure to communicate?
2. Can you communicate it more effectively by text or tabular presentation?
3. Will the figure duplicate information already provided in other ways?
4. How will the figure complement information presented in other forms?
5. What type of figure (e.g., graph, drawing, photograph) will be best?
6. If using a graph, what type of graph (e.g., histogram, bar graph, pie graph, line graph) will be the best?
7. How will you produce the figure (e.g., will you prepare it with software, have a professional draftsperson draw it, reproduce a photograph)?

You are ready to begin preparing your figures once you have answered these questions. As with tables, there are numerous conventions applied with varying consistency to figures. Let's spend a few moments reviewing these conventions. We will not discuss the various types of charts and graphs you might select; you'll find good descriptions and examples in the *Publication Manual* (APA, 2020, Chapter 7) and in Tufte (2006), Cleveland (1995), and Wainer (2007). Additionally, numerous online resources are available. Examples of graphs along with the software to create them are available in spreadsheet or presentation programs such as Excel, Google Sheets, PowerPoint, OpenOffice Calc, and Numbers. In addition, the graphics software found in most major statistical software packages (e.g., IBM SPSS Statistics, R, SAS) often creates suitable graphs to copy directly into your figures.

We cover only a few high points of graphic presentation, mixing generally accepted conventions with some preferences of our own. Refer to the *Publication Manual* for suggestions covering electrophysiological and radiological (imaging) data (APA, 2020, Section 7.31). Such figures can be especially challenging because the data are often complex and their content and format may be more variable.

When constructing a graph with Cartesian coordinates (i.e., lines at right angles to one another), the dependent variable typically is represented on the vertical or y-axis (ordinate) and the independent variable or time (or both) on the horizontal or x-axis (abscissa). Place axis labels parallel to the axes and numbers and other labels horizontally. A rule of thumb is that the length of the y-axis should be approximately two-thirds the length of the x-axis. The y-axis should include the entire range possible on the dependent variable. For example, if you are presenting percentages, the intercept of the axes should be at 0 and the last number on the ordinate should be 100, unless, of course, your percentages could exceed 100. If your scores actually occupy only a portion of the entire range, consider showing a discontinuity or interruption in the ordinate.

Figure 11.1 illustrates these points. The data in Panel A of the figure give a somewhat different impression from those in Panel B. This is because they do not emphasize just how far from being 100% appropriate the verbal behavior actually is. In Panel A, the pre- to posttest changes shown by the first two data points seem quite large. When the "distance to go" is made clear by including the entire range, as in Panel B, the impression of the impact of the intervention may change. Both axes should be labeled clearly with the name of the variable being measured and the unit of measurement. In Figure 11.1, appropriate verbal behavior is the variable, and it is measured in terms of percentage.

Figure 11.2 illustrates additional conventions. Again, notice the discontinuity on the ordinate. This time we also show a discontinuity on the abscissa. Notice that the general layout of the data in Figure 11.2 communicates the type of design (A-B-A-B) used in the study. Notice also that each of the phases is labeled and separated by a dashed vertical line. It is useful to name the phases descriptively (e.g., "Feedback") because this communicates more information than generic labels (e.g., "Treatment"). Figure 11.2 presents data from four groups. Generally, four lines in a line graph would be the maximum for readability. If the data are close, however, even four may be too many. Note also that we have included a legend for the groups. It is good to put a box around a legend, and it is conventional to include the legend within the border of the figure.

Once you decide on symbols for your lines on the graph, be consistent. In Figure 11.2, we used squares for girls and triangles for boys. We also kept these same symbols for both grade levels, using open and filled versions to indicate second and fourth grades. If you use symbols in more than one figure, keep them consistent. In other figures for this study, we would always represent boys with triangles, girls with squares, fourth grade open, and so on.

Figure 11.2 also illustrates some other useful conventions. Data points are not connected between phases, allowing easier evaluation of differences

FIGURE 11.1. Comparing Line and Bar Graphs With the Same Hypothetical Data

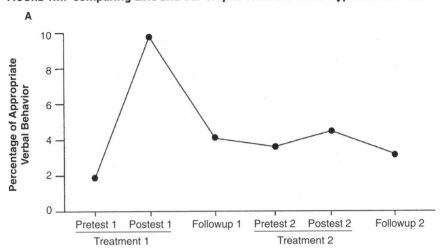

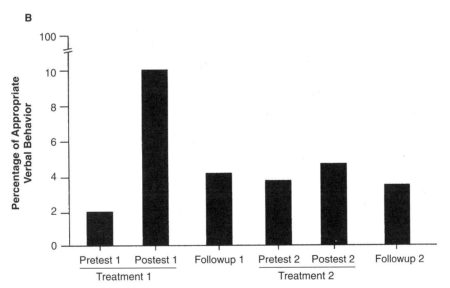

Note. Panel A: Discrete data in line graph format, with no scale break on an attenuated *y*-axis. Panel B: Identical data in bar graph format, with scale break. From "The Analysis and Presentation of Graphic Data," by B. S. Parsonson and D. M. Baer, 1978, in T. R. Kratochwill (Ed.), *Single Subject Research*, p. 117. Academic Press. Copyright 1978 by Academic Press. Reprinted with permission.

FIGURE 11.2. Mean Subtraction Problems Correct for Second- and Fourth-Grade Girls and Boys Across Four Phases of the Study and at Follow-Up

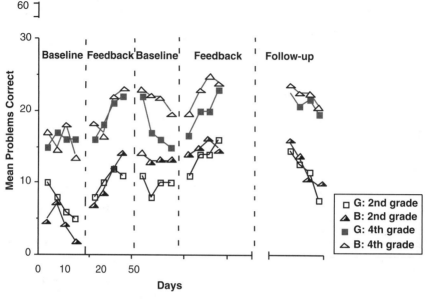

Note. G = girls; B = boys.

between phases. Missing data are indicated by a blank space (e.g., immediately after Day 20 in the Feedback phase). Points on either side of the missing data are not connected across the missing day. The phase lines (vertical hashed lines between phases) within the axes should be narrower than the axes themselves.

Sometimes you may wish to present the results for more than one dependent variable in the same figure. This can be tricky when the scale of measurement differs for the variables. Figure 11.3 illustrates a solution for this problem. In this figure, we use two ordinates. One line of the figure is referred to the left ordinate, and the other to the right. This figure shows quite graphically the different directions of change associated with the treatment for each of the dependent variables. This presentation makes it easy to compare the variables, and the entire presentation is more economical than drafting two different figures.

Finally, select the type of graph that is most appropriate to your data. Major spreadsheet programs give many options and make it easy to use your own data to see which graphs give the clearest picture. Generally, line graphs are inappropriate for discontinuous data. Panel A of Figure 11.1 illustrates this. When the actual data path between the plotted points is not known, as in this case, the bar graph shown in Panel B is more appropriate.

Lest we give the impression that the humble bar graph is the best choice in many instances, let's look at something better. Consistent with the move toward more complete data description in psychology and other sciences

FIGURE 11.3. Mean Negative Statements (Left Ordinate) and Affect Ratings (Right Ordinate) for Depressed Clients at Pre- and Posttreatment Assessments

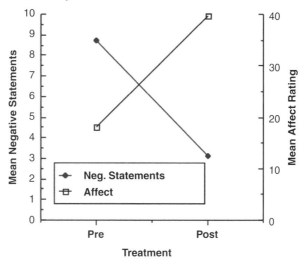

(e.g., Cumming, 2014) are suggestions for creating graphs that give a clearer picture of study findings. An example can be seen in Figure 11.4, taken from Lane and Sándor (2009). In the top panel of the figure is a bar graph showing the means of experimental and control groups across three conditions of a hypothetical study. As the authors noted, there appear to be large differences between the groups in Condition A, moderate differences in Condition C, and minimal differences in Condition B. Although such bar graphs are easily interpreted, more extensive information is provided by the simple additions represented in the box plots in the bottom panel of the figure. As noted in the figure note, not only are the means shown for the experimental and control groups of each of the three conditions, but information about the shapes of the distribution and variability is provided as well using score ranges, medians, and interquartile ranges.

With manuscripts submitted for publication in APA Style, figures may be embedded within the text after they have been mentioned, or each figure can be displayed on a separate page after the references. In theses and in dissertations, you may have more latitude in placement. As with tables, check with your committee chair for preferences regarding placement of figures in the text near where they are being discussed as opposed to at the end of the document.

The last step for most of us in creating a figure is deciding how to title it and what to include in the explanatory note. The title is placed above the figure image, and the note is placed below it. The information in titles and notes should be sufficient to allow figures to stand by themselves. That is, readers should not have to search the text to understand the data the figure presents. As with tables, the figure titles listed at the beginning of your document should

FIGURE 11.4. Hypothetical Data in Two Different Presentations

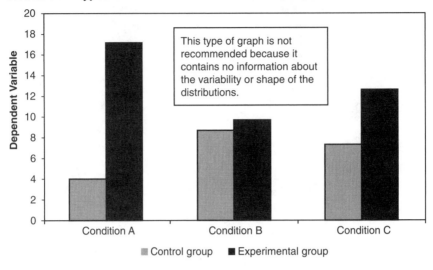

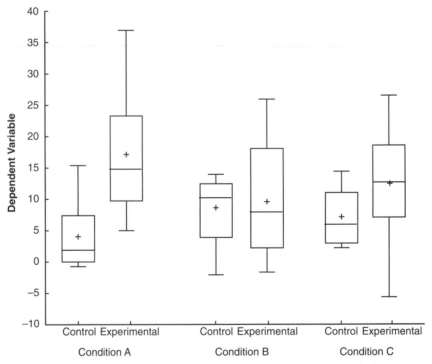

Note. Top panel: Typical bar graph seen in many behavior science journals. Bottom panel: The same data with the addition of information about the shapes of the distribution for each of the six groups. The means are represented by the plus signs, medians are shown by the horizontal lines inside the boxes, and the 75th and 25th percentiles (the interquartile range) are shown by the tops and bottoms of the boxes, respectively. The small horizontal lines above and below the boxes show the highest and lowest scores (the range), respectively, for each group. From "Designing Better Graphs by Including Distributional Information and Integrating Words, Numbers, and Images," by D. M. Lane and A. Sándor, 2009, *Psychological Methods*, *14*(3), pp. 240–241. Copyright 2009 by the American Psychological Association.

help readers locate a figure of interest. In composing a title, describe the contents of the figure. This can usually be accomplished in a brief sentence or phrase. *Brief* and *descriptive* are the most important characteristics of figure titles. An example of a too-brief title for Figure 11.3 is "Verbal Behavior and Affect Levels Pre- and Posttreatment." Compare this title with the more descriptive one provided with the figure. Remember to edit your figures so that the font, line thickness, symbols, and abbreviations are consistent across the figure, including the title and the note, and are easily read. See the *Publication Manual* (Chapter 7) for more suggestions.

Just as was true for tables, crafting figures well takes repeated practice. The *Publication Manual* (Chapter 7) covers many additional details pertaining to figures and, as with tables, it also includes a useful checklist specifically for them (see Section 7.35). As we suggested with tables, try out different versions of your figures before committing to a final version. Ask friends or your committee chair for their reactions, and then revise your figure. Once satisfied, you can create a final version with your own software or have it prepared professionally.

The availability of graphics software has made production of publication-quality figures much easier. We recommend that you take the time, preferably early in your graduate career, to become familiar with such software. If you are uncertain what software to use, several excellent options are listed in the Supplemental Resources.

At this point, you have collected and analyzed your data and arranged the results in a way that presents a compelling story. The heavy lifting is really done. In the next chapter, we talk about putting it all together—discussing your results, pointing out their implications, and convincing readers that your interpretations make sense. This is the fun part of your thesis or dissertation writing, where you remind readers of why you started the journey and what you have learned along the way.

✓   **TO DO . . .**

PRESENTING THE RESULTS

☐ Present data related to the purposes of your study.

☐ Present preliminary analyses.

☐ Present primary (hypothesis-testing) analyses.

 – Sequence the results in order of hypotheses.

 – Include relevant information in text and tables.

   • Name of statistic

   • Relevant details about the statistic

- Statistical values for significant effects

- Means

- Standard deviations

- Sample size

- Effect sizes

- Confidence intervals

  - Word your results clearly.

  - Follow conventions concerning the presentation of statistics.

☐ Describe supplemental analyses.

☐ Prepare appropriate, well-designed, clear tables.

☐ Prepare suitable, well-crafted, clear figures.

SUPPLEMENTAL RESOURCES

American Psychological Association. (n.d.). "10 posts categorized 'Statistics.'" *APA Style Blog.* http://blog.apastyle.org/apastyle/statistics/

Bigwood, S., & Spore, M. (2003). *Presenting numbers, tables, and charts.* Oxford University Press.

Dixon, M. R., Jackson, J. W., Small, S. L., Horner-King, M. J., Lik, N. M. K., Garcia, Y., & Rosales, R. (2009). Creating single-subject design graphs in Microsoft Excel™ 2007. *Journal of Applied Behavior Analysis, 42*(2), 277–293. https://doi.org/10.1901/jaba.2009.42-277

Heppner, P. P., & Heppner, M. J. (2004). *Writing and publishing your thesis, dissertation, and research.* Thomson Brooks/Cole.

Sternberg, R. J., & Sternberg, K. (2010). *The psychologist's companion: A guide to writing scientific papers for students and researchers* (5th ed.). Cambridge University Press. https://doi.org/10.1017/CBO9780511762024

Tufte, E. (2006). *Beautiful evidence.* Graphics Press.

Wallgren, A., Wallgren, B., Persson, R., Jorner, U., & Haaland, J. (1996). *Graphing statistics & data.* Sage.

Wilkinson, L., & Task Force on Statistical Inference. (1999). Statistical methods in psychology journals: Guidelines and explanations. *American Psychologist, 54*(8), 594–604. https://doi.org/10.1037/0003-066X.54.8.594

Software

Apache Software Foundation. (n.d.). *OpenOffice.* http://www.openoffice.org

Chart in OpenOffice contains the charting functions for all of the applications in the OpenOffice suite, including Calc, the OpenOffice spreadsheet application. If you are unfamiliar with charting in either OpenOffice or Microsoft Office, we recommend you explore OpenOffice first. It is free and completely compatible with Microsoft Office files.

Apple Inc. (2019). *Numbers*. https://www.apple.com/numbers

Numbers, the spreadsheet in Apple's iWork productivity suite, is available for iOS and Mac OS X Version 10.4 or newer.

Auerbach, C., & Zeitlin, W. (2019). *SSD for R: Analyzing single-system research data*. https://www.ssdanalysis.com/

SSD for R is a set of functions written in R for the analysis of single-system research design data. It is open source (free of charge) and is compatible with Windows, OS X, and Linux.

Epskamp, S., & Nuijten, M. B. (n.d.). *Statcheck manual*. http://rpubs.com/michelenuijten/statcheckmanual

Statcheck is useful in checking manuscripts for accidental inconsistencies in analyses. You can apply it to a draft of your thesis or dissertation before submitting it to your chair and holding your defense. If you are unfamiliar with R, you can use a version of Statcheck that includes its basic functions (http://statcheck.io).

Google. (n.d.). *Google sheets*. https://www.google.com/sheets/about/

Sheets is Google's spreadsheet application.

Microsoft. (2019). *Office 365*. https://products.office.com/

Microsoft makes versions of Office for both PC and Mac users. Excel is the spreadsheet application, and it contains the charting functions for the suite.

R Foundation. (n.d.). *The R project for statistical computing*. https://www.r-project.org/

R is a free, open-source programming language that can be used to analyze data in many of the same ways as more familiar commercially available software packages (e.g., those above, IBM SPSS Statistics, SAS; see Chapter 10).

12

Discussing the Results

This chapter provides an overview of the typical content of a Discussion section and includes

- questions to help you think about the meaning and implications of your results
- possible outlines and writing suggestions for a Discussion chapter
- guidance on final steps to pull the dissertation draft together

Read thoroughly if

- you are writing your first independent Discussion section
- you are not sure about what a Discussion section of a thesis or dissertation contains

Skim or skip if

- you have written a thesis or article Discussion section that followed a similar format

During your data collection and analysis, you may have filed away your proposal and the associated literature in order to focus on the nuts and bolts of conducting your study. Writing your Discussion section will require that you reengage your skills in conceptually thoughtful, logically sound, and technically tight writing. Assuming you have already drafted your results, a good way to

https://doi.org/10.1037/0000161-012
Dissertations and Theses From Start to Finish: Psychology and Related Fields, Third Edition,
by D. J. Bell, S. L. Foster, and J. D. Cone

ease back into this more conceptual kind of writing is to update your literature review and Method sections, then to work on the Discussion section. Think of your thesis or dissertation document as a series of linked parts. The hypotheses, methods, and results are the substance of your document, describing what you did and found. The hypotheses and methods guide your analyses. The literature review and Discussion sections are the "bookends" of your study. The literature review puts your study in the context of what is known about your topic. The Discussion section examines how your findings contribute to and extend that body of knowledge.

UPDATE YOUR LITERATURE REVIEW AND METHOD SECTION

If you did a thorough, high-quality literature review during the proposal stage and gathered your data in a timely fashion, your literature review should need few changes. Nonetheless, you will need to peruse the major journals in your area to add literature that has been published since your proposal meeting and to see which in-press citations have been published. In addition, you may need to make changes that your thesis or dissertation committee requested when they approved your proposal. If you produced an abbreviated literature review for the proposal, you now must pay your dues and do that comprehensive literature review that you put off. Note that by *abbreviated*, we mean preliminary or otherwise incomplete. If your program or committee allowed (or encouraged) a concise but complete publication-length literature review for the proposal, this should be fine for the final document as well.

Just as a well-done literature review at the proposal stage means fewer revisions later, you can easily revise a clearly written Method section in the proposal by doing three things. First, if you wrote your Method section in the future tense, change it to the past tense now. Second, alter your descriptions of participants, procedures, and so on, if there are differences between what you actually did and what you had planned to do. Don't worry too much about explaining (in the document) any changes between the proposed and actual study. Your chair or committee has likely already approved those changes, and this final document should describe what you actually did, not what you intended to do. Remember our advice in Chapter 6—the thesis or dissertation is not the place to outline all the twists and turns your study took from initial conceptualization to completion; rather, it is a clear, logically sequenced description of the study. Third, add the results of the analyses you conducted that are more appropriate in the Method section than in the Results section. These may include details about your actual sample (e.g., a description or table of participant characteristics for each group you included), any analyses you conducted to show the adequacy of your measures (e.g., internal consistency for scores you analyzed, interrater agreement data for your study), and details regarding data cleaning. When these revisions are complete, it is time to make the numbers in your Results section come alive. This happens when you turn them into cogent prose in your discussion of your findings.

Write Your Discussion

The last big chunk of writing that you do will probably be your Discussion section. Students sometimes tell us they don't know what to say in the discussion—they've said everything already. It is easy to understand why they believe this, but it really is not so. The Discussion section is where you interpret your findings, place them in the context of your hypotheses and the literature you reviewed, examine their implications and limitations critically, and suggest future research related to your findings.

To assist you in this process, we pose numerous questions that may apply to your study. As you read them, think about the answers. Keep notes on your thoughts, and consider integrating these points into your Discussion section. In addition, if you kept a log while you were collecting and analyzing your data, revisit it and see if your observations give you some ideas. We also describe components that are usually included in the Discussion section. These apply both to "traditional length" dissertation discussions and to shorter "article length" discussions; of course, article-length discussions will need to be more succinct than longer discussions. If you conduct a portfolio-model dissertation, your final document may include Discussion sections for each individual study, as well as a general discussion that ties all of the studies together. Think about which points fit best in each section so that you maximize impact and minimize redundancy.

Finally, we often find it useful to think about the big picture before we start writing. What do your findings tell you in general about the phenomenon you are studying? What are the take-home messages when you look at your findings as a whole? We like to make what we call a "cheat sheet" of results before writing a discussion for publication—that is, a short list (less than one page) of significant relationships and other notable findings of the study. Seeing these all on a single page helps writers integrate findings and see larger patterns (or their absence) more clearly. Your understanding of the larger scope of your results will change as you actually write the discussion and think through your results in depth, but having a general idea before you start can help you begin to see the forest and not just the individual trees.

Summarize Your Findings

Most Discussion sections begin with an integrative summary of the results. This should not reiterate your statistics; you should not state F and p values, nor should you repeat technical details of the analyses. Instead, describe your results clearly, using as little statistical jargon as possible. It might be tempting to say, "There was a significant main effect for condition on the vigilance and recall variables." But first apply the "layperson test": How would you describe your results to educated people so that they will understand them? "Students told to expect a later memory test were more vigilant and showed better recall than those who were not" would pass the layperson test.

One good way to organize your summary of the results is around whether they did or did not support each of the hypotheses; alternatively, you might organize it around how the results speak to each of your research questions. This summary can lead logically to a discussion of the possible reasons why you found what you did (or did not). If you choose this route, you will need to think about the order in which you will discuss hypotheses (or sets of related hypotheses). The most common approach is to discuss them in the order that you originally listed them in your literature review subsection on research questions and hypotheses. Briefly restate each hypothesis so that the reader will not have to turn back to the earlier section. This approach should also mirror the order in which your results section unfolded. This organizational structure is most appropriate when each hypothesis or set of hypotheses is conceptually distinct. Beware, however, that unless you are careful, hypothesis-by-hypothesis discussion can lead to a repetitive, unintegrated discussion.

An alternative way of summarizing the results is to present major findings together. This is a more challenging route, but it often produces a richer discussion because it forces you to think thematically. Here, ask yourself how the findings cut across variables and measures. Once you've identified cross-cutting themes, write about them. For example, Laura Goyer (2005) asked boys of varying delinquency levels to view videotapes of other boys talking together. She compared boys' reactions to tapes characterized by high rates of rule-breaking with their reactions to tapes showing more normal discussion. She proposed a series of hypotheses on the basis of how she thought delinquent and nondelinquent boys would differ in their observed and self-reported affective reactions to the different types of discussions. She collected supplemental observational and paper-and-pencil data and looked as well at boys' attention and interpersonal judgments of the boys in the videotapes.

Laura's results did not support her initial hypotheses: Delinquent and nondelinquent boys did not differ in any of their responses to the videos on either the dependent variables involved in her hypotheses or on her supplemental variables. Instead, virtually all of the variables differed depending on whether the tape showed rule-breaking or normative talk. Thus, it made much more sense for Laura to organize all of her findings around the two main themes: (a) the difference between the two types of discourse and (b) the failure to find the predicted differences related to delinquency level. She integrated results for affective and supplemental dependent variables within each section.

Do not forget *adventitious* findings—results of analyses you did not plan originally or did not expect to be significant. Sometimes the unexpected provides the most interesting outcome. If you compared groups of individuals, did you find any unexpected differences between the groups? Did these differences relate to your dependent variables? For example, one of our students (Sikora, 1989) examined the relationships among divorce, recent life changes, and preschool children's behavior with peers. Unfortunately, children of divorced parents and of adults who indicated a great deal of life change came from significantly poorer families than the control children. Surprisingly, divorce and reported life change related very little to behavior, but socioeconomic status (SES) correlated strongly with it. This relationship became a major focus of the discussion that followed, even though Sikora's hypotheses had not mentioned SES.

Interpret Your Findings

Summarizing the results sets the stage for the most important part of your discussion—your interpretation of the findings. What do your results mean? What do they tell you about the relationship between the independent variables and the dependent variables? Were there relationships? Did they apply to several or only selected dependent variables? Were there confounds or mediators that accounted for the findings?

Some of you will be lucky. Your study will turn out exactly as you predicted. Interpretations will come easily because you thought about them when you designed the study. If you are among these lucky few, you can progress to discussing alternative explanations for your findings and exploring what they mean for theory, practice, and the world at large.

Most of you, however, will be less fortunate. Some things will turn out as you hoped; others will not. Be grateful: This gives you lots to talk about! It could even provide the opportunity for the field to grow in a new and unexpected direction. Consider *which* variables showed predicted relationships and which did not. Then ask yourself *why* this was the case. Do significant variables share any commonalities? Point them out. Why did nonsignificant variables turn out that way? Examine why the differences exist and what these differences might tell you about the phenomenon you are studying or the method you used to examine it.

Consider these explanations for why your findings did not always match your predictions: (a) instrumentation problems (Did you measure the dependent variables well? Were measures reliable enough to detect true effects?); (b) inadequate documentation or manipulation of the independent variable (You *think* you assessed or manipulated it well, but did you *really* do so? Was the "dose" of the independent variable strong enough to make a difference?); (c) inadequate sample size (Did your study have enough power to detect an effect?); (d) specific procedural aspects of the study may have suppressed the effects of the independent variable; and (e) true relationships between the independent and dependent variables differ from the ones you predicted (Do you need to rethink how the independent variable works? Do additional mechanisms or moderators need to be proposed?). Consider each of these in turn, discussing reasons why it is or is not a plausible explanation for your failure to find what you expected.

As you consider these explanations, think about whether and how some of your results might provide evidence for or against them. Consider conducting supplemental analyses for this purpose. For example, if you used a relatively new measure with minimal reliability and validity information, you may be able to correlate that measure with other measures used in the study that have known reliability and validity data. These correlations might support the validity of the new measure, or they might challenge it. If you think gender might have been a moderator in your study, look at whether the relationships among variables differ for males compared with females—or perform some exploratory analyses with gender included as a moderator in the analyses. Clearly, these sorts of supplemental analyses go beyond your proposal. However, using the data at your disposal to clarify your results is an instance in which going beyond the "contract" agreed upon with your committee is appropriate. As an added bonus, it impresses your committee!

Occasionally, a student will find no significant results at all. If this happens to you, look for reasons. Consider the factors just described. Conduct supplemental analyses to check out hunches for the lack of findings. For example, suppose your data are highly variable and you suspect that only a subset of your participants responded to your independent variable as predicted. Identify that subset (you can use manipulation checks or other analyses to do this), analyze data for that group only, and look at your effect sizes. If you suspect that certain demographic variables were responsible for your lack of findings, correlate those variables with your dependent variables. Be sure to present these analyses in the Results section and discuss them as supplemental (and if your sample sizes are quite small, preliminary).

Do not despair if you find little to crow about. Science advances through an accumulation of information. Some of that involves failed predictions. Failed predictions can be as important as supported predictions in a well-designed study with adequate power and psychometrically sound measures. In these cases, failed predictions may suggest that the framework that led to the hypotheses needs revision. Remember, however, that the absence of significant findings does not confirm the null hypothesis. Consider a full range of plausible explanations.

In the absence of significant findings in other areas, you can always correlate your demographic variables with your dependent variables and your dependent variables with each other. This will provide additional information to discuss in the absence of more substantive findings.

Place Your Findings in Context

Your study is not the only research dealing with the issue you investigated. In fact, you probably spent many a page describing related studies when you wrote your literature review. Do not, therefore, write your discussion as though your study was the only one in the field! As you summarize and describe your results, consider how they do and do not fit with your earlier literature review. To do this, think about how your study compares with earlier research in terms of population characteristics, measurement tools, independent variables (and how they were verified), research design, and procedures. Then, think about whether your results converge with, clarify, or contradict past findings.

If your results converge with those reported by other investigators, think about how differences between your methods and those of others may *extend* earlier findings. For example, imagine that researchers have repeatedly found that couples' attributions measured in the laboratory correlate with marital satisfaction and that you found something similar using daily logs of attributions. Now you can discuss how well the relationship holds using measures taken daily in the natural environment.

Your results might also clarify contradictions in the literature. If so, point this out. Often, researchers can explain contradictory findings as they examine new and finer grained distinctions in population parameters, measurement domains, and independent variables. If you make these kinds of distinctions, your results can help others understand existing literature better. Suppose, for example, previous studies used men and women as participants without looking for gender differences. You examine these gender differences, and they are significant. This has two important implications: (a) Future research should consider gender as an important variable, and (b) past research may have *failed* to find effects when genders were combined, because of the variance attributable to gender. Past samples comprising mainly men would likely show patterns for the males, whereas those comprising mainly women would show patterns for the females.

If you don't find what others found, consider why. What are the differences between your study and others' investigations? Consider methodological explanations. Could different measures, procedures, or samples account for the discrepancy? Discuss what your failure to replicate others' results says about limitations to the generalizability of their findings. Do your findings suggest that new distinctions might need to be made in the literature going forward? If your failure to replicate previous findings is not an artifact of methodological problems, you may have discovered something important about the phenomenon you examined.

Consider what your research contributes to the existing literature. Remember that a dissertation is supposed to provide new knowledge. A thesis may provide less novel information, but it should certainly add to what is already known. Regardless of how familiar the study now seems to you, it adds to the literature in some way. Point this out. What did you do that no one else did? How did this improve on past investigations? And what did this improvement yield in terms of findings?

Consider the Implications of Your Findings

What do your findings imply? How do they improve the understanding of the phenomenon you investigated? How should they alter the way people think about the issues you researched? When you think about the implications of your findings, consider how they might speak to theory, research, and practice.

With respect to theory, think first about the prevailing theoretical models in your research area. What do these models postulate? What are their implicit assumptions? What would they predict about your findings? Are your results consistent with one or more of these theories? Why or why not? Your findings do not prove or disprove a theory: They just support or fail to support it. Although it would be nice if your findings were consistent with only a single theory, they may be explained equally well by more than one. That's fine—discuss this fact and describe how future researchers might design studies to pit the two explanations against one another.

With respect to research methodology, remember that understanding of a phenomenon advances as important distinctions are made. Did your study imply any new distinctions or any factors that are important to control in further investigations? For example, consider Sikora's (1989) dissertation on preschool children described earlier. Her finding that SES correlated consistently with social behavior has two implications: (a) Future researchers in peer relations should control for socioeconomic status, and (b) they should describe that characteristic of their participants.

Research also advances with improvements in design and measurement. Do your results have implications in these areas? If you used observational measures when others used only self-reports, do your results indicate that future studies should follow your lead? Research often progresses from general to specific, and from weak designs to strong. To illustrate: Suppose you used a longitudinal design and failed to find what cross-sectional studies have found. You may use your results to lobby for continued use of stronger designs that yield results that are more conclusive.

What do your findings have to say for practice in your field? If you are a psychology student in an applied area, for example, what do they say for the clinical, educational, or industrial–organizational practice of psychology? If you are studying a more basic area, what might the implications be for "real world" phenomena? Who might be interested in your findings and why? How should these potential readers change their thinking or practice on the basis of your findings? Even disappointing results can indicate that applied psychologists should consider your issue more carefully than they have in the past. For example, suppose that your findings challenge customary assumptions about problems experienced by adult offspring of people with alcoholism. Or suppose they lead to questions about whether a particular commonly used assessment device produces reliable and valid scores for an immigrant population. What would this mean for mental health professionals using interventions or assessments that are based on these assumptions? What would it mean for the lay public reading undocumented "pop psychology" books full of these "facts"?

Some studies have more implications for practice than others, to be sure. Studies that involve clinical or business populations, for example, are likely to have a great many practical applications that basic science investigations in physiological psychology lack—but basic science studies will certainly have implications beyond those of the specific results. As you think about potential implications, be sure to consider the limitations of your findings. You will likely want to speculate about their generalizability. As you do, be sure to acknowledge your speculations and to describe the kind of research needed to bridge the gap between your findings and the applications you discuss.

This brings us to the important issue of the role of speculation in Discussion sections. Many students err in their discussion by sticking too closely to their data, restating their findings over and over in different ways. As a result, there is little or no *discussion* in their Discussion section! When you talk about your findings, balance scientific skepticism with speculation. In practice, this means it is acceptable to speculate, but don't stray too far from the data. Use language that clearly indicates that you are speculating and discussing possibility as opposed to fact. Also, be aware of the assumptions you are making when you speculate and point them out. Support your logic with your own findings or those of others whenever possible. The keys are to be explicit about your speculations and to discuss evidence for and against them, when such evidence exists.

Include a Humility Subsection

A Discussion section is certainly a place to brag (subtly, of course) about the quality of your project and the importance of your findings. Temper this boasting with the recognition that your study is not perfect. Writing a "humility" subsection, as one of our colleagues refers to it, allows you to point out the caveats on your findings or the limitations of your study. This has two wonderful benefits: (a) It demonstrates that you understand research methodology and the inevitable trades-off that accompany research decisions, and (b) it might preempt your committee from tearing your study to pieces during your defense meeting.

Limitations of your study generally come from two sources: (a) decisions made about how to conduct the study in the first place and (b) problems that came up when actually conducting it. Decisions about criteria for subject inclusion, procedures, measures, and design all may have limitations as well as strengths. In this subsection of the Discussion section, consider those trade-offs. Of course, you may have anticipated some of the potential problems and taken steps to circumvent them. If so, you can now humbly point out how you dealt with the potential limitation.

Unavoidable problems that limit your findings may also have come up as you collected your data. Your sample may have been smaller than planned, limiting statistical power. Consent rates may have been low. Participants may have dropped out. Different groups of individuals may have diverged on demographic variables. Perhaps you overlooked some other confound that you should have assessed. Observations conducted in the natural environment may not have been very reliable. True, these were headaches during the study. Now, however, they provide material for your humility section. Remember, the key word here is *discuss*. This is not a complaint section. Whining about the problems you encountered will not interest your reader. Discussing how they may or may not have affected your outcomes will.

Think about possible limitations in four major areas. The first area is the design of the investigation and involves issues of internal validity: limitations in whether you can attribute causal status to the independent variables, potential confounding variables, and so on. The second lies in external validity: generalizing your findings to other racial or cultural groups, tasks or situations, levels of your independent variable, nonexperimental settings, and so on. The third involves the reliability, validity, and scope of your measures, along with response sets or other problems in measurement that may have contributed to your findings. Finally, there are limitations related to the statistical analyses you selected. Your study may not have limitations in all of these areas, but you should consider each as you appraise its strengths and weaknesses. Let's consider each area separately.

Note Internal Validity Concerns

Design issues always involve compromises. Any design that is relational or quasi-experimental and does not involve random assignment of the independent variable does not permit you to say that the independent variable "caused" differences in the dependent variable. *Unless you manipulated it, you cannot say unequivocally that the independent variable affected any of your dependent variables.* If your research is nonexperimental, you must consider alternative explanations for relationships between your independent and dependent variables. These include reverse causation (the variable called the dependent variable caused the independent variable), third-variable causation (a confound caused both the independent and dependent variable), and reciprocal or circular causation (increases in the independent variable caused changes in the dependent variable; increases in the dependent variable also caused changes in the independent variable). To be sure, if you controlled potential confounds, you may be able to rule out some of these explanations. This will give you stronger support for a causal hypothesis than if you failed to control these variables. However, you still cannot make unequivocal causal statements in such designs.

Problems in attributing causality also occur when a mixed design is used. These designs involve at least one independent variable that is experimental (i.e., manipulated by you) and another that is not. For example, consider a study in which older and younger participants complete one of two experimental memory tasks. Differences in performance between the two tasks can be attributed to differences you created in the conditions, but differences related to age cannot necessarily be ascribed to age per se, because age was not manipulated. You can review specific considerations regarding internal validity of particular designs by looking at Kazdin's (2016a) and Shadish et al.'s (2002) discussion of experimental and quasi-experimental designs.

You might also discover, in retrospect, that you failed to collect certain kinds of information that would help make sense of your findings. Or there may be a potential confound that you did not control. Here is a good place to mention this if you did not discuss it earlier.

Note External Validity Limitations

Even the best, most carefully controlled experimental designs are not without limitations. The control necessitated by true experiments usually entails some compromises in external validity. Think about and discuss generalizability across situations, stimuli, and procedures to important real-life situations. Analog and laboratory studies have limits on the generalizability of their findings by the very nature of the controls incorporated in them.

Other elements of investigations, regardless of design, can also limit their generalizability. These include the characteristics of the sample (e.g., diversity-related variables) and the specific operationalization of the independent variable (whether your findings generalize to other operationalizations or variations). If you used a sample from an underrepresented group, consider whether the implicit assumptions about cross-group similarity you made might not apply (e.g., Are the constructs you assessed relevant for the group you studied? Were they operationalized appropriately?). If you used a more diverse sample, might your findings largely result from the responses of the largest subgroup in your sample? Do they generalize to members of subgroups that were included but had very small ns in your study?

Note Measurement Issues

Your measures, too, may have limitations. Reliability and validity information for the particular sample you used might be insufficient, particularly with different ethnic or cultural groups. Using self-report as a surrogate for observable behavior in the absence of data showing correspondence is another common problem. Possible reactivity to measurement procedures, insufficiently reliable ratings or observations, missing data, and possible biases that could influence your results (e.g., response sets, such as social desirability) may also be considered if they are potential problems. Finally, consider whether your measures did a good job operationalizing your variables: Did you select an instrument that was less than perfect for your purposes (perhaps because it has been widely used in the literature)? If so, consider how its imperfections might affect your results.

Note Statistical Problems

Perhaps there are problems with your analyses. Did your data meet the assumptions of the statistics? Were your statistics overly conservative or overly liberal? Did your sample size limit the power of your statistics to detect anything but the strongest effects? Did you control for Type I error by limiting the number of statistical tests you performed, setting your alpha level to control for the number of tests you used, or using appropriate multivariate procedures? Did you use a new statistical procedure that lacks full elaboration of its assumptions and its problems?

Ideally, you encountered none of these statistical problems. If you did, however, revisit your Results section and take care of the problem to the extent that you can before you give your completed write-up to your committee. If, after doing these things, statistical concerns remain, discuss these in your limitations subsection.

One danger in writing humility sections is that because so many studies have the same types of limitations, students sometimes include these limitations almost "by rote." Don't just list the usual limitation suspects; consider them thoughtfully and weigh their importance for your study. Another danger is that you identify so many limitations that you begin to think your study is worthless. This conclusion is rather unlikely. As you write, recall that no research is perfect. The results of each study must be considered in light of its limitations. Scientists reach final conclusions on the basis of a body of evidence, not on a single investigation. Remember, the choices you made seemed the best at the time. Furthermore, every weakness may have a corresponding asset as its flip side. For example, controlled laboratory experiments gain tight experimental control at the expense of external validity, whereas natural-environment and quasi-experimental studies gain generalizability at the expense of internal validity. Keep a balance. Consider the pros and cons of your choices as you acknowledge the limitations of your study.

INCLUDE COMMENTS ABOUT FUTURE DIRECTIONS

Ordinarily, your Discussion section will end by identifying directions for future research. Here you tell others the questions and issues to examine in light of your results. Researchers often say that each study raises more questions than it answers. In your writing to this point, you will have thought of many questions that warrant future research. Organize and elaborate them in this subsection of your Discussion section.

Many discussions of future directions begin with recommendations to extend the study to other samples. You can go beyond this expected recommendation with several additional questions. Ideally, the first to consider will pertain to the theory underlying your study and the methods used to examine it. What additional independent variables need further research? What additional levels of existing independent variables should investigators explore? What important dependent variables should they examine, and what is the best way to assess them? What design improvements are needed? What methodological changes should researchers make in future studies?

In addition, what new distinctions might be made in sample characteristics, independent variables, and dependent variables? These distinctions can suggest future research comparisons. For example, suppose your results suggest that a certain form of cognitive behavior therapy affects different types of thoughts in different ways. Logical next steps would include developing reliable and valid ways of measuring different classes of thoughts, implementing the form of cognitive behavior therapy, and seeing how it influences these different measures.

A good way to think about future directions is to ask yourself what follow-up studies you would do, given your results. What questions do your findings provoke? What more do you need to know to understand fully the issue you set out to address in your study? What dissertation would you advise a graduate student following in your footsteps to pursue? What would you do with unlimited resources? Here is the place to dream. Ground your dreams in reality, however, and be sure you can justify why the information gleaned from your menu of future studies would be important for theory, research, or practice.

USE THESE TIPS TO ORGANIZE AND WRITE YOUR DISCUSSION

Think About the Big Picture

One challenge that students often have in crafting a discussion lies in integrating their findings and connecting them to the larger body of research in which the dissertation is embedded. It is easy to get mired in the specifics of your results, especially if interpreting the results of your individual statistical tests was difficult for you. Step back now and think thematically about what you found. What are the general patterns you see in your results? In your interpretations? In the limitations of the study? Even inconsistent or isolated effects can give rise to a theme—for example, that the results depended on the method used to assess key variables or that findings failed to replicate across procedures. Thinking about themes and what they tell you about your research area will help you to write a more integrated discussion that pulls the findings into a cohesive whole that advances the reader's understanding of your topic.

Be a Critical Thinker

As you consider your conclusions, play the devil's advocate. What would a critic say in response to your points? Anticipate the criticisms and weave your rebuttals into your discussion. This both fills up pages and demonstrates your intellectual agility—assuming, of course, your logic is sound!

Remember to show the steps in your logic. Do not assume that simply presenting your findings will make your conclusions obvious. If you make assumptions in drawing your conclusions, point them out. Your conclusions may seem simple once you arrive at them, but remember how much thinking it took to figure out what the results mean. Assume you need to guide your reader through the same process.

Avoid Common Problems

A series of common problems often arises in the Discussion sections of dissertations, theses, and published articles. Here are some no-nos:

1. *Do not discuss nearly significant or nonsignificant findings as though they were significant.* They were not, even if they might have been in the right direction. Thus, a statement such as "The finding that boys were more active than girls approached significance. Boys' greater activity could be the result of . . ." treats a nonsignificant finding as if it were significant. You may, however, consider whether power problems limited your ability to detect effects and consider your effect sizes compared with those of other studies. Saying "Boys' activity level failed to differ significantly from that of girls. This may have been due to the relatively small sample size, however: the effect size was moderate, but confidence intervals were broad. Future studies should explore this question with a larger sample . . ." would be more acceptable.

2. *Do not use causal language when discussing relational findings.* Many writers describing relational studies pay homage to the problems of assuming causation in their obligatory humility section, but they use terms such as *affect, influence,* and *produced* throughout the discussion! If your study was not a true experiment, replace verbs that imply causation with phrases such as "correlated with," "was associated with," and "related to."

3. *Do not equate statistical significance with effect size.* A p value of .05, .01, or .00001 is in part a function of the magnitude of effect relative to chance, but it is also influenced by sample size. With a sample of 100, for example, correlations of .19 will be significant at the .05 level. Yet the two variables share less than 4% of their variance! When discussing correlations, be especially careful to focus your discussion on the magnitude of significant relationships. The same applies to differences between means—the magnitude of the p value tells you nothing about the magnitude or practical significance of differences between groups. Avoid saying a difference was "highly significant," and discuss your effect size and confidence intervals instead.

4. *Avoid language that assumes the self-report or informant reports of events means the actual events occurred.* Stating "clinic mothers reported that their children were more deviant than did nonclinic mothers" is preferable to saying that "clinic children were more deviant than nonclinic children." The more

precise language also suggests two alternative explanations for your findings: Clinic children actually behaved in more deviant ways, or one or both sets of mothers see and/or report behavior in biased ways.

5. *Do not present new analyses for the first time in the Discussion section or discuss results that were not reported in the Results section*. If you wish to discuss a supplemental analysis, first describe the analysis and its outcomes in the Results section.

6. *Do not simply regurgitate the Results section*. As we have emphasized repeatedly, go beyond mere summary to interpret, synthesize, analyze, and critique your findings. Show your reader your logic as you go along and acknowledge speculation when you engage in it.

Select an Appropriate Organization

There are many ways of organizing the Discussion section, but in our experience two common structures work well. The first more or less follows the headings listed in the previous sections of this chapter. You progress from summary to interpretation and implications, to integration with existing literature, to limitations, and, finally, to future directions. The second structure involves organizing the discussion around major findings, and integrating implications, others' findings, and specific limitations into your discussion of each finding. Exhibit 12.1 presents two hypothetical outlines for a Discussion section that follow these different formats. You can also blend these formats. For example, you might discuss caveats, limitations and future directions that pertain to specific findings after you describe the finding, then discuss aspects of these topics that pertain to the study as a whole in a separate section later in the document.

Be sure to end your Discussion section with a wrap-up paragraph (or as one of us calls it, the "ta-da!" paragraph). This should pull the discussion together and highlight some of your main points, without being a summary. End the discussion, as you began, with general statements. Be upbeat. One of our favorite endings involves emphasizing the importance of a full understanding of the area under investigation, to remind the reader of how understanding the processes or individuals under investigation will improve theory, research, or practice. Then, having written your last sentence, congratulate yourself and celebrate! You deserve it!

PRODUCE THE FINAL PRODUCT

You will likely breathe a sigh of relief as you submit the draft of your discussion to your chairperson. Now is a good time to deal with the final details to get your manuscript in "defense-ready" shape. Check your references. Make sure everything in the text is in the reference list and vice versa. Write your

EXHIBIT 12.1

Two Hypothetical Outlines for a Discussion Section

Outline 1: Findings organized by hypotheses

   I. Summary and integration of results

      A. Hypothesis 1

      B. Hypothesis 2

      ⋮

      Z. Additional findings

  II. Explanations for findings

      A. Hypothesis 1

      B. Hypothesis 2

      ⋮

      Z. Additional findings

 III. Integration of findings with past literature

      1. Convergent findings

         a. Description of how findings converge with relevant findings of others

         b. Explanations of convergence

         c. Implications of convergence

      2. Divergent findings

         a. Description of how findings diverge from relevant findings of others

         b. Explanations of divergence

         c. Implications of divergence

      3. Contributions of findings to literature

         a. How findings resolve current issues

         b. What findings suggest about new distinctions and controls

 IV. Implications of findings

      A. Theoretical implications

      B. Research implications

      C. Applied implications

  V. Limitations

      A. Design and internal validity

      B. External validity and generalizability

      C. Analyses and statistical power

      D. Measurement

 VI. Future directions

EXHIBIT 12.1 (*Continued*)

Two Hypothetical Outlines for a Discussion Section

Outline 2: Findings organized thematically

I. Summary and discussion of findings

    A. Finding 1

        1. Summary and fit with hypotheses

        2. Explanation of finding

        3. Convergence or divergence with past literature

            a. Explanations for convergence or divergence

            b. Implications of convergence or divergence

        4. Limitations related to finding

        5. Specific research needed to clarify or extend finding

        ⋮

    Z. Finding *n* (topics covered as above)

II. General implications of findings

    A. Theoretical implications

    B. Research implications

    C. Applied implications

III. General limitations of study (covers issues not discussed under specific findings)

    A. Design and internal validity

    B. External validity and generalizability

    C. Analyses and statistical power

    D. Measurement

IV. Future directions

---

abstract (check your local requirements and *ProQuest* for length and format requirements; a thesis or dissertation abstract is usually longer than a journal article's abstract). Revise your table of contents (don't forget to add lists of figures, tables, and appendixes). Make sure your appendixes are complete: Include copies of noncopyrighted measures, informed consent/assent forms, extended coverage of the literature, supplemental tables or analyses, written materials that would be needed to replicate the study, and so on. Prepare your title page and signature sheets. Usually you will be required to submit a complete copy of the thesis or dissertation, minus acknowledgments and dedication pages, to your committee prior to your defense.

Check your local requirements for other details that need to be taken care of to graduate. You are almost to the finish line. This is no time to let ignorance of some form or requirement keep you from crossing it!

✓   **TO DO . . .**

DISCUSSING THE RESULTS

☐ Revise your literature review.

☐ Revise your Method section.

  – Change future to past tense.

  – Alter descriptions to match what you actually did.

  – Add demographic and other information.

☐ Summarize your findings.

  – Avoid technical detail.

  – Use clear language.

☐ Interpret your findings.

☐ Place your findings in context.

  – Consider how your findings converge with, clarify, or contradict past findings.

☐ Consider the implications of your findings.

  – Theoretical

  – Methodological

  – Applied

☐ Include a "humility" subsection, including issues with

  – Internal validity

  – External validity

  – Measurement

  – Statistical analyses

☐ Comment about future directions.

☐ End with your wrap-up/ta-da paragraph.

☐ Use these tips:

  – Think thematically.

  – Think critically.

  – Avoid common problems.

  – Select an appropriate organization.

☐ Polish the final document.

  – Revise the table of contents.

  – Write the abstract.

  – Make sure the appendixes are complete.

  – Add any additional sections.

  – Check your references.

☐ Check final requirements for graduation.

SUPPLEMENTAL RESOURCE

Heppner, P. P., & Heppner, M. J. (2004). *Writing and publishing your thesis, dissertation, and research.* Thompson-Brooks/Cole.

Provides samples of write-ups of different sections of a Discussion section.

13

Managing Committee Meetings

Proposal and Oral Defense

This chapter describes the details of proposal and defense meetings,
including
- how to prepare yourself
- logistics and content of the meetings themselves
- handling postmeeting requirements and finishing touches

Read thoroughly if
- you have not been through a proposal or defense meeting before
- you want a refresher to help you "get your head in the game" before your
  meeting

Skim or skip if
- you are already well-acquainted with the logistics and content of these
  meetings

The thesis or dissertation candidate commonly has two formal meetings
with the committee: the first to present and discuss the proposal, and the
second to defend the final outcome. The proposal meeting occurs *before* you
begin to collect data. The oral defense occurs *after* you have analyzed your
data and written up your project. Although proposal meetings are not always

https://doi.org/10.1037/0000161-013
Dissertations and Theses From Start to Finish: Psychology and Related Fields, Third Edition,
by D. J. Bell, S. L. Foster, and J. D. Cone

required, oral defenses of the dissertation are. Defenses of master's thesis research may be more variable.

During the proposal meeting, committee members and the student meet to discuss the proposed research. Usually this occurs after the student has prepared a complete proposal (i.e., literature review, methodology, proposed data analyses, references, and appendixes) and the chairperson is satisfied with this product. The student then submits the document to the committee and schedules a 1- to 2-hour meeting after some agreed-upon interval, often a minimum of 2 weeks.

Proposal meetings generally follow variants of one of two formats: (a) an implicit problem-solving format or (b) a minidefense model. In the problem-solving model, the meeting largely revolves around committee members asking questions to clarify the proposal; raising potential problems they see with the project; and suggesting alternative procedures, measures, and so on. The underlying theme is cooperative; committee members work with the student and chairperson to produce a better product. In the minidefense model, committee members expect the student to defend the content of the proposal; the focus is on the student's skills at articulating the rationale for various aspects of the proposal and defending the choices they have made. In many ways this resembles the oral defense, and in fact, the questioning may be just as or more rigorous and intense as at a defense meeting. After all, this is when committee members get the chance to guide the study's hypotheses, methods, and analyses. With both models, committee members expect that the proposal may be altered on the basis of their discussion. Of course, meetings can contain a mixture of problem-solving and minidefense components.

The oral defense is generally more formal than the proposal meeting, in part because its major purpose is to evaluate whether you have the research competence to be granted the master's or doctoral degree. This evaluation is based on both the written document and on your performance in the oral defense. Thus, committee members will ask you to explain what you did, what you found, what it means, and to discuss your research intelligently in the context of others' findings in the area. They will be looking for evidence that you (a) understand what you did and why, (b) can think about your project from a scientific (as opposed to a commonsense or intuitive) perspective, and (c) can describe your research and its findings to others. Faculty members generally expect more expertise and polish from dissertation than from master's thesis students.

Students have a range of expectations about these meetings, with some students believing that their committee's goal is to find enough faults to fail them and others believing that these meetings are pro forma exercises. The truth is most likely somewhere in between. Most students do pass their proposal and defense meetings, largely because they and their committee chair have worked hard to ensure that their documents and the students themselves are sufficiently well-prepared to respond effectively to questions and suggestions. But we also know of students who have failed their oral defense. Others have been sent back to the drawing board after a disastrous proposal meeting. We therefore recommend taking both the proposal meeting and the defense very seriously and preparing appropriately.

Departments vary widely in how they structure proposal meetings and oral defenses. Therefore, investigating local rules and norms is essential to preparing adequately for these meetings. Exhibit 13.1 presents a series of questions to ask other students and faculty about the proposal meeting and the oral defense. The answers to these questions will give you a good idea of the logistics, variability, tone, and scope of these meetings.

EXHIBIT 13.1

Information to Seek About the Proposal Meeting and Final Orals

When does the meeting usually occur in the thesis/dissertation process?

Who schedules it, reserves the room, and arranges any equipment?

How far in advance should committee members get the written document?

What forms need to be filed before having the meeting? How far in advance?

Is there any sort of formal review of the document or the defense by nonmembers of the committee (e.g., sending out the dissertation for formal external review, appointing an extra member to the committee for the defense)? If so, what form does this take, and how is it arranged?

What is the general format of meetings? Does each committee member ask his or her questions one after the other, or do members take turns?

Who chairs the meeting?

How long is the meeting?

Are students expected to bring refreshments?

Does the student make a formal presentation? How long? What is included? Are slides or other visual aids expected?

Do questions focus only the dissertation, or do they pertain to other areas as well?

Who records suggestions regarding changes in the proposal/final document?

What is the general tone of meetings? Do members respond to your answers?

What are the rules about quorums? Do all committee members have to be present? Can a member be included via telephone or videoconference? If so, who arranges these?

Who else may attend besides the committee and the student?

How does the meeting end?

What forms must be signed at the meeting? Who provides these and where can you obtain copies? Where do the forms go once they are signed?

What happens after the meeting? How do you alter the document to reflect changes?

Must committee members approve changes in the documents themselves after you make alterations, or can the chair do this?

THE PROPOSAL MEETING

Know the Format

The format and length of proposal meetings differ from one program to another. In some you will be asked at the outset to provide a brief formal overview of your proposal. Such an overview should summarize your rationale for the study and focus primarily on the methodology you plan to use. Following the overview, committee members will ask questions. These will take three basic forms: (a) What do you plan to do? (asking for greater clarity or expanded information); (b) Why are/aren't you doing ____? (inquiring about the evidence base supporting your study, consideration of alternative methods or measures, and general rationales and decision-making) and (c) What will you do about problem ____? (an issue that the member believes is likely to arise). Ordinarily, these questions will focus on your specific study. At the same time, committee members may also raise questions about why your research question is important; findings in the general area in which you are working; methodological issues related to your measures, design, and procedures; and statistical matters. Committee members will also make suggestions they believe will improve the project.

You, not your chair, should answer these questions and respond to suggestions. The best preparation for questions, of course, is to know exactly what you are doing and why you have selected your particular research questions and your data collection and analysis methods and not others. Be sure to think about methodological and theoretical reasons for your choices, as well as practical ones. Present these reasons first when articulating your responses to committee members' questions. Committee members do not respond well to answers like, "I'm including 20 participants per group because I need to finish soon and don't have time to run more than that," or similar answers that imply that you put convenience above scientific integrity. Similarly, an answer such as, "That's what other studies in this area have done," without being able to articulate the reasoning behind the methods, does little to demonstrate your understanding of the subject matter and research process. Better responses would be, for example, "I did a power analysis based on pilot data. My pilot data suggest that my effect will be quite strong and the power analysis showed this n should be sufficient to detect it," or "I plan to record EEG from 20 scalp locations. Although more exploratory studies use up to 32 locations, several studies have demonstrated that for assessing reward processing, this smaller set of locations is sufficient."

Committee members' suggestions about improving the study may vary considerably in importance and in the work required to accomplish them. In responding, ask yourself first whether and how each suggestion would add to the quality of your research. If it would add substantially, you may want to follow it, even if it involves significant extra work. Never dismiss a suggestion simply because you are horrified by the amount of work it will entail. If it involves altering an aspect of the methodology you have already thought about, it is fine to discuss the pros and cons of the suggestion with committee members.

Does this mean you have to add independent and dependent variables to your study at the whim of committee members? No, and you might respond to an unreasonable request by saying, "That would be an interesting aspect of this issue to address, but I believe it is beyond the scope of this study. I will certainly comment on it in the discussion section," and then pray that your chairperson backs you up. Indeed, many chairs will help you sidestep suggestions that they believe to be unreasonable. Of course, you can certainly raise practical issues, but discuss these from a scientific perspective as much as possible. For example, the following might be a good response:

> I agree that restricting my sample to middle-class, married, employed females who have just given birth to their first children and have a reliably diagnosed major depressive disorder (and no concomitant medical or psychological problems) would be the best way to do the study, but such a homogeneous sample is not available to me here in Podunk in sufficient numbers to do the study. I tried to expand the participant parameters in ways that wouldn't jeopardize the findings. Do you see special problems with this, or can you suggest ways that will allow me to recruit a larger sample?

Responding competently to committee members' suggestions requires that you be reasonably articulate and able to think quickly on your feet. If you have difficulties in either of these areas, take the time you need to think through a suggestion. One way to buy time is to restate the suggestion or question: "So, you are suggesting that . . ." You can then comment on the pros and cons of the idea. By the end of this process, you may have an opinion. A second way to buy time is to say, "Give me a minute to think about that." Then sit quietly and think about what you want to say. Either your committee will sit quietly, or—more likely—another committee member or the chair will jump in with a comment or opinion.

Overall, think about the proposal meeting as your best opportunity to pick the brains of a group of intelligent people who likely have considerable expertise that may or may not be directly relevant to your study. Most committee members have good ideas and sincerely want to help make your study better. Respect their expertise and ideas. At the same time, recognize that their expertise, however valuable, may not be specifically relevant to your study, and their ideas may not always be feasible for a thesis or dissertation (versus, for example, their own grant-funded, multiyear programmatic research). Take their input seriously, and consider alternatives. Stick to your proposed methods in areas where your choices are well supported by the literature. Raise questions when you think the input may call for changes that are beyond the scope or feasibility of your thesis or dissertation.

Keep Track of Meeting Input

Your committee members will undoubtedly provide input about how they think the study or the document can be improved. Someone should write down this input. Before the meeting, clarify with your chairperson who will do this. One of us routinely does this for her students, so that students can pay more attention to the meeting than to their note-taking. Even if you want to take notes for yourself, a separate set of notes from your committee chair can help fill in gaps or provide clarity for your notes.

Committee input is often in the form of "suggestions." Clarify whether these are truly suggestions—things you may simply want to consider— or politely worded required changes. With the former, committee members will likely accept your discretion in taking or rejecting the suggestion as long as you demonstrate good decision making (i.e., based on the theoretical or empirical literature, logical consideration of the pros and cons, and so on). With the latter, whether you ultimately pass your defense meeting will depend in part on whether you made the changes "suggested" in your proposal meeting. Finally, clarify when, where, and how the committee expects to see the suggested or required change. Sometimes committee members expect to see the change reflected in the final document they receive prior to the oral defense (which means you must remember to make it!). But sometimes they will want to see the change before you embark on your research; this typically occurs when they want to make sure you understand how to implement the change they are requesting. Other times committee members suggest changes that they don't truly expect to see in the thesis or dissertation document at all. Rather, they are offered for the student to keep in mind for a publication version of the document or for future research. To check your understanding and make sure the committee shares that understanding of their comments, make sure someone reads the specific changes discussed aloud before ending the meeting, with clear articulation of required as opposed to optional changes, when the changes are expected, and who will verify that they have been made.

Concluding the Meeting

At the end of your proposal meeting, one of several things may happen. You may be asked to leave the room so that your committee can discuss the proposal meeting. Your committee may formally approve your proposal (ordinarily with the suggested revisions). A list of required revisions may need to be typed and circulated or incorporated into a revised version of the proposal, or simply incorporated into the study and then described in the final document. In some cases, the committee returns the proposal to the student for more work before they will approve it. Committees that require revisions differ in how they handle final approval. Some committees may want to meet again. More often, committees will ask to have the changes circulated to one or more members for approval. Occasionally, the committee will ask the chairperson to review and approve changes on their behalf and will simply expect to see evidence of the changes in the final document.

In rare instances, the proposal will be disapproved. Outright disapproval can occur if the study is fatally flawed, the committee believes that the proposal demonstrates incompetence in research design or scientific writing, or the study poses major ethical problems (or any combination of these). The student usually then has the option of preparing another proposal, perhaps with a new committee.

After the Meeting

After the meeting, you should have two priorities: (a) jump into your study and (b) celebrate! We advise doing these in the reverse order—after all, you've just survived an important milestone! Even if you must make changes or even go back to the drawing board on one or more parts of your study, you deserve to congratulate yourself for making it to, and through, the proposal. But first, we recommend that you pause to take stock of where you are and finalize your plan for next steps. You probably already have a plan for how to move forward, including submitting an institutional review board (IRB) proposal or beginning to recruit participants, but some things may have changed on the basis of your proposal meeting, and you'll need to take these into account in your plan. One of us meets with her students immediately after the proposal meeting (sometimes with a favorite beverage to begin the celebration) to compare meeting notes and make explicit plans for handling changes agreed to in the proposal meeting. This kind of debriefing allows you to discuss the proposal meeting while it is still fresh in your mind, capitalize on the momentum and motivation created in the meeting, and set deadlines for finishing the additional tasks emerging from it. With this accomplished, you can move to a celebration and brief postreinforcement pause knowing that you have a plan for staying on track and moving forward.

THE ORAL DEFENSE

Know the Format

For the oral defense, you should be prepared to begin with a formal presentation. Dissertation orals are usually open to the academic community, although programs vary widely in how they implement this. Sometimes the scheduling is handled by the larger university wherein there are formal university-wide requirements vis-a-vis scheduling, announcing, outside members, and so forth. In some cases, orals will be scheduled in an auditorium or large classroom and advertised to the department or even more broadly. In other cases, the defense is simply scheduled between the student and committee. Although, technically, others could attend, they are not invited or even informed of the meeting. Your audience and committee preferences will influence the type of presentation you will give. If your only audience is your committee, they may or may not want to hear a lengthy presentation. If the written document was very clear and your committee is confident that both you and they have a good grasp of the study, they may ask for a very brief overview or move directly to questions.

If your audience includes noncommittee members or your committee wants to give you the opportunity to practice or demonstrate oral presentation skills (e.g., you are preparing for job talks, professional oral communication has been an area of relative weakness for you, your written document was very complex or somewhat unclear), a formal presentation is in order. For this, you might decide to use audio/visual aids, such as slides, usually prepared with presentation software (e.g., PowerPoint, Prezi). We discuss these later. Expect your audience to be intelligent, but not necessarily expert in your study or the research area. Noncommittee members may not have read your document. For these reasons, plan your presentation as though it were a talk you were about to give to a room full of professionals at a regional or national conference. Just as you would have a strict time limit at a conference, find out your time limit for the presentation and rehearse your talk so you will stay within those limits. Enquire whether committee members prefer to raise questions during the presentation or hold these until after the presentation concludes.

Some departments have a standard format for the presentation—for example, a 20- to 30-minute conference-style talk. Your committee chair can tell you what to expect. Occasionally, a chairperson may ask you to prepare one or more versions of a presentation if committees at your institutions vary in how much formal presentation they wish to hear. For example, one of us asks her students to prepare two possible presentations—a 1-minute oral synopsis (the "elevator speech") in case committee members are anxious to jump into questions (which frequently happens in this department) and a longer presentation complete with visual aids.

You may have some say in the kind of presentation you give. Although you can't really say "no thanks!" to a committee's request for a formal presentation, you can ask to give one even if they're willing to forego it. Why would you do this? Why create more work and potential stress for yourself? As noted earlier, this can be great practice for other presentations like conference or job interview talks. It's also a great way to boost your oral presentation skills with an audience whose job is to facilitate your professional development. Finally, giving a presentation ensures that everyone is on the same page in the defense; may preempt some questions; and reduces the time available for other, potentially unexpected questions!

When you finish your description, questions will begin. As in the proposal meeting, your committee will ask about your procedures, why you did certain things, what you found, and how you arrived at your conclusions. You may be asked to comment on alternative explanations offered by committee members. You will be asked some big picture questions as well. These can include "future directions questions" that focus on how you think this line of research should move forward, as well as your plans for the future (e.g., publishing this study, conducting more research, using knowledge gained from the research in your professional activities). Exhibit 13.2 lists generic questions that are common in an oral defense. In addition to these, prepare

EXHIBIT 13.2

Common Oral Defense Questions

What do you see as the problems in your study? What limitations affect what you can say about your findings? How would you correct these in future studies?

If you want to improve this measure, procedure, and so on, how would you do it?

You note that your results approached, but did not reach, significance. What could you have done differently to increase the likelihood of significant findings?

Are you sure about the degrees of freedom for the *F*-test in Table ___? It seems it should be ___.

Which current theory or model best explains your findings?

How would someone using a _____ theoretical framework interpret your results?

How do you explain the discrepancy between your findings and those of Dr. X?

What implications do your results have for future research methodology in this area?

What do you see your study contributing to the literature? What is the most important take-home message from your research?

What have you learned about this area from doing this research?

What would be the next logical study to do as a follow-up to this one?

What implications, if any, do your findings have for applied psychological practice?

If you had your study to do over again, with unlimited resources, how would you do it?

What do you plan to do next with your data? Do you plan to publish it and if so, where?

What do you plan to do next in your career (i.e., after graduation)? How will this research experience influence what you plan to do?

What should we have asked you but didn't? What questions do you have about your study?

for questions that focus on the details of your specific topic, methodology, and analytic approach.

At the end of the meeting, the committee will excuse you and any visitors from the room. They will then discuss the written document and your oral performance. Discussions can be brief or lengthy. Lengthy discussions do not mean you are in trouble: Faculty members may be arguing about a minor point of your findings or methodology and not about your performance! Occasionally, committee members will even veer into discussion of ideas that were inspired by but irrelevant to your defense. Although committees try to stay on task, aware that you're in the hallway anxiously awaiting their decision, this detour happens frequently enough that one of us always reminds both the student and the committee of this possibility, both to help the student avoid unnecessary anxiety and to remind the committee to stay on task.

After committee members conclude their discussion, they will call you back into the room and tell you the results of their deliberation. You may pass both of the written and the oral components, pass one but not the other, or fail both. In some departments and schools, you remediate a failure with a second try. Even if you passed, committee members will usually require changes in the written product after the defense (otherwise, some believe they haven't done their job properly). Prepare for this. As with the proposal meeting, make sure you know which changes are required and which are suggested, whether suggestions are intended for the document itself or to be considered for publication or future research, and who will oversee and approve each of the changes. Someone should write this information down and review it aloud to ensure all agree. Finally, if you are in the "passed both" category, pop the champagne corks and start the celebration!

How can you increase the chances you'll be celebrating at the end of your oral defense? First and foremost, prepare a good written document. If the manuscript you distribute to your committee is thorough, thoughtful, well written, and carefully prepared, you will begin your orals with a favorable impression that is based on your excellent document. Do not let your eagerness to finish or your personal timetables mislead you into pressuring your chairperson or committee to meet when your written document needs more work, as this is likely to backfire (Yates, 1982). Just because you think you have good reasons for speeding along, do not assume your committee shares your sense of urgency. A chairperson who does not think your document is ready is unlikely to support you if you find yourself in hot water for lack of preparation.

Second, prepare for the defense by informing yourself thoroughly about what is likely to happen, planning your talk, and rehearsing how you will deal with probable questions. Finally, develop an action plan for managing excess arousal that can interfere with optimal performance. The pages that follow explore these topics in detail.

Don't forget to find out the additional steps you will need to complete *after* you successfully defend your project and do any suggested revisions. Most universities require that students submit their completed dissertations to a university office or to the university library as well as to ProQuest, a national archiving service that serves as an important source for disseminating dissertation research to the academic community. University offices may also check the dissertation to ensure that it meets university format and style requirements. They are likely to have timelines for how long this takes, when you may (and may not) submit your project, and the like. Know these requirements and build them into your planning.

Prepare Your Talk

The story that you tell at the start of your meeting will set the tone for the rest of it. It is worth your time to write or outline this story and practice it until you can give a professional-sounding, coherent overview of your study in the time available. For this talk, 10-, 20-, or 30-minute time limits are common.

The major parts of your talk should parallel the sections of an APA Style publication. For a 20-minute talk, allow about 3 minutes for introducing your study, 6 to describe your methods, 6 for your results, and 5 for your discussion; for a longer presentation, allow proportionately longer times to cover each of the four sections.

Do not feel wedded to a four-section, one-by-one presentation of introduction, methods, and so on. Remember that a talk is not the same as a written document. If your talk is to be brief, you may want to integrate some of these sections—for example, present results and discuss them as you go. Expect to spend more time on the Method and Results sections than on the other two, although this will vary depending on where the complexities of your study exist. A complex theory that drives your research may require a longer introduction, whereas complicated methods or analyses will require more time for those sections.

Some polished speakers like to start presentations by telling a joke. This breaks the ice and indicates your humanity and that you have a sense of humor. If you are not a joke teller, however, this is probably not the time to launch a stand-up comedy career. Another ice-breaking strategy is to thank the committee for coming and openly acknowledge (with a smile) your sheer terror at standing before them. Make eye contact with members of the audience early and often.

Start at the beginning. Tell the audience how you got interested in this research and why it's important. Keep it professional and brief. Your colleagues are not interested in the fact that you have always had a problem with weight yourself, or that it runs in the family, and so on. Something more along the lines of "Dr. Ahab and his research group, of which I am a member, have studied whale blubber for the past 3 years. We became interested in why some people eat more of it than . . ."

Then launch into a brief review of the relevant research in the area, setting the context for your study. Recall the discussion in Chapter 5 about organizing your literature review in the form of a funnel, starting broadly and leading the reader skillfully to the conclusion that the next most logical study to do in the area is precisely the one you are about to describe. In the short time available you will not be able to start very close to the mouth of the funnel. Assume some familiarity with the general area and focus instead on the literature most relevant to your project. Briefly summarize the progression of studies leading up to yours, highlighting major findings. If your research is guided by a specific theory, present it here. Give a general integrative overview rather than a boring litany of names and dates. Then, review the shortcomings of previous theory or research and lay the groundwork for your own study and how it was designed to overcome some of these. Be humble here. Every study, including yours, will have problems. Do not go overboard in criticizing others or you might be setting yourself up for a similar fate during the question period that follows. Any figure of the theoretical model you are testing or table summarizing pertinent research might be presented now if time permits. After presenting the context for your study, state your research question and specific hypotheses. A slide may assist with this. Then move into your methodology. Follow the customary APA Style format, starting with a description of your participants and research setting. Describe recruitment procedures and inclusion and exclusion criteria. Mention informed consent. Next, describe your independent variable(s) and dependent measures. Again, slides of any unusual apparatus, tests, checklists, or observation codes can be useful. Mention the reliability and validity of your measures, and indicate how you trained raters or observers, if used, and how you ensured their continued high reliability during the data collection phase. Weave in a description of the procedures followed by each participant and how debriefing occurred after they finished.

At this point, your design is likely to be apparent. If it isn't, however, describe it. Verbal description will suffice for straightforward designs. More complex designs may require a diagram. You will obviously not be able to present every detail of your methodology in the brief time available. Leave out details that listeners will not be able to follow or that are less important to your study. In an observational study, for example, knowing the word-for-word definitions of each observation category is unnecessary. If you are unsure what to include, pick the 10 most important facts to mention, adding or deleting from this list as time permits. If you have additional information that you think your committee may ask about, create supplemental slides or handouts that you hold in reserve to use if questions arise or time permits.

Next, present your results. Do this in the order in which you introduced your hypotheses. If you used multiple dependent measures to test each hypothesis, decide an order for their presentation and stick with this for each hypothesis. As with the Method section, you will have more data than you can present in the allocated time for this section. Cull the data carefully, and select only those results pertaining most directly to testing your hypotheses or that yield the most important findings. When many variables show the same patterns of results, summarize these rather than going through each variable one by one.

Here more than anywhere, simplicity is best. Do not state your F and p values in your talk. Just present the name of the analysis and its findings in plain English. One way to keep your presentation simple is to present only those data that relate to your hypotheses and major findings. Skip nonsignificant findings or mention them only briefly. Check your time at this point, adding more information only if time permits. Be selective and clear; do not throw every number at your audience, at the risk of confusing them. As with your methods, you can create supplemental slides or handouts to have ready if questions arise.

Either during or after presenting your results, discuss their implications. Do this in the order in which you stated your hypotheses originally, which should be the order you just used to present the results. Begin your discussion with a restatement of the purpose of the research, and then launch into the first hypothesis. If you had many hypotheses, see if you can integrate findings relevant to several of them at once. Refer frequently to how your research fits with studies of others, and note how your results might alter prevalent thinking in the area.

In addition to an enthusiastic discussion of the implications of your findings, include a brief humility section, as you did in your written Discussion section (see Chapter 12). Here you should acknowledge some of the inevitable shortcomings of your research and lay the groundwork for future improved studies. Avoid being overly self-critical. Acknowledge obvious shortcomings, and point out limits to the generalizability of your findings. The latter is always a safe place to be humble because all studies have some limitations in this regard. A good way to end your presentation is by giving two or three specific suggestions for future research, unless you have integrated these into your discussion earlier.

Prepare Audiovisual Materials

It is difficult to imagine a research presentation that lasts longer than 5 minutes without some form of audiovisual (A/V) assistance. A/V aids can help get your message across and keep your audience interested. The number and type of aids you use depends on your setting and the length of your talk. Even a 5-minute presentation can benefit from a few slides or handouts, however.

We have developed several guidelines for using A/V aids over the years. First, select a medium of presentation that is readily available and reliable. Slides using computer-based presentation software are the norm for most presentations, including conference or job talks, class lectures, and, yes, even thesis and dissertation defense presentations. Presentation software is widely available, and university classrooms are increasingly equipped with permanently installed computers, projectors, and screens that make showing your presentation as simple as logging into your account or inserting your flash drive. If the room you use for your defense does not have a complete computer-based A/V set-up, you may be able to bring your own laptop to plug into a projector. Alternatively, many departments and campuses have laptops and projectors available for checkout or rental for a modest fee. If you're meeting with only your committee, simply using a laptop at the head of a conference table may suffice.

Using slides has many benefits. Slides can typically convey the research context more adequately than oral presentation and make your story more real to the audience. For example, showing pictures of a child sitting in front of the experimental apparatus, or of the street intersection where data on seat belt use were taken, can help bring your presentation to life. You can also alter or add to your slides easily if you want to change your presentation after you rehearse it. As noted earlier, we suggest that students make supplemental slides with material that they will not present in their talk but may want for the question-and-answer period of the defense. Examples of these include copies of measures, frequency distributions of variables, and tables of data that are not used in the presentation but might be relevant to committee questions.

If you are using computerized presentations for the first time, our advice is to follow the old military K.I.S.S. maxim: "Keep it simple, stupid." The Murphy's Law of presentations is that anything that can go wrong will, especially where equipment is concerned. Rehearse all details more than once before the orals. Make sure that you know how to (a) transfer your presentation to the computer you will use to show the slides, (b) hook up the computer, and (c) get the projector running. We also recommend that you have a set of printed handouts of your slides as backup just in case of last-minute equipment failure. Whatever equipment you use, get to the room early and check it out again, immediately before your presentation. Know where a backup can be found in case something breaks or a bulb burns out. (It happens, believe us!) Sit in different parts of the room to check sound and picture quality. Coordinate with anyone who will be assisting to dim lights, distribute handouts, set up refreshments, and so forth.

Despite the many benefits, there can be problems with slide use. Presentations in which the presenter merely reads the slide can be deadly. Other common dangers include using too many slides, squeezing too much data or text on a slide, or using fonts that are too small to be read easily from the back of the room. Too much text or too many data are particularly problematic because they force the audience either to listen to the speaker and ignore the slide (which cannot be read and digested simultaneously) or to read the slide and miss what you are saying about it. This results in a presentation that can be hard to follow and mind-numbingly tedious. Most of us have experienced such presentations in classes and at conferences. Remember, slides are *aids* to your oral presentation, not substitutes for it.

So, be selective. Instead of putting the entire rationale for your study on a slide, use key phrases that highlight your ideas. Avoid the temptation to make slides of tables from your thesis or dissertation just because they are readily available or you love the way they look in your text. Often this information is not easy to digest when it appears briefly on a screen. Pare down the tables. Put the data in several new slides if you absolutely need them to make a point. Keep your tables uncluttered. It is better to use more tables with fewer numbers in them than the reverse. Leave out nonessential statistical details (e.g., F values, beta weights). Use bolding, font, or animations (e.g., sequential entry of different hypotheses or pieces of a figure) to help direct audience attention to the points you will be talking about. Make sure that your text and numbers will be readable from the back of the room.

Video clips provide another good way to bring life to your talk. Most presentation software allows you to integrate video into your production, either as an embedded clip or a link to an online video. Test your transition to the video. Do this in the exact room and with the exact equipment you will be using. Last-minute discoveries of different computers, presentation software versions, or internet access quality can easily derail your plans. Have a backup plan in case your embedded or linked clip does not work, such as saving the clip as a separate document that you can have open in another window and switch to if needed. If you mix slides with playing DVDs or other video recordings, make sure to cue up the video to the correct spot ahead of time, so you can show just the material you want your audience to see. Finally, sit in different places of the room so that you can be sure viewers can see and hear clearly throughout the room.

If you elect or are limited to a lower tech approach, consider using hardcopy handouts. Paper handouts also require advance planning to prepare and print the material, but, once in hand, you can be confident that your material won't be adversely affected by equipment malfunction. In our experience, handouts are most useful when you have a small audience, such as committee members only, and would like to show one or two items that were not included in the thesis or dissertation document. Committee members can also use a handout of slides presented in the defense as a reference when they ask questions later in the defense.

Develop Strategies to Handle Questioning

Many students are terrified when they think about being questioned during their oral defense. This terror can be managed by knowing something about what committee members will probably ask (see Exhibit 13.2) and by rehearsing your answers ahead of time. Developing general strategies for responding to questions can also help. We described some of these strategies in the Proposal Meeting section of this chapter; we list others next.

Respond to questions professionally in your role as a scientist. Even if you know your committee members well, now is not the time to joke around informally. As Yates (1982) cogently pointed out, now is not the time to get angry or defensive, even if the question seems pointless or unnecessarily antagonistic. At the same time, don't feel compelled to agree with perceived criticisms too quickly. Remember that you are probably much more familiar with your study (and perhaps the general content area) than your committee, and committee members may have missed something you said in the document. Pretend your committee is a professional audience at a national convention, and comport yourself accordingly—give complete answers that demonstrate your thinking, and be respectful of the questioner but also of yourself and your work. Part of what your committee is evaluating is your ability to communicate in a competent professional manner.

Answer questions succinctly. Answer the question you were asked, not the question you wish you had been asked. After doing that, it can be appropriate to answer the question you thought a committee member was going to ask or *should have asked*. Sometimes, you'll get a question that addresses one layer or version of an issue that you wrestled with in your study, such as "Why did you omit data from the three stepfathers?" In addition to answering this, you might want to address how you made decisions about which reporters to include or exclude more generally. Addressing the broader issues can demonstrate your conceptual and decision-making skills. That said, do not give long lectures or go off on tangents that are not clearly related to the question. And do not throw in fancy jargon or mention concepts that you may not understand fully. Using a term incorrectly is like waving a red flag in front of a bull; it invites committee members to ask probing questions to see if you really understand what you are talking about.

Most students are faced with one or more convoluted, hard-to-follow questions in their oral defense. If you don't understand the question, other committee members may not, either! Take the time to paraphrase such questions to make sure you heard them correctly and to allow the questioner to correct any misperceptions you might have.

Don't be surprised if you are unsure of answers to some of the questions. If you really do not know the answer to something, rather than guessing, say "I don't know" or "I'm not sure." An occasional "don't know" won't flunk you (unless, of course, this is in response to questions like, "Who were your participants?" and "What measures did you use?"). A stupid guess, on the other hand, communicates two things: (a) You did not know the answer, and (b) you failed to recognize your ignorance. Some questions have no right or wrong answers. These "thought questions" may require speculation. It is fine to speculate as long as you acknowledge this. Being able to speculate on the logical extensions of your findings demonstrates an important scientific skill, especially if you mention the evidence you might use to test your speculation.

Don't be surprised if you encounter a bit of grandstanding. One of our colleagues, Albert Farrell, tells his students to remember that committee members ask questions during the orals for three reasons. The first is because they genuinely want to know the answer. The second, more common reason is that they want to know if *you* know the answer to the question. The third reason is that they want to show other committee members that *they* know the answer to the question. Grandstanding, as reflected in the last reason, often takes the form of lengthy questions or responses to your answers. This does not imply that you have handled yourself incompetently—it is not about you. Don't compete with a grandstander should one appear on your committee. Let grandstanders do their thing, make an appropriate comment like "that's a really important/interesting/intriguing point," and move on.

Sometimes, committee members will launch into extended discussions or debates among themselves, almost seeming to forget that the student is in the room! Again, this may have nothing to do with you. It could be an outcome of the grandstanding just described, or it could be committee members exploring a point on which they disagree. Occasionally, this discussion may occur when mentors feel like their students are being treated unfairly by another committee member. In most cases, this discussion will resolve quickly on its own or the chair will refocus the committee on your defense. If you can contribute to resolving the discussion or moving it forward, do so. For example, one of our students, after listening to her committee members dissect a particular issue, joined the conversation by saying, "I think I can address that issue" and then succinctly offering her understanding of the literature on the issue, her rationale for approaching it in a particular way in the dissertation, and then suggesting that adding a sentence or two to the dissertation that acknowledged the complexity of the issue might strengthen the document. The student's committee quickly realized that (a) they'd disappeared down a rabbit hole that was beyond the scope of the defense meeting, and (b) the student knew her stuff!

Correctly reading whether committee members like your answers can be difficult. We suggest you spend your time trying to provide good answers rather than evaluating what committee members think of your performance. A committee member may smile congenially and nod but be dissatisfied with your response, and another may sit stony-faced yet love what you are saying. Sitting in on others' defenses will help you see whether the general tone of these meetings at your school is somber or lively. One dependable indicator that things are going well is the occurrence of frequent, lively exchanges among committee members and between you and them. Most likely this means that everyone is having a good time and you are doing fine. The absence of lively exchange, however, does *not* mean that you should start searching the want-ads for a new profession!

Finally, find out which materials are appropriate to bring with you to your defense. Definitely take a copy of the complete document that you gave to your committee to defend; questions such as "What do you mean by such and such on page ___?" are common. If allowed, we recommend that you also take your printouts, copies of measures, and key articles you used in the literature review—even copies of notes you made in preparation for your oral defense. Take these as e-copies organized in files that you can easily retrieve on your computer should you need them. If you must take paper copies, stash them unobtrusively under your table or in a corner. We have heard questions during orals about whether the numbers in Table 46 really were correct, whether Smith and Jones really produced a 3- and not a 4-factor structure with the *xyz* measure, and what items were included on a particular dependent measure. If you suspect you might need to refer to one of these items during your defense, see if you can take it with you.

Rehearse Your Oral Defense

The oral defense is important enough, particularly for the doctorate, to spend some time rehearsing. If possible, schedule a "mock orals," so that you can practice your oral presentation and responses to audience questions. Fellow graduate students (especially those who have been through or observed an oral defense) and your chairperson are ideal audience members, if you can persuade them to spare the time. A favorite beverage or snack always helps here!

Before giving your mock presentation, ask your chairperson to review an outline of your talk. After suitable changes, conduct your rehearsals. We recommend the two-rehearsal format in which you give the talk once to yourself, audio- or video-recording it for later review, and once for an audience. Review the recording of the first rehearsal with timer in hand before doing the second one. Time the lengths of the various sections and the total talk, and plan where you will expand or economize the next time around.

For both rehearsals, prepare completely ahead of time. Have your notes and A/V equipment ready and use them as you plan to during the actual presentation. Select a place to rehearse that is as much like the orals setting as possible. Conduct the rehearsal at the same time of day. You might even want to wear the clothes that you plan to wear during your defense. The more cues from your eventual presentation context that you can build into your rehearsal, the more useful the rehearsal will be. Give members of your audience a handout with your slides and a place for them to make notes about things that are not clear, can't be read, and so forth.

After your talk, get your audience to ask you questions like those you anticipate committee members will ask. Prime your audience to ask questions you fear (e.g., about theoretical or statistical issues), because this is a low-risk time to practice and get feedback. Emphasize to your audience that this is not the time for unconditional positive regard (that support can come after your presentation!). Rather, the audience will be of the most help to you if they help you identify all needed improvements.

In addition to questions from your mock audience, allow enough time to get their general reactions. Prepare a few items to ask about the talk and about how you handled questions. Review these when you view or listen to your recorded presentation as well. Figure 13.1 presents a simple checklist of some important behaviors to note during the presentation and questioning. You might even ask your rehearsal audience to fill out a checklist like this as a way of directing their attention to specific aspects of your presentation. You may want to record this discussion or to ask a friend to take notes for you.

If a specific portion of the talk worries you (e.g., how clearly you described the design of the study or presented the results of the factor analysis), solicit the audience's reaction. Ask how it might have been done differently. Be open and reflective and avoid defensiveness. Remember, these are your friends. They are doing you a favor. Hear their suggestions and take their comments seriously.

Manage Your Arousal Constructively

The oral defense (and, for some, the proposal meeting) seems to produce at least twinges of anxiety even in the most eloquent speakers. Some students experience overwhelming anxiety as they think about the oral examination. Some arousal is normal and, indeed, necessary. The oral defense is the last step toward an important degree, it is an evaluative situation, and the rules for

FIGURE 13.1. Checklist of Important Behaviors for Oral Presentations and Responses to Questioning at Proposal Meetings and Defenses

Yes	No	For oral presentations:
☐	☐	1. Did you make an appropriate opening comment?
☐	☐	2. Did you vary your voice level and intonation throughout?
☐	☐	3. Did you smile appropriately?
☐	☐	4. Did you make eye contact with the audience?
☐	☐	5. Did you look energetic, engaging, and confident, avoiding sitting down and/or leaning your chin on your palm on a table?
☐	☐	6. Did your presentation appear carefully prepared but natural (e.g., avoided reading your talk)?
☐	☐	7. Did you make major points clearly?
☐	☐	8. Did you use good transitions between sections of the talk?
☐	☐	9. Did you allocate your time appropriately?
☐	☐	10. Were your A/V assists clear and easy to read from all parts of the room?
☐	☐	11. Would any additional A/V materials make your talk clearer?
☐	☐	12. Did you minimize "uhs," "ahs," throat clears, and other speech interrupters?
☐	☐	13. Did you use advance organizers, that is, tell you audience where you were going at the beginning?
☐	☐	14. Could your audience follow your results easily?
☐	☐	15. Did you keep your talk simple and to the point?
☐	☐	16. Did you avoid unnecessary detail?
☐	☐	17. Did you avoid distracting mannerisms (excessive movement, fiddling with clothing, mustache, or hair)?
☐	☐	18. Did you use scientific vocabulary appropriately?
☐	☐	19. Did you explain complex procedures clearly?

Yes	No	For oral questioning:
☐	☐	20. Did your answers address the questions?
☐	☐	21. Were your answers concise?
☐	☐	22. Did you appear confident during questioning?
☐	☐	23. Did you qualify your remarks appropriately (e.g., acknowledging speculation as such)?
☐	☐	24. Did you respond nondefensively to antagonistic questions?
☐	☐	25. Did you rephrase hard-to-understand questions before attempting to respond?

what to expect and how to handle the defense are ambiguous. One expert on anxiety, David Barlow (2000), theorized that "a sense of unpredictability and uncontrollability is at the heart of anxiety" (p. 1254). Although the defense is neither completely unpredictable nor uncontrollable, it *is* true that you will not be the only one in charge of the process.

That said, we believe the old inverted U-shaped arousal function is relevant to the oral defense: A medium level of arousal facilitates performance by helping to focus one's attention to the task. Too much arousal, however, can impede your ability to think on your feet and to express yourself clearly. One key to a successful proposal meeting and oral defense lies in managing one's arousal constructively.

Researchers have for many years described three sometimes related but more often nonconvergent elements of anxiety (e.g., Barlow, 2002; Lang, 1971). The first, the cognitive component, involves the subjective experience of anxiety: the things you say to yourself about the situation and how you label your feelings. The second, the physiological component, pertains to the physical substrate of arousal (e.g., unnecessary tensing of muscles, increased heart rate and nervous system activity, perhaps noticed by you as sweaty palms or shortness of breath). The third component, the motor, relates to your observable performance (e.g., pacing, clearing your throat, making eye contact with the audience). Managing these three components will help you deal more effectively with the proposal meeting and oral defense.

Manage Your Thoughts

Two general cognitive factors can contribute to "orals anxiety": (a) fear of the unknown (What will they ask? Will I be able to answer?); and (b) irrational thinking (I'm sure I'll fail and be unemployed for the rest of my life). To see if either of these haunts your thoughts, think about the orals. Listen to what you say to yourself. Does this self-talk revolve around fear of the unknown or the potential catastrophic consequences of failure? If so, read on.

If the ambiguity and uncertainty of oral presentations worry you, make the process less ambiguous and uncertain. Reading this chapter should help. In addition, talk with people who have gone through oral defenses about what happened. Gather a list of common questions from other students and from your chairperson and add these to the ones in Exhibit 13.2. Dissertation defenses are usually open to the public, so go to some in your department to see what they are like (choose someone who is likely to pass so that you can see a successful coping model). All of these preparations together should decrease the ambiguity of the situation for you substantially, and you will feel better prepared.

What about irrational thinking? Over 50 years ago, Ellis (e.g., Ellis & Harper, 1961) proposed the notion that irrational beliefs are associated with feelings of depression, anxiety, anger, and the like. One key irrational belief related to anxiety involves catastrophic thinking: "If things do not turn out as I wish, it will be just awful." A second relates to perfectionism: "I must handle myself flawlessly in all circumstances." Either of these beliefs can be associated with performance anxiety, and together they can be quite debilitating.

The key to dealing with irrational self-talk is to challenge it and talk back more rationally. First, let's look at perfectionism. Do you really have to handle your orals perfectly? No, you just have to handle them competently. Correcting a misstatement, taking time to think through your answers, and encountering occasional problems in understanding or answering a question will not lead you to fail your orals. Recognize and plan for the fact that you may not be as articulate on your feet as you are on paper. That is perfectly natural and no one expects you to be.

What about catastrophes? Some students fear they will not be able to answer questions correctly. They then say to themselves, "I will fail the orals. Then all my work will be down the drain and I will be homeless and unemployable and no one will love me." Let's examine the assumptions behind these thoughts more rationally. First, what is the evidence that you will not be able to answer the questions? You know what you did, right? You know why you did it, right? At this point, you should know more about your specific topic area than anyone in the room, with the possible exception of your chairperson. A reasonable prediction is that you will be able to answer most questions easily and that a few will be more difficult for you. Believe it or not, it is even possible to have fun during your orals: It can be intellectually stimulating and enjoyable to have a group of bright individuals discuss your project with you for a couple of hours.

Will occasional difficulty with a question lead you to fail the orals? Probably not. Overall, you are likely to handle the easy questions well and the difficult questions satisfactorily. After all, the best predictor of future behavior is past behavior, and if you have done well in graduate school, you will likely do fine in the orals, too. Even if you muff a question or two, you are unlikely to fail your orals. Remember, the faculty have an investment in you. They really want you to succeed. They have also typically seen you perform in many other situations—they've seen you demonstrate what you know, they've seen you when you weren't anxious, and they'll likely know to chalk up some of your difficulty to nerves.

And what if you do fail? What is the worst that can happen? Many schools allow students to retake the orals if they fail them but passed the written portion of the dissertation or thesis. Embarrassment is rarely fatal, and no doubt you would survive. Unless you have forged ahead in your program despite repeated feedback that you should consider another line of work, completely flunking at this point is unlikely. In her book on how to finish a dissertation, Miller (2009) presented several of the cognitive traps that can interfere with your progress and offered suggestions for coping with them.

Manage Your Physiology

Another key to managing anxiety is to reduce your arousal level. Working on irrational thoughts may help reduce your arousal. In addition, many techniques work directly to modulate physiological arousal, including progressive relaxation, meditation, mindfulness-based stress reduction, autogenic training, self-hypnosis, exercise, breathing training, biofeedback, and pleasant imagery. See the supplemental resources at the end of the chapter for references to workbooks to consult about some of these.

To manage the physiological components of your anxiety, experiment and find a strategy that works for you. Some like to visualize the threatening scene ahead of time, while seeing themselves performing deliberately and competently. Many athletes are trained in this form of imagery or visualization. Others can lower their anxiety by sitting in a quiet place, closing their eyes, and imagining a relaxing setting like a favorite beach or place in the mountains. Or perhaps it will work for you to move from the tips of your toes to the top of your head (or the reverse), deliberately tensing and relaxing each body part as you come to it. Many medical centers and universities offer instruction in relaxation or biofeedback that may prove helpful if these skills do not come easily to you.

Another way to manage your physiology is to breathe in ways that reduce rather than exacerbate anxiety. Under stressful conditions, many people breathe faster and more shallowly than usual, and this can lead to physical sensations associated with anxiety (e.g., dizziness, numbness in the hands; Gevirtz, 2002). The solution to this is to breathe slowly and deliberately from the diaphragm, a large muscle under the ribcage. Many forms of yoga teach this type of breathing. You can learn to breathe with your diaphragm by placing your hand on your stomach, then inhaling so your stomach goes out, and exhaling so it goes in. Imagine that you are inflating then deflating a balloon. Several minutes of sitting quietly and focusing on regular diaphragmatic breathing (try for 5–7 complete breaths/minute) helps many people reduce the fear butterflies.

Mindfulness-based stress reduction is an increasingly popular approach to managing potentially interfering physiological, cognitive, affective, and motor arousal. Incorporating physiologically focused techniques—such as meditation, breathing, and yoga, as well as cognitive strategies—such as acceptance and mindfulness—emphasizes attending to the present with an attitude of openness and acceptance. Addressing unnecessary motor behavior by noticing it and eliminating it via progressive relaxation is also useful. Many universities have online resources and classes well-suited to graduate students. For example, UCLA's Mindfulness Awareness Research Center (http://marc.ucla.edu) offers free online guided meditations, online and in-person courses, and an extensive bibliography covering research, therapist manuals, and self-help resources. Developing mindfulness skills can help you approach your thesis or dissertation from a calmer, more centered, and more fully present perspective.

Finally, another way of managing one's physiology involves medication, whether pharmacologic or agricultural. Taking a pill or a toke is easier than learning arousal reduction skills, but these can sometimes carry the risk of also slowing your cognitive processes. We do not recommend these coping aids unless you have used them before and are certain that they will not create untoward side effects in the situation.

In addition to selecting and learning ways to manage your physiological arousal, schedule time to use them right before your oral defense. One student we know scheduled her doctoral defense so she would have time for a vigorous workout and shower before it started!

Manage Your Motor Behavior

The final component of anxiety, the motor component, has to do with how you appear to others. Remember, the motor, physiological, and cognitive components of anxiety need not covary. Thus, although inside you may be shaking, this does not have to show in your behavior. Many of the best performers confess to feeling anxious inside—anxiety that their audience cannot detect.

As with most of our advice, the key to looking like a professional in your orals lies in planning and practice. Think of which of your professors or fellow students come across effectively and emulate the behaviors that give that impression. Remember that you do not have to feel competent—you just need to *pretend* that you are. Rehearsal, too, can help considerably. You can use something like the Social Performance Rating Scale (Fydrich, Chambless, Perry, Buergener, & Beazley, 1998; Harb, Eng, Zaider, & Heimberg, 2003) to identify performance cues that make you look anxious (e.g., fidgeting, rigid posture, frequent pauses, inaudible or harsh voice). Minimize these. Use the rating scale to rate a video-recorded version of your talk—you may be surprised at how calm you can appear. Many of us look much more competent than we feel.

Address Serious Anxiety Problems

As we've said, some anxiety during an oral defense is normal, even desirable. If you generally experience serious anxiety in public speaking or other social situations, however, you may want to obtain treatment for your anxiety before you get to the oral defense. For minor cases of speech anxiety, participating in Toastmasters can be useful (http://www.toastmasters.org). This is an international organization with chapters in many towns and cities. Contact the chapter nearest you. Taking a class in improvisation can also do wonders for your skill and confidence in speaking before others. Search for "improv classes" and be surprised at how many there are in your community. For more serious cases, seek assistance from a qualified, competent specialist in empirically supported strategies for anxiety management. Many professional organizations (e.g., Association for Behavioral and Cognitive Therapy, Anxiety Disorders Association of America) have websites with referral information about behavior health professionals specializing in treating anxiety. The Anxiety Disorders Association of America also lists recommended self-help books.

Final Preparations

Reread Your Document

We strongly recommend that you reread your document in the last week or two before your defense. Do not wait until the night before your meeting to do this. You want to have time to refresh your memory as to what you did. You may have written some sections of the document months or even a year or two before the defense. Do you remember exactly how you scored the data, handled missing values, screened participants? Do you know exactly where to look in your document to find details related to measures and analyses? Do you remember important details of the key studies that guided your work and that are most similar to yours? Could you discuss them knowledgeably?

If the answer to any of these questions is *no,* you need to refresh your memory about what you wrote and your procedures for collecting and analyzing the data. One student we know almost failed her defense when she could not answer a question about whether she had reverse-scored some of the items in a key questionnaire she had used. This scoring error would have explained some unusual results—along with invalidating them. She *had* scored her data correctly, but in the heat of the moment, she could not remember her scoring procedures.

Because she defended the project well otherwise, the committee passed her provisionally, pending review of her scoring procedures. Had she scored the data incorrectly, she would have been required to redo the defense with a new document. The key point here, however, is that she could have avoided all this had she reviewed her document and procedures during the week before the defense. We've seen other students handle similar questions with ease because they knew their document inside and out. Prior planning prevents poor performance!

Last-Minute Logistics

As we noted at the beginning of this chapter, the proposal and defense meetings will go more smoothly if you stay on top of several logistical issues, such as scheduling, forms, and meeting etiquette. Forms are particularly important: You do not want to have to track down committee members to get their signatures because you brought the wrong forms or no forms for them to sign. If you will be graduating from your program immediately after finishing your dissertation, check for additional forms required for graduation— graduation and the dissertation defense are not synonymous! Be sure to check with your chairperson, other students, and whomever else they recommend (e.g., the director of graduate studies or Graduate Office administrative assistant) to find the answers to the questions in Exhibit 13.1. Some of the questions have to do with department or university requirements or policies, and some have specific right answers. Others have more to do with department culture or chairperson preferences, and you can do whatever you and your chair find most comfortable. Here, we address two issues that seem to show a great deal of variability: dress code and refreshments.

Appropriate meeting attire is well-defined in some departments and given almost no thought in others. In some departments, a business suit would be considered appropriate, whereas in others, the answer to "What should I wear?" is likely to be "clothes." As with other aspects of these meetings, the proposal meeting is likely to be less formal than the defense. Think about how you want to represent your institution and yourself as a professional, especially if your defense will be attended by individuals from other departments or the public. If your meeting will be limited to your committee or people in your department, just go with normal attire for teaching, meetings, or clinical work. We recommend that you not wear your normal "student" attire, particularly if it is very casual. Although you are a student, you are also demonstrating your professionalism and, especially at the dissertation defense, your readiness to enter the workforce. As the saying goes, dress for the job you want, not the job you have.

The second issue concerns refreshments—should you bring them or not? People tend to be split on this issue, with some viewing it as a gesture of hospitality and others viewing it as a potentially awkward inducement to encourage positive evaluation of your defense. We recommend that you ask your committee chair; in our experience students sometimes develop a culture of "escalating refreshments," feeling the need to bring home-baked goods or an entire meal to avoid falling short of expectations. In general, if your department culture supports providing refreshments, think small. IRB regulations indicate that participant incentives should not be large enough that they could be perceived as providing undue influence on participants; similarly, your refreshments should not be large enough to be perceived as an attempt to influence your committee. A pot of coffee, bottled water, and a small snack should be sufficient. And think of refreshments as a snack, not as a celebration. Don't do as a legendary student in one of our programs did and bring a bottle of wine to your defense meeting! Although we admit that a nice glass of wine pairs well with many tasks, your oral defense is not one of them.

Plan for the Worst, Expect the Best

Remember, proposal meetings and oral defenses can be scary or they can be enjoyable and productive. You've spent several years developing the necessary knowledge, research skills, and professional communication competencies for your project, and a year or more seeing the project to completion. Now it's time for the final step. As with virtually every step of the research process, some advance investigation and preparation can increase the chances that this aspect of your project will go smoothly and successfully.

FINISHING TOUCHES

Let's assume that all has gone well, you passed your defense, cleaned up the document incorporating suggestions from your committee and any additional formatting required by your institution, and deposited your opus and required forms at the appropriate office. Don't forget to give your committee members a final copy of the document! In the excitement of moving forward, it can be easy to forget this step, but your committee will appreciate having the clean and complete version of your project. In the old days, it was customary to provide hard- or softbound copies to each committee member. Now, an electronic copy will often suffice. Check with your committee chair regarding expectations.

Next, it's time to share your findings with the world! Chapter 14 discusses this step.

✓   TO DO . . .

MANAGING COMMITTEE MEETINGS

The Proposal Meeting

☐ Prepare for the meeting.

  - Find out typical format—see Exhibit 13.1, list of questions to ask about the meeting.

  - Prepare a brief presentation, if applicable.

  - Prepare for questions.

☐ Manage the meeting.

  - Keep track of committee input.

  - Clarify what input is suggested versus what is required (and at what stage of the project—at proposal, final document, publication).

☐ Moving forward after the meeting.

  - Take stock of meeting input, and develop a plan for moving forward.

  - Go! Implement your thesis/dissertation plan.

The Defense Meeting

☐ Prepare for the meeting.

  - Find out typical format—use the list in Exhibit 13.1.

  - Prepare brief or extended presentation and A/V materials.

  - Make sure you will have appropriate A/V equipment.

  - Prepare for questions (see Exhibit 13.2).

  - Rehearse! Use mock orals or other practice.

  - Ask for feedback (can use Figure 13.1).

☐ Manage your arousal.

  - Learn (and use) skills for managing mild to moderate cognitive distortions, anxiety.

  - Consider more intensive intervention for severe anxiety.

☐ Final preparations

  – Reread the document.

  – Dress for success.

  – Final logistics—snacks, verify meeting room availability and equipment.

☐ Ready, set, defend!

  – Deliver presentation, answer questions.

  – Keep track of committee input.

☐ Postmeeting wrap-up

  – Complete changes to the document as required by the committee and by the institution (e.g., formatting).

  – Meet with the committee as needed and secure final approval, signatures, forms.

  – Deposit a final copy of the document and forms to the institution.

  – Give final document copies to the committee.

SUPPLEMENTAL RESOURCES

Defense Process and Tips

Miller, A. B. (2009). *Finish your dissertation once and for all! How to overcome psychological barriers, get results, and move on with your life.* American Psychological Association.

Pyrczak, F. (2000). *Completing your thesis or dissertation.* Pyrczak.

Managing Anxiety

Anxiety Disorders Association of America. http://www.adaa.org/

Bourne, E. J. (2001). *Anxiety and phobia workbook* (3rd ed.). New Harbinger.

Davis, M., Robbins-Eshelman, E., & McKay, M. (2000). *The relaxation and stress reduction workbook* (5th ed.). New Harbinger.

Ellis, A. (2001). *Overcoming destructive beliefs, feelings, and behavior: New directions for rational emotive behavior therapy.* Prometheus Books.

Hayes, S. C., & Smith, S. (2005). *Get out of your mind and into your life: The new acceptance and commitment therapy.* New Harbinger.

Kabat-Zinn, J. (2005). *Full catastrophe living: Using the wisdom of your body and mind to face stress, pain, and illness: Fifteenth anniversary edition.* Bantam Dell.

Roemer, L., & Orsillo, S. M. (2009). *Mindfulness- and acceptance-based behavioral therapies in practice.* Guilford Press.

Smalley, S. L., & Winston, D. (2010). *Fully present: The science, art, and practice of mindfulness.* Da Capo Lifelong Books.

Toastmasters International. http://www.toastmasters.org/

UCLA Health. (n.d.). *UCLA Mindful Awareness Research Center.* https://www.uclahealth.org/marc/default.cfm

14

Presenting Your Project to the World

This chapter is about ways to disseminate your findings to the world, including
- presentations at professional meetings
- publication in professional journals and online
- articles in the popular press, and discussions via blogs and podcasts

Read thoroughly if
- you are unfamiliar with the process of submitting your work for presentation or publication
- you are not sure it is worth the extra effort for you to make your work widely known

Skim or skip if
- you already know how to use contemporary forms of dissemination, like professional presentation and publication

It's over. You've defended your research, made the necessary revisions, and presented the required copies to your institution. Whew! Now, on with your life, right? Wrong! Well, at least not without ever looking back at your project. You began your research months and possibly years ago, when you started looking for an idea that could be molded into the project you've just

https://doi.org/10.1037/0000161-014
Dissertations and Theses From Start to Finish: Psychology and Related Fields, Third Edition,
by D. J. Bell, S. L. Foster, and J. D. Cone

completed. That process, as Yogi Berra once said, ain't over until it's over. And research, in a sense, is never really over. As Figure 14.1 shows, research is a cyclical process that begins with a question and begins again, when the answers to that question have been presented to the research community. In truth, your study probably raised additional questions that you or others will pursue in the future. So, research is probably best thought of as an evolutionary process, rather than as something with definite boundaries and end points.

Nonetheless, there are times when major portions of research (e.g., specific studies in a program, specific thesis or dissertation projects) are complete and can be shared with others. In a sense, you have already done this, albeit in a limited way. You have shared your findings with your committee, turned in your thesis or dissertation document, and its written form is now available to others. This chapter is about additional dissemination of your findings in ways that are likely to call them to the attention of like-minded scholars who can take your results and build on them. We speak here of both oral and published ways of disseminating.

When should you present the results of your hard work? Usually, as soon as possible after your oral defense. We encourage speed because you will have a natural tendency to slow down and relax a bit after your defense. Life moves on, and you risk losing momentum, and perhaps even never touching your document again. This is a mistake. For one thing, although your completed

FIGURE 14.1. The Research Cycle

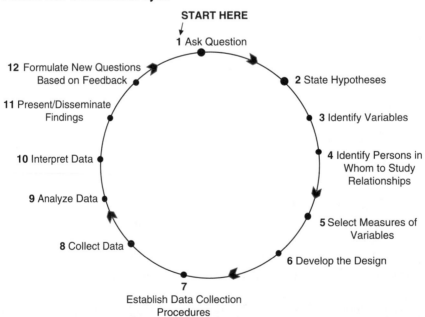

Note. From *Evaluating Outcomes: Empirical Tools for Effective Practice* (p. 41) by J.D. Cone, 2001. American Psychological Association. Copyright 2001 by the American Psychological Association.

thesis is certainly a praiseworthy accomplishment, its limited distribution means relatively few people will have the opportunity to learn from your work. Your completed dissertation will probably have wider distribution because most universities archive them and make them available through sources like ProQuest. However, these archives can still be difficult for interested readers to access and often do not contain your complete document. And, knowingly or not, you have incurred certain obligations in the process of completing your research. For example, you have a responsibility to share your findings with the broader scientific community. Additionally, at times there are ethical obligations to disclose your results in a timely manner. For example, if your study evaluated an existing program, you may have a responsibility to both a sponsor and to program participants to present your findings within a reasonable period after completing the evaluation.

As we said in Chapter 4, research is a cumulative process. Each study builds on those that went before. If yours is not there for others to see, they cannot build on it and they cannot come to you with questions that might improve the quality of their own research. In addition, sharing your results with others communicates something important about how you value the time and effort you have expended and the sacrifices you have asked others (e.g., your participants, research assistants, committee members, family) to make on your behalf. Was it really so bad that you never want to talk about it again? Were all those sacrifices only for the sake of a diploma to hang on a wall?

Finally, on a less philosophical, more practical note, presenting and publishing your work may help you in the job search now or in the future. Any potential employer will be impressed that you took the time and were organized enough to present your findings. If you plan an academic career, want to apply for postdoctoral research fellowships, or are interested in research-oriented clinical internships, having presentations, publications, and submissions on your vita will be essential to the success of your application. If you just finished a master's thesis and want to apply to doctoral programs, be aware that most faculty look favorably on students who took the initiative to present and publish their theses.

Although some master's research may lack the necessary scope for publication, many thesis and dissertation projects will be suitable for presenting at a conference and publishing in a journal. So, assuming we have convinced you to share the good news of your findings, let's talk strategy. How should you go about getting your research to the scientific and other communities?

PUBLISH IT ONLINE FIRST

In earlier editions of this book, we suggested that readers present their work first, usually orally, at some meeting organized to share scientific information. This might be as informal as a departmental brown bag lunch or as formal as a national or international meeting of a professional organization. The logic for suggesting an oral presentation first stems from the value of getting and using feedback from those in attendance. This would be the basis for improving how you tell your story. Incorporating these improvements into a formal written journal submission increases the likelihood of its being accepted for publication.

With the availability of a greater variety of digital outlets for reaching others (e.g., blogs, podcasts, social media, online publishing), we now suggest you take advantage of some of these first. For example, the American Psychological Association (APA) recently endorsed the use of an online repository of scientific information (PsyArXiv) to which prepublication drafts of papers can be submitted (APA, 2017a; see http://www.apa.org/news/press/releases/2017/08/open-science.aspx). Developed by the Society for the Improvement of Psychological Science and maintained by the Center for Open Science, PsyArXiv accepts as yet unpublished papers, works in progress, and even those currently under review. PsyArXiv provides a free, open access to psychological science, even for papers that are ultimately published in journals that are only accessible to subscribers.

Papers in this easily searchable archive are immediately available at no cost to a worldwide audience of anyone with access to the internet. Placing your paper in the archive allows others working in your area to know about your work much sooner than they would if they had to wait to hear or read about it through conventional means. They can then communicate with you and share suggestions you might not have considered. If you avail yourself of such a service as soon as your thesis or dissertation proposal is accepted by your committee, with the preregistration process described in Chapter 5 you can benefit from feedback that might help you improve the quality of your research as it progresses. If you update your registration at points along the way (e.g., data collected, analyses completed, results discussed), you may receive feedback that contributes to the overall quality of your finished product. When you have defended this product and revised it, you can update your registration with the accepted document. At this point any feedback you receive can assist you in formal oral and written presentation of your work as you complete Step 11 of the research cycle in Figure 14.1.

You may worry that registering your paper in an online public archive such as PsyArXiv might lead others to steal your idea before your research is conducted and appears in print. *Au contraire, mon cher/ma chérie.* As noted in Chapter 5, the very act of registering your intentions certifies, with a time-and-date stamp, that you are the originator of the idea. And if you are still concerned, you can register your paper privately for a period of time, making it public later (e.g., after publication).

In addition to establishing a presence on a widely available resource such as PsyArXiv, you might also consider starting a blog. In fact, if you do this even earlier when you have initially decided the outlines of your project, you can use it to share your progress broadly. This opens the possibility of interactions with like-minded researchers that can be very beneficial. There are literally hundreds of psychology blogs on the internet. Some of these focus on giving psychology to nonpsychologists (e.g., https://writerswrite.co.za/top-100-psychology-blogs-a-fabulous-resource-for-writers/ [retrieved February 16, 2018]). There are also quite a few resources for how to start and maintain a blog (e.g., Novotney, 2014; see https://www.apa.org/monitor/2014/06/blogging).

Another means of openly sharing your work is through podcasts. These are showing a steadily increasing user base with a reported 67 million Americans listening to at least one a month (Stringer, 2017; see http://www.apa.org/monitor/2017/12/create-podcast.aspx). Although this may be a type of media that is more useful *after* you have completed your studies and launched a career, it is still worth considering as a way of disseminating the findings of your thesis or dissertation research. Be aware that these are totally open forms of sharing that, unlike PsyArXiv, do not provide a registration that you are the originator of the material.

Unless you have a job lined up that starts immediately, you may have time on your hands right after completing your project and can add creating a podcast to your efforts to submitting a paper to a conference or a journal. If you decide to do this, first look into some of the readily available "how to create a podcast" material you can find on the Internet. Stringer (2017) provided some practical advice to consider before you commit to doing one. One caution: Be aware that you are committing yourself to an ongoing effort. As with a blog, podcasts are not a one-shot production in the way that presentations or publications are. You get into them with the idea of continuing a weekly, monthly, and so on, presence at specific times, much as a television or radio show. If what you say is interesting, your listeners will want to tune in again. Of course, your podcast can be archived and listened to on demand. It is not that you must "go live" at a specific time each week. People will just want to know when the next podcast can be expected so they can look for it. If you make a new one available on a dependable schedule, you will be more likely to keep your followers and grow their numbers.

There can be substantial rewards for successful bloggers or podcasters. If your career is in academia, for example, the skills of communicating with people (by writing, lecturing, submitting grant applications) all involve storytelling (Hu, 2016). If you hone the skills needed to attract and keep people downloading your written or spoken material, you will increase your influence and make a bigger impact in and for your field. You may attract an audience (interest group) of like-minded scholars who begin interacting around your blog or podcast and synergistically expand the work in your area. If you go into business for yourself (e.g., private practice), you can use blogs and podcasts to attract interest and build a clientele. Whatever your motivation, you should expect to commit both time and money to the effort (Hu, 2016).

PRESENT IT IN PERSON

As we suggested in the previous section, the first step in disseminating your findings is to establish your presence in your chosen research area to others doing work in that area as well. By preregistering your project and then submitting a description of your work-to-date to an online archive such as PsyArXiv, you stake a claim, much like a gold miner of old, and others will have to acknowledge your prior work and cannot claim it as their own.

At this point, those who do access your archived writing can contact you and ask questions, give suggestions, and so on. Now you can turn to disseminating and getting feedback on your research by presenting your findings to groups of professionals. Then you can incorporate this feedback into your own thinking about the research and prepare a formal submission for publication. This permits the research to benefit from the gradual shaping provided by the peer-review process. In addition, presenting (particularly at conferences) inevitably leads to conversations with others interested in your work, expanding your professional network and providing support and encouragement for your efforts. Think about the Big Names cited in your references. Wouldn't it be a thrill if one of them came up and complimented you on your study?

A continuum of outlets exists for presenting research results. At one end are informal discussions of your findings with other students over coffee. At the other is the formal presentation of your research to the Committee for Nobel Laureates at the Nobel Institute in Stockholm. In between, there are departmental colloquia; informal media presentations (e.g., as a guest on a radio or television show); research presentations during job interviews; and formal presentations at state, regional, national, and international professional conferences. Most of us spend our research careers somewhere in the middle of this continuum, with a much smaller number who are lucky and talented enough to present their work as they are accepting accolades as the newest APA Distinguished Scientist or recipient of the Nobel Prize.

Many departments routinely schedule colloquia during which students, faculty, or invited visitors present their research to anyone interested in attending. Sometimes, these are periodically or regularly scheduled events in classrooms or auditoriums. Others occur more informally as brown bag lunch affairs. If your department has such colloquia, we strongly recommend presenting your findings in this forum. In some departments, it will be appropriate to present soon after completing your defense. In effect, this will be your second presentation, because you already gave one and exposed yourself to the peer review process when you met with your committee for your defense. This sort of presentation is great practice for an upcoming conference presentation or job talk. In other departments, these seminars are used for people to present their work earlier in the process—as a place to get feedback on different ways of presenting the findings or to practice for a thesis or dissertation defense meeting.

You may be thinking, "Okay, okay, I'll present a paper, but I think I'll skip the local presentation because the audience is probably not important enough for me to bother." Nothing could be further from the truth—presenting in front of your "home crowd" is priceless. At the same time, the thought of standing in front of your whole program or department can be pretty daunting. You might be thinking, "I have to see these people every day. What if my research presentation is absolutely horrid? Do I want to have to slink along the hallways or come to school only at night to avoid the scorn or pity of my colleagues?" These concerns are quite normal. In reality, local presentations are sometimes the most challenging because your colleagues are more likely than others to know some of the real issues and to feel comfortable discussing them with you. Thus, they are less likely to pull punches in questioning you about your research procedures and findings. At the same time, these are the faculty who admitted you to graduate school and the peers with whom you spend every day. They are (professionally speaking), the people who know and love you, and, believe it or not, they want you to succeed! Their feedback will help make your presentation better, so that it's ready to take "on the road." This is why some people say that if you can present at home, you can present anywhere.

Beyond the department, there are state-level professional meetings, as well as regional, national, and international ones. Where you choose to submit your research will depend on several factors, including whether the meeting invites research presentations in the first place, the schedule (i.e., time of year the meeting is held), the cost of attending, and the professional and personal advantages. Assuming the meeting welcomes research presentations, the most important of these considerations may be the professional advantages that can accrue. If you will be looking for a job immediately after completing your study, you should consider submitting your research to a meeting that may help you find a job. If your interest is in an applied position and you have definite geographic requirements, consider a state or regional meeting. These often have placement facilities and procedures for arranging interviews with representatives of organizations that are currently hiring in the geographic area where the meeting occurs. Even if no formal placement facilities exist, presenting at a state or regional meeting will expose you to people in the area and increase your chances of hearing about suitable positions.

As you may have gathered from the above, professional meetings are about sharing information. This can be scientific, vocational, or personal/social information, and there is overlap among them. As conferences are inherently social, you will be wise to *be* social when attending them. Don't hide out in your room. Make it a practice to attend the receptions, cocktail hours and banquet dinners. Linger after presentations and join the group of attendees surrounding the speaker after they finish. Whether you have a question to ask is not critical. Others will, and listening to them and the responses they get provides an entree for you to engage the questioner with, "That was an interesting question. What did you think of her/his answer?" Don't stand quietly in lines either. Engage those around you. Multiple interactions like these across the days of the meetings will extend your professional network and increase the likelihood of learning about things that can advance your own research, practice, and career.

If your career aspirations tend toward the academic, you will almost certainly want to present your work at national conferences. Get into the habit of presenting at such conventions early. In addition to the professional connections that sharing your research at such venues will facilitate, many professional associations' annual meetings include networking events and other placement services for the next stage of your career, such as internship, postdoctoral training, or a job. You can find out more about relevant conferences by talking with your advisor and lab-mates, looking through recent issues of publications from professional organizations, and going to organizations' websites.

Be warned that abstracts often must be submitted long before the conference. For example, the Association for Behavioral and Cognitive Therapy, which meets in November each year, usually requires that submissions be received by March. APA requires submissions to be received by mid-November for their meeting, which is ordinarily held the following August. Presenting your study in a forum such as these obviously takes some advance planning. This is such an important part of the thesis-dissertation—job-finding sequence, however, that we strongly recommend that you build such presentations into the time schedule you developed in Chapter 3.

When you begin exploring presentation possibilities, you will find a variety of formats, including online, poster presentations, individual papers presented orally, papers presented as part of organized symposia, workshops, panel discussions, and invited addresses. Submissions of individual projects such as a thesis or dissertation are often most appropriate for poster sessions or paper presentations. However, there are also symposia to consider. If your study is part of a research program, you may be able to talk your chairperson into organizing a research symposium that includes several presentations around a particular theme. Yours could be one of them. If you are an advanced student with an active research program and some experience presenting, you might consider organizing a symposium yourself. Your study could be included as one of the submissions. Finding others to fill your symposium line-up is a great opportunity for you to gain recognition and build relationships with other researchers in your area.

Pare to Prepare for Presentation

Much of getting a thesis or dissertation ready for dissemination involves paring it to a manageable size. When you prepared for your defense (see Chapter 13) you might have used software (e.g., *Google Docs Presentation*, PowerPoint) to organize your material. In doing, so you have already pared it significantly. Using the material you created at that point to facilitate formal submission to a professional conference will save time now.

If you wish to present your research at a conference, you will have to submit an abstract of your study. Producing a good abstract requires that you pare your 100 or more pages to just a few hundred words. The abstract of your thesis or dissertation is a good place to begin. The abstract should contain the rationale for your research, methodology, results, and brief reference to its significance and implications. Approximately 60% of the allocated words should describe method and results. These sections should communicate the most important details of the study because this is what the program committee will use to decide whether to accept or reject it. For this reason, make clear to the reviewer what you did and the methodological soundness of your procedures. Exhibit 14.1 is an abstract based on the collaborative work from two students' dissertation (Hausman, Kim, Bell, Lee, & An, 2016) that was submitted and accepted for presentation at a meeting of the Association for Behavioral and Cognitive Therapies. It is typical of such submissions and might be a useful model in planning your own.

Assume that a program committee or group recognizes the worth of your research and schedules your presentation at a conference. Or, perhaps, someone invites you for a job interview. The next round of paring involves producing your talk or poster. Preparation for these two events differs somewhat. However, both have much in common with the preparations necessary for the proposal and defense meetings discussed in Chapter 13.

Oral Presentations

First, consider how much of your study you should present. That depends on a number of factors. How much time will you have? Who is likely to be in the audience? Will audiovisual or computer equipment be available? Will you have internet access? Ask these questions before preparing any presentation. Regional or national meetings will typically allow you 10 to 20 minutes for your talk and usually provide a projector, although you might have to bring your own laptop to attach to it. They may provide internet connection so that you can retrieve material you have stored in the cloud or so that you can link to websites (e.g., you might want to include a short segment of a YouTube video). It is probably a good idea to develop contingency plans for inconveniences such as poor internet connection or lack of compatibility between your presentation software and theirs. Bringing your presentation on a flash drive, bringing your own computer, and having some screen shots that you can use in case a video won't load are all ways to keep your presentation on track despite technology glitches.

During job interviews or at local departmental research colloquia, expect somewhere around an hour to be allocated. In these cases, plan to hold your remarks to about 40 to 45 minutes to allow time for questions, late starts, equipment ambivalence, and so on. Chapter 13 presents numerous suggestions for preparing an oral presentation, including percentages of time to allocate to different sections (e.g., introduction, method), so we won't repeat them all here.

EXHIBIT 14.1

Sample Abstract for a Poster Presentation: The Relationship of Regulation of Positive Affect and Adjustment Across Cultures

Research and theory suggest that anxiety and depression are disorders of deficits in emotion regulation. Much of this literature has focused on regulation of negative affect (NA), while research about how positive affect (PA) is regulated in depressed and anxious individuals is in its infancy. Regulation strategies that enhance PA, such as positive rumination, are associated with lower depressive symptoms and higher self-esteem, while strategies that diminish the experience of PA, such as dampening, are related to lower life satisfaction and self-esteem and higher anxious and depressive symptoms (Eisner et al., 2009; Feldman et al., 2008; Quiodbach et al., 2010). The majority of this research has predominantly included European and European American samples, but there is emerging evidence that the regulation of PA varies across culture (e.g., Miyamoto & Ma, 2011). Further, because of differences in cultural values on optimal positive emotional experience and expression, there may be differences in the relationships of PA regulation to indices of adjustment across cultures. Few studies have examined these relationships across cultures.

The present study extends the literature on regulation of positive emotions by examining relationships of dampening and positive rumination to depression, anxiety, and well-being in a sample of South Korean nationals compared to a predominantly European American sample from the United States. Participants were 371 American and 182 South Korean undergraduates, ages 18–29, recruited from introductory psychology courses at U.S. and South Korean universities. Participants completed an online survey battery in their own native language, assessing internalizing symptoms, affect, and regulation of positive emotions (via dampening and positive rumination), negative emotions (via rumination), and life satisfaction.

To investigate the relative importance of regulation of PA on adjustment across cultures, regression models were conducted predicting depressive symptoms, anxious symptoms, and life satisfaction. Both dampening and lower positive rumination predicted higher depressive symptoms across both samples. For anxious symptoms, being American and having higher dampening both predicted higher anxious symptoms. The combination of lower dampening and higher positive rumination predicted higher life satisfaction in our U.S. sample, with dampening showing a relatively large effect. In our South Korean sample, only higher positive rumination predicted higher life satisfaction, also a relatively large effect. Findings may have important implications for understanding regulation of PA in different cultural contexts and suggest that optimal interventions involving regulation of PA may differ in part for South Koreans and Americans. The focus of treatment for internalizing symptoms may be common across cultures (e.g., target dampening), but may require a more nuanced approach when considering interventions to optimally enhance life satisfaction for Americans and South Koreans (e.g., target dampening for Americans, increase positive rumination for South Koreans).

Note. Abstract submitted by E. Hausman, S. Kim, D. Bell, H. Lee, and D. An and accepted for presentation at the annual meeting of the Association for Behavioral and Cognitive Therapies, 2016. Reprinted with permission.

When we discussed the oral defense, we emphasized the benefits of practicing your talk. The same logic applies here. You'll need an audience. The most useful audience will include your chairperson or other faculty members, graduate student colleagues, and significant others (hence our "present at your local seminar!" advice). Other good possibilities for dress-rehearsal audiences would be undergraduate classes that you or your colleagues are teaching or research seminars or journal clubs at an agency where you are doing a practicum or internship.

Overall, when preparing your talk, think about accomplishing the two I's: (a) inspiring and (b) informing your audience. Accomplishing both requires you recognize that although some of your audience may be quite knowledgeable in your area, others will not know much about the area and may not be convinced that they should care much about it! Helping people understand why they should listen to you—why your research matters (significance, impact) and why they can trust it (methodological and analytic clarity and soundness and rigor)—will make your talk engaging and impactful rather than being the type of dry and boring talk that people often associate with academic researchers. Incidentally, a sound and engaging talk will serve you especially well on the job market. Although job talks are a platform for demonstrating skill in conducting high-quality research, they are also important for demonstrating that you can communicate and teach about research in a way that reaches your audience, teaches them something, and keeps them engaged.

Poster Presentations

Most regional or national professional organizations are more likely to accept individual studies for presentation during poster sessions than during a series of oral talks. The advantage of this format is that you can discuss your work with interested attendees who circulate among the posters in your session.

There are many resources available online that make this process much easier than it used to be (e.g., http://guides.lib.unc.edu/posters/pptwindows2016 and http://prezi.com/ix7pbexccxbc/?utm_campaign=share &utm_medium=copy). If you have already used a program such as PowerPoint in presenting your findings at your defense, select a template that uses it as well. This will save time in converting what you've already done to the poster you are preparing now. Typically, posters will be approximately 3 feet high by 5 feet long paper sheets that can be attached to something that looks like a free-standing bulletin board. Sometimes the allowable size will be smaller or you may be required to put your poster on a rigid backing (e.g., a trifold poster stand).

For a poster session, prepare a visual layout of your study that parallels the organization and content that you would present orally or in a formal journal submission: abstract (although sometimes this section is excluded from a poster), introduction, method, results, and so on. Poster guidelines discuss the importance of presenting your information so that people can walk by and take in information about your study pretty quickly, which means that paring your prose is a must (more on this later).

Poster sessions are usually scheduled so that similarly themed posters are presented together (e.g., human learning, assessment and diagnosis). Numerous presenters display their posters for a designated time period (e.g., 1.5 hours) in rooms or areas of the conference center (e.g., in the exhibitions hall) dedicated to poster presentations. As the author, you are expected to stand beside your poster and discuss it with conference attendees as they wander by.

The rules governing poster presentations vary somewhat from conference to conference. In general, poster guidelines (e.g., http://www.psychologicalscience. org/conventions/annual/call-for-submissions/rules-guidelines#id2) specify that (a) the type size (e.g., 20 points or larger) must be readable at a distance of 3 feet, (b) copies of the complete presentation must be available to conference attendees (e.g., emailed after the conference to interested individuals or paper copies available at the poster session), and (c) at least one author of the paper must be present throughout to discuss the poster. Incidentally, hard-copy handouts have become increasingly rare at conferences as digital forms of communication have emerged. Provide a means by which interested persons can leave their address, so that you can mail or email information to them later. Alternatively, you can provide a web address or QR code that conference attendees can use to link directly to a copy of your poster, supporting materials, or your research website.

To decide what goes into your poster, first decide on your general format and set some space or page limits. Poster constructions used to be a fairly low-tech affair. All three of us "grew up" in academia preparing several typed pages with enlarged print, then attaching them to stiff colored backing with a half- or three-quarter-inch border around the entire page. The current standard is to use PowerPoint or similar presentation software to create your poster as a single slide, with desired formatting, and then print that slide as a poster. One of us favors a 3-column PowerPoint slide format, with a left-hand column devoted to the introduction and research questions; a center column containing methods, results, tables, and figures; a right-hand column for the discussion and references; and a title and author banner across the top. Column widths can be adjusted as needed to accommodate the material, although generally, the center column containing the "meat" of the study takes about half of the poster's width. If you are using typed pages, we suggest the following: no more than one double-spaced page in a large font for the introduction and rationale for the study; two pages for the method; one or two pages for the results, supplemented by tables or figures; and one page for discussion (sometimes results and discussion can be combined). With either format, we suggest keeping the combination of tables and figures to three or fewer. Because your poster will be in large type, concise, clear prose is essential. Bullet points, rather than complete sentences, can also be useful. Attendees will want to walk by, peruse the poster quickly, and get the gist of the study. We find it useful to use the abstract as a basis for the poster and build up, adding details in order of importance until we have met our page or word limits.

Remember, when you give such a presentation, you represent not only yourself but your coauthors and school as well. The visual appearance of your poster makes an important statement that complements its written content. Most of us have seen poorly prepared poster presentations and been thankful that they did not have our school's name attached to them. We have also seen brightly colored Las Vegas–style posters that clearly represent style over substance. Taste, clarity, and ease of reading are the most important criteria for posters, given that the program committee considered their content important enough to be accepted.

Once you've decided on your poster content, we suggest that you go back to the guidelines provided by the program committee. This is not the place to get creative. Remember, they have their rules for a reason. Many conference websites include suggested poster layouts that can give you an idea of how to arrange your space. In addition, keep it simple. You will have to carry your poster with you to the conference, often on an airplane. You will have to set it up and take it down in as little as 1 to 2 minutes. The only materials you can count on being provided will be the poster board to which you attach your materials (unless, as noted above, there are specific requirements for you to provide the actual poster backing or support). Although most conferences will provide these, it is helpful to take along a supply of pushpins or tacks, in case your poster board's supply has been raided!

As noted above, the current standard is to prepare a poster as a single large sheet, typically in color, using a poster printer. At many universities, graduate students have access to free or low-cost (e.g., ranging from $10 to $60) poster printing as part of the services covered by their student fees. Check with your department, graduate school, library, or audiovisual center to see what is available at your institution. If your university doesn't provide access to a poster printer, you can take a flash drive containing your presentation to a copy or office supply shop for printing. This option is generally a bit pricier, but it offers good quality. Note that the office store may offer you some very fancy options, most of which may not be necessary. If budget is an issue, ask whether producing a black-and-white version is less costly. Some of our students have produced professional-looking, eye-catching, low-cost posters making liberal use of grayscale instead of color. And do you really need glossy photo-quality paper? Matte finish, everyday paper is typically sufficient and more affordable. You can roll this up in a mailer or poster tube (available at most office supply stores or your campus bookstore) and carry it on the plane with you. Putting up the poster is a simple process of unrolling and pinning. Even easier is to have a service such as PosterSmith print your poster on foldable and wrinkle resistant fabric that can be tucked into your suitcase thus avoiding hassling with another piece of luggage (https://postersmith.com/).

Although we emphasize the structural and written communication aspects of poster presentations here, it is important to acknowledge that talking with people about your poster may actually be the most important part of the poster session. One of us recommends that students think of poster attendees as very smart and interested people who may be jet-lagged, suffering conference fatigue, hungry, and trying to get through 47 posters in an hour. For these people, the poster serves best as a hook to encourage them to stop, a quick read from which they can glean important points at a glance, and as a prop to guide more in-depth conversation. In this context, your bullet points, tables, and figures become critical—they provide the foundation for additional detail your visitor may want and serve as visual aids that you use to walk your visitor through your findings.

It is also well to consider our earlier comments about the broader social aspects of professional meetings. Standing before your poster and interacting with the people looking at it provide an excellent opportunity to expand your professional contacts—you're not just talking about your poster, you're talking *with people* about your broader body of work, your ideas and plans for further work, your career goals, and so on. Often, this leads to discovery of shared interests, cool complementary work in other labs, or ways that the practical applications of your research can be tested or implemented. Vicens and Bourne (2007) noted that "many a lifelong collaboration has begun in front of a poster board" (p. 1). In their "Ten Simple Rules for a Good Poster Presentation," Erren and Bourne (2007) noted other social opportunities of this format and suggested working the crowd, engaging and making eye contact with each visitor, and remaining curious and open to input.

One temptation that we encourage you to avoid is getting engrossed in conversation with your coauthors, grad school buddies, or friends from other programs. It's fine to chat (it would look odd if you stood there silently!), but make sure you always keep one eye on people who are anywhere near your poster, so that you're ready to greet them and discuss their questions and ideas. The Cain Project at Rice University provides a very useful guide to ways of interacting while showing your poster (see the Supplemental Resources at the end of this chapter and Exhibit 14.2).

EXHIBIT 14.2

Preparing to Represent a Poster

Making the physical poster is only part of preparing for a poster session. You MUST practice also. Interacting with the audience demands thinking on your feet, applying your social skills, and drawing on short, concise explanations without fumbling or mumbling.

- Practice 2, 5, and 10-minute versions of your poster presentation.

- Make sure you can sum up your poster's key points and conclusions in 2–3 sentences.

- Practice starting your spiel from different sections of your poster.

- Think about which parts of your poster will be the most challenging to explain.

EXHIBIT 14.2

Preparing to Represent a Poster (*Continued*)

- Anticipate people's questions and how you will answer them.

- Produce supplemental handouts and/or photocopies of publications related to the work described in your poster. Don't substitute a handout for a good oral explanation—the handout is a "take away" piece for reinforcing your message.

Presenting Your Talk

- **Greet people with a smile and show your enthusiasm** for your work.

- **Find out why they are interested in your poster BEFORE you launch into your spiel** so that you are able to address their needs and expectations.

- **Do not stand in front of your poster** where you might block people's view. Stand to the side or turn sideways at the side of the poster without blocking the adjacent poster.

- **Maintain eye contact with people as you present your poster.** Do not read directly from your poster or from a prepared script. Reading signals "lack of knowledge" to the audience.

- **Use hand gestures to illustrate and reinforce key concepts and relationships.** As you talk through your poster, use a pointer or your hands to refer to particular parts of the poster so that people can follow your talk. Do not put your hands in your pockets or behind your back.

- **Spend extra time explaining the figures and tables** on your poster.

- **Summarize each section of the poster** before moving on to the next section. For example, "Now that I've described the need to XXX, I'd like to explain the process we developed to do it."

- If people approach your poster after you have begun your spiel, **pause to welcome them** and identify where you are in the spiel, "Hi, I'm in the middle of explaining the methods we used to characterize the XXX protein."

- **Check your audience's understanding** of the more complex concepts presented in your poster by paying attention to non-verbal cues or by asking them whether YOU have been clear or should go into a little more detail. DO NOT ask whether THEY understand what you've said.

    For example, say, "Should I say a little more about how the algorithm operates?" "Have I been complete enough?" or "Would you like me to go over any of the parts again?"

    DO NOT SAY "Do you understand how this works?" or "Do you get this?" Such questions seem to blame the audience or seem designed to reveal their ignorance.

- **Maintain your professionalism.** Thank people for listening and talking with you about your project: "Thanks for stopping to talk with me." "Thanks for your feedback on the XXX mechanism." Make your comment show YOU WERE LISTENING TO THEM, not just talking at them. (Don't use a cliché such as "thank you for your time," and don't apologize, either). Remember that the people attending the poster session may be your future employers or research collaborators.

Note. From The Cain Project in Engineering and Professional Communication. Copyright 2003 by Rice University. Reprinted with permission.

PUBLISH YOUR STUDY

After you have presented your findings to various professional audiences and received feedback from them (or sometimes even before), plan to submit your study for publication. Again, speed and brevity are important considerations. Avoid the temptation to shove your document in a drawer and forget about it. Capitalize on the completion momentum and write it up for publication as soon as possible. Depending on how much opportunity you have for feedback at your home institution, you may be able to work on your conference presentation and manuscript at the same time or, at a minimum, you may be able to begin your manuscript immediately after you get your presentation in good shape. This lets you maintain momentum and write while you still have a good memory of the excellent points that simply wouldn't fit in your poster but that you want to include in a manuscript. *A good rule of thumb is to present the paper and submit it for publication within 12 months of your defense.*

There are many excellent sources for information about preparing submissions for professional journals (e.g., APA, 2020; Bem, 1995; Kazdin, 2016b). We encourage you to supplement the material below by examining these additional resources as well.

Select a Publication Medium

There is a wide variety of publication possibilities. We recommend, however, that you limit your focus to professional outlets that involve peer review. There are two major approaches to consider: online and print. Until recently, the latter dominated the field of academic peer-reviewed outlets. Online outlets have been appearing over the past 15 years, taking advantage of widely available sophisticated technology that allows more efficient and rapid publication. Both online and print approaches operate similarly in their submission management, peer review, and editorial processes.

With respect to online options, the two largest and most developed are the Public Library of Science (PLOS) and Frontiers. Both of these are riding a wave of increased support for openness and transparency in scientific research, and both have their roots in the quest for speedy dissemination of the results of that research. Nowhere is this more apparent than in the medical and public health fields, where rapid distribution of effective interventions for disease and illness can save lives. PLOS is an open access nonprofit publisher that started its first journal, *PLOS Biology*, in 2003. Like Frontiers, it aims to get research findings to the public more efficiently by focusing on scientific quality during the review process while eliminating judgments about significance. Currently, the PLOS suite of publications includes journals in nine content areas (e.g., psychology, biology, medicine, computational biology).

PLOS gets money for its operation from charitable donations and from the fees it charges to publish accepted papers. Fees currently range from $1,495 (PLOS-One-psychology) to $2,900 (medicine, biology). Reviewers are expected to return their evaluations within 10 days, a process that commonly takes months with traditional print journals. Accepted papers are classified and categorized immediately and placed online. Users can go on the site https://www.plos.org and search using familiar terms to access thousands of papers that can be downloaded and saved or printed directly from the website without charge. The obvious benefits of rapid publication and open worldwide access are likely to increase use of PLOS and Frontiers rapidly in the next few years. It is noteworthy that publishing with PLOS does not preclude submitting the paper to a print journal. Different journals will have different views as to the acceptability of such a submission, so it is wise to inquire of the journal's policy before submitting to it.

Frontiers currently publishes journals online in 59 academic areas (e.g., aging neuroscience, cell and developmental psychology, communication, immunology, oncology, marine science). *Frontiers in Psychology* was started in 2010 as an open-access, peer-reviewed journal that covers a broad range of all topics in psychology. As with PLOS, Frontiers charges a fee for publishing manuscripts that it accepts. Its archives of accepted papers are freely available, readily searchable, and allow downloading without charge. Users can go on the site https://www.frontiersin.org to find out more about Frontiers' publication procedures and the extent of its archives.

We recommend that you consider submitting your work to one of these online publications first if you can swing the fees, which may be possible if you have a faculty coauthor with access to grant or publication funds. Both PLOS and Frontiers are committed to open science and are set up to get information freely distributed worldwide as soon as possible. Because their technology permits practically instantaneous posting of accepted manuscripts on their websites, they will get your work seen by others more quickly than traditional print media, which usually take months or even years to have journals on the shelves—although many APA journals have recently cut this time considerably with an "online first" publication option that provides for accepted papers to appear in digital form before they eventually appear in print.

Select a Journal

With your paper safely archived and available online, proceed to getting it into print. First, select an appropriate journal. You may have begun this process long before now, perhaps considering potential outlets as you designed and conducted your study. Now that your results are in hand, it's time to finalize your decision. Although there are dozens of possibilities, remember to limit your consideration to ones that are peer reviewed. These will generally be more selective and of higher quality than nonrefereed outlets, and publishing with them will do more to get your career off to a good start.

Because each journal has different submission requirements, it makes sense to find out about them at the outset. This permits selecting the most appropriate outlet for your work, tailoring your submission to it, and increasing your chances of having it accepted. To do this, first get a copy of the journal's instructions to authors. These can usually be found toward the front or back of each issue or online at the journal's website. They describe the type of work the journal publishes, along with format and submission requirements. Make sure your work fits the journal's stated mission and scope. If you have followed our recommendations to publish online first, check that the journal allows this form of prior publication. If it does, conform to any requirements unique to this type of submission.

Selecting an appropriate journal can be a formidable task. Among the many journals from which to choose some will be more appropriate than others (see http://www.psycline.org/journals/psycline.html). Kazdin (2016b) suggested criteria that can make the process easier. For example, look at the journals cited in your references. Which ones occur most frequently? These may be ones that attract researchers and readers doing similar work. In addition, your committee chairperson or student peers with experience publishing in your area may suggest an appropriate outlet. Possibly, your study is part of a research program that normally directs its submissions to one or two journals. Which journals publish most of the research in this area? If the journals you are considering are not on this list, look at their tables of contents. Do you see papers similar to yours? Would the content and methodology of your paper fit with those you see?

Be aware that journal "pecking orders" exist, with some journals being much more selective than others. Many journals of the APA and the Association for Psychological Science, for example, receive hundreds of submissions each year and have 80% or higher rejection rates. Only the strongest studies, with the most rigorous methods, compelling results, and largest potential impact, make it into these journals. If your study did not turn out as well as you wanted or had some obvious problems, you might want to try a less selective or more specialized journal and avoid the pain of an almost-certain rejection. If your findings and methodology are solid, and if you have a thick skin and don't mind the fact that you may have to revise and submit the article to your second-choice outlet, you might try for a more prestigious or widely circulated journal.

In general, you want to publish your work in the best journal you can. But how do you evaluate journal quality? In addition to rejection rates, which indicate selectivity, a journal's reputation is quantified in terms of its *impact factor*, a measure of how frequently the journal's articles are cited in other outlets. Although the use of impact factors to judge journal quality or the quality of individual scholars' work is not without controversy (see Alberts, 2013, for more on this issue), impact factors and rejection rates are currently the most generally accepted measures of journal quality.

Prepare the Manuscript

As with preparing a presentation, paring is essential to get your study ready to submit to a journal. Start by rereading the journal's instructions to authors. Many research-based journals expect a maximum of 25 double-spaced manuscript pages; this maximum generally includes every part of your manuscript (e.g., title page, abstract, text, references, tables, figures). Journals that publish primarily reviews of the literature (e.g., *Perspectives on Psychological Science, Psychological Bulletin, Developmental Review, Psychological Review,* and *Clinical Psychology Review*) often accept longer papers, but some data-type journals (e.g., medical publications) require considerably shorter ones. It is well to examine your target journal's average article length.

An important warning: Do not simply cut and paste from your thesis or dissertation. This leads to disjointed papers. As we mentioned earlier, one idea is to build up from your poster presentation, dissertation talk, or abstract rather than pare down from your thesis or dissertation. To create a very compact poster, you had to include only the most important details. Add the next most important points, then the next, and so on, until your paper reaches the target length.

As you write, consider the specific requirements and typical content of articles appearing in the journal you have selected. Download a few sample articles addressing topics similar to yours and look at how the authors present their work. How much emphasis do authors give to theoretical issues, methodological ones, or discussion? What kind of details do they provide on the ins-and-outs of their methods and statistics? Tailor your paper to the specific requirements of the journal, both explicit and implicit, whenever possible.

Be sure to attend to details. If a phrase or sentence is not clear to you, it will not be clear to the reviewer who has never heard of your work. Have a colleague read your paper, checking in particular for inadequate or unnecessary detail and for clarity. Finally, proofread carefully for typos and make sure you conform to the journal's format requirements. These are reasonably consistent across journals that use APA Style and often conform closely to those of the *Publication Manual of the American Psychological Association* (seventh ed.; APA, 2020; see Chapter 2, "Paper Elements and Format"). A sloppy paper can lead readers to prejudge how carefully the research it describes was actually conducted.

Discuss with your chairperson and other coauthors how to orchestrate the write-up. Often, the student writes a first draft, and coauthors edit it and make comments. Making a publicly agreed-to schedule for completion of drafts helps get the manuscript ready in a timely fashion. For example, one of us has found that the best path to a submitted dissertation is to meet monthly or biweekly with former students, with manageable goals for each meeting (e.g., "next month you will draft the methods and I will edit and comment on your introduction").

Decide Authorship

Standard 8.12b, Publication Credit, of the *Ethical Principles of Psychologists and Code of Conduct* (APA, 2017b) governs authorship issues. Usually dissertations are submitted for publication under the joint authorship of the student and the student's committee chair. As noted in the APA *Publication Manual*

(7th ed.; APA, 2020; see Chapter 1, "Scholarly Writing and Publishing Principles"), authorship is accorded to those who make "substantial scientific contributions" to the research and is not reserved only for those who do the actual writing. In general, "substantial professional contributions may include formulating the problem or hypothesis, structuring the experimental study design, organizing and conducting the analysis, or interpreting the results and findings" (p. 24). Minor intellectual contributions and supportive and other forms of nonintellectual contributions (e.g., building an apparatus, collecting data, making suggestions for statistical analyses, recruiting participants, or obtaining animals) can be acknowledged in the author note. The significance of each person's contribution generally determines the order of authorship, with the person making the greatest contribution listed first. With rare exceptions, because a dissertation or thesis can represent an original and independent contribution, "whether students merit principal authorship on papers based on master's-level or other predoctoral research will depend on their specific contributions to the research. When master's-level students make the primary contribution to a study, they should be listed as the first author" (APA, 2020, p. 25).

Following principal authorship, the Ethics Committee of the APA indicated that second authorship for committee chairs may be considered obligatory if they designate the primary variables, make major interpretative contributions, or provide the database. It also noted that authorship is a courtesy if the chair suggests the general research area, is substantially involved in the development of the design and dependent measures, or contributes substantially to writing the published report. Alternatively, a committee chair with these contributions may take the last author position, consistent with convention in the medical literature and growing convention in psychology that this authorship position is reserved for the person who serves as senior mentor and in whose lab the research is conducted.

For committee chairs whose contributions are minor, such as editorial suggestions, encouragement, or provision of physical facilities, the APA Ethics Code indicates that authorship is not warranted (APA, 2017b). For this input, acknowledgment in a footnote or introductory statement is appropriate. Several resources discuss authorship issues. Fine and Kurdek (1993) discussed it for non–thesis/dissertation papers in more detail. Shawchuck, Fatis, and Breitenstein (1986) suggested a process to follow in working out authorship arrangements. An excellent downloadable source on authorship determination may be found at http://www.apa.org/science/leadership/students/authorship-paper.pdf

It is sometimes difficult to ascertain the relative significance of contributions among authors at the completion of a research endeavor. As a result, disputes about authorship or order of authors are common, and they are not very pleasant. A good way to avoid them is to decide at the *beginning* of a collaborative research effort what the individual responsibilities will be and what the relative contributions mean in terms of eventual authorship. In other words, even though we discuss these issues after the steps of selecting a journal and preparing the manuscript, discussion of publication authorship issues should begin early (even as you are just beginning your thesis or dissertation) and continue as your project and individuals' contributions evolve.

Because dissemination is such an important part of the research process, it is unwise to leave issues regarding presentation and publication unspoken. Especially with dissertations, a good deal of both student and faculty time will be devoted to the research, and its completion demands some form of presentation at least, and publication at best. After deciding on your research question, think about making a formal agreement with your chairperson (perhaps in writing) covering jointly determined dissemination plans. The agreement should state what forms dissemination will take: the approximate time after completion these forms will be pursued (recall the 12-month rule above); individual responsibilities of the student, chair, and any others who will be involved; and the order of authorship you anticipate. The agreement should also provide contingencies should one or more of the parties alter the level or timing of their participation. Do not underestimate the pull of your next academic requirements (e.g., comprehensive exams following the thesis), an internship, or a new job. Priorities change, time seems to melt away, and the longer the delay in submitting a manuscript, the more frustrated all authors become. A clear, written agreement produced in advance can help prevent strained relationships later, and it will do a lot to ensure that the project advances to publication.

Submit the Manuscript

When you are ready to send your slimmed-down opus to the previously selected journal, consult the journal's guidelines for authors again to review the exact submission procedures and determine what materials to include with your submission. Virtually all journals use an electronic submission platform, but read carefully to see whether your chosen journal is the rare exception that still requires hard-copy submission. If so, verify where you should send the manuscript, how many copies to send, and so on. Be sure that your copies are legible and complete and that pages are in the proper order. Do not staple or otherwise bind pages together. A paper clip will suffice.

For electronic submission, the process will be smoother if you identify submission details ahead of time and have documents ready before you begin. For example, some submission systems require that you upload separate documents containing the title page with authors, abstract, and de-identified manuscript; others require that you cut and paste the abstract into a text box. If you have prepared your manuscript according to APA Style, you likely have key words listed on the title page, but online submission portals will often have separate text boxes or drop-down menus for this information. In addition to all of the manuscript components, find out what else should accompany your submission. If you created a measure, does the journal require that you submit a copy of it for reviewer examination?

Accompany your submission with a cover letter indicating that the paper is not simultaneously being considered by any other journal and that it is not published elsewhere (or that is currently published online if this applies). Mention that all participants (human or nonhuman animals) have been treated in accord with the ethical standards of the APA concerning research and with appropriate institutional review board approvals. If any copyrighted material appears in your submission, be sure to enclose copies of any permission you have for its use. If the journal allows you to choose between anonymous (i.e., masked) or unmasked reviews, state your preference in the letter. If the journal allows you to name potential reviewers for the paper or to request that certain individuals *not* provide reviews, talk with your faculty mentor about this. Suggesting reviewers may be helpful if your work is in a very new, esoteric, or small area that does not have a well-known group of individuals knowledgeable enough to provide an informed review. Providing a "do not use" list is typically reserved for areas of research with two (or more) well-known warring factions who will reject any manuscript that is not consistent with their camp; fortunately, this is rare. Finally, indicate a phone number and address (usually an email address will suffice) where you can be reached. If your address changes while the article is under review, notify the editor handling the submission promptly. Chapter 12 of the APA Publication Manual (APA, 2020) provides additional details regarding manuscript submission.

Editors of most journals assign papers to an associate editor with expertise in the general area that the research addresses, reserving a few papers to handle themselves. The associate editor then seeks comments from two or three reviewers. One or more of these will usually be an expert on your specific topic. These individuals evaluate the strengths and shortcomings of your paper, provide feedback to help the editor or associate editor make a publication decision, and furnish comments to be shared with you and your coauthors. The feedback that reviewers share with editors (but that is not passed along to you) often includes ratings on specific aspects of the paper's quality, such as its significance or importance, clarity, methodological and analytic soundness, and accuracy of interpretation, as well as a recommendation regarding publication. Reviewers also provide written comments about the strengths and weaknesses of the paper, and these will come back to you at the end of the review process.

Most editors will acknowledge receipt of your manuscript in writing; for online submissions you will often receive two notifications—one automatically generated to acknowledge a successful submission (important for those of us who sometimes forget to hit a final submit button!) and one when the action editor (the editor or associate editor who will handle your manuscript) is assigned. This correspondence may also specify a date by which you can expect to receive the reviews and the publication decision. It usually takes 60 to 90 days for a paper to be reviewed, so you do not need to start checking your email obsessively for a while. Use the waiting period as time to get busy with other writing projects. You have probably earmarked time in your schedule to write up your project. By viewing this as "sacred writing time" you will want to preserve it for that purpose. Before nonwriting activities start to creep into this time slot, get going on your next writing project! This will reinforce a component of your work ethic that will pay dividends throughout your career.

If you have not heard from the journal by a week or two after the target date, check on its status. Online submission portals often allow authors to track the progress of their manuscript; although the information is often general (e.g., noting "assigned to reviewers" or "out for review"), it will often tell you whether there is a holdup because only two of three requested reviews have been received or because the paper has been sitting in the editor's inbox awaiting decision for a while. If it looks like all reviews have been in for at least a few weeks or if there is no online tracking, you can call or email the person handling your manuscript and inquire politely about its status. Polite, repeated inquiries at 2-week intervals can prompt a slow editor to complete the review process on your manuscript.

When you receive an editorial decision, your work is not over. Journal editors ordinarily use four categories of response. The least frequent is an outright acceptance with no requirement for revision. The most common is a rejection, accompanied by one or more reviews, usually anonymous, detailing the reviewers' reactions to the paper. A third type of decision involves conditionally accepting the paper based on your agreeing to make certain changes. The fourth type of decision is really no decision at all. It involves telling the authors that the reviewers and editor could not decide. The paper had several strengths, but it also had enough weaknesses that an acceptance, even with the promise of changes, could not be rendered at this time. The editor invites the authors to revise the paper as suggested by the reviewers and resubmit it for additional consideration. In such cases, the editor often treats the paper as a new submission, sending it through the entire review process again.

The revise–resubmit verdict often devastates first-time submitters, who conclude that their paper is ultimately doomed. The truth is that such a decision from a good journal that has a high rejection rate can be excellent news. It means your paper was good enough to get a second chance! If you and your coauthors think it is possible to make the suggested changes within a reasonable amount of time, your best bet is to resubmit to that journal. If you have significant disagreement with the changes recommended or they will take too much time (or both), you may prefer to revise and submit the paper to another journal.

Pick Yourself Up, Dust Yourself Off, and Start All Over Again

Because approximately 80% of the papers submitted to the best journals are rejected, it is reasonable to assume that your study may meet a similar fate the first time you submit it. Even if the paper is accepted, it will likely receive criticisms. First-timers often react to such criticism with excessive anger or depression. Stay centered at this point. Be constructive. Act out the advice of the old Dorothy Fields and Jerome Kern song in the heading above. See the rejection as an opportunity to get back in the game—and at a higher level of participation.

In responding to reviewers' comments, it is helpful to remember several points. First, editors ask reviewers to indicate how the paper can be improved. The reviewers' comments can seem like criticism, but it is usually constructive commentary on how to make things better. Second, whereas strengths can often be stated briefly, it takes more space to explain a weakness. Third, the review tradition emphasizes critical rather than laudatory commentary. For these reasons, it is very likely that most comments you receive will focus on weaknesses of the manuscript. Even papers that are published in excellent journals usually go through at least two revisions to handle reviewers' criticisms. Don't take the comments personally.

The high likelihood of initial rejection is another good reason for getting your project ready for submission as soon after your defense as possible. This is because you may have to try again, revising your paper and sending it out a second time. The good news about a rejection is that it is usually accompanied by excellent suggestions from experts in your area as to how the paper and your research can be improved. If you attend to these carefully and make the changes that are appropriate, the chances for acceptance of your next submission will increase considerably. Even more important, attending to the comments of these experts can improve your own critical thinking and any future research you might do in this or other areas. Yes, that's right. Your learning does not end with the completion of your dissertation or thesis, and you really don't want it to! Exposing yourself to feedback from others in your field will lead to continued refinement of your skills and overall professional repertoire.

Note that it is considered professionally unacceptable to submit your manuscript to a second journal without revision. Different journals sometimes use the same reviewers, and these hardworking colleagues do not take kindly to seeing a paper a second time when its authors have not bothered to respond to suggestions for improving the first version. The peer-review process is an important mechanism for advancing science, and it behooves all of us to respect it.

When (as is likely) you do receive a rejection of your initial submission, you may be inclined to put the paper away and forget about it. This is a very natural reaction. After all, although some of the comments of the reviewers simply reflect their misunderstanding of what was done or found, some were rather telling criticisms of the study as well. You might be tempted to conclude that the research is so flawed it is not worth disseminating further. Avoid this temptation. Remember, a committee of scholars at your school approved what you have done and contributed substantially to it. It must have *some* merit. Most carefully conceived and conducted research efforts have something worth sharing with others. When you get your reviews, we suggest you read them and show them to your chair. Set a time to discuss them after a week or so. During this cooling off period, put the reviews away and forget about them until just before meeting with your chair. At this point, you will have a fresh, somewhat less defensive perspective. You will be ready to consider how the reviewers' concerns can be addressed in a revision. When you do meet with your chair, you can decide jointly how the various concerns will be handled and who will be responsible for each. If you do not have a resubmit option from the initial journal, decide where to send the revised version and consult that journal's instructions to authors. Be sure to agree on timelines for completing and submitting the revision.

CONSIDER DIVIDING MAJOR PROJECTS FOR MULTIPLE SUBMISSIONS

Approach submission of your research for publication systematically. This is especially critical with a dissertation that can produce multiple scholarly products. In fact, you might have a publication program worked out from the very beginning. You might decide at the outset that your literature review will be of such comprehensiveness and quality that it will warrant submission to a discussion or review-type journal, such as *Psychological Bulletin*. If so, an excellent source to guide this is Bem (1995). You might develop an apparatus or computer software for conducting your study that could be described in a separate paper submitted to an appropriately specialized journal. You might produce treatment manuals describing your intervention programs in sufficient detail to warrant publication as a short book. Or you might develop and produce sufficient information about a new assessment instrument that you could write a stand-alone article describing it. All these spinoffs from the major thrust of your research could be parts of your publication program. Finally, if your dissertation is a multistudy, program-of-research type project, you will almost certainly have multiple submissions.

If you consider submitting more than one paper from your dissertation, consult the APA's warnings about duplicate publication (APA, 2017b). Duplicate publication involves "the publication of the same data or ideas in two separate works" (APA, 2020, p. 17). Say, for example, you plan to submit two separate papers based on the work you did for your thesis or dissertation—one literature review paper and one research paper. The research paper's introduction must be substantially different from the literature review paper. Prudence dictates informing the editors receiving either submission of the other paper so that they will have the opportunity to decide whether duplicate publication is an issue.

Note that we are talking about submitting papers describing independent parts of the larger project. We are not advocating piecemeal publication of several reports deriving from one data base. "Piecemeal publication is the unnecessary splitting of the findings from one research effort into multiple works" (APA, 2020, p. 17). This practice often constitutes duplicate publication (because of substantial overlap). There are legitimate instances (e.g., results of individual assessment occasions in a longitudinal study or consideration of different research questions that can be addressed with large multi-site, national, or international datasets) in which multiple publications from the same database would be warranted, however, and we encourage you to consult the APA *Publication Manual* for more discussion of these.

WEIGH THE BENEFITS OF DISSEMINATION IN THE POPULAR PRESS

Up to now, we have restricted our discussion to disseminating your findings to professional audiences. The general public may be another appropriate audience. Not only does your profession benefit from informing the public of significant research in the academic community, you may benefit personally. For example, imagine you have an interest in behavioral economics, a discipline that studies how emotional and cognitive behavior can influence people's investment decisions. Suppose further that your dissertation shows substantial individual differences in the extent to which people spread hypothetical large sums of inherited money across different investments or concentrate it in one or two. Moreover, you show that willingness to diversify is positively correlated with scores on a measure of risk aversion. Media interviews could inform the public of this finding and include carefully worded implications that it might have for personal investing. Articles citing your work might appear in the business section of major city newspapers. Being mentioned as a potential expert in this area could help launch your career in the psychology of personal finance!

If you are pursuing an academic career, you can also benefit from having information about your work appear in the popular press. If your research requires cooperation of local agencies, schools, and so on, a good way to be introduced can sometimes be a newspaper story about the "fascinating research of Dr. Blank, newly appointed assistant professor at O.U.K.D." Timing such a story to precede your contact with agencies can do a lot to open doors.

We speak here of stories in local newspapers and appearances on radio or local television talk shows. These do not usually involve publication of major portions of your findings. There are other popular outlets (e.g., magazines, trade books), however, in which a substantial part of an applied research project might be published. It is now relatively easy to have a book published yourself. For example, Amazon's Create Space offers an array of self-publishing services including editing, designing the book, and marketing it. Now a completed book can be printed and ready to distribute in literally hours (see https://www.createspace.com).

Outlets such as these may or may not be appropriate to your professional objectives, and warnings are in order. These are not peer-reviewed journals and, thus, will not carry much weight in the academic community. Established and well-respected publishers of scholarly books (e.g., APA, Sage) will lend greater legitimacy to your publication, but these will still not be held in the same esteem or as useful for academic promotion as peer-reviewed scholarly work.

In addition, it is easy to lose control of the content of stories appearing in popular media. Your carefully phrased, appropriately qualified interpretations can be sensationalized rather quickly into more newsworthy proclamations that go way beyond the scope of your study. Ask to have final approval of any article or story that is based on your research, especially if it includes direct quotes from you. Finally, consider that previous publication in popular outlets such as these might foreclose publication in professional journals because of the duplicate publication prohibition. Weigh your dissemination options carefully. If you decide to reach the public through the media, be sure to follow the APA guidelines for appropriate public presentation (APA, 2020).

Dissemination is the important last step in the research cycle. Do not avoid it in your natural inclination to get the dissertation process behind you and move on with your life. Your research benefited from the fact that others presented and published their work. You learned from their advances and their mistakes. It is time to allow others to learn from you. Besides, publishing your results provides another reason to celebrate. And, face it, it's fun to see your name in print and to track how many times people view and cite your work!

✓   **TO DO . . .**
PRESENTING YOUR PROJECT PUBLICLY

☐ Submit your research for presentation.

- Meet with chair and decide authorship.

- Identify outlet and due dates for submissions.

- Submit an abstract.

☐ Prepare your presentation.

- Identify format and length of oral talks.

- Identify page limits for posters.

- Create a clear, readable poster.

- Prepare to share your poster with others (e.g., handouts, webpage links).

- Obtain any supplies needed during poster session (e.g., tablet, push pins).

☐ Publish your study.

- Select a journal.

- Examine instructions to authors.

- Write the manuscript.

- Submit the manuscript.

- Be ready for feedback and be ready to deal with it constructively.

☐ Divide major projects for multiple submissions.

☐ Consider dissemination in the popular press.

SUPPLEMENTAL RESOURCES

General Publishing Guidelines/Suggestions

American Psychological Association. (2020). *Publication manual of the American Psychological Association* (7th ed.).

Cooper, H. (2018). *Reporting quantitative research in psychology: How to meet APA Style journal article reporting standards* (2nd ed.). American Psychological Association.

Suggestions for Preparing Poster Presentations

Association for Psychological Science. (n.d.). *Submission rules and guidelines.* http://www.psychologicalscience.org/conventions/annual/call-for-submissions/rules-guidelines

Cain Project. (2003). *A guide to presenting a poster.* http://www.owlnet.rice.edu/~cainproj/presenting.html

Recommendations for presenting posters and talks.

Price, M. (2011). *The perfect poster: Experts reveal the art behind displaying your science.* American Psychological Association. http://www.apa.org/gradpsych/2011/01/poster.aspx

UNC Library. (n.d.). *Designing effective posters.* http://guides.lib.unc.edu/posters/pptwindows2016

REFERENCES

Abraham, W. T., & Russell, D. W. (2008). Statistical power analysis in psychological research. *Social and Personality Psychology Compass*, *2*(1), 283–301. https://doi.org/10.1111/j.1751-9004.2007.00052.x

Aiken, L. S., & West, S. G. (1996). *Multiple regression: Testing and interpreting interactions*. Sage.

Aiken, L. S., West, S. G., & Taylor, A. B. (2007). Correlation methods/regression models. In D. McKay (Ed.), *Handbook of research methods in abnormal and clinical psychology* (pp. 79–106). Sage.

Alberts, B. (2013). Impact factor distortions. *Science*, *340*(6134), 787. https://doi.org/10.1126/science.1240319

Alisic, E., Barrett, A., Bowles, P., Conroy, R., & Mehl, M. R. (2016). Topical review: Families coping with child trauma: A naturalistic observation methodology. *Journal of Pediatric Psychology*, *41*(1), 117–127. https://doi.org/10.1093/jpepsy/jsv016

Allen, J. P., & Wilson, V. B. (2003). *Assessing alcohol problems: A guide for clinicians and researchers* (2nd ed.). National Institute on Alcohol Abuse and Alcoholism.

American Educational Research Association. (2011). Code of ethics. *Educational Researcher*, *40*(3), 145–156. https://doi.org/10.3102/0013189X11410403

American Psychiatric Association. (2013). *Diagnostic and statistical manual of mental disorders* (5th ed.). American Psychiatric Publishing.

American Psychological Association. (2017a). *APA Journals Program collaborates with Center for Open Science to advance open science practices in psychological research* [Press release]. http://www.apa.org/news/press/releases/2017/08/open-science.aspx

American Psychological Association. (2017b). *Ethical principles of psychologists and code of conduct: Including 2010 and 2016 amendments*. http://www.apa.org/ethics/code/index

American Psychological Association. (2017c). *Multicultural guidelines: An ecological approach to context, identity, and intersectionality.* http://www.apa.org/about/policy/multicultural-guidelines.pdf

American Psychological Association. (2020). *Publication manual of the American Psychological Association* (7th ed.).

American Psychological Association Ethics Committee. (1983). *Authorship guidelines for dissertation supervision.*

Anderson, N., Schlueter, J. E., Carlson, J. F., & Geisinger, K. F. (Eds.). (2016). *Tests in Print IX.* Buros Center for Testing.

Andrews, F. M., Klem, L., O'Malley, P. M., Rodgers, W. L., Welch, K. B., & Davidson, T. N. (1998). *Selecting statistical techniques for social science data: A guide for SAS users* (3rd ed.). SAS Institute.

Antony, M. M., Orsillo, S. M., & Roemer, L. (2001). *Practitioner's guide to empirically based measures of anxiety.* Springer.

Appelbaum, M., Cooper, H., Kline, R. B., Mayo-Wilson, E., Nezu, A. M., & Rao, S. M. (2018). Journal article reporting standards for quantitative research in psychology: The APA Publications and Communications Board task force report. *American Psychologist, 73*(1), 3–25. https://doi.org/10.1037/amp0000191

Baer, L., & Blais, M. A. (Eds.). (2010). *Handbook of clinical rating scales and assessment in psychiatry and mental health.* Humana Press. https://doi.org/10.1007/978-1-59745-387-5

Bailar, J. C., III, & Mosteller, F. (2009). Guidelines for statistical reporting in articles for medical journals. In J. C. Bailar, III, & D. C. Hoaglin (Eds.), *Medical uses of statistics* (3rd ed., pp. 266–273). Wiley.

Bakeman, R., & Quera, V. (2011). *Sequential analysis and observational methods for the behavioral sciences.* Cambridge University Press. https://doi.org/10.1017/CBO9781139017343

Barlow, D. H. (2000). Unraveling the mysteries of anxiety and its disorders from the perspective of emotion theory. *American Psychologist, 55*(11), 1247–1263. https://doi.org/10.1037/0003-066X.55.11.1247

Barlow, D. H. (2002). *Anxiety and its disorders: The nature and treatment of anxiety and panic* (2nd ed.). Guilford Press.

Barlow, D. H., Allen, L. B., & Choate, M. L. (2004). Towards a unified treatment for emotional disorders. *Behavior Therapy, 35*(2), 205–230. https://doi.org/10.1016/S0005-7894(04)80036-4

Barnett, L. (2005). *The universe and Dr. Einstein.* Dover.

Baron, R. M., & Kenny, D. A. (1986). The moderator–mediator variable distinction in social psychological research: Conceptual, strategic, and statistical considerations. *Journal of Personality and Social Psychology, 51*(6), 1173–1182. https://doi.org/10.1037/0022-3514.51.6.1173

Beavers, A. S., Lounsbury, J. W., Richards, J. K., Huck, S. W., Skolits, G. J., & Esquivel, S. L. (2013). Practical considerations for using exploratory factor analysis in educational research. *Practical Assessment, Research & Evaluation, 18*(6). http://www.pareonline.net/getvn.asp?v=18&n=6

Beck, A. T., Rush, A. J., Shaw, B. F., & Emery, G. (1979). *Cognitive therapy of depression.* Guilford Press.

Bellack, A. S., & Hersen, M. (1977). Self-report inventories in behavioral assessment. In J. D. Cone & R. P. Hawkins (Eds.), *Behavioral assessment: New directions in clinical psychology* (pp. 52–76). Brunner/Mazel.

Bell-Dolan, D. J., Foster, S. L., & Sikora, D. M. (1989). Effects of sociometric testing on children's behavior and loneliness in school. *Developmental Psychology, 25*(2), 306–311. https://doi.org/10.1037/0012-1649.25.2.306

Bem, D. J. (1995). Writing a review article for *Psychological Bulletin. Psychological Bulletin, 118*(2), 172–177. https://doi.org/10.1037/0033-2909.118.2.172

Bickel, R. (2007). *Multilevel analysis for applied research: It's just regression!* Guilford Press.

Bigwood, S., & Spore, M. (2003). *Presenting numbers, tables, and charts.* Oxford University Press.

Bird, K. D., & Hadzi-Pavlovic, D. (2014). Controlling the maximum familywise Type I error rate in analyses of multivariate experiments. *Psychological Methods, 19*(2), 265–280. https://doi.org/10.1037/a0033806

Bock, R. D. (1997). A brief history of item theory response. *Educational Measurement: Issues and Practice, 16*(4), 21–33. https://doi.org/10.1111/j.1745-3992.1997.tb00605.x

Bolker, J. (1998). *Writing your dissertation in 15 minutes a day.* Henry Holt.

Bourne, E. J. (2001). *Anxiety and phobia workbook* (3rd ed.). New Harbinger.

Brown, T. A. (2015). *Confirmatory factor analysis for applied research* (2nd ed.). Guilford Press.

Bruning, J. L., & Kintz, B. L. (1997). *Computational handbook of statistics* (4th ed.). Pearson.

Bryan, S. (2017). *The psychological effects of body talk between gay and heterosexual men* [Unpublished dissertation proposal]. California School of Professional Psychology.

Buhrmester, M., Kwang, T., & Gosling, S. D. (2011). Amazon's Mechanical Turk: A new source of inexpensive, yet high-quality, data? *Perspectives on Psychological Science, 6*(1), 3–5. https://doi.org/10.1177/1745691610393980

Butcher, J. N., Graham, J. R., Haynes, S. N., & Nelson, L. D. (Eds.). (1995). Special issue: Methodological issues in psychological assessment research. *Psychological Assessment, 7*(3).

The Cain Project in Engineering and Professional Communication. (2003). *A guide to presenting a poster.* http://www.owlnet.rice.edu/~cainproj/presenting.html

Cairns, R. B., & Green, J. A. (1979). How to assess personality and social patterns: Observations or ratings? In R. B. Cairns (Ed.), *The analysis of social interactions* (pp. 209–226). Erlbaum.

Campbell, D. T. (1960). Recommendations for APA test standards regarding construct, trait, and discriminant validity. *American Psychologist, 15*(8), 546–553. https://doi.org/10.1037/h0048255

Campbell, D. T., & Fiske, D. W. (1959). Convergent and discriminant validation by the multitrait–multimethod matrix. *Psychological Bulletin, 56*(2), 81–105. https://doi.org/10.1037/h0046016

Carlson, J. F., Geisinger, K. F., & Jonson, J. L. (Eds.). (2017). *The Twentieth Mental Measurements Yearbook.* Buros Center for Testing.

Christensen, T. C., Barrett, L. F., Bliss-Moreau, E., Lebo, K., & Kaschub, C. (2003). A practical guide to experience-sampling procedures. *Journal of Happiness Studies, 4*(1), 53–78. https://doi.org/10.1023/A:1023609306024

Clark, L. A., & Watson, D. (2016). Constructing validity: Basic issues in objective scale development. In A. E. Kazdin (Ed.), *Methodological issues and strategies in clinical research* (4th ed., pp. 187–203). American Psychological Association. https://doi.org/10.1037/14805-012

Clatworthy, J., Buick, D., Hankins, M., Weinman, J., & Horne, R. (2005). The use and reporting of cluster analysis in health psychology: A review. *British Journal of Health Psychology, 10*(3), 329–358. https://doi.org/10.1348/135910705X25697

Clauser, B. E., & Clauser, J. C. (2016). Applications of generalizability theory. In C. S. Wells & M. Faulkner-Bond (Eds.), *Educational measurement: From foundations to future* (pp. 89–104). Guilford Press.

Cleveland, W. S. (1995). *Visualizing data*. Hobart Press.

Cohen, J. (1988). *Statistical power analysis for the behavioral sciences* (2nd ed.). Erlbaum.

Cohen, J. (1992). A power primer. *Psychological Bulletin, 112*(1), 155–159. https://doi.org/10.1037/0033-2909.112.1.155

Cohen, P., Cohen, J., West, S. G., & Aiken, L. S. (2003). *Applied multiple regression/correlation analysis for the behavioral sciences* (3rd ed.). Erlbaum.

Cone, J. D. (1978). The Behavioral Assessment Grid (BAG): A conceptual framework and a taxonomy. *Behavior Therapy, 9*(5), 882–888. https://doi.org/10.1016/S0005-7894(78)80020-3

Cone, J. D. (1992). Accuracy and curriculum-based measurement. *School Psychology Quarterly, 7*(1), 22–26. https://doi.org/10.1037/h0088243

Cone, J. D. (1999). Observational assessment: Measure development and research issues. In P. C. Kendall, J. N. Butcher, & G. N. Holmbeck (Eds.), *Handbook of research methods in clinical psychology* (2nd ed., pp. 183–223). Wiley.

Cone, J. D. (2001). *Evaluating outcomes: Empirical tools for effective practice*. American Psychological Association. https://doi.org/10.1037/10384-000

Cone, J. D., & Dalenberg, C. J. (2004). Ethics concerns in outcomes assessment. In M. E. Maruish (Ed.), *The use of psychological testing for treatment planning and outcomes assessment* (3rd ed., Vol. 1, pp. 307–334). Erlbaum.

Cone, J. D., & Foster, S. L. (2006). *Dissertations and theses from start to finish: Psychology and related fields* (2nd ed.). American Psychological Association.

Cooper, H. (1998). *Synthesizing research: A guide for literature reviews* (3rd ed.). Sage.

Cooper, H. (Ed.). (2012). *APA handbook of research methods in psychology* (Vols. 1–3). American Psychological Association.

Cooper, H. (2018). *Reporting quantitative research in psychology: How to meet APA Style journal article reporting standards* (2nd ed.). American Psychological Association. https://doi.org/10.1037/0000103-001

Cooper, H., Camic, P. M., Long, D. L., Panter, A. T., Rindskopf, D. & Sher, K. J. (Eds.). (2012). *APA handbook of research methods in psychology: Vol. 1. Foundations planning, measures, and psychometrics*. American Psychological Association.

Cooper, H., Hedges, I. V., & Valentine, J. C. (Eds.). (2009). *The handbook of research synthesis and meta-analysis* (2nd ed.). Russell Sage Foundation.

Cooper, J. O., Heron, T. E., & Heward, W. L. (2007). *Applied behavior analysis* (2nd ed.). Pearson Education.

Corcoran, K., & Fischer, J. (Eds.). (2013). *Measures for clinical practice and research, 2-volume set* (5th ed.). Oxford University Press.

Cortina, J. M. (1993). What is coefficient alpha? An examination of theory and applications. *Journal of Applied Psychology, 78*(1), 98–104. https://doi.org/10.1037/0021-9010.78.1.98

Cotter, R., Burke, J., Loeber, R., & Navratil, J. (2002). Innovative retention methods in longitudinal research: A case study of the developmental trends study. *Journal of Child and Family Studies, 11*(4), 485–498. https://doi.org/10.1023/A:1020939626243

Coxe, S., West, S. G., & Aiken, L. S. (2009). The analysis of count data: A gentle introduction to Poisson regression and its alternatives. *Journal of Personality Assessment, 91*(2), 121–136. https://doi.org/10.1080/00223890802634175

Crego, C., & Widiger, T. A. (2016). Convergent and discriminant validity of alternative measures of maladaptive personality traits. *Psychological Assessment, 28*(12), 1561–1575. https://doi.org/10.1037/pas0000282

Cresswell, J. W. (2017). *Qualitative inquiry and research design: Choosing among five approaches* (4th ed.). Sage.

Croasdale, N. (2016). *How to keep your data accurate with CLASS Calibration.* http://info.teachstone.com/blog/class-calibration-keep-yourself-honest

Cronbach, L. J. (1951). Coefficient alpha and the internal structure of tests. *Psychometrika, 16*(3), 297–334. https://doi.org/10.1007/BF02310555

Cronbach, L. J. (1990). *Essentials of psychological testing* (5th ed.). HarperCollins.

Cronbach, L. J., Gleser, G. C., Nanda, H., & Rajaratnam, N. (1972). *The dependability of behavioral measurements.* Wiley.

Crowne, D. P., & Marlowe, D. (1960). A new scale of social desirability independent of psychopathology. *Journal of Consulting Psychology, 24*(4), 349–354. https://doi.org/10.1037/h0047358

Crump, M. J. C., McDonnell, J. V., & Gureckis, T. M. (2013). Evaluating Amazon's Mechanical Turk as a tool for experimental behavioral research. *PLoS One, 8*(3), e57410. https://doi.org/10.1371/journal.pone.0057410

Cumming, G. (2014). The new statistics: Why and how. *Psychological Science, 25*(1), 7–29. https://doi.org/10.1177/0956797613504966

Cunningham, P. B., Foster, S. L., Kawahara, D. M., Robbins, M. S., Bryan, S., Burleson, G., . . . Smith, K. (2019). Midtreatment problems implementing evidence-based interventions in community settings. *Family Process, 58*(2), 287–304. https://doi.org/10.1111/famp.12380

Darley, J. M., Roediger, H. L., & Zanna, M. P. (Eds.). (2003). *The compleat academic: A practical guide for the beginning social scientist.* American Psychological Association.

Davis, M., Robbins-Eshelman, E., & McKay, M. (2000). *The relaxation and stress reduction workbook* (5th ed.). New Harbinger.

Delwiche, L. D., & Slaughter, S. J. (2012). *The little SAS book: A primer* (5th ed.). SAS.

DeMars, C. (2010). *Item response theory.* Oxford University Press. https://doi.org/10.1093/acprof:oso/9780195377033.001.0001

DeVellis, R. F. (2003). *Scale development: Theories and applications* (2nd ed.). Sage.

DiLalla, D. L., & Dollinger, S. J. (2006). Cleaning up data and running preliminary analyses. In F. T. L. Leong & J. T. Austin (Eds.), *The psychology research handbook: A guide for graduate students and research assistants* (2nd ed., pp. 241–253). Sage. https://doi.org/10.4135/9781412976626.n16

Dionne, R. R. (1992). *Effective strategies for handling teasing among fifth and sixth grade children* [Unpublished doctoral dissertation]. California School of Professional Psychology.

Dixon, M. R., Jackson, J. W., Small, S. L., Horner-King, M. J., Lik, N. M. K., Garcia, Y., & Rosales, R. (2009). Creating single-subject design graphs in Microsoft Excel 2007. *Journal of Applied Behavior Analysis, 42*(2), 277–293. https://doi.org/10.1901/jaba.2009.42-277

Dodeen, H., & Al-Darmaki, F. (2016). The application of item response theory in developing and validating a shortened version of the Emirate Marital

Satisfaction Scale. *Psychological Assessment, 28*(12), 1625–1633. https://doi.org/10.1037/pas0000296

Edwards, A. L. (1957). *The social desirability variable in personality assessment and research*. Dryden Press.

Edwards, A. L. (1970). *The measurement of traits by scales and inventories*. Holt, Rinehart & Winston.

Edwards, A. L. (1990). Construct validity and social desirability. *American Psychologist, 45*(2), 287–289. https://doi.org/10.1037/0003-066X.45.2.287

Ellis, A. (2001). *Overcoming destructive beliefs, feelings, and behavior: New directions for rational emotive behavior therapy*. Prometheus Books.

Ellis, A., & Harper, R. A. (1961). *A guide to rational living*. Wilshire.

Emanuel, E., Abdoler, E., & Stunkel, L. (2016). Research ethics: How to treat people who participate in research. In A. E. Kazdin (Ed.), *Methodological issues and strategies in clinical research* (4th ed., pp. 513–523). American Psychological Association.

Embretson, S. E., & Riese, S. P. (2000). *Item response theory for psychologists*. Erlbaum.

Enders, C. K. (2010). *Applied missing data analysis*. Guilford Press.

Erceg-Hurn, D. M., & Mirosevich, V. M. (2008). Modern robust statistical methods: An easy way to maximize the accuracy and power of your research. *American Psychologist, 63*(7), 591–601. https://doi.org/10.1037/0003-066X.63.7.591

Erren, T. C., & Bourne, P. E. (2007). Ten simple rules for a good poster presentation. *PLoS Computational Biology, 3*(5), e102. https://doi.org/10.1371/journal.pcbi.0030102

Fabrigar, L. R., Wegener, D. T., MacCallum, R. C., & Strahan, E. J. (1999). Evaluating the use of exploratory factor analysis in psychological research. *Psychological Methods, 4*(3), 272–299. https://doi.org/10.1037/1082-989X.4.3.272

Fagan, J. C. (2017). An evidence-based review of academic web search engines, 2014–2016: Implications for librarians' practice and research agenda. *Information Technology and Libraries, 36*(2), 7–47. https://doi.org/10.6017/ital.v36i2.9718

Fallon, L. M., Sanetti, L. M. H., Chafouleas, S. M., Faggella-Luby, M. N., & Briesch, A. M. (2017). Direct training to increase agreement between teachers' and observers' treatment integrity ratings. *Assessment for Effective Intervention, 43*(4), 196–211. https://doi.org/10.1177/1534508417738721

Faul, F., Erdfelder, E., Lang, A. G., & Buchner, A. (2007). G*Power 3: A flexible statistical power analysis program for the social, behavioral, and biomedical sciences. *Behavior Research Methods, 39*(2), 175–191. https://doi.org/10.3758/BF03193146

Faulkner-Bond, M., & Wells, C. S. (2016). A brief history of and introduction to item response theory. In C. S. Wells & M. Faulkner-Bond (Eds.), *Educational measurement: From foundations to future* (pp. 107–125). Guilford Press.

Feingold, A., Tiberio, S. S., & Capaldi, D. M. (2014). New approaches for examining associations with latent categorical variables: Applications to substance abuse and aggression. *Psychology of Addictive Behaviors, 28*(1), 257–267. https://doi.org/10.1037/a0031487

Ferrari, J. R. (2010). *Still procrastinating? The no regrets guide to getting it done*. Wiley.

Field, A. (2018). *Discovering multivariate statistics using IBM SPSS Statistics* (5th ed.). Sage.

Field, A., Miles, J., & Field, Z. (2012). *Discovering statistics using R*. Sage.

Field, A. P., & Wilcox, R. R. (2017). Robust statistical methods: A primer for clinical psychology and experimental psychopathology researchers. *Behaviour Research and Therapy, 98*, 19–38. https://doi.org/10.1016/j.brat.2017.05.013

Fine, M. A., & Kurdek, L. A. (1993). Reflections on determining authorship credit and authorship order on faculty–student collaborations. *American Psychologist, 48*(11), 1141–1147. https://doi.org/10.1037/0003-066X.48.11.1141

Finhamict. (2016). *Creating a Gantt chart in Google Sheets* [Video file]. https://www.youtube.com/watch?v=ibdDmhipDOQ

Fink, A. G. (Series Ed.). (2003). *The survey kit* (2nd ed.). Sage.

Floyd, F., & Widaman, K. F. (1995). Factor analysis in the development and refinement of clinical assessment instruments. *Psychological Assessment, 7*(3), 286–299. https://doi.org/10.1037/1040-3590.7.3.286

Foster, S. L., & Cone, J. D. (1995). Validity issues in clinical assessment. *Psychological Assessment, 7*(3), 248–260. https://doi.org/10.1037/1040-3590.7.3.248

Furr, R. M. (2018). *Psychometrics: An introduction* (3rd ed.). Sage.

Fydrich, T., Chambless, D. L., Perry, K. J., Buergener, F., & Beazley, M. B. (1998). Behavioral assessment of social performance: A rating system for social phobia. *Behaviour Research and Therapy, 36*(10), 995–1010. https://doi.org/10.1016/S0005-7967(98)00069-2

Galvan, J. L., & Galvan, M. C. (2017). *Writing literature reviews: A guide for students of the social and behavioral sciences* (7th ed.). Routledge.

Gao, X., & Harris, D. J. (2012). Generalizability theory. In H. Cooper (Ed.), *APA handbook of research methods in psychology, Vol. 1. Foundations, planning, measures, and psychometrics* (pp. 661–681). American Psychological Association. https://doi.org/10.1037/13619-035

Gevirtz, R. (2002). Physiological perspectives. In B. Horwitz (Ed.), *Communication apprehension: Origins and management* (pp. 114–136). Singular.

Gorsuch, R. L. (2015). *Factor analysis* (classic ed.). Routledge.

Goyer, L. E. (2005). *Responsiveness to deviancy training among highly deviant, moderately deviant, and non-deviant early adolescent males* [Unpublished doctoral dissertation]. Alliant International University.

Graham, J. W. (2009). Missing data analysis: Making it work in the real world. *Annual Review of Psychology, 60*, 549–576. https://doi.org/10.1146/annurev.psych.58.110405.085530

Hallgren, K. A. (2012). Computing inter-rater reliability for observational data: An overview and tutorial. *Tutorials in Quantitative Methods for Psychology, 8*(1), 23–34. https://doi.org/10.20982/tqmp.08.1.p023

Harari, G. M., Lane, N. D., Wang, R., Crosier, B. S., Campbell, A. T., & Gosling, S. D. (2016). Using smartphones to collect behavioral data in psychological science: Opportunities, practical considerations, and challenges. *Perspectives on Psychological Science, 11*(6), 838–854. https://doi.org/10.1177/1745691616650285

Harb, G. C., Eng, W., Zaider, T., & Heimberg, R. T. (2003). Behavioral assessment of public-speaking anxiety using a modified version of the Social Performance Rating Scale. *Behaviour Research and Therapy, 41*(11), 1373–1380. https://doi.org/10.1016/S0005-7967(03)00158-X

Harris, S. R. (2014). *How to critique articles in the social sciences*. Sage.

Hausman, E. M. (2017). *The costs and benefits of dampening of positive affect in youth* [Unpublished doctoral dissertation]. University of Missouri.

Hausman, E. M., Kim, S., Bell, D., Lee, H., & An, D. D. (2016, October 27–30). *The relationship of regulation of positive affect and adjustment across cultures* [Poster presentation]. 50th annual meeting of the Association for Cognitive and Behavioral Therapies, New York, NY.

Hayes, A. F. (2013). *Introduction to mediation, moderation, and conditional process analysis: A regression-based approach.* Guilford Press.

Hayes, S. C., Barlow, D. H., & Nelson-Gray, R. O. (1999). *The scientist practitioner: Research and accountability in the age of managed care* (2nd ed.). Allyn and Bacon.

Hayes, S. C., & Smith, S. (2005). *Get out of your mind and into your life: The new acceptance and commitment therapy.* New Harbinger.

Haynes, S. N., & Heiby, E. (Eds.). (2004). *Comprehensive handbook of psychological assessment, Vol. 3. Behavioral assessment.* Wiley.

Haynes, S. N., Richard, D. C. S., & Kubany, E. (1995). Content validity in psychological assessment: A functional approach to concepts and methods. *Psychological Assessment, 7*(3), 238–247. https://doi.org/10.1037/1040-3590.7.3.238

Heinrich-Heine-Universität Düsseldorf. (2018). *G*Power: Statistical power analyses for Windows and Mac.* http://www.gpower.hhu.de/en.html

Helmes, E., & Holden, R. (2003). The construct of social desirability: One or two dimensions? *Personality and Individual Differences, 34*(6), 1015–1023. https://doi.org/10.1016/S0191-8869(02)00086-7

Heppner, P. P., & Heppner, M. J. (2004). *Writing and publishing your thesis, dissertation, and research.* Thomson Brooks/Cole.

Hersen, M., & Bellack, A. S. (Eds.). (1988). *Dictionary of behavioral assessment techniques.* Percheron Press.

Hochhauser, M. (1999). Informed consent and patient's rights documents: A right, a rite, or a rewrite? *Ethics & Behavior, 9*(1), 1–20. https://doi.org/10.1207/s15327019eb0901_1

Hoier, T. S. (1984). *Target selection of social skills for children: An experimental investigation of the template matching procedure* [Unpublished doctoral dissertation]. West Virginia University.

Hoier, T. S., & Cone, J. D. (1987). Target selection of social skills for children: The template matching procedure. *Behavior Modification, 11*(2), 137–163. https://doi.org/10.1177/01454455870112002

Holmbeck, G. N. (1997). Toward terminological, conceptual, and statistical clarity in the study of mediators and moderators: Examples from the child-clinical and pediatric psychology literatures. *Journal of Consulting and Clinical Psychology, 65*(4), 599–610. https://doi.org/10.1037/0022-006X.65.4.599

Hox, J. J. (2010). *Multilevel analysis: Techniques and applications* (2nd ed.). Routledge. https://doi.org/10.4324/9780203852279

Hu, J. C. (2016). Scientists ride the podcasting wave. *Science.* https://doi.org/10.1126/science.caredit.a1600152

Huberty, C. J., & Morris, J. D. (1989). Multivariate analysis versus multiple univariate analyses. *Psychological Bulletin, 105*(2), 302–308. https://doi.org/10.1037/0033-2909.105.2.302

Iacobucci, D. (2010). Structural equations modeling: Fit indices, sample size, and advanced topics. *Journal of Consumer Psychology, 20*(1), 90–98. https://doi.org/10.1016/j.jcps.2009.09.003

Irvin, K. (2017). *Association between positive emotion regulation strategies and the reward positivity effect* [Unpublished master's thesis proposal]. University of Missouri.

Jackson, D. L., Gillaspy, J. A., Jr., & Purc-Stephenson, R. (2009). Reporting practices in confirmatory factor analysis: An overview and some recommendations. *Psychological Methods, 14*(1), 6–23. https://doi.org/10.1037/a0014694

Jaffe, E. (2013). Why wait? The science behind procrastination. *Observer, 26*(4). https://www.psychologicalscience.org/observer/why-wait-the-science-behind-procrastination

John, O. P., & Srivastava, S. (1999). The Big Five trait taxonomy: History, measurement, and theoretical perspectives. In L. A. Pervin & O. P. John (Eds.), *Handbook of personality: Theory and research* (pp. 102–138). Guilford Press.

Johnston, J. M., & Pennypacker, H. S. (1993). *Strategies and tactics of human behavioral research* (2nd ed.). Erlbaum.

Judd, C. M., McClelland, G. H., & Culhane, S. E. (1995). Data analysis: Continuing issues in the everyday analysis of psychological data. *Annual Review of Psychology, 46*, 433–465. https://doi.org/10.1146/annurev.ps.46.020195.002245

Junco, R., Heiberger, G., & Loken, E. (2011). The effect of Twitter on college student engagement and grades. *Journal of Computer Assisted Learning, 27*(2), 119–132. https://doi.org/10.1111/j.1365-2729.2010.00387.x

Kabacoff, R. I. (2017). *Quick-R: Power analysis.* https://www.statmethods.net/stats/power.html

Kabat-Zinn, J. (2005). *Full catastrophe living: Using the wisdom of your body and mind to face stress, pain, and illness: Fifteenth anniversary edition.* Bantam Dell.

Kazdin, A. E. (2016a). Experimental and observational designs: An overview. In A. E. Kazdin (Ed.), *Methodological issues and strategies in clinical research* (4th ed., pp. 155–180). American Psychological Association. https://doi.org/10.1037/14805-011

Kazdin, A. E. (2016b). Publication and communication of research findings. In A. E. Kazdin (Ed.), *Methodological issues and strategies in clinical research* (4th ed., pp. 647–662). American Psychological Association. https://doi.org/10.1037/14805-040

Kazdin, A. E. (2016c). *Research design in clinical psychology* (5th ed.). Pearson.

Kelley, M. L., Reitman, D., & Noell, G. H. (2003). *Practitioner's guide to empirically based measures of school behavior.* Springer.

Kelley, T. L. (1927). *Interpretation of educational measurements.* World Book.

Kenny, D. A., Kashy, D. A., Cook, W. L., & Simpson, J. A. (2006). *Dyadic data analysis.* Guilford Press.

Keppel, G., & Wickens, T. D. (2004). *Design and analysis: A researcher's handbook* (4th ed.). Pearson Prentice-Hall.

Kerlinger, F. N. (2000). *Foundations of behavioral research* (4th ed.). Harcourt Brace.

Keselman, H. J. (2015). Per family or familywise Type I error control: "Eether, eyether, neether, nyther, let's call the whole thing off!" *Journal of Modern Applied Statistical Methods, 14*(1), 24–37. https://doi.org/10.22237/jmasm/1430453100

Khabsa, M., & Giles, C. L. (2014). The number of scholarly documents on the public web. *PLoS One, 9*(5), e93949. https://doi.org/10.1371/journal.pone.0093949

Kidwell, M. C., Lazarević, L. B., Baranski, E., Hardwicke, T. E., Piechowski, S., Falkenberg, L.-S., . . . Nosek, B. A. (2016). Badges to acknowledge open practices: A simple, low-cost, effective method for increasing transparency. *PLoS Biology, 14*(5), e1002456. https://doi.org/10.1371/journal.pbio.1002456

Kies, D. (2018). *Evaluating grammar checkers: A comparative ten-year study.* https://papyr.com/hypertextbooks/grammar/gramchek.htm

Kirk, R. E. (2013). *Experimental design: Procedures for the behavioral sciences* (4th ed.). Brooks/Cole Wadsworth. https://doi.org/10.4135/9781483384733

Klem, L. (1995). Path analysis. In L. G. Grimm & P. R. Yarnold (Eds.), *Reading and understanding multivariate statistics* (pp. 65–97). American Psychological Association.

Kline, R. B. (2015). *Principles and practice of structural equation modeling* (4th ed.). Guilford Press.

Knapp, S. J. (Ed.). (2012). *APA handbook of ethics in psychology.* American Psychological Association.

Koyré, A. (1965). *Newtonian studies.* Chapman and Hall. https://doi.org/10.4159/harvard.9780674181861

Kraemer, H. C. (2013). Statistical power: Issues and proper applications. In J. S. Comer & P. C. Kendall (Eds.), *The Oxford handbook of research strategies for clinical psychology* (pp. 213–226). Oxford University Press.

Kratochwill, T. R., & Levin, J. R. (Eds.). (2014). *Single-case intervention research: Methodologies and statistical advances.* American Psychological Association. https://doi.org/10.1037/14376-000

Kuder, G. F., & Richardson, M. W. (1937). The theory of the estimation of test reliability. *Psychometrika, 2*(3), 151–160. https://doi.org/10.1007/BF02288391

Kuhn, T. (1970). *The structure of scientific revolutions* (2nd ed.). University of Chicago Press.

Kuntsche, E., & Labhart, F. (2013). Drinking motives moderate the impact of pre-drinking on heavy drinking on a given evening and related adverse consequences—An event-level study. *Addiction, 108*(10), 1747–1755. https://doi.org/10.1111/add.12253

Lakin, A. (1974). *How to get control of your time and your life.* Signet Books.

Lane, D. M., & Sándor, A. (2009). Designing better graphs by including distributional information and integrating words, numbers, and images. *Psychological Methods, 14*(3), 239–257. https://doi.org/10.1037/a0016620

Lang, P. J. (1971). The application of psychophysiological methods to the study of psychotherapy and behavior modification. In A. E. Bergin & S. L. Garfield (Eds.), *Handbook of psychotherapy and behavior change* (pp. 75–125). Wiley.

Leffingwell, T. R., Cooney, N. J., Murphy, J. G., Luczak, S., Rosen, G., Dougherty, D. M., & Barnett, N. P. (2013). Continuous objective monitoring of alcohol use: Twenty-first century measurement using transdermal sensors. *Alcoholism: Clinical and Experimental Research, 37*(1), 16–22. https://doi.org/10.1111/j.1530-0277.2012.01869.x

Leong, F. T. L. (Ed.). (2014). *APA handbook of multicultural psychology.* American Psychological Association.

Leong, F. T. L., Schmitt, N., & Lyons, B. J. (2012). Developing testable and important research questions. In H. Cooper, P. M. Camic, D. L. Long, A. T. Panter, D. Rindskopf, & K. J. Sher (Eds.), *APA handbook of research methods in psychology, Vol. 1. Foundations, planning, measures, and psychometrics* (pp. 119–132). American Psychological Association. https://doi.org/10.1037/13619-008

Levitt, H. M., Bamberg, M., Creswell, J. W., Frost, D. M., Josselson, R., & Suárez-Orozco, C. (2018). Journal article reporting standards for qualitative primary, qualitative meta-analytic, and mixed methods research in psychology: The APA Publications and Communications Board task force report. *American Psychologist, 73*(1), 26–46. https://doi.org/10.1037/amp0000151

Licht, M. H. (1995). Multiple regression and correlation. In L. G. Grimm & P. R. Yarnold (Eds.), *Reading and understanding multivariate statistics* (pp. 19–64). American Psychological Association.

Lipsey, M. W., & Wilson, D. B. (2000). *Practical meta analysis*. Sage.

Liu, X. S. (2014). *Statistical power analysis for the social and behavioral sciences: Basic and advanced techniques*. Routledge.

Loehr, J., & Schwartz, T. (2003). *The power of full engagement: Managing energy, not time, is the key to high performance and personal renewal*. Free Press.

Lord, C. (2005). *Indirect aggression and social support among elderly retirement community residents* [Unpublished doctoral dissertation]. Alliant International University.

Lord, F. M. (1952). A theory of test scores. *Psychometrika Monographs*, Whole No. 7. Psychometric Corporation.

Luborsky, L., Rosenthal, R., & Diguer, L. (2002). The dodo bird verdict is alive and well—Mostly. *Clinical Psychology: Science and Practice, 9*(1), 2–12. https://doi.org/10.1093/clipsy/9.1.2

MacCallum, R. C., Widaman, K. F., Zhang, S., & Hong, S. (1999). Sample size in factor analysis. *Psychological Methods, 4*(1), 84–99. https://doi.org/10.1037/1082-989X.4.1.84

MacKinnon, D. P., Fairchild, A. J., & Fritz, M. S. (2007). Mediation analysis. *Annual Review of Psychology, 58*, 593–614. https://doi.org/10.1146/annurev.psych.58.110405.085542

Maher, B. A. (1978). A reader's, writer's, and reviewer's guide to assessing research reports in clinical psychology. *Journal of Consulting and Clinical Psychology, 46*(4), 835–838. https://doi.org/10.1037/0022-006X.46.4.835

Mahoney, M. J., & Mahoney, B. K. (1976). *Permanent weight control*. Norton.

Maxwell, S. E., Delaney, H. D., & Kelley, K. (2018a). Chapter 3 extensions. In *Designing experiments and analyzing data: A model comparison approach* (3rd ed.). Routledge. https://designingexperiments.com/supplements/

Maxwell, S. E., Delaney, H. D., & Kelley, K. (2018b). *Designing experiments and analyzing data: A model comparison approach* (3rd ed.). Routledge.

Mehl, M. R. (2017). The electronically activated recorder (EAR): A method for the naturalistic observation of daily social behavior. *Current Directions in Psychological Science, 26*(2), 184–190. https://doi.org/10.1177/0963721416680611

Merriam-Webster. (n.d.-a). Dissertation. In *Merriam-Webster online dictionary*. https://www.merriam-webster.com/dictionary/dissertation

Merriam-Webster. (n.d.-b). Plagiarize. In *Merriam-Webster online dictionary*. https://www.merriam-webster.com/dictionary/plagiarize

Merriam-Webster. (n.d.-c). Thesis. In *Merriam-Webster online dictionary*. https://www.merriam-webster.com/dictionary/thesis

Mertler, C. A., & Vannatta, R. A. (2016). *Advanced and multivariate statistical methods* (6th ed.). Routledge.

Meyers, L. S., Gamst, G., & Guarino, A. J. (2017). *Applied multivariate research: Design and interpretation* (3rd ed.). Sage.

Miller, A. B. (2009). *Finish your dissertation once and for all! How to overcome psychological barriers, get results, and move on with your life*. American Psychological Association.

Miller, D. C. (2002). *Handbook of research design and social measurement* (6th ed.). Sage. https://doi.org/10.4135/9781412984386

Miller, G. (2012). The smartphone psychology manifesto. *Perspectives on Psychological Science, 7*(3), 221–237. https://doi.org/10.1177/1745691612441215

Miller, G. A., & Chapman, J. P. (2001). Misunderstanding analysis of covariance. *Journal of Abnormal Psychology, 110*(1), 40–48. https://doi.org/10.1037/0021-843X.110.1.40

Moher, D., Liberati, A., Tetzlaff, J., & Altman, D. G.; PRISMA Group. (2009). Preferred Reporting Items for Systematic reviews and Meta-Analyses: The PRISMA statement. *PLoS Medicine, 6*(7), e1000097. https://doi.org/10.1371/journal.pmed.1000097

Mueller, P. A., & Oppenheimer, D. M. (2014). The pen is mightier than the keyboard: Advantages of longhand over laptop note taking. *Psychological Science, 25*(6), 1159–1168. https://doi.org/10.1177/0956797614524581

Munafò, M. R., Nosek, B. A., Bishop, D. V. M., Button, K. S., Chambers, C. D., Percie du Sert, N., . . . Ioannidis, J. P. A. (2017). A manifesto for reproducible science. *Nature Human Behaviour, 1*, 0021. https://doi.org/10.1038/s41562-016-0021

Munder, T., Flückiger, C., Gerger, H., Wampold, B. E., & Barth, J. (2012). Is the allegiance effect an epiphenomenon of true efficacy differences between treatments? A meta-analysis. *Journal of Counseling Psychology, 59*(4), 631–637. https://doi.org/10.1037/a0029571

Munsey, C. (2009). Summer session: 8 tips for funding your dissertation. *APA Monitor on Psychology, 40*(7), 64. www.apa.org/monitor/2009/07-08/dissertation.aspx

Murphy, K. R, Myors, B., & Wolach, A. (2014). *Statistical power analysis* (4th ed.). Routledge.

Nagy, T. F. (2005). *Ethics in plain English: An illustrative casebook for psychologists* (2nd ed.). American Psychological Association.

Nangle, D. W., Hansen, D. J., Erdley, C. A., & Norton, P. J. (Eds.). (2010). *Practitioner's guide to empirically supported measures of social skills*. Springer.

National Association of Social Workers. (2017). *Code of ethics*. https://www.socialworkers.org/About/Ethics/Code-of-Ethics.aspx

National Institutes of Health. (n.d.). *Grant writing tips sheets*. https://grants.nih.gov/grants/grant_tips.htm

NCSS Statistical Software. (2005). *Power Analysis and Sample Size: PASS* [Computer software].

Nelson, G. L., Cone, J. D., & Hanson, C. R. (1975). Training correct utensil use in retarded children: Modeling vs. physical guidance. *American Journal of Mental Deficiency, 80*(1), 114–122.

Newton, R. R., & Rudestam, K. E. (2013). *Your statistical consultant: Answers to your data analysis questions* (2nd ed.). Sage. https://doi.org/10.4135/9781506374673

Nezu, A., Ronan, G. F., Meadows, E. A., & McClure, K. S. (2000). *Practitioner's guide to empirically based measures of depression*. Springer.

Nosek, B. A., Ebersole, C. R., DeHaven, A. C., & Mellor, D. T. (2018). The preregistration revolution. *PNAS, 115*(11), 2600–2606. https://doi.org/10.1073/pnas.1708274114

Nosek, B. A., Spies, J. R., Cohn, M., Bartmess, E., Lakens, D., Holman, D., . . . Giner-Sorolla, R. (2015, June 12). Open Science Collaboration.osf.io/vmrgu

Novotney, A. (2014). Blogging for mental health. *Monitor on Psychology, 45*(6), 42. https://www.apa.org/monitor/2014/06/blogging

Nunnally, N. C., & Bernstein, I. H. (1994). *Psychometric theory* (3rd ed.). McGraw-Hill.

Osborne, J. W. (2010). Data cleaning basics: Best practices in dealing with extreme scores. *Newborn and Infant Nursing Reviews, 10*(1), 37–43. https://doi.org/10.1053/j.nainr.2009.12.009

Osborne, J. W. (2013). *Best practices in data cleaning*. Sage.

Osborne, J. W., & Overbay, A. (2004). The power of outliers (and why researchers should always check for them). *Practical Assessment, Research & Evaluation, 9*(6), 1–8.

Oxford English Dictionary. (n.d.-a). Dissertation. In *AskOxford.com online dictionary*. https://en.oxforddictionaries.com/definition/dissertation

Oxford English Dictionary. (n.d.-b). Thesis. In *AskOxford.com online dictionary*. https://en.oxforddictionaries.com/definition/thesis

Pallant, J. (2013). *SPSS survival manual: A step-by-step guide to data analysis using SPSS* (5th ed.). Open University Press.

Parsonson, B. S., & Baer, D. M. (1978). The analysis and presentation of graphic data. In T. R. Kratochwill (Ed.), *Single subject research* (pp. 101–165). Academic Press. https://doi.org/10.1016/B978-0-12-425850-1.50009-0

Paul, G. L. (1969). Behavior modification research: Design and tactics. In C. M. Franks (Ed.), *Behavior therapy: Appraisal and status* (pp. 29–62). McGraw-Hill.

Paulhus, D. L. (1991). Measurement and control of response bias. In J. P. Robinson, P. Shaver, & L. S. Wrightsman (Eds.), *Measures of personality and social psychological attitudes* (pp. 17–59). Academic Press. https://doi.org/10.1016/B978-0-12-590241-0.50006-X

Pedhazur, E. J. (1997). *Multiple regression in behavioral research: Explanation and prediction* (3rd ed.). Harcourt Brace.

Pedhazur, E. J., & Schmelkin, L. P. (1991). *Measurement, design, and analysis: An integrated approach*. Erlbaum.

Peters, G.-J. Y. (2014). The alpha and the omega of scale reliability and validity: Why and how to abandon Cronbach's alpha and the route towards more comprehensive assessment of scale quality. *The European Health Psychologist, 16*(2), 56–69.

Preacher, K. J., & MacCallum, R. C. (2003). Repairing Tom Swift's electric factor analysis machine. *Understanding Statistics, 2*(1), 13–43. https://doi.org/10.1207/S15328031US0201_02

Pyrczak, F. (2000). *Completing your thesis or dissertation*. Pyrczak.

Ramírez-Esparza, N., Mehl, M. R., Alvarez-Bermudez, J., & Pennebaker, J. W. (2009). Are Mexicans more or less sociable than Americans? Insights from a naturalistic observation study. *Journal of Research in Personality, 43*(1), 1–7. https://doi.org/10.1016/j.jrp.2008.09.002

Raudenbush, S. W., & Bryk, A. S. (2002). *Hierarchical linear models: Applications and data analysis methods* (2nd ed.). Sage.

Ray, W. J. (2011). *Methods: Toward a science of behavior and experience* (10th ed.). Cengage Learning.

Raykov, T., & Marcoulides, G. M. (2006). *A first course in structural equation modeling* (2nd ed.). Erlbaum.

Rodgers, W. (1995). Analysis of cross-classified data. In L. G. Grimm & P. R. Yarnold (Eds.), *Reading and understanding multivariate statistics* (pp. 169–216). American Psychological Association.

Roemer, L., & Orsillo, S. M. (2009). *Mindfulness- and acceptance-based behavioral therapies in practice*. Guilford Press.

Ronan, G. F., Dreer, L., Maurelli, K., Ronan, D., & Gerhart, J. (2014). *Practitioner's guide to empirically supported measures of anger, aggression, and violence.* Springer. https://doi.org/10.1007/978-3-319-00245-3

Rosenthal, R. (1969). Interpersonal expectations: Effects of the experimenter's hypothesis. In R. Rosenthal & R. L. Rosnow (Eds.), *Artifact in behavioral research* (pp. 181–277). Academic Press.

Rothstein, H. R. (2012). Accessing relevant literature. In H. Cooper, P. M. Camic, D. L. Long, A. T. Panter, D. Rindskopf, & K. J. Sher (Eds.), *APA handbook of research methods in psychology, Vol. 1. Foundations, planning, measures, and psychometrics* (pp. 133–144). American Psychological Association. https://doi.org/10.1037/13619-009

Rudestam, K. E., & Newton, R. R. (2015). *Surviving your dissertation* (4th ed.). Sage.

Sales, B. D., & Folkman, S. (Eds.). (2000). *Ethics in research with human participants.* American Psychological Association.

Sanchez-Hucles, J., & Cash, T. F. (1992). The dissertation in professional psychology programs: I. A survey of clinical directors on requirements and practices. *Professional Psychology: Research and Practice, 23*(1), 59–61. https://doi.org/10.1037/0735-7028.23.1.59

Sandstrom, G. M., Lathia, N., Mascolo, C., & Rentfrow, P. J. (2016). Opportunities for smartphones in clinical care: The future of mobile mood monitoring. *The Journal of Clinical Psychiatry, 77*(2), e135–e137. https://doi.org/10.4088/JCP.15com10054

Saris, W. E., & Andrews, F. M. (2004). Evaluation of measurement instruments using a structural modeling approach. In P. P. Biemer, R. M. Groves, L. E. Lyberg, N. A. Mathiowetz, & S. Sudman (Eds.), *Measurement errors in surveys* (pp. 575–597). Wiley. https://doi.org/10.1002/9781118150382.ch28

Schafer, J. L., & Graham, J. W. (2002). Missing data: Our view of the state of the art. *Psychological Methods, 7*(2), 147–177. https://doi.org/10.1037/1082-989X.7.2.147

Schlueter, J. E., Carlson, J. F., Geisinger, K. F., & Murphy, L. L. (Eds.). (2018). *Pruebas publicadas en Español II: An index of Spanish tests in print.* Buros Center for Testing.

Schulz, K. F., Altman, D. G., Moher, D., & the CONSORT Group. (2010). CONSORT 2010 statement: Updated guidelines for reporting parallel group randomized trials. *Annals of Internal Medicine, 152*(11), 726–732. https://doi.org/10.7326/0003-4819-152-11-201006010-00232

Schumacker, R. E., & Lomax, R. G. (2016). *A beginner's guide to structural equation modeling* (4th ed.). Routledge.

Schwarz, N., & Oyserman, D. (2001). Asking questions about behavior: Cognition, communication, and questionnaire construction. *American Journal of Evaluation, 22*(2), 127–160. https://doi.org/10.1177/109821400102200202

Shadish, W. R., Cook, T. D., & Campbell, D. T. (2002). *Experimental and quasi-experimental designs for generalized causal inference.* Houghton Mifflin.

Shawchuck, C. R., Fatis, M., & Breitenstein, J. L. (1986). A practical guide to the assignment of authorship credit. *The Behavior Therapist, 9*(10), 216–217.

Shiffman, S. (2000). Real-time self-report of momentary states in the natural environment: Computerized ecological momentary assessment. In A. A. Stone, J. S. Turkan, C. A. Bachrach, J. B. Jobe, H. S. Kurtzman, & V. S. Cain (Eds.), *The science of self-report: Implications for research and practice* (pp. 277–296). Erlbaum.

Siegel, S. (1956). *Nonparametric statistics for the behavioral sciences.* McGraw-Hill.

Sikora, D. M. (1989). *Divorce, environmental change, parental conflict, and the peer relations of preschool children* [Unpublished doctoral dissertation]. West Virginia University.

Silvia, P. J. (2007). *How to write a lot: A practical guide to productive academic writing.* American Psychological Association.

Silvia, P. J. (2018). *How to write a lot: A practical guide to productive academic writing* (2nd ed.). American Psychological Association.

Singer, J. D., & Willett, J. S. (2003). *Applied longitudinal data analysis: Modeling change and event occurrence.* Oxford University Press. https://doi.org/10.1093/acprof:oso/9780195152968.001.0001

Smalley, S. L., & Winston, D. (2010). *Fully present: The science, art, and practice of mindfulness.* Da Capo Lifelong Books.

Smith, J. D. (2012). Single-case experimental designs: A systematic review of published research and current standards. *Psychological Methods, 17*(4), 510–550. https://doi.org/10.1037/a0029312

Smyth, J. M., & Stone, A. A. (2003). Ecological momentary assessment research in behavioral medicine. *Journal of Happiness Studies, 4*(1), 35–52. https://doi.org/10.1023/A:1023657221954

Solso, R. L., & MacLin, M. (2002). *Experimental psychology: A case approach* (7th ed.). Allyn & Bacon.

Sonuga-Barke, E. (2017). Editorial: Science unskewed—Acknowledging and reducing 'risk of bias' in parenting research. *Journal of Child Psychology and Psychiatry, and Allied Disciplines, 58*(1), 1–3. https://doi.org/10.1111/jcpp.12676

Steneck, N. H. (2007). *Introduction to the responsible conduct of research.* Government Printing Office. https://doi.org/10.1037/e638422011-001

Sternberg, R. J., & Sternberg, K. (2010). *The psychologist's companion: A guide to writing scientific papers for students and researchers* (5th ed.). Cambridge University Press. https://doi.org/10.1017/CBO9780511762024

Stone, A. A., Turkan, J. S., Bachrach, C. A., Jobe, J. B., Kurtzman, H. S., & Cain, V. S. (Eds.). (2000). *The science of self-report: Implications for research and practice.* Erlbaum.

Stringer, H. (2017). How to create your own podcast. *Monitor on Psychology, 48*(11), 58.

Stuart, R. B. (Ed.). (1977). *Behavioral self-management: Strategies, techniques and outcome.* Brunner/Mazel.

Suen, H. K., & Ary, D. (2014). *Analyzing quantitative behavioral observation data.* Erlbaum. https://doi.org/10.4324/9781315801827

Tabachnick, B. F., & Fidell, L. S. (2013). *Using multivariate statistics* (6th ed.). Pearson.

Taplin, P. S., & Reid, J. B. (1973). Effects of instructional set and experimental influence on observer reliability. *Child Development, 44*(3), 547–554. https://doi.org/10.2307/1128011

Thompson, B. (Ed.). (2003). *Score reliability: Contemporary thinking on reliability issues.* Sage. https://doi.org/10.4135/9781412985789

Thompson, B. (2004). *Exploratory and confirmatory factor analysis: Understanding concepts and applications.* American Psychological Association. https://doi.org/10.1037/10694-000

Thompson, R. H., & Borrero, J. C. (2011). Direct observation. In W. W. Fisher, C. C. Piazza, & H. S. Roane (Eds.), *Handbook of applied behavior analysis* (pp. 191–205). Guilford Press.

Tracy, B. (2004). *Time power: A proven system for getting more done in less time than you ever thought possible.* AMACOM.

Trull, T. J., & Ebner-Priemer, U. (2013). Ambulatory assessment. *Annual Review of Clinical Psychology, 9,* 151–176. https://www.annualreviews.org/doi/10.1146/annurev-clinpsy-050212-185510

Trull, T. J., & Ebner-Priemer, U. (2014). The role of ambulatory assessment in psychological science. *Current Directions in Psychological Science, 23*(6), 466–470. https://doi.org/10.1177/0963721414550706

Tufte, E. (2006). *Beautiful evidence.* Graphics Press.

Urbina, S. (2014). *Essentials of psychological testing* (2nd ed.). Wiley.

U.S. Department of Health and Human Services. (2017). *Office for Human Research Protections: Regulations.* https://www.hhs.gov/ohrp/regulations-and-policy/regulations/index.html

van der Linden, W. J. (Ed.). (2016). *Handbook of modern item response theory* (Vols. 1–3). CRC Press.

Vazire, S., & Mehl, M. R. (2008). Knowing me, knowing you: The accuracy and unique predictive validity of self-ratings and other-ratings of daily behavior. *Journal of Personality and Social Psychology, 95*(5), 1202–1216. https://doi.org/10.1037/a0013314

Vernoff, J. (2015). Writing. In K. E. Rudestam & R. R. Newton, *Surviving your dissertation* (4th ed., pp. 259–280). Sage.

Vicens, Q., & Bourne, P. E. (2007). Ten simple rules for a successful collaboration. *PLoS Computational Biology, 3*(3), e44. https://doi.org/10.1371/journal.pcbi.0030044

von Eye, A., & Mun, E. Y. (2005). *Analyzing rater agreement: Manifest variable methods.* Erlbaum.

Wainer, H. (2007). *Graphic discovery: A trout in the milk and other visual adventures.* Princeton University Press.

Wallgren, A., Wallgren, B., Persson, R., Jorner, U., & Haaland, J. (1996). *Graphing statistics & data.* Sage.

Webb, E. J., Campbell, D. T., Schwartz, R. D., & Sechrest, L. (1966). *Unobtrusive measures: Nonreactive research in the social sciences.* Rand McNally.

Weisberg, H. F., Krosnick, J. A., & Bowen, B. D. (1996). *An introduction to survey research, polling, and data analysis* (3rd ed.). Sage.

Weston, S. J., & Yee, D. (2017). Why you should become a UseR: A brief introduction to R. *Observer, 30*(3). https://www.psychologicalscience.org/observer/why-you-should-become-a-user-a-brief-introduction-to-r

Wettstein, A., & Scherzinger, M. (2015). Using camera-glasses for the assessment of aggressive behaviour among adolescents in residential correctional care: A small-scale study. *Journal of Aggression, Conflict and Peace Research, 7*(1), 33–46. https://doi.org/10.1108/JACPR-04-2014-0117

White, T. L., & McBurney, D. H. (2013). *Research methods* (9th ed.). Wadsworth Cengage.

Wiggins, J. S. (1959). Interrelationships among MMPI measures of dissimulation under standard and social desirability instructions. *Journal of Consulting Psychology, 23*(5), 419–427. https://doi.org/10.1037/h0047823

Wilcox, R. R. (2017). *Introduction to robust estimation and hypothesis testing* (4th ed.). Academic Press.

Wiley, E. W., Webb, N. M., & Shavelson, R. J. (2013). The generalizability of test scores. In K. F. Geisinger, B. A. Bracken, J. F. Carlson, J. C. Hansen, N. R. Kuncel,

S. P. Reise, & M. C. Rodriguez (Eds.), *APA handbook of testing and assessment in psychology, Vol. 1. Test theory and testing and assessment in industrial and organizational psychology* (pp. 43–60). American Psychological Association.

Wilkinson, L., & Task Force on Statistical Inference. (1999). Statistical methods in psychology journals: Guidelines and explanations. *American Psychologist, 54*(8), 594–604. https://doi.org/10.1037/0003-066X.54.8.594

Wolf, E. J., Harrington, K. M., Clark, S. L., & Miller, M. W. (2013). Sample size requirements for structural equation models: An evaluation of power, bias, and solution propriety. *Educational and Psychological Measurement, 73*(6), 913–934. https://doi.org/10.1177/0013164413495237

Wright, D. B., London, K., & Field, A. P. (2011). Using bootstrap estimation and the plug-in principle for clinical psychology data. *Journal of Experimental Psychopathology, 2*(2), 252–270. https://doi.org/10.5127/jep.013611

Yates, B. T. (1982). *Doing the dissertation: The nuts and bolts of psychological research.* Charles C Thomas.

Yoder, P. J., & Symons, F. (2010). *Observational measurement of behavior.* Springer.

Zimbardo, P., & Boyd, J. (2008). *The time paradox: The new psychology of time that will change your life.* Simon & Schuster.

Zinsser, W. K. (2006). *On writing well: The classic guide to writing nonfiction* (7th ed., rev.). HarperCollins.

INDEX

ABOUT THE AUTHORS

Debora J. Bell, PhD, is a professor of psychology and associate chair for clinical science at the University of Missouri–Columbia. She received her doctorate in psychology from West Virginia University after completing a clinical internship at the Western Psychiatric Institute and Clinic of the University of Pittsburgh School of Medicine. She has been at the University of Missouri since receiving her degree and has served as the director of clinical training and director of the clinical doctoral program's training clinic, the Psychological Services Clinic, for 20 years. Dr. Bell has held several national leadership positions in graduate psychology education, including current roles as editor of *Training and Education in Professional Psychology* and chair of the Council of Chairs of Training Councils and previous roles as chair of the Council of University Directors of Clinical Psychology, and as commissioner and chair of the American Psychological Association's Commission on Accreditation. She is a fellow of the Association for Behavioral and Cognitive Therapies and is the author of numerous articles, book chapters, and a book in the areas of graduate education, girls' adjustment, and youths' internalizing problems, social information processing, and regulation of positive emotions.

Sharon L. Foster, PhD, is a Distinguished Professor Emerita at Alliant International University in San Diego, California. She received her doctorate in psychology from the State University of New York at Stony Brook after completing a clinical internship at the University of Washington Medical School. She also taught at West Virginia University. Dr. Foster served as an associate editor for the journals *Behavioral Assessment* and the *Journal of Consulting and Clinical Psychology*, and she was a fellow at the Center for Advanced Study in the Behavioral Sciences. She is the author of four books and numerous articles and chapters on children's peer relations, assessment and treatment of adolescent externalizing behavior problems, and research methodology.

John D. Cone, PhD, earned his BA in psychology from Stanford University and his master's degree and doctorate from the University of Washington. He has taught at the University of Puget Sound, West Virginia University, the University of Hawaii, United States International University, San Diego State University, and Alliant International University. He is a fellow of both the American Psychological Association and the Association for Psychological Science, a member of the Association for Behavior Analysis, and a board certified behavior analyst. His research interests include the development of idiographic assessment methodology; autism intervention; and the development, implementation, and evaluation of large-scale service delivery systems, especially those for persons with developmental disabilities. An executive coach and frequent organizational consultant, Dr. Cone is the author of several books, including *Evaluating Outcomes: Empirical Tools for Effective Practice* (2001). When not being professionally active, he spends his time jogging, working on his 55′ yacht (*Context*), and cruising the waters of the blue Pacific.